CASES IN HOSPITALITY MARKETING AND MANAGEMENT

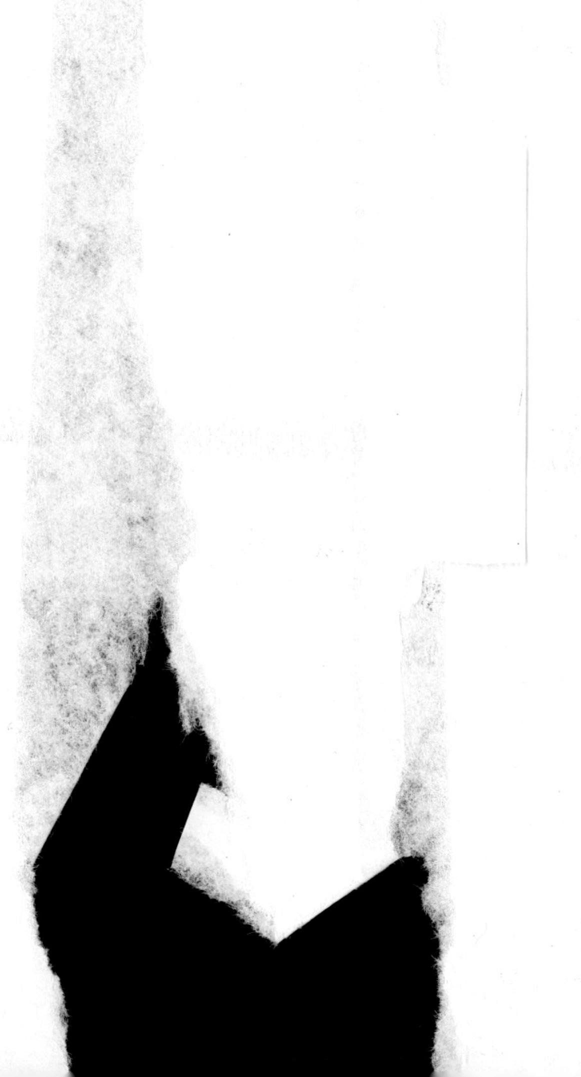

CASES IN HOSPITALITY MARKETING AND MANAGEMENT

ROBERT C. LEWIS
University of Massachusetts

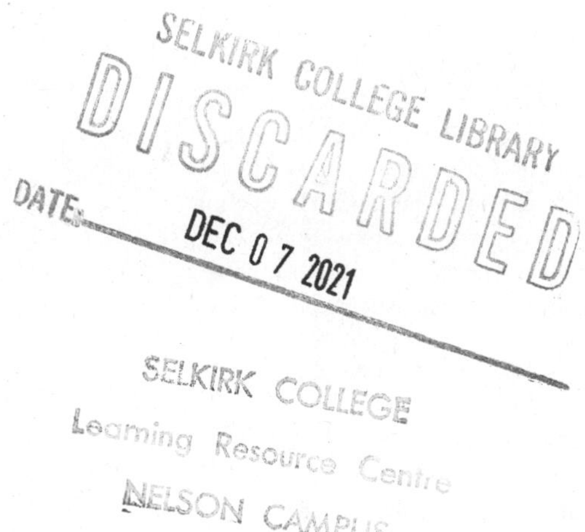

John Wiley & Sons
New York Chichester Brisbane Toronto Singapore

ISBN 0-471-50898-5

Printed in the United States of America

10 9 8 7 6 5 4 3 2 1

PREFACE

The use of case studies as a pedagogical tool has long been prevalent in many disciplines including, most relevant here, business schools. Their use, however, has been sorely limited in hospitality programs. There has been a very real reason for this: there just weren't cases readily available and current. This book is written specifically to alleviate that problem. Personally, the author has found the case study method to be such a powerful learning tool with tremendous acceptance by students at all levels, that he sometimes wonders how he ever taught without them.

The major thrust of the cases in this book is on hospitality marketing. Its use, however, is not limited to those classes. First, if you accept the premise, as the author contends, that every act of hospitality management is also an act of marketing because it impacts the customer, then it becomes clear that this text can also be used in a management course. Each case clearly deals with management situations. Second, these cases contain information that relates to many facets of hospitality management. For example, in various cases can be found elements of food and beverage costs, financial statements, organizations, human resources, ownership relations, franchise agreements, architecture and design concepts, and a multitude of other factors that continuously revolve around us in this eclectic industry.

Similarly, although the book is divided into six major topic headings, these headings are anything but mutually exclusive. Every case has elements of major marketing tools, be it segmentation, positioning, competitive analysis, the marketing mix, strategy, or whatever, these elements simply cannot be separated from one another. The categorizations, thus, are somewhat arbitrary and the user may want to rearrange them.

Each section begins with a mini-case of two to four pages. We call these quickies. They can be used to demonstrate quickly the major points of that section. They are useful for quick classroom discussion, as well as for quizzes. We find them useful in preparing for the longer cases that follow, sort of like a trial run. The last case, The Omni Park Central Hotel, is a very comprehensive case that has many possibilities. In this case can be found many, many elements of management and how closely they interrelate with marketing. At the same time the case is very versatile. We have used it over five three-hour classes at the graduate level. We have used it as a half day, full day, and two day case in executive seminars. And we have used it, without most of the exhibits, in an hour and a quarter class at the undergraduate level.

In between these two extremes, the mini-case and the comprehensive, are 15 moderate length, moderately complex, cases. They are about evenly divided between hotel and restaurant situations. They are also about evenly divided between what we call a "discussion" case or a "problem" case. The latter, of course, can also be used as a discussion case but usually not vice versa because a discussion case will often lack enough information to reach a solution, although there are always suggested directions.

Similarly, the cases are of varying levels of difficulty, most of them can be used at more than one academic level. In fact, each case has been classroom tested at various levels. Some obviously fit better than others, but as each instructor has her or his own way, we think that this is a question of self-determination. In general, we have found that at least half the cases in the book can be used in one semester at any level. For example, at the intro level we use all seven mini-cases and a selection from cases 2, 4, 7, 8, 9, 12, 13, and 19. We do not explore these cases in great depth; rather, we use them to illustrate the principles and foundations of those sections.

At the intermediate level, we will use the same cases plus any of the others, except the Omni case in its full form. Here the use depends upon prior courses. Some cases can be used to demonstrate foundations, while others can be probed in depth and used in search for solutions. In the advanced or graduate course, we would recommend cases 2, 5, 9, 10, 14, 15, 17, 20, 21, and 22.

Because of the varied use of cases, and use at different levels, we do not specifically suggest any one way of approaching each case. Instead, we recommend that the instructor make these suggestions, and we have provided alternative ideas in the instructor's manual. Not infrequently, at advanced levels, we deliberately do not give direction, i.e., we let the students find their own direction. This is consistent with our own philosophy that students need to learn to think and determine their own direction, like they would have to do in the real world, rather than be spoon-fed down the primrose path.

Case studies can be used as the basis around which a course is developed. In fact, beyond the intro course, this author has been doing this for almost 10 years and has found it extremely effective. Harvard uses cases almost exclusively without supplemental reading in its graduate business school. Except at the advanced or executive level, however, this can be a less than satisfactory process. A student can get quite good at case handling and problem solving, without really understanding why they do what they do. The result may be that the next time, when things are different, it doesn't work. Therefore, I always assign some reading, be it from a text or an article, along with cases in order to test some foundation or principle.

Harvard also practices a policy of "never tell them the answer." I've tried this and found it does nothing but frustrate students and leave them bewildered. I do, however, emphasize that, especially in marketing, there may be more than one solution and, in fact, the optimal solution may never really be known. Some students have a problem with this. They have long been taught that two and two must add up to four. In marketing, however, two and two may add up to almost any number, so to speak, and it is important to understand this conceptualization process at a higher level of abstraction than that to which most students are accustomed.

The important emphasis, that needs to be made, is how you get to the solution. Have you utilized all the available information? Have you appropriately analyzed it? Have you interpreted it correctly? And so forth. Two students may have done this but arrived at somewhat different solutions. I give credit for the process and the ability to think and conceptualize.

ACKNOWLEDGMENTS

Many people have worked on these cases as well as another 40 or so cases that were left out of the book in order to keep it the proper length. All cases, with some apologies to secondary sources, are original with the sole exception of Case 10, Andy's Barbecue, which was originally written and published by Roger Kerin, Professor of Marketing at Southern Methodist University. It has been updated for this book.

Some cases derive from consulting or research work by the author. Some have come from participants in executive seminars. In all other cases, the original research and writing was done by graduate students. Their help has been monumental and is hereby acknowledged by name: Nancy Cedrone, Rosa Liu, Laurie Walsh, Salim Ouchi, Norm Nichols, Rick Spola, Rick Warfel, Susan Morris, John Wolper, LingYu Wang, Helaine Rockett, Chris Dipre, Richard McCallum, Barbara Hammond, and Rosemary Klein. In addition, two other students did extensive work in word processing and formatting: Nancy Charves and Beth Dugan. To all these people I am most grateful. I am also grateful to those industry people who were, and are, willing to share information and experiences so that others may learn from them.

It is important to note that these cases were prepared as a basis for class analysis and discussion rather than to illustrate effective or ineffective handling of an administrative or managerial situation.

A NOTE ON PRODUCTION

The text for this book was composed by the author using WordPerfect 5.0 word processing, and camera-ready copy was printed on an NEC 5200 24-pin dot matrix printer. I can testify that word processing technology has not reached perfection in user-friendliness; neither has the author in mastering it. In spite of all precautions taken, you will no doubt find typos, columns that don't line up perfectly, formatting errors, and other flaws in this book.

Why was it done this way, you might ask. The primary consideration was speed. Both publisher and author wanted to get books to instructors and students while the material was still current. Another concern was flexibility. I hope to update the book with new cases within three years. This is subject to whether there is sufficient demand, which is complicated by the question of how many instructors will copy the cases and distribute them to their classes instead of having students purchase the book. I lean on the integrity of my colleagues in this situation. If you make copies instead of ordering, this project will turn out not to have been viable, and all this work will have been in vain.

In spite of all the help, I stand responsible for the end result. Any and all comments are welcome and will help to improve the next edition.

Robert C. Lewis
Amherst, Massachusetts
Winter 1989

CONTENTS

CASES IN HOSPITALITY MARKETING AND MANAGEMENT

INTRODUCTION

THE CASE METHOD

For many students, use of this book in a course will be their first introduction into the use of the case method. Thus, some explanation is in order. For those who have previously worked with case method instruction, we will also suggest some ways of looking at marketing cases.

Probably, the primary reason for using cases at all is their verisimilitude, or their approximation of reality. Although cases will not give us all the information we would like to have, or probably all that we could have in the real world, where we still never have all that we would like to have, they come as close as possible to that situation in an academic setting. Similarly, as in the real world, we have in cases more information than we need, or at least more than is relevant to the present situation. We must then separate the wheat from the chaff, the relevant from the irrelevant. We must define the problem(s), understand its causes, symptoms, ramifications, consequences, and repercussions, organize the facts, synthesize and analyze them, formulate possible solutions, verify them, and choose and defend a particular solution or application.

Thus, what the case process really does is to bring theory, concepts, and facts into a stage of application. You may, for example, understand perfectly well the concepts of segmentation and positioning but these will mean little to you until you have to actually apply them. In the case method of learning you get a chance to do this.

There are two things that are inherent in using cases in education. One is that you have to *think*! By that we mean that doing case studies is not an exercise in memorization. Like the real world, there is no place to look up answers. Instead, you have to *read between the lines*, assimilate and synthesize various pieces of information, apply concepts and theories, and project all this into a realistic situation. This takes a lot of *thinking!*

The second inherent factor in using case studies is *participation.* While much can be learned from the information that is in a case, and much can be learned from the cognitive process in analyzing the case, the ultimate test will come in being able to articulate and explicate this process. You may be the genius who has the secret to eternal life but if you can't 1) articulate it, and 2) persuade someone to use it, then it will amount to naught. You may be asked to do this in writing, and you may be asked to do it orally. Regardless, being able to articulate is an important part of the case method learning process.

ANALYZING CASES

There are a number of ways suggested for analyzing cases. Which way is best depends alot on the type of case, the information in the case, what kind of decisions and/or applications are to be made, and finally, what works best for you. One thing, however, is fairly unanimously agreed: read the case through first without taking notes, marking the case, or in any way trying to break it down. The idea, first, is to get the total picture.

The second time through, mark the case or make notes on what is pertinent and relevant. Depending on the case, you will need to define the problem, gather the facts, analyze the information, define alternatives, and arrive at solutions. These steps are fairly standard for handling any problem oriented case. Some cases in this book will be used as discussion cases. In these cases, arriving at a solution is not as critical; in fact, the case may lack enough information to do that and part of your job may be to determine what information is needed and how to go about getting it. In discussion cases, used as such for educational purposes, the emphasis will be more on identifying and applying the tools you are learning in your courses.

What follows is more specific for the cases in this text, essentially marketing management cases. We will, in fact, suggest two models that we have found to be very useful in handling marketing management cases. The first of these is called the strategic systems model and is shown in Exhibit 1.

THE STRATEGIC SYSTEMS MODEL

This model depicts as a system all the elements and factors that impact upon marketing processes and decisions. Although the model is depicted as flowing from one stage to the next, and it does, there is essentially *no* decision made in marketing that does not contain some vestige of every element in this model. The point of the flow is that, as shown, one stage follows from the previous one at a lower level of abstraction. A problem often occurs when this flow does not logically occur. For example, you will find cases in this book where the functional strategies, or even tactics, are decided without deciding, or without relevance to, the master and operational strategies. This usually leads to trouble as you will discover.

Although every case will contain every element of the model, and you should look for them, each case will more or less concentrate on one particular stage, as broken into sections in the table of contents. This does not mean, for example, in a "segmentation" case that you should ignore the product/service, the communication, or the distribution. Rather, you should see how these other elements fit into the segmentation issue.

Thus, Exhibit 1 can be used as a checklist. You have not really stated the case, and you cannot fully analyze it, until you have looked at each of the parts to see how they fit in to the whole.

EXHIBIT 1 The Strategic Marketing Systems Model

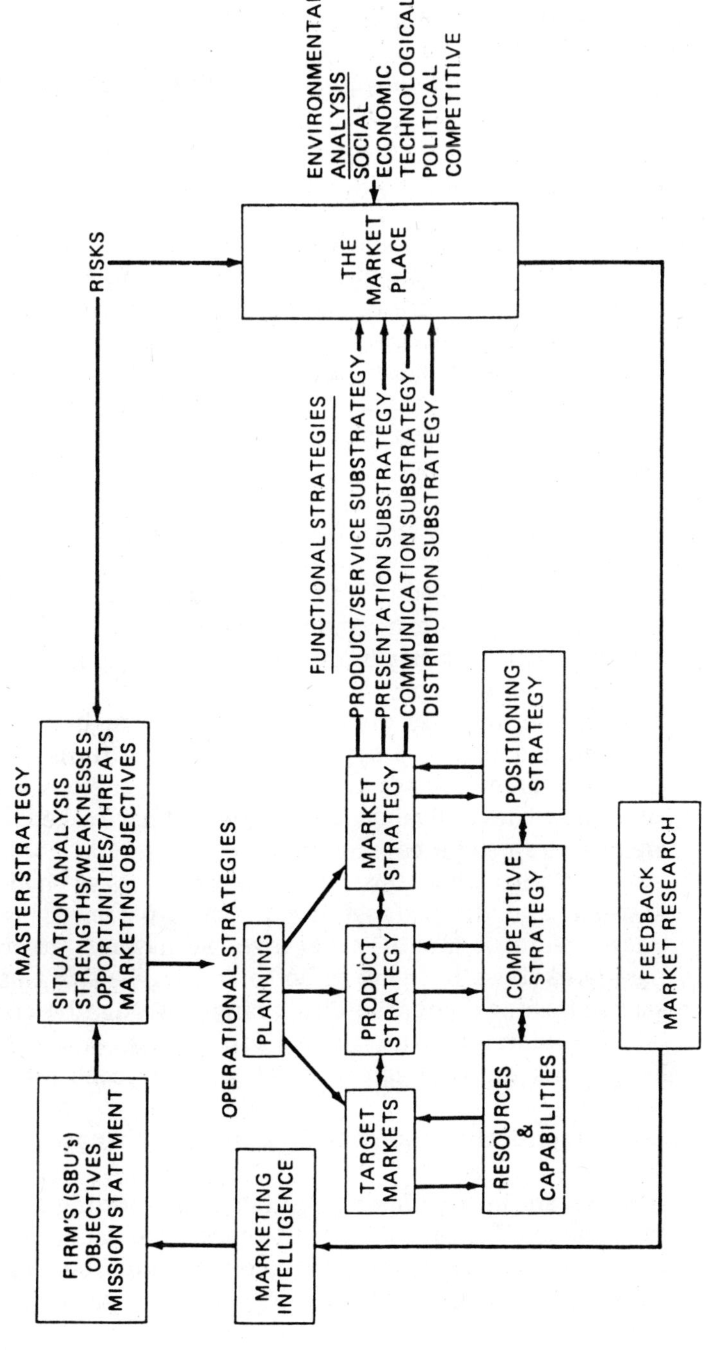

DEVELOPING MARKETING STRATEGIES

The second model we recommend is also a checklist model that breaks down the parts, one by one, to get at the real issues and to see where they lead. Although you may not be developing marketing strategies in each case, you will find this analysis very useful in dissecting the cases.

Our first checklist asks the questions to which we will need answers, either now or later.

1. Why is there a problem?

   The answer to this should be factual and measurable. This is usually what management sees as its problem, e.g., occupancy is down, covers are off, we are losing market share, etc. Note an important distinction: This is *why*, not *what*. The answer to this question, and this is important, is not the solution to the problem. It is simply why it exists, and we need to identify that first in order to guide our direction in looking for a solution.

2. What is the critical question(s)? What is the root problem?

   At this stage we need to find the question that will lead us to the answer after we have done the analysis. To make this clear, we will work backwards in a simple example. Suppose the "why there is a problem" above is, "We've been open six months and are only doing forty covers a night." The root problem, jumping to a hypothetical solution, turns out to be that the market doesn't know we exist, i.e., there is a lack of awareness. The critical question we would have asked is "Why aren't more people coming here?

   Notice that this question could have had many answers, e.g., the product is poor, it is perceived as overpriced, word of mouth is negative, we haven't targeted the right market, we're trying to do something we don't have the capabilities for doing, the positioning is wrong, the competition is undercutting us, and so forth. First, as you see, we have to ask the *right* question. Then we proceed with,

3. What are the critical factors? What has to be changed?

   Now we are into gathering the facts, and sorting the wheat from the chaff. Here we have to analyze the data (Don't skip over those exhibits! They may contain important information!). We're really just gathering information at this stage, but we want it to be the right information, which is why we define the critical question first. Once we have done this, but before we analyze it, we need to see if there are any,

4. Conditions for solution.

This is important because it helps to keep us from going astray. For example, in a case with a deteriorating hotel property students will often define the solution as "renovate." Of course, if renovation means $50 million and the owner is not about to spend it, then that "solution" isn't of much help. Conditions may be values or beliefs. Sometimes these may be overcome, sometimes not. It is important to know what they are. The best solution is useless if it can't be implemented.

5. Situation analysis.

This may be the most important part of marketing and/or management, but many people don't want to bother to do a proper job at it. It is easier to say, "Business is off, let's increase the advertising," which may, in fact, make the situation worse if the reason business is off is a negative perception. Marketing decisions are relatively easy if you've done the analysis right. You will read a number of cases in this book where highly paid executives made poor decisions because either they didn't do, or wouldn't accept, what the analysis clearly showed.

Following is a list of areas that you need to especially look at, but you have to read between the lines. For example, don't expect the case to say "the generic demand is..." You may find that answer in a graph, in a table, in a comment, in a financial breakdown, or any one of a number of places. Or, you may not find it at all - you may have to infer it from the best information you have and decide if it is worth going after additional information. The questions after each item on the the list are suggestive, *not* exhaustive by any means. Your marketing courses, texts, and instructors will give you many more ideas.

Generic demand: who is it, why is it, what are the needs, are they fulfilled, are there trends, are there complementary products, where is the product class on its life cycle?

Brand demand: who is it, why, what segment and target market, how do they use us, what benefits do we offer, what problems do we solve, what are awareness and preference levels, what is our market share, where are we on the brand life cycle?

Customer profile: what do they look like, are they heavy or light users, how do they make the decision, what influences them, how do they perceive us, what do they use us for, where else do they go, what needs/wants do we fulfill?

Competition: who are they, where are they, what do they look like, how are they positioned against us, in what segments are they stronger/weaker, why do people go there, what do they do better/poorer, what is their market share?

Product/service: what is it, what benefits does it offer or problems does it solve, how is it perceived, positioned, what are complementary lines, what are strengths/weaknesses?

When you have answered these questions, and many more, and decided which ones are critical factors in the case, you should then look at them more closely. What you have done is determined the "facts," or at least the facts as they can best be determined. This is from information in the case, or information you have inferred from the case. As far as you know, it is the best information you have.

Now you need to ask: What assumptions can I make from this information? What further questions do I need to ask? What is missing? Is it worth the time and effort to get it? Is research needed? When you have answered these questions, and done the additional work called for, you can then say, "Okay, what tentative conclusions can I draw from this?" For example, you might have made the assumption that there is a lack of awareness in the marketplace. Your conclusion, then, would be that you need to increase awareness.

From the situation analysis, you should be able to identify not only the problems and causes, but also the opportunities and what it takes, and what precludes, to take advantage of those opportunities.

Now, and only now if this is a solution oriented assignment, should you start thinking about solutions. If you think about them earlier, you are likely to bias your analysis. For example, a case might say that the business did no advertising. You start thinking that a solution is to do advertising. As you proceed through the analysis you look for information to support that solution, which may not be the right solution at all.

The only difference when cases are used as discussion cases, is that the solution may be somewhat elusive for lack of information. Your situation analysis, however, does not change.

FINALLY

After you have done all this work, you need to put it all in perspective. Whether you have been told to turn in the work or not, *organize it*! For many students, this may be the most important thing you will learn in a case course. Frankly, if you cannot organize your thoughts in a way that others can follow, explicate them succinctly, and articulate them clearly, you will not go far in business no matter how smart you are, or what your GPA is.

Check you work against your original questions. Why is there a problem? Does your solution address it? Did you answer the critical question(s)? If not, you may have the wrong answer - or the wrong question. Did you satisfy the conditions for solution? What are the risks? Are the resources available? What are the advantages/disadvantages - no solution is ever perfect or without some problem. What will happen if you do? What will happen if you don't? Who is going to implement it?

If you can answer these questions, you should be ready to go into the classroom, or put down on paper, or, in the real world, present to your superiors, a cogent, clear, concisive, succinct argument for your position - and hold your own against anyone. Holding your own doesn't mean not listening to other viewpoints, not considering new information or a new way to look at the information, or not accepting an alternative that may be better than yours. That's all part of the process. Even the President's cabinet disagrees, yet decisions have to be made.

What it means is: don't be shy, speak up, don't be afraid to argue and defend your position, and don't be afraid to compromise and accept someone else's position. Thinking clearly, using and analyzing the best information available, explicating, and articulating are what the real world is all about. What better place is there to learn it than here?

SECTION 1

THE CONCEPT OF MARKETING

CASE 1

WE DO IT ALL FOR YOU

In 1990, McDonald's celebrates its 35th anniversary. It has long since been the largest foodservice organization in the world and its success story is unparalleled in the foodservice industry. In 1993, McDonald's anticipates selling its 100 billionth hamburger. In 1984, the American Marketing Association awarded McDonald's its supreme accolade of marketing company of the year. How did McDonald's get this way? The answer to that question demonstrates the concept of marketing.

Ray Kroc, McDonald's founder, probably never heard of the marketing concept. No doubt he would have failed the final exam in Marketing 101 had he been required to take it. Yet Kroc, and McDonald's, is probably the best example we have in the hospitality industry of a marketer *par excellence*.

McCONCEPT

Kroc found a particularly successful restaurant in San Bernadino, California and approached the owners (the McDonald brothers) with the idea of franchising their fast food (then an unknown term) concept. When they finally reluctantly agreed, Kroc converted a product orientation into a marketing orientation that has since spelled out the reasons for McDonald's success.

Major demographic shifts were taking place on the American landscape in the 1950s and early 1960s. First, there was a massive movement of the middle-class population to the suburbs. This population was families, typically with 2.7 children, a wife and mother who stayed home, a casual life style, and many trips to shopping centers and other suburban locations with the children in the back of a station wagon. There was also a perceptive increase in discretionary dollars for these families.

Kroc saw in these demographic movements a need for foodservice establishments that provided uniformity and cleanliness, wherever and whenever a family might choose to eat, at affordable prices. Typically, in those days, one of a mother's most frustrating experiences was to enter a restaurant with children. Enduring the long wait for service was a harrowing experience, not to mention the usual "greasy spoon" ambience, and the unreliability of the product.

Recognizing these problems, Kroc developed the concept of QSC - quality, service, and cleanliness. Quality meant that the food was hot and tasted good. Rigid standards were established as to the beef used in hamburgers, the potatoes used for french fries, and the recipe used for milkshakes. Service meant that it was quick and courteous and produced without hassle. Cleanliness meant that the surroundings would be clean and neat, both inside and out. This included personnel, equipment, and product presentation. Perhaps Kroc's greatest coup in this respect was the large windows in the front of his stores which revealed everything inside. Cleanliness not only existed, it was there for all to see. In 1955, this concept was totally unique.

Kroc initially identified his market as the large number of families across the United States who wanted budget-priced hamburgers produced fast in clean surroundings. Early advertising was targeted at this market and McDonald's research revealed that over three-fourths of the company's sales were to families influenced by children. The early McDonald's sales pitch was aimed almost entirely at these children.

According to Kroc, McDonald's success was derived from finding something the market wanted, something that was basic and simple, and something that could be sold in volume and sold fast. "What could be more natural than meat and potatoes - that's what we sell at McDonald's," he said. McDonald's initial emphasis was on the hamburger. Thirty-five years later it was still on the hamburger.

McPROGRESS

Of course, menu expansion occurred. There was the Big Mac in 1968, and still going strong, and the Quarter Pounder in 1972. There was the filet-of-fish sandwich, hot apple pie, triple ripple ice cream, McDonald Land cookies, egg McMuffin, chicken McNuggets, McD.L.T., and many others. Innovative styrofoam packaging was developed for takeout orders. Some of these innovations succeeded and some did not, but almost all new menu items originated with franchisees. They then went through extensive testing in McDonald's cooking labs, as well as in the field. In fact, Kroc himself was never very successful as an innovator, most of his suggestions failed in the marketplace.

Although McDonald's has more than held its own in product development, it didn't always command the marketing spotlight. New products were slow to come out of hamburger headquarters in Oak Brook, Illinois, the home of McDonald's corporate offices and also the home of Hamburger University where McDonald's "weeds out" its managers. There have been times, such as the late 1970s and early 1980s, when customers seemed to tire of hamburgers. Rivals Wendy's and Burger King pumped out new products and revamped menus and formats to cope with downturns in the industry. Nevertheless, it was McDonald's that changed America's habits when it rolled out "Breakfast at McDonald's," an act that Burger King is still trying to catch up to.

McDonald's stuck with its original strategy and its continued reverence for the principles of Ray Kroc. Consistently, in good times and bad, McDonald's has been able to maintain, if not increase, market share against its rivals who "do or die" to catch the leader. McDonald's stays positioned according to Ray Kroc's original formula - be the lowest price, look for new markets, and put efficiency above all else. More than that, McDonald's never takes its eye off the customer. This strategy led to overseas expansion, although initially unprofitable, while other chains concentrated on saturating the domestic scene. Today, over 25 percent of McDonald's are outside the United States compared to the ten percent Burger King's, its closest rival.

It was Kroc's vision, as well, that led to resistance to an industry trend to higher priced menus. This strategy paid off when consumers traded down during inflationary periods. The original strategy still served McDonald's well 34 years later.

Originally, McDonald's was a chain of drive-ins featuring candy-stripe buildings of red and white tile. Today, these buildings no longer exist. In their place is every kind of imaginable structure or location. Although drive-throughs have come back after almost disappearing, there are now facilities with indoor dining, seating capacity for 125 people, and locations in shopping malls, office buildings, universities, institutions, interstate highways, and most any other conceivable place. Although the golden arches are omnipresent, McDonald's has continuously adapted to the local environment, decor, and architecture from Wisconsin Dells (adapted to Frank Lloyd Wright concepts) to the Champs Elysee in Paris. Built adjacent to restaurants where feasible, or integrated into the interior design of the dining area, is a McDonald's playland which provides children a place to eat and play while families eat their meals at McDonald's.

McDonald's advertising strategy has been consistent with its master strategy. Objectives of this strategy have been,

* presell the market by making them aware of their eating out needs,
* inform the market of the special values that make it ad vantageous to buy from McDonald's, and
* maintain and enhance competitive position in the market.

McFUTURE

McDonald's spends most of its advertising money on special promotions and commercial television. In fact, it is one of the largest television advertisers in the country. Unlike its competitors, however, rarely does McDonald's feature its physical product in its commercials. Instead, it features the intangible product - good fun and sociableness. These attributes, along with the symbolic presence of Ronald McDonald, have become McDonald's trademarks.

In 1975, McDonald's inaugurated its "At McDonald's we do it all for you" campaign on the premise that McDonald's offers people more than just "quality, service, cleanliness." The campaign was designed to communicate that McDonald's was an experience that was the sum total of food, folks, and fun found there. That theme, although not in those words, has continued until today and the emphasis remains on the experience that one has at McDonald's, each and every time.

In addition to national programs, local operations participate frequently in community development and local programs developed from local concerns such as safety, ecology, and nutrition. When communities suffer hardships, McDonald's is the first one there giving coffee to fireman, feeding victims, raising relief funds, and contributing to the cause. Ronald McDonald Houses, supported by local McDonald's restaurants, the medical community, and volunteer groups, served as homes away from home for nearly 100,000 family members whose children were treated at nearby hospitals in the United States, Canada, and Australia.

A strong marketing research department conducts ongoing surveys to measure the company's strength with consumers and to provide direction for marketing strategy. In 1970, research found that most of McDonald's customers were young married couples with small children, children who led their parents to McDonald's. In 1989 these children, and those of the baby-boom generation that preceded them, had all been weaned on McDonald's, and led their own children in that direction. From sponsoring Saturday morning cartoons on television, McDonald's now sponsors the Olympics and major golf tournaments.

At McDonald's, they still "do it all for you."

CASE 2

THE HOWARD JOHNSON SAGA

In 1965 Howard Johnson's sales exceeded the combined sales of McDonald's, Burger King, and Kentucky Fried Chicken combined. It is said that Bill Marriott remarked at about that time, "I hope one day we can be as big as Howard Johnson's." Twenty years later, when the Howard Johnson company was sold for the second time, to Marriott, its sales were less than three-fourths of a billion dollars, Marriott's were $3.5 billion. The Howard Johnson story is a study in hospitality marketing. To put it in the proper perspective, we need to trace its history from the beginning.

THE BEGINNING

Howard Johnson Sr., like Kemmons Wilson of Holiday Inns and Ray Kroc of McDonald's, was one of the pioneers of the hospitality industry. These men performed marketing coups. They identified a need in the marketplace, identified the market, and built a product to fill the need. Figuratively speaking, Kemmons Wilson put clean, dependable, affordable lodging on every highway corner in America. Ray Kroc put fast, clean, inexpensive food at the fingertips of every American. Howard Johnson Sr. made dependable, moderate priced eating-out available to many American families. Holiday and McDonald's continue their legacies today, Howard Johnson's does not.

In the 1950s, from roots that began in 1925, Howard Johnson's was No. 1 in the foodservice hearts of millions of Americans. It was a household name that customers could count on for quality, service, and a reasonable meal at a reasonable price. The symbolic orange roofs dotted the American landscape by the hundreds and were a welcome sight for weary travelers. They stood for old-fashioned American values, and places where you could always get the best fried clams and the best 28 flavors of ice cream available anywhere. Later on, you could stay at a Howard Johnson's motel as well, but the real Howard Johnson's institution was a restaurant institution.

Howard Johnson Sr., was a true entrepreneur in the American tradition. He had a love for his work and his destiny and a tremendous drive to succeed. He also had a true appreciation of the restaurant business and the need to provide a quality product and quality service. Like what happens to many entrepreneurs, however, the business grew beyond Howard Johnson Sr. The tried and true formula and the cookie-cutter approach began to lose its lustre. Quality of food and service slipped, and cleanliness slipped. Competition began to spring up with new ideas, new concepts, and new ways to serve the customer. Howard Johnson's motels, like Holiday Inns' motels the forerunners of today's modern motor inn, became functionally and technologicaly obsolete. Holiday Inns changed theirs, albeit barely in time, but Howard Johnson's did not. Thin walls, imitation Danish furniture, dark corridors, and shoddy appearances were behind the times.

Howard Johnson Sr. died in 1972 but he had turned the reins over to his son in the 1960s. The company became real estate and bottom line oriented. The orange roofs became a symbol for shoddy service, dreary food, lack of cleanliness, sour attitudes, and poor price/value. The customer went elsewhere.

It was not only Howard Johnson's that changed. More important, the customer changed. The customer now had choices, he and she became more demanding. He and she now had different needs and wants than basic food and accommodations from a cooky-cutter mold. The world drove past Howard Johnson's.

THE LATE 1970s

By the late 1970s, Howard Johnson's had become a multi-brand company. Howard Johnson Jr. had put together a new management team in an attempt to revive the ailing situation. Long study led to the conclusion that the company would have to be repositioned, to the recognition that the customer had changed, and to the realization that things would have to be done differently. The company was reorganized into divisions, each with its own group vice president.

THE ORANGE ROOF DIVISION

Dramatic changes were assigned to take place in the oldest and largest division of the company (644 company owned and 244 franchise units). This division included four different restaurant concepts: Howard Johnson's, New Edition, The Choice is Yours, and toll road restaurants. Rising costs and flattening sales trends had left their mark. An extensive renovation program was begun and over $15 million was spent on rehabilitation in 1978. According to this division's head, "Six or seven years ago we didn't put as much money into refurbishing as we should have. Now we're playing catch-up."

Howard Johnson's Over 200 of the orange roof restaurants were rehabbed with wicker chairs, marble-like table tops, potted ferns, gazebo salad bars, and plush cocktail lounges. Liquor sales increased to 30 percent of sales from the former 10 percent. The traditional Howard Johnson's menu, however, was retained.

New Edition Fourteen New Edition restaurants (with 20 more sites approved) bore the same basic new look as the orange roof restaurants except that peacock chairs, linen napkins, and wooden signage were added, plus an oversize, full color, completely revamped glossy menu costing over $5.00 to produce. Portions were oversized, "a major drawing card to increase the customer's perception of value." The menus were revised four times in less than two years to reflect customer preference or labor intensity of the selections. Menus also merchandised cocktails, wines, and cordials. Eggs Benedict, among other things, went on the breakfast and late night menus, deli sandwiches went on the lunch menus, and dinner menus featured seafood platters, beef kabobs and chicken chasseur. The target was a 15 percent increase in customer count and a 40 percent increase in check average.

The company was extremely bullish on the New Edition concept. New units opened with a 40 percent increase in customers and almost a 100 percent increase in check average in the first two weeks. All new or rehab-bed orange roof restaurants were planned to be New Edition units.

The Choice is Yours The third entry in the orange roof division was the Choice is Yours restaurants. The first three units were opened in the south. The concept of these restaurants was to give people a choice in portion, price, and variety. Menu items were priced on a unit basis so customers could order, for example, one egg and three sausages, or the reverse, and pay for each on a unit basis. The concept was initially aimed at senior citizens with limited income and limited appetites, but future units were planned for different demographic and income areas. Check averages doubled to over three dollars. Newspaper ads explained the concept:

> If you're tired of restaurants that don't give you a choice, come to the Choice is Yours. If you'd like a little veal with your spaghetti, or if you'd like a little spaghetti with your veal, come to the Choice is Yours.

Decor was country kitchen style with round wooden tables and a kitchen hearth with a kettle of soup and mugs for self-service. Menu items included frankfurters, both traditional and exotic hamburgers, sauteed beef liver, London broil, and broiled fish.

Turnpike Units Over 90 traditional orange roof Howard Johnson's turnpike units were converted to cafeterias to speed up service and raise volume. On the West Virginia turnpike, however, six units were refurbished to feature dining room service, fast food, and a decor similar to New Edition.

Truck Stops In the southwest, a fifth orange roof concept was deve-loping. These were truck stops located in service plazas with a limited menu, shower facilities, and TV rooms.

All orange roof restaurants were opened on a 24 hour basis. This was reported to be successful with late night travelers plus "it had the added attraction of reducing fire problems almost completely." The number of orange roof units being constructed was almost on a par with those being closed so total number of units remained about he same.

THE SPECIALTY RESTAURANT DIVISION

There were three restaurant concepts in the Howard Johnson's specialty division: 128 Ground Round units, 32 Red Coach Grills, and a new Lucky Lil's concept.

Ground Round In 1979, Ground Round was scheduled for a major franchising effort with as many units planned as there were orange roof restaurants. One hundred company operated units had been built since 1969 to refine the concept before franchising it.

The Ground Round concept was a beef based menu in a turn-of-the-century saloon atmosphere. Peanut shells on the floor and popcorn on every table went with the continuous oldtime movies to establish a fun atmosphere. On one side of the units, lighting and entertainment were geared to the family, on the other side they were geared to singles and couples.

Ground Rounds were intended to serve the local community in its tastes and promotions, and were built or converted in clusters of six units. The menu consisted of moderate priced hamburgers, sandwiches, steaks and seafood items. Drinks were sold singly or by the pitcher and flyers pushed frozen daiquiris, margaritas, and brandy Alexanders. A 16 unit St. Louis based restaurant chain was purchased with plans to convert all units to Ground Rounds. With average unit volumes at $750,000, additional units were planned for New England, New Jersey, Pennsylvania, Washington D.C., and Virginia.

Red Coach Grills The Red Coach Grills were part of a 40 year old chain of upscale, fine dining establishments considered to be a pet project of Howard Johnson Sr. It had evolved from a staid, conservative concept to one catering to all market segments. To increase price/value perception, prices had been lowered, the atmosphere was relaxed, and promotions encouraged family business. Another idea was on the horizon and a prototype had been built. This was the addition of discotheques in Lightfoot's Lounge, a 150 seat wood, brick, and leather decor bar. In the prototype unit, total sales had increased by 40 percent. The aim was to increase gross profits through higher liquor sales because of the opposing high food costs.

Lucky Lil's Lucky Lil's was a plush fine dining restaurant opened on the rich suburban Long Island north shore. It was a 200 seat, opulent, neo-Victorian unit that was planned for new Howard Johnson's hotels if it proved successful. It was converted from a former Red Coach Grill and attached to an historical landmark. The menu ranged from shrimp in cognac sauce, quiche, and crepes for appetizers to steak, seafood, shrimp, chicken, and sandwich items. Lavish deserts were also featured as were specialty drinks and an 18 choice wine list.

COMPANY STRATEGIES

Howard Johnson's corporate headquarters were near Boston, Massachusetts but President Howard B. Johnson had his office in Rockefeller Plaza in New York. Interviewed there, he had the following to say about the company's direction.

> Some of the changes might be more cosmetic than total, because the same fellow who was running the company 10 years ago is still running it today. The fundamental elements will stay the same: the emphasis on quality products, the commissary system, the supporting retail system, the strong conservative approach, the liquidity of finacial status and the blending of the franchised and company operated system.
>
> [In the past] we've changed subtly. Now we're changing with a little more punch. In the old days, the changes were largely architectural, now our food and liquor service are changing too.

Johnson worried about repositioning a company whose image was engraved in so many minds. He was not particularly optimistic about the future of the foodservice industry in general, in spite of the fact that he was spending millions of dollars to be ready for the 1980s. The 1980s, Johnson felt, would bring many changes. For example, he noted that "women don't want to cook anymore." That he considered a plus, but admitted that there were problems for which he did not have solutions such as adjusting the consumer's perception of price/value as costs of doing business continued to increase.

Johnson commented that the competition was "tough and intelligent." He wondered about using TV to woo customers versus simply offering good food and good service. He stated,

> I still don't think that the food business is a marketing business. If you think that you can cut portions and food quality and raise prices just so long as you advertise, I don't think you'll stay in business very long.
>
> We all want the dinner business, but you have those horrible margins involved in putting out the plate. So we have to sell a lot of liquor, but in a coffee shop you can't sell more than seven or eight percent liquor.

I don't have the key yet. I'm sure that we're making the right long term moves, but I don't have the key to shrinking return on investment or profit margins yet.

NEW OWNERSHIP

In June 1980, Imperial Group PLC, a leading British tobacco and food conglomerate, completed the purchase of Howard Johnson's for $630 million. The price was 18 times earnings, more than twice book value, but Imperial described Howard Johnson's as part of the American way of life, attuned to changing consumer preferences and circumstances.

For a year and a half Howard Johnson's floundered as Imperial tried to figure out what to do with it. Howard Johnson remained at the helm. Sales remained flat while operating income dropped. The major marketing effort was in advertising, but in fiscal 1982 operating profits dropped 33 percent to $27 million. Exhibit 1 shows the type of national ad that was run in 1980 and 1981.

On January 1, 1982 G.Michael Hostage became chairman, president, and chief executive office of the company. Hostage was recruited by Imperial from ITT Continental Baking Company, the makers of Wonder Bread. He had previously spent 15 years with the Marriott Corporation where he had been Restaurant Group president and an executive vice-president. Hostage spent 10 months putting together his plan to revive the ailing company and to fulfill his mandate from Imperial to turn the company around in five years.

In November, Hostage flew to London to present his plan to Imperial. He returned with what he wanted. Imperial agreed to finance a huge building program including $700 million for a new chain of hotels. An additional $78 million would be spent to refurbish existing lodges and Howard Johnson's restaurants would get money to revamp their image and menus. Hostage stated, "We're basically catching up with the rest of the industry." Industry observers, however, were less sanguine. Most contended that Howard Johnson's biggest problem was in implementing change.

Hostage's plans included a new hotel chain with 40 hotels in cities, suburbs, and at airports. Rooms would average $55 a night, $15 higher than present rates. Howard Johnson's would buy, remodel, and build these hotels.

Howard Johnson's owned and operated 75 percent of its 800 orange roof restaurants. Hostage intended to fix these up so that they would support and complement the lodges that they usually adjoined, and close about 60 that could not be turned around. He also intended to revamp menus and increase liquor sales. "HoJo restaurants," said a competitor, "for years have squeezed customers with higher prices, poor service, and outdated entrees." To cut costs, Hostage would allow managers to buy from sources other than Howard Johnson's central commissaries.

EXHIBIT 1 Howard Johnson's Advertising in 1980 and 1981

Why Jimmy Connors' business manager makes Howard Johnson's her first choice.

Gloria Connors, president of Tennis Management Associates and mother of the company's biggest asset, tells why she likes Howard Johnson's.

"From Longwood to Hollywood, there always seems to be a Howard Johnson's nearby."

"In my business, a big, comfortable room isn't a luxury, it's a necessity."

"After two double-tiebreakers, believe me, I need to relax. A tall cool drink, a dip in the pool or a little music in the lounge can work wonders."

"As a business woman, I like knowing I can dine right where I'm staying. And because many Howard Johnson's restaurants are open 24 hours, I can have a meal or snack anytime I want."

HOWARD JOHNSON'S

First choice of more and more business travelers.

Hostage also planned to increase occupancy at existing lodges from the present 63.5 percent, which was below industry averages. He wanted to add amenities such as racquetball courts to lure business travelers, as well as corporate discounts, a new reservations system, and to start a national television advertising campaign. He would offer low interest loans to the 120 franchisees to encourage them to refurbish.

The Ground Round chain was to be expanded and the 26 lagging Red Coach Grills would be sold or turned into Ground Rounds. What was left of the New Edition, Choice is Yours, and Lucky Lil's units would be phased out, converted, or sold.

Industry commentators noted the difficulties with Hostage's plans. The plans offered nothing that the industry did not already offer. The new hotel chain would need a new name because the old one had a dowdy reputation. This image persisted with the restaurant chains. Said one critic, "Howard Johnson's will have to run hard just to keep up. Forget about sales gains." Said a former employee, "The problem is more in execution. HoJo's has been a sleeping giant for years. If Hostage can wake it up , the competition better watch out."

IMPLEMENTING THE NEW PLAN

1983 saw the beginning of a carefully planned, major reorganization of the way Howard Johnson's manages and markets its restaurants and lodges. Potentially most important was a program to eliminate separate management of restaurants and lodges. This was intended to allow a general manager to develop a program of high margin room service and banquet sales. Tests of this new organization, at two locations where the company had new upscale Chatt's restaurants, were considered successful. One problem, however, was that three-fourths of the lodges were franchised while most the restaurants were company owned and operated.

Consumer research had been conducted in 1982 to determine strategy for competing in the family restaurant arena. The research revealed what appeared to be a deficiency of fast food restaurants in the family market. Fast food customers with children were found to be highly susceptible to an appeal to bringing their families to a concept with tableservice and metal flatware. New advertising copy was rolled out to take advantage of this opportunity. Ads headlined, "If it's not your mother it must be Howard Johnson's." Other promotional spots highlighted specific menu items such as roast beef, clams, and chicken. Regional menu items were also adopted at certain locations featuring options like crab cakes, sticky beans, catfish, red beans and rice, and barbecued pork.

Sixteen of the remaining 19 Red Coach Grills were sold. Plans were made for expanding the Ground Round chain by 25 to 30 units in the next year, but were hampered by the lack of experienced unit managers. Actual chain average unit sales had dropped in 1982 to about $900,000 from the previous $1.25 million range. This was largely blamed on inexperienced management. A new restaurant training center was established to correct this problem. In several other units, it was planned to build a greenhouse-like dining space on one side of the building to make the restaurant brighter in color, lighter, and more airy. It was intended to do away with the old peanuts-on-the-floor look and appeal more to the family segment.

By mid-1983 Howard Johnson Company (the apostrophe s had been dropped) was testing a range of new casual theme and family restaurants. Prototype openings came on the heels of a push into full service hotels, fast food, and an expanded contract management business. The new strategy was to gain entry into many demographic groups.

Bumbershoots was a casual theme concept designed to compete with the likes of Houlihan's, Bennigan's and TGI Friday's, a hot and highly competitive market segment at the time. Paddywacks was an upscale coffee shop, and Halligan's was a dinnerhouse with a menu similar to Bumbershoots but more formal. Franchised Burger King outlets were opened on the Pennsylvania Turnpike and others were planned.

Ground Round, now 222 units strong, had its menu revised to lighter fare along with the change in decor, to build check averages and volumes and to draw customers from more upscale casual-theme competitors. The menu would include everything from hamburgers and chicken to a pasta of the day. "Americans have developed into eclectic eaters," said the woman who planned the menus. "They get bored easily. A successful restaurant must have a varied menu." These changes were expected to increase unit sales by more than 15 percent.

Michael Fuller, the vice president who headed Ground Round, said the company would fill in existing markets before entering new ones. He was unfazed by competition such as TGI Friday's and Bennigan's, which he called "fern bars." "Ground Round has a unique niche," Fuller said. "Both families and singles are comfortable with us. We have done the one thing other chains have failed to do: marry the family trade with strong liquor sales."

The Howard Johnson restaurants, 490 company owned, 86 on turnpikes, and 225 franchised, also had a new program designated "Up, up and Away." The traditional stodgy signage would give way to an updated look and menus would also be modernized. Exterior changes were planned including greenhouses, sunroofs, and possible elimination of the orange roofs. Said one executive about the $150 million spent in the past seven years, "We spent all that money, but we didn't tell the public we were doing anything different." The company also had plans for a "Super Howard Johnson" designed by an outside consultant.

OTHER CHANGES

The first full service hotel was under construction and was scheduled to open in 1985. In the 500 unit motor lodge system (60,000 rooms, 11,000 company owned), a refurbishing program was beginning to help shift the market mix to a greater share of commercial travelers. Twenty-six million dollars was scheduled for revamping during the next two years. A program had also been instituted by which entire floors of lodges were segregated for traveling businessmen who were provided with special amenities including free breakfast for four to five extra dollars per night.

Meanwhile, major changes were made in personnel administration. These included some reduction in work week hours for salaried employees, a boost in incentives, and a certification program for employees who come into contact with the public. This program was designed to eliminate, or avoid hiring of, employees who were prone to be rude to customers.

In spite of all this movement, industry watchers tended to be sceptical and impatient for results. Those close to the situation, however, praised Hostage for having taken a conservative, real estate oriented company and moved it slowly toward a marketing oriented company. Some felt that if Hostage had moved more swiftly he might have torn the tradition-laden company apart.

Hostage also brought in new top executives to blend with existing personnel, rather than do an overall house-cleaning. He stated, "There's nothing wrong with the people who worked so loyally for Howard Johnson for so many years. It's just a case of reorienting the thinking under new leadership."

More important than anything, perhaps, was the newly expressed philosophy of management. Said Thomas Russo, president of the restaurant and lodging group, "When Howard Johnson's started out, we were the only company out there doing what we did. So we could do what we wanted. But eventually the customer became important. It's taken us a while to recognize that." Russo attributed this new consumer consciousness to the arrival of Mike Hostage. "We have to create a marketing oriented atmosphere."

"We know we've been in a time warp at Howard Johnson's," said Russo. "We're bringing it into the '80s and preparing it for the '90s. We've kept what's good - ice cream, for example - and added some new dimensions. We're not married to an orange roof. They'll probably change eventually, to what color I don't know."

THE NEW HOTELS

In spring 1984, Hostage and Manuel Ferris, Howard Johnson hotel group head, introduced the Plaza-Hotel concept at a New York City press conference. Hostage said the company had begun undoing a "decade of neglect." "We aim to introduce a new generation of commercial travelers to Howard Johnson's," Ferris said. "As a group, they are people who never really thought of staying at Howard Johnson's before."

Each new hotel would carry the words Plaza-Hotel preceded by its location, e.g., the Washington Plaza-Hotel. At the time, two acquired hotels were open (Washington D.C. and Minneapolis) and two were under construction (J.F.Kennedy Airport and Baltimore's Inner Harbor). Each hotel offered a full range of amenities, meeting facilities, and services. Most would have separate executive sections.

The hotels were positioned in the mid-price range of the market at $45 to $65 per night, depending on location. Major competition was perceived to be Ramada, Holiday and Marriott's Courtyard, just introduced. Costs for new hotels were pegged at about $55,000 per room. Eighty to 100 were planned within the next five years including new construction, acquisitions, and conversion of existing full service Howard Johnson properties. Locations would be downtown, suburban and airport sites with special emphasis on developing the west coast where Howard Johnson was under represented.

The designation "A Howard Johnson Hotel" would appear in prominent places around each new property. "We're not trying to keep Howard Johnson's role a secret," said Ferris, "but we are trying to show this concept is different from anything we've been involved in before." Hotels would contain an extremely upscale coffee shop as their full service dining room and would not resemble the other Howard Johnson restaurants.

"The most important thing for Howard Johnson was to get out and get moving again, and we've done that," said Hostage.

THE NEW RESTAURANTS

A year after opening the first unit, Bumbershoots tripled its business compared to the previous operation. Customer research showed a 95 percent intent to return. A second one was being built in New Jersey.

In May 1984, the company opened a new "fun-and-food" concept with a separate lounge called Pickle Lilys in Burlington, Massachusetts. Lower priced than Bumbershoots, this concept was a variation of the Ground Round theme and appeared "promising." Hostage also had high hopes for another concept called Deli Baker Ice Cream Maker, a full service restaurant with take out counters featuring deli fare, ice cream, and baked goods. Paddywacks, meanwhile, had not met projections and was being considered for termination.

In November 1984, Howard Johnson completed the nationwide rollout of a new menu for its orange roof restaurants. The menu, according to a company spokeswoman, is an indicator of "a return to traditional values and thinking" on Howard Johnson's part. Capitalizing on customer nostalgia, Howard Johnson also resurrected its Simple Simon and the Pieman logo, originally developed in the 1930s, and positioned it prominently on the menu's cover. Exhibit 2 shows the original version.

EXHIBIT 2 Howard Johnson's Original Simple Simon Logo

The new menu was more different from the previous one in terms of the graphics than in its offerings, although several new dishes had been added. In addition some "old favorites" were brought back. Like the old Howard Johnson's menu, the new one was an all day menu designed to "keep customers coming in throughout the day." The spokeswoman also explained that renovation of Ground Rounds and development of new concepts were two main components in Howard Johnson's efforts to upgrade the image of its restaurants, which had long been held back by sluggish sales. "One of the things the company has failed to do in the past," she said, "is to change. These are some of the ways we're trying to correct the problem."

For fiscal 1984, Howard Johnson's sales were a little over $700 million, barely $100 million more than where they were when Imperial PLC bought the company. Operating income was about $27 million, about what it had been four years before. Even cash flow had turned negative. Imperial PLC announced that it might sell the company.

BREAKING UP THE COMPANY

In November 1985, Imperial sold all of Howard Johnson to Marriott Corporation for $300 million, less than half of what it had paid. In British pounds, however, Imperial broke even because of the better exchange rates caused by weakening of the dollar. An Imperial spokesman stated, "Profits were artificially high when we bought it. Because its asset values were very low, depreciation charges were also low. Its reinvestment had been neglected. Pennies had been pinched on staffing, menus and renewal. It was milking the business by not reinvesting." Howard Johnson's restaurants had become overpriced and understaffed purveyors of pallid food, hamstrung by outdated ideas. Howard Johnson, it was said, had stood fast with a diversified menu while it was being segmented to death. Howard Johnson, himself, commented on the situation:

> Shaking it all down, that's probably where the difficulty lay - [business travelers in motor lodges didn't want HoJo restaurants]. The more we tried to adjust our restaurants to what the motor lodge's business clientele wanted, the more difficult our restaurant operation became. We spent 15 years trying to do what was probably an impossible task. We tried just about everything. New layouts, new architecture, cocktail lounges and discos. But it kept coming back. We needed two different restaurants. Frankfurters and ice cream just didn't mix with martinis and rock music.

Another commentary stated,

> There was no real marketing plan. Howard Johnson ran the company more with an accountant's eye than with an entrepreneur's. The preoccupation was with controlling expenses instead of monitoring changing consumer opinions. Said Johnson, 'We ran a very tight operation. We kept our expenses low. We wanted to have earnings improvement. We were on top of the numbers daily.' To gauge customer satisfaction and changing tastes, HoJo largely relies on comment cards left at its restaurant tables. Competitors Marriott and Denny's run sophisticated market-testing operations. Not only do those tests tell competitors what customers do like, they also tell them what they don't like - Howard Johnson's.

Said a competitor,

> Every time I saw Howard Johnson he was always telling me how he was going to cut costs further. I don't think he spent enough time at his restaurants. If he'd eaten in his own restaurants more instead of lunching at '21,' he might have learned something.

Although Marriott paid Imperial $300 million for all of Howard Johnson, it kept only the 418 company owned HoJo restaurants. This provided Marriott with prime real estate locations that were gradually to be converted to Marriott concepts. Marriott sold the 199 franchised restaurants plus all of the mostly franchised lodging properties to Prime Motor Inns.

PRIME MOTOR INNS AND HOWARD JOHNSON

Prime Motor Inns was a successful hotel management company that had been a Howard Johnson franchisee, and also owned franchises of other companies. It quickly sold off the 199 unit still orange-roofed Howard Johnson restaurant franchise system. Prime then disclosed its plans for dramatically expanding the Howard Johnson hotel chain. Michael Hostage, now chairman of Prime's Howard Johnson division, announced a concept similar to Marriott's Courtyard except that, unlike Courtyards, the units would be franchised. The new hotels were to be called Howard Johnson Park Square Inns (Exhibit 3). Three hundred were planned by 1990.

EXHIBIT 3 The Howard Johnson Courtyard Concept

Curtis Bean, vice president of franchising, called Park Square Inn a unique product. He stated,

> I think it's important to emphasize that what we're going through now with Howard Johnson is going back to basics. [Our competitors who are geared for the midprice segment] have lost focus. I see us as being in that very niche to a more sophisticated traveler, and to a businessman who wants a quality room and is still looking for price and value in a room.

Hostage announced a $10 - $12 million marketing program for the 500 existing (125 company owned) hotels and plans to refurbish all properties. Some units were sold with Prime retaining management contracts.

In June 1986, the Howard Johnson Hotel Company kicked off a five million dollar ad campaign in an effort to improve an image that a company spokesman said, "could use a little dusting off." Howard Johnson wanted to inform the public that the company had changed dramatically since Prime took it over. Howard Johnson now wanted to position solely as a lodging chain. As VP - Sales and Marketing Roland Watters Jr. put it,

> What we're saying here is, 'Hey,folks, we've got a really good product here and don't be discouraged by what we were in the past. Now we're strictly in the hotel business. If you try us, chances are you're going to like us and want to come back.' To capitalize on the ownership change, we wanted a campaign that would cut through all the clutter. We wanted our customers to know that something is changing at Howard Johnson.

Phase I of the campaign used television commercials and print advertising to note the change (Exhibit 4). Phase 2, used later, was designed to establish the identity with the tag line, "This is Howard Johnson" showing Howard Johnson properties.

The ad campaign was based on research that indicated a connection between the lodging properties and Howard Johnson's familiar orange roof restaurants, as well as the fact that the quality of the properties had slipped.

"Alot of the negative image of Howard Johnson is related to the restaurants," said Watters. (Approximately 300 remained in the Marriott fold, another 190 belonged to owners/operators under franchise agreements, and still bore the familiar orange roof. From May 1986 through April 1987, *Consumer Reports* magazine surveyed 220,000 diners' opinions about the nation's largest restaurant chains in terms of taste, selection, service, atmosphere, cleanliness, value, and child accommodations. Howard Johnson received the lowest rating of all family restaurant chains.) "We've been going through a refurbishing program and we're well on the way to getting that completed."

Prime lacked expertise in restaurant franchising and therefore chose not to retain the Howard Johnson restaurants. The company did not, however, shy away from food and beverage operations, which it had found very profitable through its Sandalwood restaurant concept in its hotels.

In 1988, Prime approved the concept for replacing the orange roof Howard Johnson restaurants that came with its hotels. Conversion began to change them to Herbie K's, chrome- and neon-filled 1950s style diners. The first conversion, in Cocoa Beach, FL, grossed $800,000 in sales its first year, more than five times its pre-conversion volume. According to vice-president David Barsky, the choice to go 50s with Herbie K's had to do with conversion costs.

> The cost of converting to a 1950s style diner was the least expensive of all the choices available to us. Most of those buildings were built in the 1950s, complete with counters. It was the easiest conversion, so why not?

The units have a lounge attached, but with a separate entrance. The menu features standard fare such as meat loaf with mashed potatoes, daily blue plate specials, chili, burgers, wet fries, egg creams, shakes, and banana split.

According to Barsky, Herbie K's is a place to be entertained with nostalgia from the 1950s while you eat. "One thing is almost guaranteed; you'll leave with a smile on your face." How can you not when a bubble gum-blowing waitress sidles over to your table, puts her arm around you and coos, "What'll you have, Toots?"

THE FUTURE

By 1988, the Howard Johnson Divison of Prime Motor Inns had five different concepts on line and was advertising heavily for franchisees (Exhibit 5). Franchise Associates, Inc., the franchisor of Howard Johnson restaurants which had bought the franchise rights from Prime Motor Inns, announced that it had hired a design firm to develop a new look for the familar orange roof concept. It had also asked the firm to develop a new look for Howard Johnson menus and uniforms.

EXHIBIT 4 **Howard Johnson Campaign to Change Its Image**

WE'RE TURNING HOWARD JOHNSON UPSIDE DOWN.

"Your eyes aren't playing tricks on you. We're making so many exciting changes at Howard Johnson, people in the travel industry are starting to say we're turning the place around (or upside down, depending on how you look at things).

Most of the rooms in our nearly 500 hotels and lodges have already been renovated and our refurbishment campaign continues. Everyday it's becoming more apparent to everyone, especially corporate travel professionals, that my management team is committed to this transformation. From top to bottom.

In addition to the physical changes, there are personal ones, too. They're reflected in the smiles on our employees' faces and the extra effort they'll extend to every guest you send to a Howard Johnson Hotel or Lodge.

One thing we're not going to change is our dedication to corporate travel professionals. So we'll continue to offer you corporate rates and fast, efficient ways to book rooms through your major airline reservation system by using our HJ access code. Or by simply calling our toll-free number: 800-654-2677.

Your eyes aren't fooling you, Howard Johnson *is* turning upside down. And we're so excited about the changes, we're doing flip-flops ourselves."

G. Michael Hostage
President and Chief Executive Officer
HOWARD JOHNSON

EXHIBIT 5 Howard Johnson 1988 Lodging Concepts and Franchisee Ad

"We liked the Howard Johnson 'Franchise' so much, we bought the company."

Peter Simon,
Chairman, Prime Motor Inns

We were Howard Johnson franchisees during the period of its greatest growth under its founder and original owners. We see significant opportunities for this fine company today under our stewardship.

Growth is, after all, what Prime is after. And we have a track record of 30 percent compound annual growth that says we know how to achieve it.

We intend to move Howard Johnson into the leadership position in the mid-priced lodging market through ambitious development, renovation and marketing over the next few years.

The mid-market products are here – full-service **Hotels**, **Plaza-Hotels**, **Plaza-Suites**, limited service **AmeriSuites** and improved **Lodges**. The aggressive marketing and advertising support is here. And Prime is here to back it all up.

Now we're looking for developers and franchisees with solid credentials of their own who know a good growth opportunity when they see it.

I invite them to join us by calling **John Buttolph, Howard Johnson's Senior Vice President of Franchise Development at (201) 882-1880.**

You'll be in good company.

THIS IS HOWARD JOHNSON TODAY!

SECTION 2

ENVIRONMENTAL SCANNING AND COMPETITIVE ANALYSIS

CASE 3

WHAT DO WE DO NOW?

Frank Lorenzo spent 20 years in the foodservice business working for others. Working his way from the ground up through all the departments, he had learned the business well. Eventually, he managed properties for Stuart Anderson's Black Angus chain, for Far West Services' theme restaurant chain, and a large steak house restaurant for an independent operator. Frank not only knew his food and beverage controls, purchasing, menu planning, amd organization skills, but he also knew how to treat employees and how to deal with customers. His employees were loyal and worked hard for him; his customers frequently asked for him if he didn't seek them out first. In fact, some said that it was Frank, not the food, service, or decor that made them patronize his restaurants.

Frank enjoyed the restaurant business and had made a good living at it. He yearned, however, to settle down in one place and run his own operation. In 1975, at the age of 40, he found the right spot, raised the necessary capital, and went into business for himself with a restaurant he called Frank's Steak Paradise.

Frank's "spot" was in an eastern city of some 200,000 population. He chose it not only for the location and because he liked the city, but also because the city lacked a good steak house. Frank felt that this offered a real opportunity.

In fact, Frank's Steak Paradise was the first really theme restaurant in town. It had a western setting with a waterfall, a stream, a small wooden bridge, cactus and other western plants, and authentic western memorabilia. The restaurant seated 200 people in various secluded arrangements and configurations that gave it a sense of privacy, as well as one of comfort and warmth. It also had a bar and lounge with a strong western motif that seated another 40 people.

The restaurant was an immediate success. The food was good, the service prompt, and Frank quickly made friends with his customers. In fact, the Steak Paradise became the talk of the town and many people arranged to meet there. Volume reached $1 million the first year and grew to $1.75 million within three years, where it leveled off other than annual adjustments for inflation. Frank was satisfied with this because he felt that this was just about the capacity he could handle and do the job right.

Frank never did any advertising or sales promotion other than local support activities such as a civic group program or the high school football team program. A good product, good relationships, and word-of-mouth did the job for him. Frank seemed to have a monopoly on the steak house market.

Between 1980 and 1985, five competitors opened within a half hour's driving radius. The new competitors had little effect on Frank's business. Frank's Steak Paradise had become an institution and growth in the city seemed to absorb the competition without seriously affecting Frank. As each new restaurant opened, Frank would experience a slight drop in volume but within a few months his volume would recover. Frank continued to do no advertising or promotion since he considered it a waste of money.

In 1986 and 1987, two major chain operations opened in the city. One featured prime rib of beef and the other featured "turf and surf" or steak and lobster. Both new restaurants had a theme atmosphere and both were in the same price range as Frank. Neither, however, did any advertising after their opening promotions.

In 1988, Frank's volume dropped below $1.5 million. In February, 1989 Frank learned of a new steak chain coming to town. Word had it that this chain was an aggressive advertiser on radio, television and in the newspaper and also conducted frequent promotions. Further investigation revealed that in cities where this chain had located, it had attained a volume of $2 million with a steak oriented menu.

The new chain was due to open by the end of the year and Frank decided he had little enough time to do some advertising.

CASE 4

TWIN OAKS RESTAURANT

Twin Oaks Restaurant[1] was purchased in 1946 by an enterprising young couple, Anne and Charlie Curran. Their desire was to operate a restaurant dedicated to the service of "delicious Yankee food in a rustic setting." Forty three years later, Twin Oaks still operated under that premise and the Currans prided themselves on owning one of the oldest restaurants in New England. Continually operating under their direction, the restaurant had always strived to serve the finest food and provide the finest service possible.

The Currans had spent their early years building a name for Twin Oaks. Charlie had designed a logo that had been associated with the restaurant for twenty five years. Anne's own recipes for corn fritters, pecan rolls, and several entrees had been used at Twin Oaks for many years and the Currans believed that the image of the restaurant was strongly associated with quality.

The Twin Oaks manager, Kay Barry, believed the restaurant to be all that it tried to be - a place with no faults and only minor, fleeting problems that served "good old-style Yankee food." She had been heard to say, "This is a family place. Everyone knows about Twin Oaks and knows us as a place to come for a special evening and a nice dinner. They see our place just the way we do and accept our prices as reasonable."

Mr. Curran, however, was reticent to say what he felt it was that brought people to Twin Oaks. The restaurant had always done a lively business, but lately it seemed as though business was dropping. He attributed much of this to the automobile that enabled people to go much further to restaurants than they could in the early years of Twin Oaks. Surely he felt, Twin Oaks was still the fine restaurant it had always been; his feeling for the restaurant had never changed. "Still," he wondered, "that's my feeling for the restaurant. Is that the way my customers see Twin Oaks?"

LOCATION

Twin Oaks was located on Route 20 five miles east of Sturbridge, Massachusetts, easily accessible from Route I-90 (Massachusetts Turnpike), the

---

1 Names and places have been disguised.

major route that ran east and west across the state, and from Route I-86 that ran into I-90 from Connecticut (Exhibit 1).

EXHIBIT 1 Location of Twin Oaks and Surrounding Area

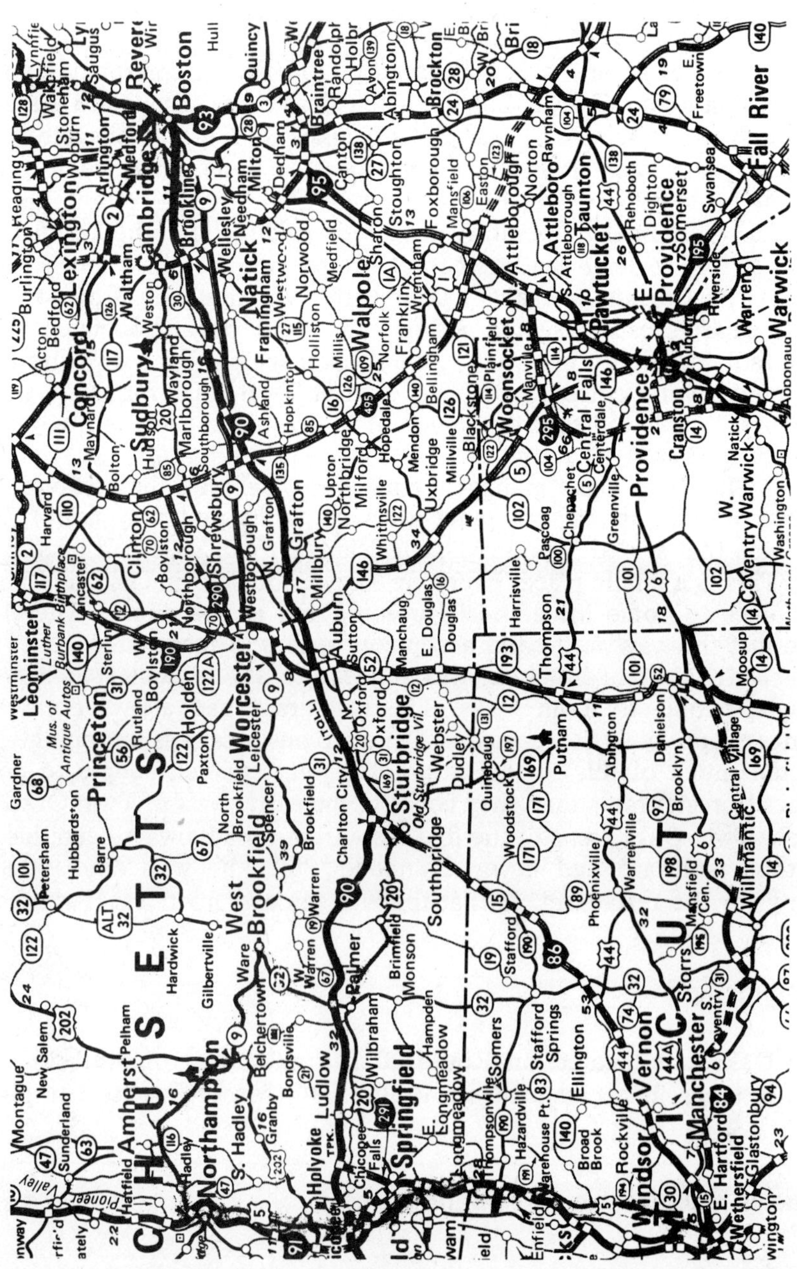

At the time Twin Oaks was purchased by the Currans, Route 20 was a major traffic route. Knowing that Routes I-90 and I-86 would eventually be built, Curran felt that the key to their success would be to establish an image of quality that would attract people to the restaurant. There would be few passersby.

Sturbridge was 60 miles southwest of Boston, 20 miles southwest of Worcester and approximately 30 miles east of Springfield. The restaurant itself was located directly on Route 20, set somewhat back from the roadside but still highly visible. Parking was ample. One side of Twin Oaks faced the mill pond where a small waterfall cascaded past the main entrance and turned into a brook. This brook ran past the twin oak trees which framed the front of the building and by the other side of the restaurant past the main dining room. As it had been built on an incline, the main dining room was approximately twenty feet above the brook, affording a view to all diners in the main room.

Access to Twin Oaks was over a covered footbridge which led to the lower entrance and cocktail lounge or over a larger footbridge which led to a stone path to the main entrance. The pond had a resident family of ducks.

RESTAURANT HISTORY

Twin Oaks was an old sawmill established in 1761. It originally provided lumber for homes in the Sturbridge area and, because of the nearby pond, was the place where townspeople took their Saturday bath. By 1900, the mill had fallen into disrepair and lay vacant until 1921 when it was turned into a summer tearoom which operated until 1942. The pair of 80 foot oak trees at the main entrance remained from the original mill days.

From the time the Currans purchased Twin Oaks and turned it into a full-service year-around operation, the restaurant staff increased from seven employees serving 25,000 customers annually to 200 workers who Curran claimed could serve 290,000 each year.

The Currans were responsible for adding the downstairs Buzz Saw Lounge and the Gift Shop to Twin Oaks without changing the original appearance of the mill. The Gift Shop utilized previously vacant space and offered local and imported handmade items. It did not generate any business of its own, but did operate at a modest profit. It was not in a location where many diners passed by.

THE ORGANIZATION

Charlie and Anne Curran were the owners and founders of the restaurant. Although Anne was semi-retired, Charlie retained his management position and acted as final decision maker for all aspects of the operation. He worked very closely with his General Manager, Kay Barry and their relationship was that of a management team. Charlie Curran maintained all financial records and sales histories for Twin Oaks Enterprises.

Kay Barry was the General Manager of Twin Oaks. She had formerly been the head waitress at the restaurant. In 1984 she returned to Twin Oaks as Food and Beverage Manager, marking the end of a fourteen year career as an interior decorator. Barry's rise to her present position was rapid and her responsibilities covered two areas: she attended to the daily operations of the restaurant and also functioned as the Sales Manager. As Sales Manager, Barry prepared mailing lists of area businesses and created promotional materials for mailings. Barry also booked all banquets.

Assistant Manager was a vacant position. The former Assistant Manager had been promoted from the position of head bartender. He was fired after six months because, according to Kay Barry, "he just couldn't handle it." Barry had assumed all responsibilities of the position and felt no immediate pressure to fill it.

Executive Chef was a position that had been vacant for one month. The previous chef had retired after twenty years and the sous chef had temporarily assumed the overall responsibility. Executive Chef duties included the preparation of the daily menu and the supervision of the kitchen. He was also responsible for control of food and labor cost, an area which was temporarily overseen by Barry and Curran.

Kay Barry considered the organizational atmosphere at Twin Oaks to be "like one big family." She believed that employees were very comfortable and that the office was open to everyone.

Each new waitress or waiter was required to undergo seven to ten days of on-the-job training and was assigned to work on a one-to-one basis with a senior employee. Training was supervised by the head waitress.

The Currans had always believed in strict discipline for their employees. Quality service was part of the restaurant's tradition so they felt that discipline in training was essential. In fact, both felt that discipline and training were two of their greatest strengths.

Many trainees dropped out of the training program before completion. Those who remained but did not attain the required level of service were dismissed. Kay had been heard to say that every waitress at Twin Oaks could be successfully employed at her choice of restaurants across the country.

THE APPEARANCE

The ten dining rooms varied in size. Total capacity of the restaurant was 650 although Curran considered 525 to be a full house. The dining rooms seated 10 to 150 and all of the larger rooms were equipped with a fireplace. Pianos, if desired, could be supplied for private functions.

Each of the establishment's rooms had print colonial wallpaper and oak beam ceilings and wide plank floors. Each room was brightly lighted, too well lighted according to some past patrons. Several area diners felt that the bright lighting detracted from the atmosphere and reduced the warmth of the restaurant.

Tables in the dining room were placed fairly close together. Many patrons felt that the close proximity of the tables detracted from the privacy they desired.

Since its opening, Twin Oaks had served complimentary, homemade corn fritters and pecan rolls to each diner. These items and others were available for purchase at a bakery counter inside the main entrance. The setting of the restaurant was generally considered to be beautiful and many people who had never dined at Twin Oaks were familiar with the name and believed it to be a quality restaurant.

The Buzzsaw Lounge The cocktail lounge, with a capacity of 55, could be reached by a private entrance without entering the restaurant. The room itself was dimly lit with a flagstone floor and fireplace. It was located underneath the main dining room so this room also benefitted from a view overlooking the brook.

Kay Barry had recently hired new lounge entertainment – an electronic keyboard player who performed Wednesday through Sunday. She believed that this was the "now" sound and would attract a clientele in their late 20's and older. She had just begun to advertise this entertainment in the local newspapers.

The contribution of liquor sales to total sales was approximately 19 percent. Curran believed this small percentage was attributable to the inconvenient location of the lounge in relation to the restaurant dining rooms. Twin Oaks dining room waitresses did not actively promote cocktails to diners although over two-thirds of all cocktail revenue came from dining room sales. Table tents were used to merchandise specialty drinks and a limited wine list was also available. Banquets were supplied with a private bar or special punch if they so desired.

The Christmas Shop A small residence on the parking lot had been converted to the Christmas Shop. The shop had not been expected to be profitable and had never proven otherwise. The Curran's opened the Christmas Shop only because the space was available and they believed it would prove to be an extra side attraction. It was traditionally open from Mother's Day through January 15th.

The Village Inn In 1954, Charlie Curran purchased land on Route 20 about 2 miles east of Twin Oaks and built The Village Inn, a Best Western motel. The Inn was built with thirty separate units which could later be renovated and sold as apartments.

The Inn operated at a high occupancy level with 80 percent repeat customers; the Currans regretted it had not been built closer to the restaurant. Despite this hindsight, the Inn continued to be highly profitable.

THE CUISINE

The hours of operation for Twin Oaks were: Monday to Friday, 11am to 10pm; Saturday, 8am to 11pm; and Sunday, 8am to 10pm with a weekend brunch. The restaurant always closed on Christmas day and offered a limited menu on Thanksgiving.

According to Curran, the kitchen staff prepared all menu items from scratch. The menu featured traditional American entrees. Although complete dinner specials had always been responsible for a substantial portion of business, there were many standard a la carte items which consistently outsold the complete dinners, such as chicken pie, prime rib, roast duck, and stuffed shrimp. The menu also featured sirloin steak, filet mignon, surf and turf, roast leg of lamb, lamb chops and seafood items such as lobster, crab, scrod, scallops, and swordfish. Twin Oaks was named "One of the World's Distinguished Restaurants" in 1969 by *Gourmet Magazine* in recognition of its Duckling with Country Gravy.

The Currans stressed that they believed in setting very high standards in food quality and consistency. They insisted on purchasing only the highest quality of ingredients and were understandably proud of their homemade baked goods, real whipped cream, butter, coffee cream, and fresh or frozen strawberries. The Currans believed that the greatest strength of Twin Oaks was the adherence to high standards they had set for good quality, service and discipline.

Area diners' perceptions of Twin Oaks would on occasion differ from those of the owners. Many guests returned to Twin Oaks often, yet others felt that some standards of quality had slipped. Pecan rolls and corn fritters remained popular but Twin Oaks was not seen as offering food as good as it had been years before.

THE CLIENTELE

Peak business periods were, first, October during fall foliage season and, second, May through September. Exhibit 2 illustrates the monthly fluctuations in sales for the past two years.

The Twin Oaks clientele tended to be older people, senior citizens, with some businessmen and local families. Most of the guests came from the Sturbridge, Palmer, Springfield and Worcester areas. The Currans believed that Twin Oaks was a primary destination for customers as, according to Charlie, 90 percent of the business was repeat. This information was obtained through reservation cards that were compiled monthly, and by recording the hometown when reservations were made by phone. Eighty percent of Twin Oaks diners made reservations.

Management believed that the primary market for Twin Oaks should be businessmen eating lunch and/or dinner in the restaurant. Management solicited meeting/banquet functions from the many local businesses in the area and also sponsored a businessman's contest. Each week featured a drawing of business cards for a $5.00 gift certificate. A mailing list was also prepared from these cards and banquet information sent to each business.

There were also several colleges in the area, one of which held an annual vegetarian banquet at Twin Oaks. Kay Barry believed that some business was drawn from the colleges, but had not actively pursued this market.

Curran stated that, after raising prices a year ago, average dinner checks ran approximately $16 per person including $2.75 from the bar, while lunch checks averaged $6.75, plus about 50 cents for beverage which sold poorly at lunch. Total meal covers were split about evenly between lunch and dinner.

Forty percent of all business was banquets and tours and the Currans had considered expanding the 150 seat room to accommodate larger groups. Bus tours accounted for a small portion of the business and Twin Oaks brochures were mailed to bus companies, senior citizens clubs, and others as far away as New York City.

EXHIBIT 2 Monthly Business Fluctuations (Fiscal years ending June 30 1988, 1989)

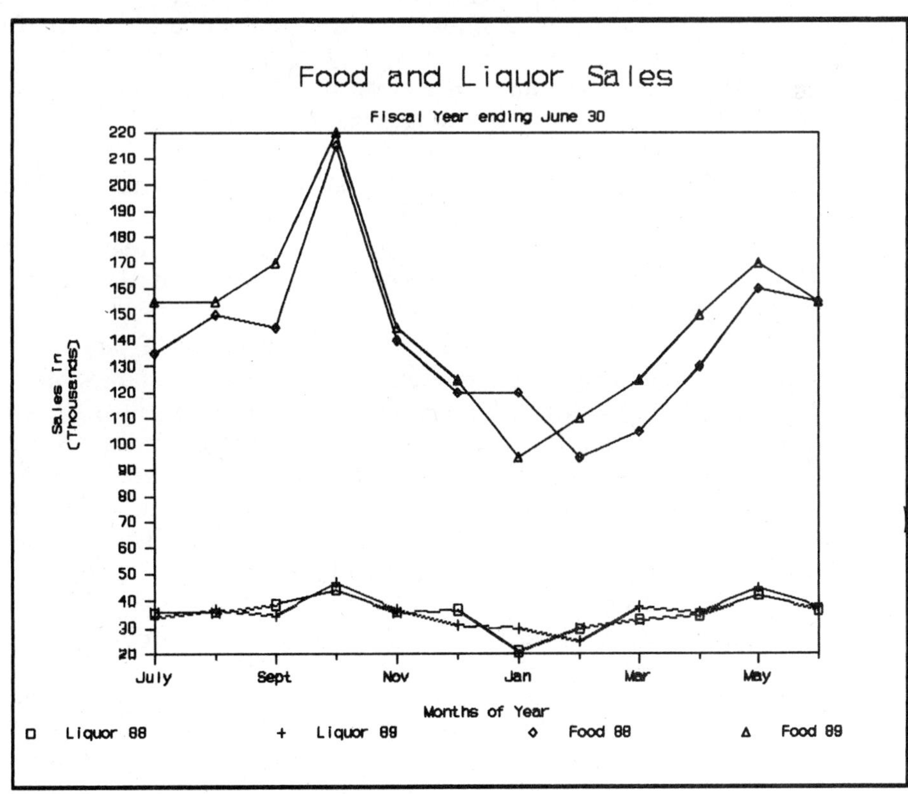

THE COMPETITION

The immediate area around Twin Oaks had no other restaurants. Its closest geographic competitor was the Nichols Tavern located about one mile away. The Tavern was directly on Route 20, but access to the restaurant necessitated slowing to a near stop on the highway in order to negotiate the sharp turn.

The Twin Oaks management felt that no other restaurant in the area could accomodate large banquets as well as they could. Although they acknowledged that the Nichols Tavern was in the same class, their prices were slightly higher and their banquet capacity was only one hundred people.

The Tavern was only four years old and drew its clientele from local businesses for lunch. Their younger clientele was attracted to the less formal atmosphere and also the complimentary hors d'oeuvres and piano entertainment.

The most direct competition for dinner business was Joseph's on Route 169 near Southbridge, approximately 10 miles to the southwest. Joseph's was situated away from a major traffic route in country surroundings. Their menu was similar to the Twin Oaks offerings, but included some continental French dishes as well.

Near Brimfield, 15 miles west on Route 20, was the Townhouse. Although this restaurant did not have banquet facilities, it was similar to Twin Oaks in cuisine although prices were higher. Area residents felt that the Townhouse had a beautiful formal decor and offered superior service. The Sunday champagne brunch was especially popular.

The Havens House in Oxford was located approximately 10 miles east of Sturbridge on Route 52, 15 miles from Worcester. This establishment was comparable to Twin Oaks in both menu and prices but boasted a banquet capacity of 200. Many Havens House diners traveled from Worcester and surrounding towns and believed that the Havens House offered more cleanliness and better service than Twin Oaks.

In Sturbridge, the Sturbridge Inn attracted a large tourist trade, especially older people. The Inn had rustic, historic finishings, but no banquet facilities. There were also motel dining rooms in Sturbridge as well as family type restaurants and fast food operations, but these were not perceived to be in the same category as Twin Oaks. One exception was the Sheraton Sturbridge restaurant. The general public perception of this restaurant, however, was one of "hotel food," and it did not have a good reputation. The Worcester market tended to avoid Sturbridge because of its touristy atmosphere.

A final restaurant which was similar to Twin Oaks was Roberto's in East Brookfield. Roberto's offered American and Italian food and could serve functions as large as 300.

Despite the solvency of the other rural restaurants, Charlie Curran contended Worcester was to blame for the drop in business at Twin Oaks. Worcester had been one of his primary markets and was now retaining a portion of his business, according to Curran, because of an increased number of good restaurants in the city and their proximity to Worcester residents.

ADVERTISING

Local business was not actively solicited by the Kay Barry. She did not believe it was necessary because of the restaurant's reputation. Barry had limited past promotional activity to distributing brochures in tourist areas during the fall foliage season and sending Christmas greetings to area businesses.

Twin Oaks also provided the nearby gas stations with small maps and information packets about the restaurant's history. Charlie Curran believed that word of mouth was the best advertising and relied on area residents to refer customers to Twin Oaks. Despite this activity, Curran felt that his advertising and promotional activity was weak. He was not able to offset the seasonal fluctuations in business and attract new customers.

The advertising expenses at Twin Oaks had been approximately one to one and one half percent of total sales each year for quite some time. Most advertising appeared in local papers during the holiday season and, to a lesser degree, during the slow season. However, Curran also listed the restaurant in *Gourmet Magazine* because he believed the images of the other restaurants listed there rubbed off on Twin Oaks.

The Twin Oaks logo of 35 years appeared in all advertising and telephone directories. Curran and Barry believed that advertising was useful only to project the established Twin Oaks image. Curran had expressed his contention that people already knew of Twin Oaks and that advertising was simply a means to reinforce the name by reminding people that Twin Oaks still existed.

CONCLUSION

Curran was satisfied with the sales volume of the Village Inn within the past few years, but was worried that the motel profits were beginning to support Twin Oaks Enterprises. He was concerned by his inability to increase restaurant sales during the traditionally slow months of January through March, and the fact that business during peak season had also tapered off. Curran's faith in the restaurant was still strong, however, and he looked to the coming year with the hope that he would be able to recoup some of his recent losses.

The 1989 income statement had shown a bare profit after a net loss in 1988 and business levels were consistently lower than they had been in recent years (Exhibit 3). In an effort to reduce costs, Curran cut back the size of his staff, but Twin Oaks remained an expensive operation and he refused to compromise on the quality of the food.

Area businesses and banquets had contributed a great deal to Twin

Oaks revenue and Curran had been considering expansion of his banquet facilities. He was just not sure what direction to take in order to restore the business of Twin Oaks to its past levels.

EXHIBIT 3 Income Statements Years Ending June 30, 1989, 1988

	1989		1988	
	Amount	Percent	Amount	Percent
Food Sales:	$1,687,763	100.00	$1,788,468	100.00
Cost of Sales:				
Food	682,146	40.42	732,517	40.96
Payroll	562,493	33.32	663,187	37.08
	1,244,639	73.74	1,395,704	78.04
Gross Profits	443,124	26.26	392,764	21.96
Beverage Sales:	395,723	100.00	429,325	100.00
Cost of Sales:				
Beverage	121,336	30.66	139,399	32.47
Payroll	65,765	16.62	85,128	19.83
	187,101	47.28	224,527	52.30
Gross Profits	208,622	52.72	204,798	47.70
Tot.Gross Profit	651,746	31.28	597,562	26.95
Other Income	20,058	0.96	21,386	0.96
Total Income	671,804	32.24	618,948	27.91
Controllable Expenses:				
Advert./Sales Prom	118,000	5.66	129,741	5.85
Utilities/ R & M	171,783	8.24	159,501	7.19
Administrative	193,324	9.28	215,198	9.70
	483,107	23.18	504,440	22.75
Gross Profits	188,697	9.06	114,508	5.16
Occup.Costs/Dep.	159,980	7.68	132,661	6.12
Inc.before Taxes	28,717	1.38	(18,153)	-0.95

CASE 5

SAO PAULO PLAZA HOTEL

In recent years, both the city of Sao Paulo and most of Brazil had been enduring a wave of economic turmoil. The value of the Brazilian cruziero relative to the American dollar had continued to decline. This, in turn, stimulated the threat of an international banking crisis with Brazil targeted as a prime debtor. As a result of this instability, the government had imposed strict regulations on importation and on the flow of money across Brazil's borders.

All forms of international commerce had decreased. Pressures to "Buy Brazilian" diverted attention from potential imports that had so far managed to survive strict regulations. High unemployment caused by factory shutdowns created labor problems, particularly in Sao Paulo which had previously boasted high employment. With a presidential election scheduled in 1985, the economy experienced a pre-election slowdown led by cautious investors awaiting the new administration.

THE CORPORATE MARKET

Sao Paulo was a Brazilian city with twelve million people in the greater metropolitan area. It had its sights set on being the second largest city in the world by the year 2000. Despite this huge size, the hotel business had always been relatively lean. Now, due to a decline in foreign business travel, the city's hotels discovered that they needed to target Brazilian travelers if they hoped to achieve an acceptable occupancy of their historically under-utilized rooms.

Compounding the problem was the relocation of many corporate headquarters from downtown Sao Paulo, where the Plaza was located, to the Paulista area on the outskirts of the city, ten to fifteen minutes from downtown, and to the Faria-Lima area which was ten miles further from downtown than Paulista. This was due to the outgrowing of available space and expansion, rather than any undesirability of the downtown area. Full use of the new space, however, never occurred due to the recession period which began in 1979.

Major room night producing companies such as DuPont, Embratel, Rohm and Haas, L'Oreal, and Hewlett-Packard (one of the Plaza's largest accounts) had moved to newly developed office buildings in Paulista, while others like Monsanto planned to relocate soon. The exodus to the Faria-Lima area was somewhat slower due to the higher cost of office rental, but growth there was steady. Despite the shift of business, downtown Sao Paulo continued to host the banking community, major airline companies, other types of industries located within walking distance of the Sao Paulo Plaza, and smaller companies that were moving into the vacated offices.

The Sao Paulo Plaza was severely impacted by the economic crunch along with all the other hotels. Since the hotel had relied heavily on the international business traveler in the past (Exhibit 1), management recognized that a different style of operation would be required to handle Brazilian business.

EXHIBIT 1 Geographic Origin of Business

Geographic Source	1982 %Occ.	1983 %Occ.	1984 %Occ.
North America	18.2	14.9	12.8
Latin America	15.1	11.1	11.1
Europe	16.7	16.3	13.2
Brazil	42.4	54.6	58.5
Other	7.6	3.1	4.4

Since the needs and wants of the smaller Brazilian companies had not been clearly defined and more hotels were now vying for fewer customers, the sales effort was recognized as challenging. A salesperson could no longer rely on a few major client companies to produce the bulk of the business, and was forced to explore dramatically different approaches to direct selling, as well as making multiple visits to more smaller companies.

The decreasing demand for hotel rooms was further aggravated by some changes in airline routes. Major airlines had begun to schedule additional morning and evening flights to accommodate corporate and government officials flying to or from Rio de Janeiro or Brasilia for the day. By encouraging same day, roundtrip customers, the airlines allowed the traveler to save the cost of a night's accommodation. This deprived the city's hotels of considerable revenue, particularly from Rio which was only a 50 minute shuttle. The trip to Brasilia, an hour and a half, was equally conducive to day trips.

THE GROUP MARKET

Corporate accounts were not the only type of business for which Sao Paulo hotels actively competed. Brazil boasted over 10,000 associations in the country, but only 150-200 could be considered major convention producers worthy of pursuit. In addition, volume and/or cyclical business from the association market was not significant. The Maksoud Place Hotel regularly undercut any other hotel and was therefore understandably the first choice of the association market. Association decision makers generally ranked the Sao Paulo Plaza as their second or third choice, although historically it was chosen most often as convention headquarters amidst stiff competition.

Non-business groups were usually one-shot deals from other countries and were largely controlled by wholesale agents in Rio. These were usually typical tour groups and the agents bargained hard for volume wholesale rates.

Sao Paulo convention business was focused at two major facilities with one other center at Brazil's largest hospital. The Ibeuratera Convention Center was located near the airport, a 15-20 minute taxi ride from downtown Sao Paulo. It was situated in a densely populated residential area and was the smaller of the two centers.

The Anhembi, the largest convention facility in Brazil, had a 3,500 person capacity and housed all large exhibitions. Since international trade had declined, it was primarily the site of trade shows within the country. The Anhembi was located 20 minutes from downtown in a poor residential neighborhood. Several attempts to build a hotel near this facility had proven futile. Shuttle buses were used to transport people from hotels.

Sao Paulo competed with three other major cities for convention business. Until five years ago when a facility was built in the east coast resort town of Recife, Sao Paulo had been known as the "only game in town." The city of Rio de Janeiro also had a municipal convention center which was promoted and supported by Embratur, the national tourist bureau. Regardless of location, convention facilities and activity were embedded in politics and difficult to control.

SAO PAULO AS A DESTINATION

Sao Paulo suffered from a poor self-image in regard to its ability to attract either the leisure or the business traveler. In the past, the hotel association, the city, and the airlines had each attempted to promote Sao Paulo as a shopping or cultural attraction, but all had failed or aborted their efforts before any positive results could be seen. State officials pessimistically wondered "who would want to come to Sao Paulo; it's such a dirty, large city."

The Sao Paulo Plaza was quite active in the 1983 organization of the Convention and Visitors Bureau. Hoping to receive government support through the Embratur, the hotel suffered a major setback when the financial backing went to Rio.

The role of Embratur was to promote Brazil as a destination to visitors from outside the country. Its management was only marginally effective and it was further hindered by poor tourism infrastructures in the many cities with potential for foreign visitors. These cities lacked organized sightseeing, and had few if any buses, taxis or car rentals. Airfares were expensive. The national airline, Varig, was favored by the government and influenced airline routes.

THE SAO PAULO PLAZA

The Sao Paulo Plaza[1] was a 25 story, 407 room hotel with three restaurants, a lounge, pool, discotheque, health club, and an extensive shopping arcade of international shops. It was managed by an American-based international hotel company with a strong international reservations system. Its location in the heart of the business district, as well as its close proximity to Viracopos International Airport, had made it attractive to the business market. However a new airport, Guarulhos International, was due to open in two years and would be considerably further away.

The hotel opened its doors in October of 1971. By 1984 occupancy was down to 51.4 percent with an average rate of US $47.20, in comparison to a 1983 occupancy of 53 percent with an average rate of US $57.82, and a 1982 occupancy of 54.5 percent with an average rate of US $64.39. Average monthly room rates and occupancy percentages for 1983 and 1984 are shown in Exhibit 2 along with the 1984 forecast figures. Exhibit 3 shows the percentage changes. The breakdown by market segment for 1984 is shown in Exhibit 4. Exhibit 5 shows a comparison with projections.

Room rack rates (US $) in 1984 were as follows:

Single	$63	$73	$88
Double	$70	$84	$98

All rooms had modern conveniences such as direct dial telephones, air conditioning, private baths, and portable refrigerators. There was a deluxe Presidential Suite, 33 one-bedroom suites, and a Penthouse Suite offering a panoramic view of Sao Paulo. The Grand Ballroom could accommodate 340 banquet style and there were other rooms with capacities of 140, 80 and 60.

---

1 Name, some dates and figures, have been disguised.

EXHIBIT 2 1983/1984 Monthly Room Rates and Occupancy

	Average Room Rates			%Occupancy		
	1983	1984	'84 Fct.	1983	1984	84 Fct.
JAN	$69.71	$59.77	$68.17	48.0%	43.2%	44.8%
FEB	66.00	43.30	61.90	50.0	55.4	49.7
MAR	60.60	49.30	71.80	69.0	63.7	66.9
APR	68.80	50.50	69.40	48.0	53.4	44.0
MAY	64.40	54.20	66.40	67.0	53.2	63.4
JUN	60.60	48.90	66.20	60.0	63.2	45.5
JUL	55.00	52.80	65.10	40.0	38.4	36.7
AUG	54.70	50.20	65.40	58.0	45.2	54.6
SEP	54.00	45.80	61.60	60.0	49.8	56.6
OCT	56.00	40.70	61.80	58.0	66.2	54.9
NOV	55.70	44.50	61.10	73.0	65.9	70.9
DEC	55.10	41.14	57.10	35.0	57.5	42.4

EXHIBIT 3 1983/1984 Rate/Occupancy Change Percentage

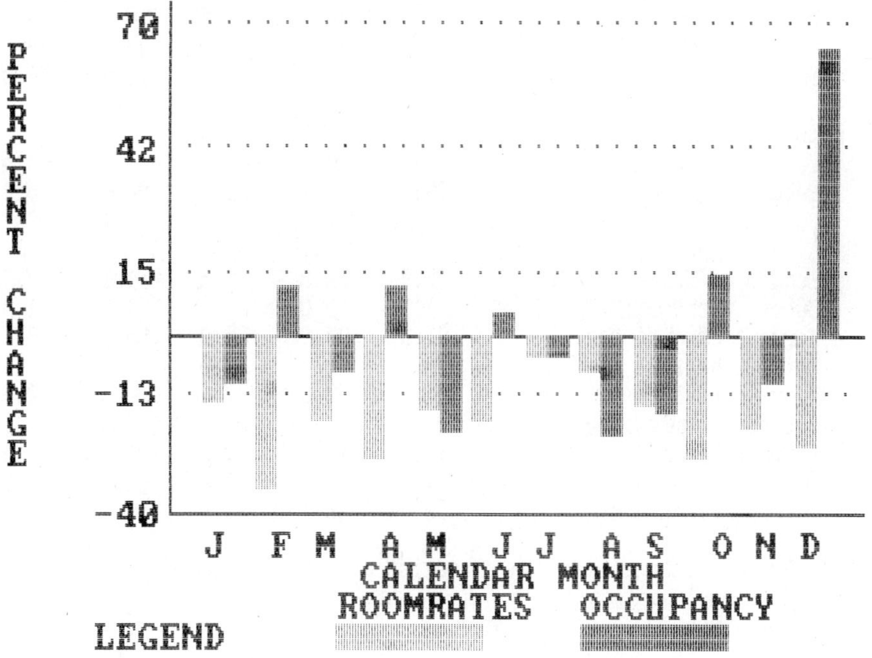

EXHIBIT 4 1984 Profile by Market Segment (Based on 10% sample)

	ALL GUESTS	EBS	FIT COMMER.	COMPANY MTG	FIT SOCIAL
OCCUPANCY					
Occupied Rooms	8036	3280	2376	783	484
Percent to Total	100.0	40.8	29.6	9.7	6.0
Complimentary	127	0	54	2	42
REGISTRATIONS					
Number	3510	1166	1090	279	261
Percent to Total	100.0	33.2	31.1	7.9	7.4
EXPENDITURE AVERAGES					
Room Rate (per Occ Rm)	39.01	36.63	46.61	27.25	42.46
Chg Per Day (Occ Rm)	49.31	46.18	59.13	32.54	49.44
Non-Room Chg/Day	10.30	9.55	12.52	5.29	6.97
Charges Per Stay	112.99	129.91	128.99	91.43	92.03
REVENUE ESTIMATES (000)					
Total Revenue [1]	396.5	151.5	140.6	25.5	24.0
Room Revenue [2]	308.5	120.1	108.2	21.3	18.8
Non-Room Revmue [3]	88.0	31.3	32.4	4.2	5.2
Percent Total Revenue	100.0	38.2	35.5	6.4	6.1
Room Rev as % of Total	77.8	79.3	77.0	83.4	78.2
Non-room Rev as % of Total	22.2	20.7	23.0	16.6	21.8
RATE CATEGORY					
Percent Rack	26.7	0.9	65.9	1.1	53.6
Percent Discount	73.3	99.1	34.1	98.9	46.4
STAY PATTERNS					
Length of Stay	2.5	2.8	2.4	3.1	2.2
Guests per Room	1.1	1.0	1.1	1.1	1.3
Percent Advance Res.	91.3	94.9	85.0	98.2	78.2
Percent Walk-in	8.7	5.1	15.0	1.8	21.8
Average Lead Time	6.8	7.3	7.6	4.8	9.3
Percent Commissionable	21.3	6.3	23.6	3.9	24.1
Percent Direct	79.6	86.1	69.6	96.8	58.6
Percent HRS	11.7	8.8	15.4	1.4	19.5
Percent First Visit	60.4	36.1	61.9	69.9	76.2

[1] Average charges per stay * Registrations
[2] Non-Complimentary Rooms * Room Rate
[3] Total Revenue - Room Revenue

EXHIBIT 4 Market Segment Profile (continued)

NON-BUS. GROUP	C'VNTION CONGRESS	PACKAGE	TOUR SERIES	CAN FIT OVERFLOW	AIRLINE CREW	INCENT.
461	330	151	73	57	25	13
5.7	4.1	1.9	0.9	0.7	0.3	0.2
20	3	0	0	0	3	3
325	122	138	35	69	16	9
9.3	3.5	3.9	1.0	2.0	0.5	0.3
35.47	32.18	47.21	57.39	32.61	15.32	32.54
43.54	41.56	78.17	77.73	38.52	35.78	27.77
8.07	9.38	30.96	20.33	5.90	20.46	-4.77
61.91	112.59	85.65	163.45	31.87	57.02	40.11
20.1	13.7	11.8	5.7	2.2	0.9	0.4
15.7	10.5	7.1	4.2	1.9	0.3	0.3
4.5	3.2	4.7	1.5	0.3	0.6	0.0
5.1	3.5	3.0	1.4	0.6	0.2	0.1
77.8	76.7	60.4	73.8	84.7	37.8	90.1
22.2	23.3	39.6	26.2	15.3	62.2	9.9
0.0	2.5	46.4	0.0	0.0	0.0	0.0
00.0	97.5	53.6	100.0	100.0	100.0	100.0
2.1	3.2	1.8	3.3	1.0	1.6	1.7
1.5	1.3	1.8	1.6	1.2	1.2	1.2
99.4	90.2	96.4	100.0	100.0	93.8	100.0
0.6	9.8	3.6	0.0	0.0	6.3	0.0
6.0	4.1	4.2	7.9	1.0	0.0	3.7
74.2	18.9	29.7	100.0	1.4	0.0	22.2
86.5	77.0	86.2	65.7	100.0	87.5	100.0
12.9	12.3	10.1	34.3	0.0	6.3	0.0
94.2	79.5	78.3	85.7	100.0	62.5	100.0

EXHIBIT 5 1984 Comparison with Projections (Based on 10% sample)

Segment	Projected Number	Projected Prct.	Actual Number	Actual Prct.	Variance Number	Variance Prct.
FIT Commercial	3174	38.7	2376	29.6	-798	-25.1
EBS	2852	34.8	3280	40.8	428	15.0
Convention/Congress	773	9.4	330	4.1	-443	-57.3
Company Meeting	718	8.8	783	9.7	65	9.1
FIT Social	384	4.7	484	6.0	100	26.0
Non-Business Group	133	1.6	461	5.7	328	246.0
Package	79	1.0	151	1.9	72	91.1
Incentive	48	0.6	13	0.2	-35	-72.9
Airline Crew	30	0.4	25	0.3	-5	16.7
Flight Delay/Overflow	0	0.0	57	0.7	57	NA
Tour Series	0	0.0	73	0.9	73	NA
Total	8191	100.0	8033	100.0	-158	-2.0

The Plaza had undergone a face lift in recent years. The main lobby was modernized as were the banquet rooms and executive floors. One hundred fifty of the guest rooms were also renovated. In November, 1983, the Roof restaurant was closed due to its unprofitability. Plans were to replace it with two meeting rooms.

The Plaza offered an assortment of distinctive dining experiences ranging from the casual to the elegant. The Tavern was remodeled to resemble an old English pub and transformed into one of Sao Paulo's hottest discos in the evening. Native Brazilian cuisine was served in the Grill Colonial which catered to the luncheon businessman. The Varavida Bar, located on the pool's terrace, was an informal yet chic lounge frequented by the "in" Sao Paulo crowd. All of the food outlets had gained a reputation for superb cuisine among business and pleasure travelers alike.

Meeting and banquet facilities were versatile in both the hotel and in its recently completed convention center. This addition featured state-of-the-art audio-visual systems in the new auditorium/exhibition foyer.

Other Plaza amenities included concierge service, beauty shops, laundry/valet service and a business center. Travelers pressed for time frequently contacted the business center for information or assistance in making appointments, sending cables or telexes, and arranging secretarial, copying, and translation services. The Plaza also developed an executive credit card for the purpose of encouraging food and beverage spending in the hotel.

The hotel had installed a toll-free 800 number (HRS) in 1981 to improve its reservation capacity. The volume of calls was low, about 100 a month, and was almost entirely generated from FIT commercial business; about 60 percent of the calls were converted into reservations. Sao Paulo was the major contributing source for business of all market segments, but Rio contributed heavily for FIT, package, non-business, and EBS (executive business service) groups.

Company meetings were predominantly of Sao Paulo origin and were almost entirely controlled within the city. This type of business was very cut-throat. Most hotels would do anything to sell a room and, in fact, offered various different rates depending on how low they had to go to get the business.

COMPETITION

The first hotel built in the Paulista region was the 177 room Caesar Park which boasted a longstanding, favorable reputation in the community. One of its selling features was the Presidential Suite which was often in demand by heads of state governments and other prestigious visitors. The Caesar Park had three food service outlets, all of which were very well received. Meeting facilities consisted of five rooms with a maximum banquet capacity of 300. The rack rates (US $) were as follows:

Single: $105–130; Double: $125–160; Suites: $230–450

The Transamerica Hotel was to be positioned to attract the "training-related" group market. This 250 room property was slated to open in late 1985. It would have state-of-the-art audio-visual equipment, closed circuit television, and other training needs. In contrast to the Sao Paulo Plaza, the Transamerica was to be a mid-range hotel competing for the specialty groups market.

The Maksoud Plaza was opened in 1979 by a well known Lebanese real estate developer. It had an impressive appearance with an atrium lobby, French restaurant, unique Scandinavian coffee shop, auditorium, and disco. The owner was a prominent local "wheeler dealer" who favored lavish, international entertainment and who bartered free hotel rooms for business-related favors.

The Maksoud Plaza was a 371 room hotel with 50 suites, a heated swimming pool, and a 420 seat theatre located in the Paulista area. It featured a health club, executive service center with office facilities, and 40 meeting rooms with the latest in meeting equipment. Rack rates (US $) were as follows:

Single: $99–122; Double: $115–140; Suites: $207–255

Maksoud's quality of service and plant maintenance was declining as the hotel neared its fifth birthday.

The Eldorado Boulevard Hotel was situated in the downtown region, approximately 7 miles from the airport. It was a 136 room property with 21 suites and the following room rates (US $):

Single: $60–$70; Double: $72–$108; Suites: $140–$170

There were two food outlets accessible by a street entrance. Function space consisted of only two rooms with a maximum capacity of 200 people.

The Mofarrej Hotel was a beautiful, new property under construction in Paulista by a wealthy Sao Paulo businessman. Each guest room was to be equipped with the latest in modern technology including American programmed television, conference calls, and video checkout. The property was intended to be a "monument" to the wealthy and was unlikely to operate profitably. It was rumored, but not confirmed, that it would be operated by Sheraton.

The 252 room Brasilton was only a short distance from the Plaza and was constructed by the same owners to absorb the Plaza's overflow. It appealed to a more price-sensitive guest than the Plaza, and had the following rack rates.

Single: $92–$99; Double: $99–$115: Suites: $162–$182

In the current competitive climate, the Brasilton took a survival stance in the battle for room nights. It had two fine restaurants, the Braseiro and the Taverna. Banquet facilities included a maximum banquet capacity of 520 people. This hotel also had a good reputation with the local community.

The 500 room Hotel Ca d'Oro was also located close to the Sao Paulo Plaza and was owned by a local Italian restaurateur. Its success in attracting a strong base in the training market allowed the construction of a new wing which made the property most competitive.

Holiday Inn, the second international hotel company to enter the Sao Paulo market, planned to open a 232 room "Crowne Plaza" hotel near Paulista in August. More upscale than the typical Holiday Inn, Crowne Plaza was expected to fall into the deluxe range.

The location of the hotels is shown in Exhibit 6.

EXHIBIT 6 Map of Sao Paulo with Location of Hotels

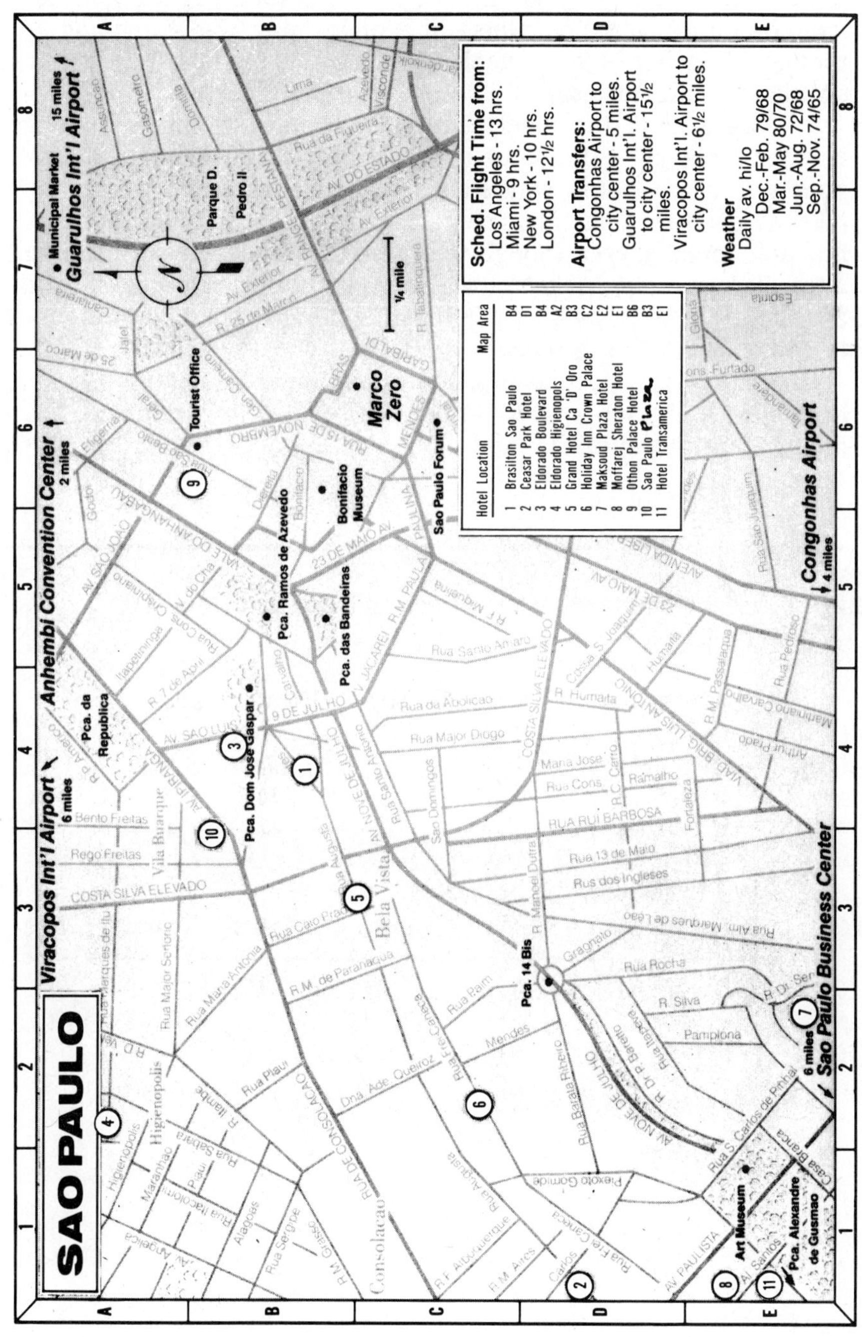

THE BUSINESS CLIMATE

The most resounding echo of competition in Sao Paulo was the result of vicious price-cutting by the hotels. The Maksoud Plaza practiced a bazaar style of rate negotiation where the philosophy was "anything to fill the room." Other hotels were quick to follow suit for fear they would lose out on the available business.

Because it was almost entirely controlled within the city, corporate meeting business tended to be the most frequent benefactor of the cutthroat price war. Many hotels consistently quoted rates which were as little as 40 percent of their minimum rack rate in order to capture the corporate function booking, even though they gave the appearance of maintaining rack rates. For example, Maksoud was known to offer corporate rates in the $40 range. Ca d'Oro, with an $80 minimum rack rate, had offered a $35 rate to company meeting groups.

Competitive occupancy figures and business mix for 1983 are shown in Exhibit 7. Figures for 1984, when the segment mix remained the same as in 1983, are shown in Figure 8.

EXHIBIT 7 1983 Competitive Occupancy and Business Mix

	Plaza	Maksoud	Caesar Pk	Brasilton	Eldorado	Cadoro	Total
No of Rms.	407	421	177	252	157	500	1914
Ann.Occ %	53	65	62	68	50	55	58
ARR	58	68	51	39	42	48	
Market Segment	% Occ	% Occ	% Occ	% Occ	% Occ	% Occ	%Occ
FIT Comm'l	75	70	60	74	65	75	71
GroupComm'l	15	12	30	4.7	11	15	14
FIT Soc'l	5	8	5	3.2	9	5	6
Group Soc'l	5	10	5	18	15	5	9

EXHIBIT 8 Occupancy Figures for 1984

	SP Plaza	Brasilton	Maksoud	Caesar	ElDorado	CaDoro	Total
AVAIL.ROOMS							
Number	407	252	421	177	157	500	1914
% Total	21.3%	13.2%	22.0%	9.2%	8.2%	26.1%	100.0%
ARR $	47	38	58	49	36	47	
OCCUPANCY							
Percent	51.4%	64.9%	74.6%	59.3%	57.0%	40.1%	56.5%
RN	76424	59695	114634	38311	32664	73182	394910
% Total	19.4%	15.1%	29.0%	9.7%	8.3%	18.5%	100.0%

Future business prospects did not appear dismal for the Sao Paulo Plaza, just highly competitive. The Maksoud Plaza had recently become the new social gathering spot for the elite of Sao Paulo. By investing heavily in lavish, international entertainment (Frank Sinatra was a frequent entertainer), the Maksoud family succeeded in overtaking the Sao Paulo Plaza as the place to be seen. The Mofarrej was expected to follow suit in head-to-head competition with the Maksoud Plaza. Neither of the owners was particularly concerned with profit; image appeared to be the primary concern.

Once a stable property, the Sao Paulo Plaza was apparently in need of a new, clearly defined identity to compete effectively in the intense environment. The economy was not projected to bounce back quickly and the available pool of rooms continued to increase in an already diluted market.

The ownership and the management of the Sao Paulo Plaza recognized that strategic marketing was the only tonic for survival in a highly competitive market. Given their limited resources, they wondered how to segment and how to position in the current marketplace, in addition to what their product strategy should be. Exhibit 9 shows the demand analysis that was projected for 1985. Exhibit 10 shows abstracts from the 1985 marketing plan.

EXHIBIT 9 1985 Projected Demand Analysis

	Plaza		Maksoud		Caesar Park		Brasilton		Eldorado	
Annual Occ %	50		59		62		64		52	
Avail. Rooms	407		421		177		252		157	
Room Nights	148,962		154,086		64,782		92,232		57,462	
Market Segment	R/N	%Occ	R/N	%Occ	R/N	% Occ	R/N	% Occ	R/N	% Occ
FIT Comm'	53179	71.4	64715	71.2	25264	62.8	43736	74.1	20562	69.5
Group Comm'	4916	6.6	5896	6.5	3302	8.2	2774	4.7	800	2.0
FIT Social	14678	19.7	11094	12.2	7773	19.3	1888	3.2	3839	13.0
GroupSocial	1708	2.3	9246	10.2	3886	9.7	10630	18.0	4378	14.8
Total	74,481	100	90,951	100	40,225	100	59,028	100	29,579	100

	Ca d'Oro		(August) Holiday Inn		(August) Mofarrej		(August) TransAmerica		Total	
Annual Occ %	59		42		37		23		55	
Avail. Rooms	450		232		250		250		2596	
Room Nights	164,700		35496		38250		15250		771220	
Market Segment	R/N	%Occ	R/N	%Occ	R/N	%Occ	R/N	%Occ	R/N	%Occ
FIT Comm'l	74115	76.4	9319	62.7	9204	64.6	2007	57.2	302181	71.3
Group Comm'l	2141	3.2	1090	7.3	1284	9.0	351	10.0	23554	5.6
FIT Social	14123	15.3	1195	12.9	3060	21.5	799	22.8	59789	14.1
Group Social	4941	5.1	2530	17.0	612	4.3	351	10.0	38362	9.0
Total	97020	100	14854	100	14240	100	3508	100	423886	100

EXHIBIT 10 1985 Marketing Plan Abstracts

To: Senior Vice President of Marketing, Corporate Office, NYC

From: Director of Marketing, Sao Paulo Plaza Hotel

Subject: 1985 Marketing Plan

Date: September 1984

Following a meeting held on September 4 with Luis Filipo on the marketing plan and strategy for 1985, here are some thoughts and additional promotional ideas for the Sao Paulo Plaza. All these ideas are subject to your agreement.

INTRODUCTION

There is no doubt that the Sao Paulo Plaza will physically enjoy a renewed image with the outstanding renovated lobby and lobby Bar. One can already hear very favorable comments by guests realizing the hotel has undertaken a serious effort to upgrade its facilities. This factor is critical to supporting any marketing actions.

However, one very essential point to consider and one that will play a tremendous role in our overall performance is "service." Sao Paulo Plaza offers a good service; marketing-wise we are convinced "service" will differentiate us from any other existing or new hotel in town.

The following ideas are suggested for achieving these specific objectives:

* Consolidate and secure our present market share despite new hotels.
* Anticipate the reaction to be caused by new hotel and minimize the impact as much as possible.
* Create new business opportunities.

These ideas focus on major market segments, aside from some others geared to the market in general.

I **EXECUTIVE FLOORS (Top Class)**

The 1983 advertising campaign had the Executive Floors as a theme. Since then, these floors have been promoted through sales personnel. Your advertising budget limitation for 1985 will not allow continued advertising of this unique service. Therefore, two ideas could be developed to consolidate the image and promotion of these floors.

A) **Executive Floors Brochure** This brochure will include detailed information on the Executive floors and the service provided. It is far more than a nice room and a lounge that we are offering and this could be clearly stressed in a single brochure. The brochure could be distributed by sales personnel when introducing this service, as well as be included in the preferential mail (sales and management correspondence). The brochure would only be utilized for direct mail when felt convenient. The layout could be a 3 panel format and printed by your printshop.

B) **ICARO International** Now that the Executive Floors will have been completed for two years, we could develop a celebration promotion by offering a bonus to Varig International passengers through its Icaro in-flight magazine international edition. It is difficult to precisely establish the volume of incremental business this program could generate since we cannot exactly know the volume of Varig international passengers that normally utilize the Executive Floors. We estimate 0.5% which would translate into 600 to 700 room nights.

II **F.I.T. (Commercial/Social)**

A) **Frequent Traveler Program** This program for FIT commercial and social business would consist of a progressive discount for a total of six visits within a period of 4 months (January - April 1985).

FIT guests, upon checking out the first time will be handed the program brochure showing the program content. On every subsequent visit of the future 5, he will be granted a specific discount according to the following schedule: 2nd stay - 10% off rack rate, each additional stay an additional 5% up to 6th stay - 30%.

The average length of stay of FIT commercial guests is 2.35 nights which means an average 20% discount will be granted over a total of 16.6 nights throughout 6 visits. Note that the purpose is to minimize the transfer of FIT business to the newcoming hotels and to ensure the FIT guest loyalty to the Sao Paulo Plaza as much as possible.

The cost for this program will only be that of producing the Frequent Traveler brochure. The program will not be available for the Executive Floors and will not be commissionable.

B) **Microcomputer for Guests** As an additional service to the guests, a room could be set up with a micro computer and technical program for the use of guests. The computer could be easily obtained from a local manufacturer such as Itautec on a promotional basis and this could be promoted as one more service. Most executives nowadays require permanent access to a computer for their data processing and it could be a meaningful tool. We could have this available on a trial basis.

C) **Interior Sales Coverage** Since 1981, 3570 guests from the state interior have increased to 1984's 5857 guests. It is clear that there is an excellent potential from that area. Sales coverage in major towns should be intensified by planning trips for 1985. Rio production has also increased from 6491 guests in 1981 to 9192 in 1984, which also indicates the need for a continued and expanded coverage of that market.

D) **Service Committee** Along the lines of permanent monitoring of service, a rotating "service committee" could be created where members are selected from staff supervisory level and changed every month. This committee would meet twice a month or at department heads meetings, to report on what they observed. No department head should be part of the committee. This initiative would help in monitoring quality and would show employees our permanent concern with their performance.

E) **Transportation Project** Considering our location problems vis-a-vis the existing airport, the Sao Paulo Plaza together with the Brasilton and Ca' d'Oro could establish a free transportation service to and from the Congonhas airport only for hotel guests. If feasible, this would mean the hotels in this part of town (versus Maksoud, Caesar, Mofarrej and Holiday Inn) will be offering a unique service until the new airport is opened. If you agree with this idea, a meeting between the 3 hotel managers could be arranged to discuss the project and we could obtain a quotation from a ground transportation agent and clearance from the airport authority.

III Executive Business Service (EBS)

The EBS business represents a significant share of our business mix and, despite our efforts to control it, we are always bound to see it moving to competitive hotels. The research New York is conducting to define a new modus operandi for this segment will be a very important step in establishing a new strategy. While we have some thoughts on this particular item, we prefer to wait for the research results before making any decision on the rate concessions. Nevertheless some other actions can be taken to help secure this business. For example:

A) EBS Stuffer Aside from a special rate, there is a variety of other services and attentions we provide EBS accounts such as speedy check-in, check-out, late check-out, room upgrade, credit, executive card, etc.

Many times the accounts do not seem to visualize the convenience of such facilities and therefore regard the EBS program as a rate concession only. A stuffer on this program's privileges can be distributed by sales personnel on their calls and by the F.O. staff to EBS guests. This will show that we offer other things to EBS customers that most hotels in town do not.

B) Executive Card The Executive Card program is coming along fairly well. Over 700 cards are already distributed, however this volume can be greatly expanded. The marketing plan for 1985 includes a specific program for this, however it will not be carried out due to advertising budget limitations. We would like to propose a different approach to promote this program.

1. A personal visit with you would be planned for top existing and potential accounts that could provide us with more business. The president or top executives of these accounts would be visited as a courtesy and upon the visit handed an Executive Card. This could open doors to two things:
    a. allow for eventual interest in the card program for other company executives upon the top man recommendation.
    b. attempt to expanding the business from these accounts with the top man approbation.
2. Intensify the card promotion in Sao Paulo by sales personnel and at the front desk for checking in/out guests.
3. Make sales trips to Brasilia, Porto Alegre, Belo Horizonte, and Rio to promote the card, plus ads in those cities.

IV. PACKAGE

37% of Package business is booked in Sao Paulo and 24% of these guests originate from here. 72% of all package reservations are booked by guests directly. Aside from the ongoing packages promotion, we thought of creating a new package called "Acredite se quiser" labelled according to the quite popular program on TV Manchete (the American "Believe it or Not").

This package which would include the basic contents of the usual weekend package could be promoted through the normal channels. However, we could try a different approach and have it displayed in one of Sao Paulo largest supermarkets, The Eldorado, just like any other product. The gimmick is that it is not usual to see this kind of promotion in such places. However, the Eldorado receives daily hundreds and hundreds of visitors (potential buyers) who, being from Sao Paulo, would be easily reached to sell a weekend package. The idea may sound fancy but it could produce weekend business. Obviously, there would be some costs involved like producing the flyer and the display. Similar displays could be placed in other shopping centers in town.

Another type of package could be arranged with a micro computer manufacturer. Courses in micro processing could be promoted on weekends at the hotel. Computers are now in fashion and we could get some manufacturer interested in joining this program, including rooms for participants from other cities.

V. Food & Beverage

With the closing of the Roof restaurant, the hotel is left with a limited number of options for entertainment. Aside from the beautiful Lobby bar and the refurbished theater, the only outlet left is the London Tavern.

We believe that a Brazilian popular music program could be organized by occasionally having typical Brazilian singers perform at the London Tavern during the week. Something along the lines of a "Cafe Concerto" where one could hear nice Brazilian music by traditional artists. This should not be a profit minded program but a PR and sales promotion approach towards the local community and one that could help establish the hotel image.

I know there is a lot to discuss about these ideas and eventually some may not be applicable for various reasons. However, one has to realize that under present circumstances and in view of the money limitation for broader advertising, the objective of these thoughts is to take advantage of the momentum whereby the hotel looks physically renewed, and to stress this by as many promotional actions as possible.

SECTION 3

SEGMENTATION

AND

POSITIONING

CASE 6

ATTRACTING THEM ALL

Amherst, Massachusetts is a college town with a permanent population of about 27,000 inhabitants. Additionally, there are a similar number of temporary inhabitants in the form of college students at both a small private college and a large state university. Amherst College is a prestigious, liberal arts, ivy league college with 2700 students. The University of Massachusetts (UMass), has about 25,000 students, including 5000 at the graduate levels, enrolled in multiple disciplines. There is a tendency among the students from the two institutions to polarize.

Downtown Amherst essentially contains one main street. In this area are most of the town's many small stores, restaurants, and bars. Amherst College is located just south of the main business area. UMass is spread over a larger area located about one and a half miles north of the main business area. About one half of UMass students live in dorms, the rest in rooms and apartments scattered throughout Amherst and nearby villages.

The numbers of bars and restaurants represent a great variety. Within the down town area can be found three ice-cream bars, three Chinese restaurants, one "freaky" cafe, one more traditional cafe, one fast food restaurant, one Mexican restaurant, one vegetarian restaurant, two regular restaurants, a hotel restaurant, one pub also serving food, and three bars also serving snack-type food. The pub has a rather large dance floor and a disc-jockey playing current music nightly. The bars have loudspeakers that blast out current fad music, TV-screens, electronic games, and other usual college student attractions. The surrounding area of Amherst has similar attractions including a half dozen more refined and adult type restaurants.

Most people working in Amherst go out for lunch, and all the restaurants and bars serve some kind of lunch. The restaurants, the traditional cafe, and the pub also serve dinner until 9:00 or 10:00 in the evening.

Early week business in the bars and restaurants is moderate but steady. Thursday, Friday, and Saturday nights are a different story. There are usually lines waiting for tables in the restaurants, but the lines of students (mostly UMass) headed for the bars and pub extend out into the street, as management allows one to enter only to replace one that leaves.

TWISTERS

Twisters Tavern opened in downtown Amherst in February 1989. It was located on the ground floor of a large, historic building in an area that had previously been a sports pub bar and lounge of a restaurant located on the first floor above. Management's objective was to establish Twisters as a comfortable, more upscale alternative to other local establishments. The desired target market was the 25 and older crowd although, as management put it, "everyone was welcome." Management sought lunch and dinner business, but also felt there was a market for a place that offered live music, particularly jazz and blues.

The layout and accoutrements of Twisters remained much as they had been under the previous management (Exhibit 1). One corner was turned over to a dance floor, which also served as a podium for the bands when they played. Walls were brick and stone, which made it warm and cozy, and were decorated with modernistic artwork depicting jazz instrumentalists. Sports broadcasts were shown on the large videoscreen from Monday through Wednesday. Sometimes Wednesdays, but always Thursday through Saturday, were reserved for bands. The tables had glass tops over table clothes. Fresh flowers were on every table and the floor was carpeted. Because of the glass-tops on the tables, drinks were served in plastic glasses that would not easily break. The back room contained dart boards as well as a pool table. When the pool table was needed for other purposes, a cover was placed on it.

Management wanted to maintain reasonable prices on the food that was served. A simple menu with popular student dishes like salads, sandwiches, soups, and burgers was put together. In accordance with the desired image, jazz-like names were used on menu items. To save money, the menu was printed on thick blue paper with the Twisters logo. The same menu was used throughout the day (Exhibit 2). A $5.25 brunch was sold on Sundays. Beverage prices were higher than those being charged in surrounding bars, although specials were offered (Exhibit 3).

To create the right atmosphere, jazz and blues are played over the loudspeakers, usually between 7 and 8 pm. As it is not always possible to get good jazz and blues groups that are not too expensive, in some cases more folk- or rock-like bands are hired.

Twisters was promoted from airplane streamers over the football stadium during UMass homegames, local FM radio which played Top 40 music, and through ads in four newspapers: student papers of Amherst College and UMass, a weekly free "cultural-liberal" paper published locally but widely distributed over a large area, and the *Amherst Bulletin*, a weekly free paper delivered to every household in Amherst (Exhibit 3).

EXHIBIT 1 Twisters Floor Layout

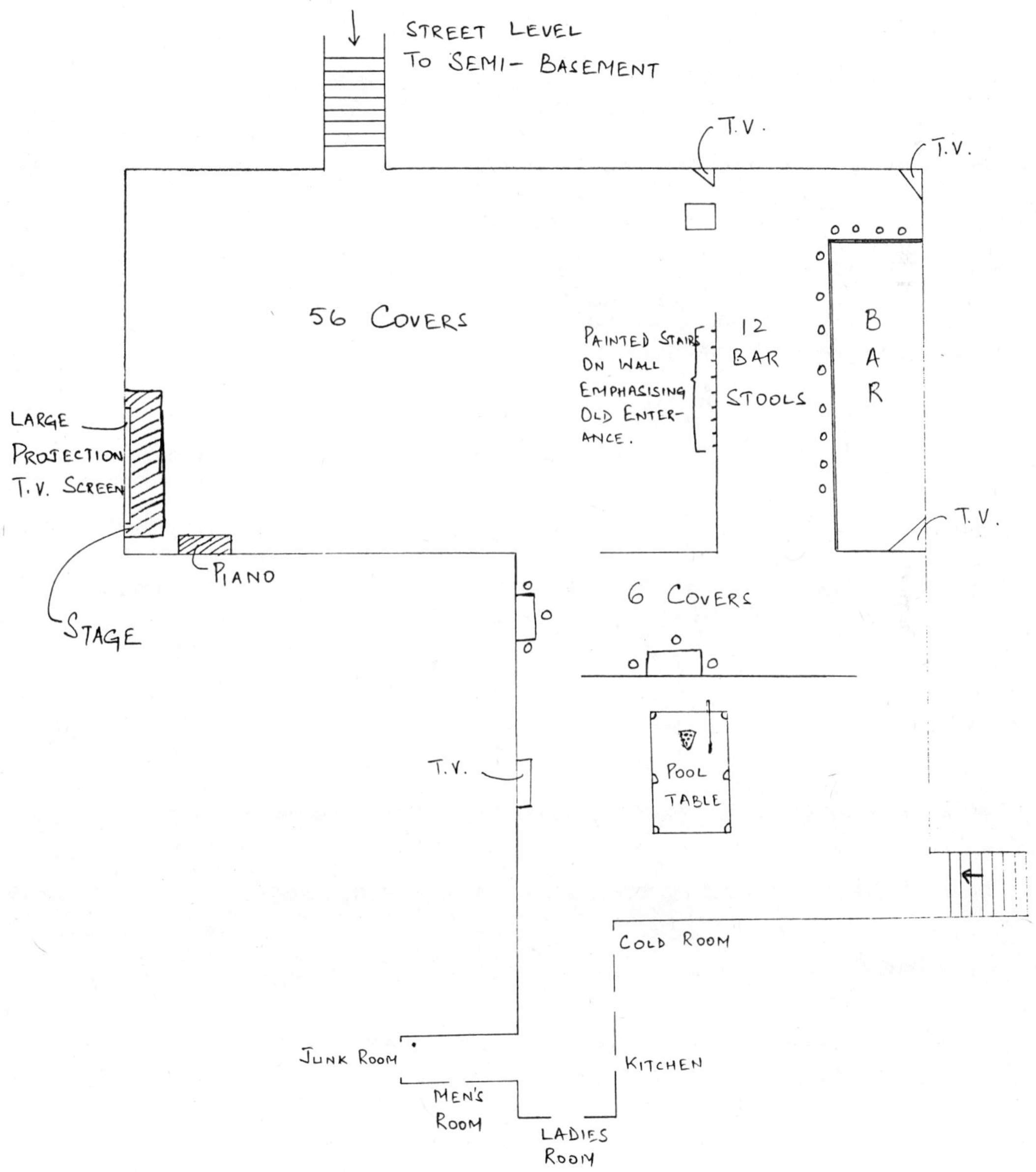

EXHIBIT 2 Twisters All-Day Menu

The Keyboard of Sandwiches

All of Twister's sandwiches are served with chips, pickle, and your choice of breads.
Add Twister's famous fries - .95

Billie Holiday Ham — Thinly sliced ham served with lettuce, tomatoe and your choice of cheese - 3.95

The Jazz Club — A triple decker turkey club with bacon, lettuce, tomatoe and mayo - 4.25

Blues Brothers Beef — Roast beef piled high, drenched with melted cheddar cheese - 4.45

The Dizzie Garden — Melted cheese over mushrooms, olives, tomatoes, peppers and onions. Grilled and topped with fresh lettuce - 3.25

Basie's BLT — The old time favorite - 3.25

The Brubeck Reuben — Corned beef, sauerkraut, melted swiss cheese, topped off with Russian dressing - 4.45

Quartet Tuna — White tuna with cheese, bacon, lettuce and tomatoe - 4.25

The Booker Bratwurst — Boiled in beer, with sauted peppers, onions and Poupon mustard on top - 3.25

A New Twist

Our "burgers" are made with either the freshest beef or a **boneless chicken breast**—all charbroiled !
Served with chips & pickle. Add Twister's famous fries - .95

Bennie Goodburger — Topped off lettuce, tomatoe and our tangy barbecue sauce - 4.15
Add cheese - .80

The Duke Deluxe — Served with lettuce, cheese, tomatoe, mayo and bacon - 4.95

Louie, Louie — Smothered with mushrooms, onions and melted cheese - 4.45

The B.B. Burger — Covered with chili and melted cheddar cheese - 4.95

Enjoy !

EXHIBIT 3 College and Local Newspaper Ads

Management had no strong opinions about their markets. They believed that for lunch and dinner they competed with most every other establishment serving food to anyone from senior citizens to young professionals, blue collar workers, and students. Evenings, they hoped to attract a clientele of jazz and blues fans of 25 years and older. When queried, however, one manager stated that the goal was to try and get a mix of everyone into the tavern, primarily "townies," students and for lunch, business people. Quoted in the local paper, before the opening, management stated, "...marketing emphasis will be toward professionals for the lunch and dinner crowd...But, obviously the student segment we do not want to ignore...We're trying to attract them all."

CASE 7

BENTLEY'S RESTAURANT

Kathy Kelleher, manager of Bentley's Restaurant on the Common,[1] was pleased to see many students seated throughout the restaurant as she scanned the sections on an afternoon in May. Kelleher attributed the high percentage of students to current advertisements in the local newspapers promoting a University of Arizona student/faculty specialty dinner for $5.95 from 4:00 to 6:00 pm daily.

Kelleher felt that many students had dismissed the idea of dinner at Bentley's in the past because they did not consider it to be within their price range. By lowering the prices during off-peak times, Kelleher felt that she could change the restaurant's image from a place to eat when Dad is paying to one that everyone can afford. She wanted all guests to feel comfortable in her establishment, and thought that the time had finally come to expose the university market to Bentley's.

THE BENTLEY GROUP

Bentley Family Restaurants was a corporation which operated several establishments in the southwest region of the country. The company was founded by Chairman of the Board Alexander Bentley 15 years earlier. The Bentley Group, as it came to be called, did not see itself as a chain organization and made every effort to create uniquely different restaurants. Concept was of paramount importance and such factors as the type of city and the architecture of the structure were considered before a concept was chosen. Alexander Bentley believed in becoming heavily involved in the respective communities in order to familiarize himself with their individual haracters and to best select an appropriate concept.

Each establishment was independently operated although the basic strategy of offering high quality at a good value was consistent. All of the properties also provided facilities for both on- and off-premise catering.

Three of the units were operated with a sporting motif under the name of Touchdown Charlie's with facilities in Tempe, Scottsdale, and Nogales. At the other extreme, there was a first rate, elegant restaurant in

---

1 Names and places have been disguised.

downtown Phoenix in addition to a variety of other establishments throughout the southwest. Bentley's on the Common was the Bentley Group restaurant in the city of Tucson, Arizona, a city of 350,000. It was the group's first endeavor close by a major college campus.

BENTLEY'S ON THE COMMON

The classic yellow and white Victorian structure located near the campus of the University of Arizona was originally a private nursing home. The Bentley Group purchased the building in 1985 after it had been closed for many years, and opened the doors as Bentley's on the Common in April 1986. Bentley's was located in the historic part of town which lent a certain charm to the converted facility, and Bentley had been careful to preserve the original structure of the building when it created the dining establishment.

Bentley's offered five dining rooms and a lounge, each with its own decor and atmosphere for a total of 220 seats (Exhibit 1). The overall sales mix was 80 percent food and 20 percent alcoholic beverages. Kathy Kelleher described the ambiance as "casually elegant," noting that she did not want the restaurant to appear "too stuffy." The five dining areas were as follows:

The Greenhouse: a very popular glass-walled, outside room with a springlike atmosphere, air conditioned or heated all year;
The Library: a more intimate, smaller and darker room with candlelight in the evenings, leather back chairs and, of course, shelves filled with books;
The Parlor: a more formally furnished dining room used mainly for Sunday brunch;
The Sun Porch: the non-smoking section,a bright but informal room with garden-style furniture, also glass-walled;
The Main Dining Room: a conventional yet comfortable dining room with nooks and crannies to accommodate wheelchairs and highchairs.

In addition to the regular dinner menu which began at 4:00 pm daily, Bentley's would also write a customized menu for private parties of 20 or more. As an unusual twist, customers were allowed to create their own menu for banquet functions if they preferred.

Webster's was an 80-seat plus bar, full service, cozy lounge located in the basement with its original brick walls. The atmosphere was more casual than in the restaurant upstairs, and there was a separate entrance to the room. The Bentley's menu was served in Webster's and there was frequently live entertainment on weekends.

EXHIBIT 1 Bentley's Dining Rooms

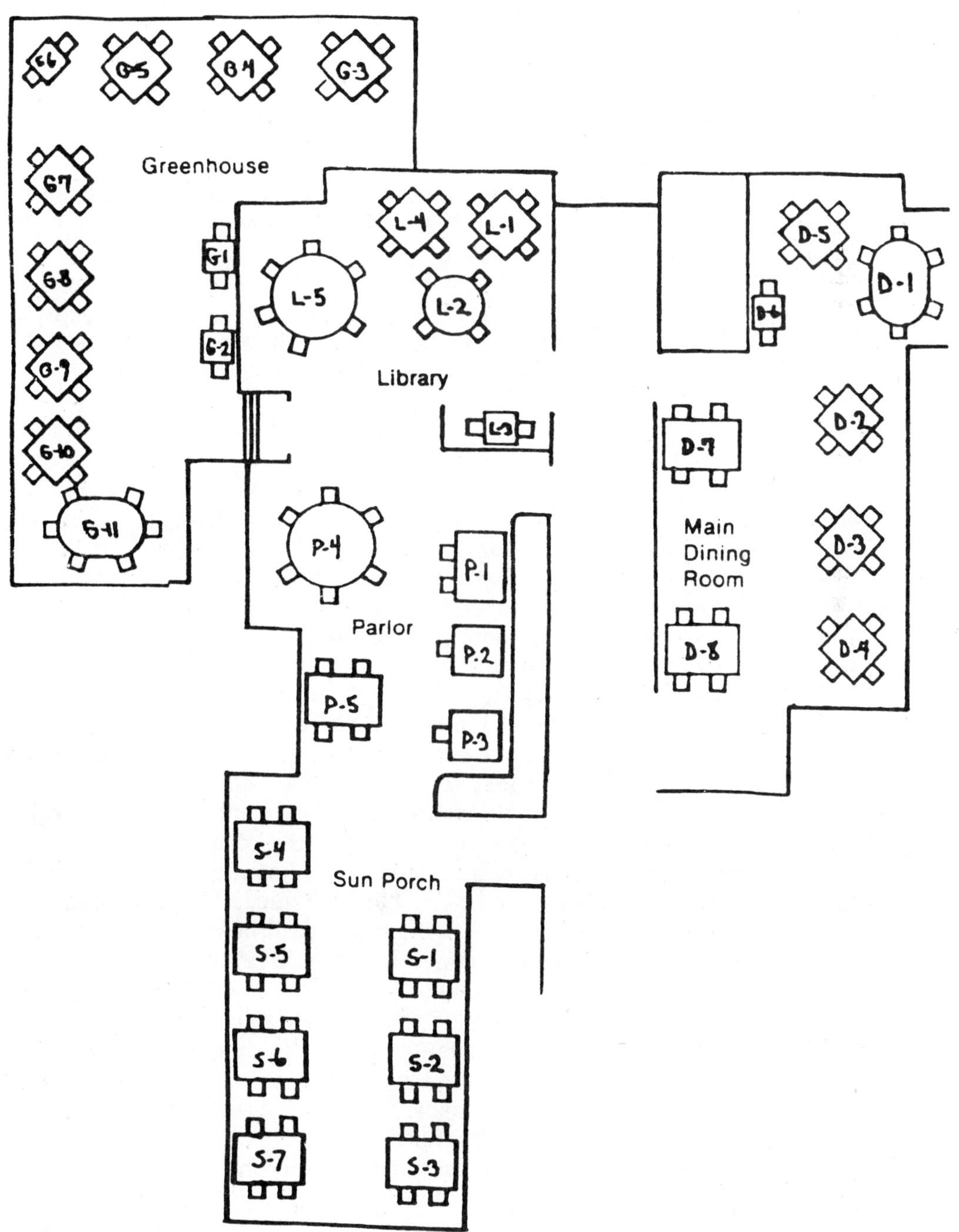

When the weather allowed, a 70-seat outdoor patio with a garden ambience and its own bar was opened for business on one side of the restaurant. Kelleher created the patio bar when she recognized that there was no other outdoor spot in town which allowed guests to enjoy a cocktail outside without ordering food.

THE MARKETING PLAN

Kelleher made her mission statement very clear. "We offer a little bit of everything for everyone," she said. "The last thing I want to do is limit the market to one particular target group."

Kelleher was committed to providing a facility which would be appealing to all. "We want the locals to come and have a good time, just as we want to make the students and the businesspeople feel comfortable," she continued,"regardless of whether they are wearing jeans or a tuxedo."

STRATEGIC CHANGES

With this goal in mind, Bentley's began to make a few changes. After over two years with just one menu for both lunch and dinner, Kelleher decided to offer two separate menus beginning in August of 1988. Although the dinner menu still featured a preponderance of the classic dinner entrees, it also offered the ever-popular potato skins, buffalo wings and deep- fried vegetables (Exhibit 2). The dinner check average including beverages was about $17.00 in May 1989.

Many of the front-of-the-house employees were unhappy with the new menus since they had to serve more customers to make the same money. The chef and the cooks were even less enthusiastic since they considered the lower priced additions to the dinner menu to be incompatible with the overall concept and not particularly worthy of their attention.

Nevertheless, Kelleher was undeterred. "If you are afraid to change to keep up with the times," she said, "today's successful restaurant can easily become tomorrow's failure." Bentley's had been only moderately successful and Kelleher was determined to increase revenues and profits.

Lunch service was eventually discontinued on weekdays in early 1989 after covers had plummeted by 75 percent. Management blamed the decrease on the construction of a building on a former parking lot in the area which had previously been used by guests of the restaurant. Many luncheon customers were simply unable to park and went elsewhere rather than waste their lunch hour looking for a space.

Kelleher was philosophical about closing for lunch on weekdays since a major portion of the business was done in the evenings. She was happy to have eliminated the significant overhead required to open during the day.

EXHIBIT 2 Bentley's Dinner Menu After the Change

Appetizers From The Sea

LITTLE NECKS ON THE HALFSHELL
freshly shucked little neck clams with cocktail sauce and lemon. $4.50

SHRIMP COCKTAIL
plump gulf shrimp accompanied by our own horseradish cocktail sauce. $6.50

CLAMS CASINO
little neck clams baked with casino butter, lightly crumbed, and topped with bacon. $4.75

OYSTERS ROCKEFELLER
succulent Long Island oysters topped with seasoned spinach and hollandaise sauce baked to perfection. $5.25

MIXED SHELLS
three each of Oysters Rockefeller and Clams Casino. $4.95

House Specialty

BAKED STUFFED MUSHROOMS
large mushrooms stuffed with a mixture of crab, scallops, vegetables, and bread crumbs. $4.50

ESCARGOT
six escargot broiled in garlic butter served with garlic toast. $4.50

Savory Soups And Chowders

BAKED FRENCH ONION SOUP GRATINEE
piping hot, loaded with sauteed onions, and topped with a blend of cheeses. $2.50

NEW ENGLAND CL[illegible]M CHOWDER
thick and creamy ser[illegible] piping hot. $2.25

SOUP DU JOUR
Our chef creates a different soup daily, generally thick and hearty.

Salads

CHEFS JULIENNE SALAD
crisp salad greens covered with ham, turkey, bacon, and swiss cheese topped with fresh green peppers, olives, tomatoes, onions, sliced egg, and your choice of dressing. $5.50

SEAFOOD SALAD SUPREME
a delightful blend of shrimp, scallops, and crabmeat tossed in a fresh, herb, mayonnaise sauce and garnished with sliced egg and tomatoes. $6.95

Assortments

POTATO SKINS GRAND AMERICAN
crispy fried potato shells loaded with cheddar cheese and bacon bits 4.25

DEEP FRIED:
ZUCCHINI OR MUSHROOMS OR ONION RINGS
dipped in beer batter and gently fried until golden.
single order. $1.95
double order. $3.25

BUFFALO WINGS
deep fried chicken wings hot, medium, or mild served with celery sticks and blue cheese dressing for dipping. $4.50

VEGETABLE PLATE
an array of fresh vegetables in season. Prepared with fresh fruit and topped with your choice of hollandaise or bearnaise sauce. $5.25

Mix And Match

ONE IF BY LAND TWO IF BY SEA
A petite broiled New York Sirloin served with two large Louisiana Shrimp stuffed with crabmeat, scallops, and mushrooms $13.95

BEEF AND BIRD
One boneless breast of our orange whiskey chicken and a petite broiled sirloin - what a couple. $11.50

EXHIBIT 2 Bentley's Dinner Menu After the Change (continued)

Poultry

ROAST DUCKLING
A half duckling, roasted until crisp and topped with a peach and Grand Marnier sauce. $12.25

CHICKEN PICCATA
Medallions of chicken dipped in a cheese and egg batter and sauteed with mushrooms in a lemon wine butter. $10.25

BROILED ORANGE WHISKEY CHICKEN
Two boneless breasts of chicken, broiled to perfection then topped with an orange whiskey sauce. $8.95

BAKED STUFFED BREAST OF CHICKEN
Boneless breast of chicken filled with seasoned stuffing and baked until golden. $8.95

From The Sea

BAKED BOSTON SCROD
Young cod or haddock baked with lemon butter and white wine and dusted with flavored bread crumbs. $9.50

BAKED STUFFED SHRIMP
Four large Louisiana Shrimp stuffed with crabmeat, scallops, and mushrooms and simmered in white wine and butter. $12.95

SHRIMP SCAMPI
Louisiana Gulf Shrimp sauteed in garlic butter and white wine served with linguine. $12.95

SOLE FLORENTINE
Fresh filet of sole wrapped around a delicate blend of spinach, crabmeat, and scallops. Baked and topped with hollandaise sauce. $9.95

SEAFOOD MEDLEY
Shrimp, haddock, scallops, and clams baked in garlic and white wine with diced peppers, onions, and tomatoes and served over linguin: $13.50

CATCH OF THE DAY
"Different se foods picked by the chef daily assuring the freshest of quality."

Noah's Choice

ROAST PRIME RIB OF BEEF
Hand cut, tender rib served in a rich Au Jus.
Traditional cut. $11.50
Hearty Cut. $13.50

WEBSTER'S PLATE
Sliced tenderloin smothered with crabmeat and broccoli, topped with hollandaise. $13.95

STEAK AU POIVRE
Our 12 oz. New York sirloin coated with freshly cracked black peppercorns and served with dijon demi-glaze laced with cognac. $13.95

SLICED TENDERLOIN
Two petite filets of tenderloin broiled to perfection and topped with bordelaise sauce and a mushroom cap. $12.95

NEW YORK SIRLOIN
A 12 oz. sirloin steak, carefully selected, well-marbled, tenderly aged, and broiled to your preference. $13.25

VEAL CORDON BLEU
This tender cutlet of veal is lightly breaded and stuffed with imported ham and cheese, sauteed and topped with a mushroom demi-glaze. $11.50

ALL DINNER ITEMS INCLUDE:
garden salad, fresh vegetable, potato
whipped butter & fresh bread

For The Children Young And Older

BROILED BREAST OF CHICKEN	5.45
BURGER, BURGER all beef burger	4.75
BAKED SCROD	4.95
PRIME RIB, au jus	7.45

served with vegetable and potato

ADVERTISING AND PROMOTION

From the very beginning, Bentley's had been committed to aggressive promotion in order to keep the public talking about the establishment. Nothing had changed in that regard.

Like most restaurants, Bentley's was slowest during the early nights of the week averaging 100 covers Monday to Wednesday, 125 Thursday and Friday, 200 on Saturday and Sunday, and 300 for Sunday brunch. These numbers had remained fairly constant since shortly after the opening. Kelleher estimated that half of the customers were "regulars." The restaurant was capable of two and a half turnovers per night. Management had attempted to fill in the slow periods by offering a number of low cost specials such as the current offering of dinner for two for $11.95 on Monday and Tuesday nights. This special allowed guests to select from a selection of four entrees which changed every month.

The restaurant also advertised a Sunday special of "chicken or steak and chocolate cake" for $8.95. These two promotions were in addition to the previously mentioned $5.95 early bird special targeted at the area's large university population.

Bentley's advertising was directed to different markets during different seasons. Since students inundated the area surrounding the restaurant during the spring and fall semesters, many locals were hesitant to venture into this collegiate part of town. A significant number visited the restaurant once a week during the summer, but would not return again until the holiday season.

Bentley's food had a very good reputation which was well-publicized in the area. Tucson television channel 13 had awarded the establishment with 4 stars, its highest rating for food quality and value. The restaurant had also been featured on PM magazine and was periodically reviewed in the local newspapers.

BENTLEY'S VS. THE COMPETITION

Kathy Kelleher believed that every food service operation was the competition, even fast food outlets such as Taco Bell and McDonald's. However, she considered Bentley's to be somewhat unique in the marketplace due to its decor, atmosphere, and classic structure. Nevertheless, she spent a great deal of her time visiting competitors in order to identify new ideas and trends to implement at her restaurant.

Comment cards were frequently distributed to guests as a means of monitoring the Bentley's experience and comparing it to the competition. As an incentive to complete the comment card, one was randomly selected each month and the customer was awarded a complimentary Sunday brunch for two.

According to Kelleher, 99.99 percent of the returned comment cards were fantastic. Both the menu and service were rated very high when guests were asked to compare them to other restaurants that they patronized, and the majority said that "nothing" could be done to make the dining experience more enjoyable. However, some customers did request less expensive menu items, which Kelleher was considering.

STRENGTHS AND WEAKNESSES

Kelleher was confident that the restaurant's menu, food, prices, decor, atmosphere, and location were strengths compared to the competition. Unfortunately, some of these could also be perceived as weaknesses, depending on the perspective.

"Take the flowers for example," said Kelleher. "We have always spent a considerable amount of money on a large arrangement for the entranceway and fresh flowers for each table, and I have no intention of changing that. However, some guests have been confused by these touches since they assumed that the restaurant was out of their price range."

The establishment was constantly working to overcome this misconception. In fact, Kelleher had originally initiated the cut-rate specials as a means of reaching the price-sensitive market.

Bentley's one glaring weakness was the lack of available parking in the immediate vicinity. At one time, Kelleher had investigated the possibility of purchasing a piece of land for this specific purpose, but there was simply nothing on the market which was geographically realistic.

Parking in the evening had always been limited but sufficient once the area business people had gone home for the day, freeing up the bulk of the spaces. Historically, it had been the lunchtime crowd which was most seriously impacted by the parking problem.

THE CLIENTELE

Kathy Kelleher summarized the Bentley's clientele in the following way,

> We don't target any one particular market and we attract a wide range of customers. I don't think there is another restaurant around with this kind of ambience where you can enjoy such a wide range of food and prices. You can come here for just dessert, or an appetizer or a hamburger, yet you can always order a full meal. As a result, we count the locals, the students, business people,and tourists as our customers. Essentially, we want everyone to come here, have a good time, and enjoy the experience.

The establishment's records showed that a great deal of business came from university departments which often held meetings at Bentley's. The restaurant was also very popular for private business meetings after the normal work day, and in the afternoon when the facility was normally closed to the public.

Historically, Bentley's had been popular with students, but only on special occasions or when someone else was paying. Kelleher knew there were over 25,000 students and faculty in the area, and she decided to focus on this group. In April of 1988, Bentley's began to advertise student specials for $5.95 from the hours of 4:00 to 6:00 pm. The price included a full dinner which could be chosen from a selection of four entrees, and students and faculty needed only to present their university ID card to qualify.

This special promotion was advertised in the local press as well as in the university newspaper, and the response was terrific. On the first night, the over 100 takers were almost entirely undergraduates, which was fine. Although demand had since softened, it was most encouraging when the older students and the faculty began to filter in with their families on subsequent evenings, often ordering cocktails or wine with their dinner. All of this was particularly satisfying since the regular clientele did not normally arrive until well after 6:00 pm.

Kelleher was encouraged that the first-time visitors had enjoyed their meals and were surprised to find that they could afford to eat at Bentley's if they timed it correctly. Although she had always wanted to offer something for everyone, she now felt that the current menu was too formal. "We set out to be a dinner house", she said, "but what we intended was not necessarily what the area needs. In retrospect, I think we made a mistake by becoming a little too stuffy for the average student."

CONCLUSION

With the overwhelming success of the $5.95 special fresh in her mind, Kelleher wondered what course of action she should take. On the one hand, she was anxious to attract even more of the university population, but she wondered if that was wise.

Would the students come in and overwhelm the restaurant, making the rest of the clientele feel out of place? Also, would the increase in volume compensate for the lower average check or would the bottom line effect be an ultimately negative one?

The more Kelleher considered the multiple variables, the more confused she became. Finally, she decided to telephone her former marketing professor for a little advice. After some considerable discussion it was decided that the first step, because it was quickest, easiest and cheapest, would be to survey the student market. Exhibit 3 shows some of the questions asked and the responses from a random sample of 150 students.

EXHIBIT 3 Selected Survey Questions and Student Repsonses

Do you go out to dinner once a month or more? Yes 91% No 9%

When you go out to dinner, how much do you spend per person for food and beverage, not including tax and tip?

$15 - 20	16%
$10 - 14	16%
$ 5 - 9	60%
Under $5	8%

Have you heard of Bentley's? Yes 97% No 3%

Have you been to Bentley's for dinner in the past 12 months?
Yes 35% No 65%

From your experience and what you have heard, how much do you agree or disagree with each of the following to describe Bentley's?

	SD*	RD*	N*	RA*	SA*
* an expensive restaurant	4	7	21	51	17
* good restaurant with average to high prices	2	0	14	63	21
* good restaurant with low prices	27	54	12	5	2
* good restaurant with wide range of prices for everyone	9	36	34	21	0
* restaurant where possible to order just sandwich or burger	18	32	29	18	3
* a restaurant worth the price	5	9	28	40	18
* a special occasion place only	13	30	25	23	9
* customers dress sporty,casual	5	11	21	47	16
* doesn't matter what you wear	42	35	14	7	2
* where you spend $15-#20 on food and beverage	14	20	5	30	31
* if Bentley's had a new concept with light meals,relatively low prices,good service and informal atmosphere,you would be likely to go there	5	7	32	28	28

Would you go there with present the concept if you had $5 to spend on food? Yes 5% No 95%

*SD strongly disagree, *RD relatively disagree, * N neutral, *RA relatively agree, *SA strongly agree

CASE 8

THE HOTEL NORTHAMPTON

For virtually all of the past decade, the historic Hotel Northampton had experienced financial difficulties and a poor local image. During this time, three different sets of owners had attempted to run a profitable operation. In March of 1987, George Page and his partner, Harry McColgan, decided to try their luck. Since Page had functioned, very successfully, as managing owner of the Northampton Hilton for the last nine years, the local community was guardedly optimistic. The feeling on the street was that if anyone could operate the Hotel Northampton at a profit, it would be George Page.

In late April of 1988, Page reflected back on the first year of operation since the re-opening. Although many changes had been implemented and the operation was clearly showing signs of improvement, the average occupancy rate was only 47 percent and the hotel was still unprofitable.

Louis Bailey, the General Manager, was mystified. "I think we should be getting more business than we are, and I don't know why we're not," said Bailey. "Our rates are lower than the competition's, but they are not so low that people would wonder why."

HISTORY

In 1923, the Northampton Chamber of Commerce proposed that a "modern community hotel" be built as a means to socially unite and promote the Northampton area. The publicly owned Northampton Hotel Corporation was formed and construction began in the spring of 1926.

The hotel was constructed adjacent to the building which had once housed the famous Wiggins Tavern, founded in 1780 by Ben Wiggins. A local descendant named Lewis Wiggins leased the hotel and it opened in 1927 with Wiggins as the manager. In 1931, Wiggins re-opened the historic Wiggins Tavern at the rear of the hotel and Northampton had a first class hotel/restaurant combination. It became the social center of Northampton, serving as a meeting place for family and friends, church groups, charity organizations, and businesses. The Chamber of Commerce had achieved its objective of creating a modern community hotel.

Upon retirement in 1946, Wiggins sold the restaurant to the Schine Hotel Corporation which took over the hotel operation through a leasing agreement. Schine purchased the hotel in 1957 and operated it as the Schine Northampton Inn. During the Schine years, the hotel's reputation as a fine lodging and dining establishment gradually deteriorated. Financial difficulties began to surface in the early 1970's, and finally necessitated that the hotel be closed for the winter of 1977–1978 in order to prevent further losses. Schine finally sold the hotel in 1978 to a local resident, Joseph Albergo.

The hotel's financial difficulties continued under Albergo and the hotel was closed for each of two subsequent winters. Maintenance and repairs were delayed in order to reduce operating expenses. Valuable antique furniture which helped to create the unique atmosphere of the hotel was sold in an effort to cover losses. As the reputation and physical condition of the hotel further deteriorated, the once prestigious center of attraction hit bottom when it didn't re-open after the winter of 1980.

Proposals for converting the hotel into offices, apartments, and condominiums were presented to the city zoning board following the closing. In March, shortly after the city had approved a zoning change for conversion into condominiums, the Northampton Development Corporation purchased the structure and announced plans to open a renovated Hotel Northampton.

The Northampton Development Corporation (NDC) was headed by a local banker and primarily consisted of seven local banks, Smith College, and the *Daily Hampshire Gazette*. This group provided the hotel's $725,000 purchase price. In May of 1981, the NDC succeeded in selling the hotel to the Northampton Hotel Associates (NHA), a Boston-based three man partnership which planned to renovate the property.

The NDC floated a bond issue raising $1 million which allowed the NHA to purchase the hotel. The NHA received additional financing to renovate the property, but mysteriously overspent its $3.8 million budget halfway through the renovation process. Eventually, the NHA raised an additional $2 million by selling limited partnership interests in the hotel.

The owners entered into a management contract with Robert F. Warner, Inc., a New York based hotel representative and marketing firm that represented 150 hospitality and travel related enterprises. The Hotel Northampton became a member of their referral network called *Distinguished Inns and Historic Hotels*, but this was Warner's first venture into actual management of an historic property. With the management contract, the Hotel Northampton gained an established management organization and an international reservation system.

A skeleton staff was selected to ready the hotel for operations. A local resident, Catherine Blinder, became director of sales and marketing. Projected occupancies were developed from a market study by the Warner company (Exhibit 1). Blinder initiated action to build a clientele, both immediately and in the long run. Releasing press statements, obtaining mailing lists, beginning sales coverage of accounts, and arranging advertising were among her activities.

EXHIBIT 1 **Projected Occupancies**

Month	1st Year	2nd Year
January	40%	48%
February	45	50
March	52	57
April	55	60
May	75	80
June	72	80
July	68	70
August	68	70
September	78	80
October	75	78
November	60	63
December	50	53

It soon became apparent, however, that the hotel would not be ready on schedule. The renovations were more involved than originally planned and demanded greater time and money. The renovation budget was increased to $5.8 million and the opening delayed until January, 1983. Further delays led to a pre-opening scheduled for April and a hard opening on May 21. Steps were taken to finalize marketing strategies and operational details.

The month of March, however, brought substantial changes in the circumstances surrounding the hotel. Catherine Blinder was replaced by Marian Whalen on March 8. Concurrently, David Scales assumed the position of General Manager, allowing the project manager to concentrate on overseeing construction. Finally, on March 20, the hotel changed advertising agencies.

THE REOPENING

On Friday, April 25, the Hotel Northampton reopened its doors to welcome guests who had come for Parent's Weekend at one of the local colleges. Sunday night Marian Whalen sat in the Currier and Ives room, empty now except for a few service personnel who were breaking down tables, where the hotel's gala reopening reception had been held Friday evening. Reflecting upon the events of the past weekend, Whalen felt that her idea of using the hotel's incomplete renovations to an advantage had been a good one.

Reservations for the weekend had been accepted long before it was evident that construction and redecorating efforts would be this far behind schedule. The hotel compensated for inconveniences to guests, such as having no lobby furniture, by providing complimentary drinks at the reopening reception, and by the staff trying extra hard to provide a high level of service and hospitality. The hotel also made light of the predicament by giving guests toy construction helmets and explaining to them that they were taking part in the history of the renovation and reopening of the historic Hotel Northampton.

Feedback from service level employees indicated to the management that, except for a few isolated incidents, guests' responses had been very positive. Many guests were already making reservations to return some time in the future.

Though she had been in her position less than two months, Whalen felt that she had a good understanding for the marketing of the hotel. The opening was only the beginning in this unique situation. The summer months ahead would be critical ones. During that time perceptions of the hotel would be reestablished in the community and with its visitors. The financing of the expensive, over-budget renovation project would also test the accuracy of the sales projections in the near future. Whalen hoped the plans she had made would carry the hotel through and beyond this critical period.

THE MANAGEMENT TEAM

David Scales' background included a degree in hotel management from the University of Surrey in England, his native country. His first general manager's position was at the Randolph Hotel in London, a 1200 room property with a high level of service. After 18 months at the Randolph, Scales was general manager for two years at the London Airport Hotel, a 350 room banquet and conference center. For five year prior to coming to Northampton, Scales managed the Club Caribbean in Jamaica.

Scales compared the Hotel Northampton to the Randolph Hotel in that they were both high quality hotels serving tourists in a university environment. He accepted the Northampton position because of its challenge and because it would permit him to practice his *mein host* philosophy of hospitality management. One of Scale's intended projects was to open a lounge in the basement of the hotel with an old English pub theme and nightly entertainment. He anticipated a young, lively college crowd to which he did not want the hotel to appear aloof.

Marian Whalen held an Associate's Degree in personnel administration from Cornell University. She had been manager of the hotel restaurant at a nearby major university, a director of an 18 school cafeteria system, and a food service director for eight restaurants in a department store in Hartford, Connecticut. Whalen felt that the Hotel Northampton should specialize in personalized hospitality. Eventually, she saw the hotel as having a five star rating, the highest given by the Mobil Travel Guide. She foresaw the hiring of a combined social director/concierge.

MARKETING OBJECTIVES

David Scales expressed a desire to make the Northampton vicinity a tourist area. A recent study had shown that the Pioneer Valley, in which Northampton was located, had the second largest mix of attractions in the state, next to Boston. Historic sights had the greatest appeal, followed by fishing and scenic sightseeing. The area counted among its attractions four museums, the national Basketball Hall of Fame, two historic villages, famous historic homes, theatres and concerts, amusement parks, four ski areas, numerous parks and wildlife attractions. It also included a number of major industrial groups and six colleges and universities.

Scales' idea was to "make Northampton a destination point from Memorial Day to Thanksgiving Day." He proclaimed, "We're going to provide early American genuine hospitality with the efficiency and conveniences of a modern hotel. The Hotel Northampton will be a five star hotel, providing personal touches and all the little things, but simply on a smaller scale." Scales described the property as large enough to be profitable, but small enough to maintain intimacy.

After achieving an anticipated occupancy rate of 62 percent in the first year of operations, Scales asserted that "without a doubt" the hotel could achieve an occupancy in the high seventies by 1985. "Wherever there is a market, we will capture and develop it; as more are found, we will serve them," he said.

In order to capitalize on strong support from the local community, Scales planned a May promotion when 30 local VIPs would be invited to the hotel for a complimentary dinner and one night stay. He explained that local restaurant and banquet business was necessary to fill gaps in projected room sales.

Marian Whalen pointed to the advantages of being a small, non-chain hotel and believed the hotel would be superior to any major chain hotel such as Marriott or Hilton. "Because we're not subject to standardization imposed by a chain affiliation, we can develop the aura of colonial and traditional charm, mixed with modern facilities. We're able to offer the best of both worlds," she said, "specializing in hospitality."

Whalen believed that the history surrounding the hotel was a great advantage, but warned that it could be overdone. "History comes and goes and the time will come when we can no longer depend on it," she said. She felt that they must constantly be looking for new angles from which to market the hotel.

Whalen also felt that the sale of rooms was critical to survival of the entire operation. "Our marketing effort must be directed at the hotel operation; Wiggins Tavern is a tack-on to my sales task," she said. Accordingly, she aimed to change current perceptions of Wiggins Tavern as the focal point of the operation. Expected to supply 55 percent of the operation's gross operating income, the restaurant depended primarily on transient business. While it was currently marketed in a generalized fashion,

Whalen intended to address specific groups when the hotel was past the tight cash flow surrounding the opening.

MARKETS

Both Scales and Whalen agreed that, primarily, the corporate executive was the type of guest that would stay at the Hotel Northampton. Small executive workshops and conferences would be associated with these guests. They also hoped to obtain the overflow of guests from other area conference facilities.

In addition to commercial travelers, Scales and Whalen planned to appeal to bus tours and independent tourists interested in the area's history and fall foliage. The area colleges were also seen as a source of business from returning alumni, visiting parents and professionals, and graduations. Other potential sources included travelers from nearby Interstate 91, and packages for travel writers and skiers. Scales stated that the overall market would be "people who have taste and want modern services," and who come primarily from an area 50 miles in radius south of Northampton, which almost reached to Hartford, Connecticut (Exhibit 2).

ADVERTISING

In late summer, 1982, Catherine Blinder had initiated advertising in preparation for the forthcoming reopening of Wiggins Tavern. It consisted of radio spots and print copy accentuating the rich historic atmosphere, fine food, and quality service (Exhibit 3). A billboard off the exit of Interstate 91 was also rented.

When David Scales arrived on the scene he expressed a preference for print media because he felt it had a longer shelf life. He planned to generate print advertising that would separately promote Wiggins Tavern, the hotel's guest rooms, and its conference and banquet facilities. He also planned a mass mailing campaign and, later, a return to radio as an advertising medium in the future.

Whalen, on the other hand, felt that Wiggin's Tavern had been adequately promoted and her first decision when she came on board in March was to promote the entire property as "The Hotel Northampton, home of Wiggins Tavern." Her other plans included initiating a cold calling campaign with a theme that asks, " Why not meet at the historic Hotel Northampton and dine at Wiggins Tavern?"

EXHIBIT 2 Map of the Northampton Area

EXHIBIT 3 Pre-opening Radio Copy

SFX: FIFE AND DRUM MUSIC. YANKEE DOODLE. UP, THEN UNDER.

ANNCR: *Northampton.... 1780. Four years after the Declaration of Independence was signed, the Wiggins Tavern first opened its doors.*

SFX: CROSSFADE BED TO TAVERN AMBIENCE: EATING, DRINKING, GENERAL MERRIMENT.

ANNCR: *Inside, the atmosphere was warm and flavorful. The talk was of the good old days. Of battles won. Of John Paul Jones. The food...always plentiful. Great steaming rounds of roast beef. Heavy tankards of ale. This was the Wiggins Tavern as it was. Now, over 200 years later, we've reopened. And the good old days have returned. The food is just as delicious. Prime rib, fresh brook trout, Maine lobster. And you'll dine as your ancestors might have, in comfortable ladderback chairs surrounded by the glow of pewter. Come to Northampton and savor a dining experience people have been enjoying for over 200 years. The Wiggins Tavern. History has never repeated itself with such taste.*

SFX: CROSSFADE BED BACK TO YANKEE DOODLE. UP AND OUT TO END.

REALITY SETS IN

The future, however, was to present a different picture. The July 13, 1983 edition of the *Daily Hampshire Gazette* told the following story.

HOTEL OWNERS OUST THEIR TOP MANAGER

The owners of the Hotel Northampton have fired their hotel's manager after four months on the job, alleging that he spent too much money and ignored Northampton while promoting the hotel to out-of-towners. [The owners] said they will run the hotel themselves until they hire a replacement for David Scales. [They] dismissed Scales and Robert F. Warner, Inc., the New York consulting firm that employed him.

[One owner] said Scales maintained a full staff at the hotel even during slow weeks, costing the hotel unnecessary amounts of money. He charged that Scales and Robert F. Warner focused their advertising on the Connecticut and New

York markets, ignoring Northampton and making local patrons feel unwelcome at the hotel.

"One doesn't judge the performance of a general manager in such a short time," said Scales. He said he brought down costs in the food and beverage department and operated on budget in the other areas. The overspending, he said, was in the construction budget over which he had no control. "The financial situation at the hotel had become critical, and I suppose some decisions had to be made," he said. The firing of Scales comes at a time when the owners are being sued by three creditors who claim they have not been paid on time.

In an interview, one of the owners said he was still optimistic the hotel still will be a success despite the difficulties. "The Warner people were staffing up, assuming somehow that the business would be at a much higher level. They did not have the kind of controls up and down the line that are necessary in an organization of this size." Neither of the owners have run a hotel before, in contrast to Scales who had two decades of experience.

A few months later, the owners hired James Lucie and his wife Diane to manage the hotel. Lucie had been food and beverage manager at the historic Red Lion Inn in Great Barrington, Massachusetts, and his entire background was in that area of operations. Lucie and his wife concentrated on improving the performance of Wiggins Tavern. Approximately six months later, in April 1984, the *Daily Hampshire Gazette* carried this news item.

HOTEL MANAGEMENT CHANGED

An Ohio firm has taken over management of the Hotel Northampton and Wiggins Tavern. G.E. Springer, Inc., a hotel management and development firm from Cleveland, has been retained to manage the hotel and tavern. The decision to enter into an agreement with Springer was said to reflect the hotel's need for ongoing professional management and national marketing representation. Springer manages 16 inns in the midwest and northeast, including Sheraton, Hilton and Marriott hotels and Howard Johnson and Holiday Inn motels.

'We will rely heavily on nationwide marketing to present the hotel to travelers as a pleasant and comfortable place in an historic setting,' said a spokesperson. 'We plan to make the hotel well-known regionally and nationally, while improving the way it has been running.' According to one of the owners of the hotel, 'initial difficulties have been

> overcome and the hotel is profitable again. Even though room occupancy has not improved dramatically in recent months, the general health of the hotel is markedly better.'

The massive $5.8 million renovation project actually took four years to final completion. It involved converting the 27 rooms on each floor to only 17, plus the installation of new bathrooms. NHA attempted to operate the property with two more successive management companies, but they eventually decided that the hotel was just not a viable moneymaker. The NHA then deeded the property back to the original consortium of banks, and this group sold the hotel to Page and McColgan at very attractive interest rates in March of 1987.

THE 1988 HOTEL NORTHAMPTON

The Hotel Northampton was a five-story brick structure with round arch windows and a large porch supported by 40 foot white pillars. Located in downtown Northampton (population 30,000), the hotel was situated across the street from City Hall and was in the center of the shopping area. Smith College (2600 students) was within walking distance, and four area colleges with a combined student population in excess of 30,000 people were within a 20 minute drive. Interstate highways 90 and 91 were nearby, thus making Northampton a good stopover point for tourists on their way from New York City and points south to the mountains of Vermont.

The April 1986 edition of *Colonial Homes* magazine described the hotel as follows:

> In the verdant hills of the Connecticut River Valley, Northampton, Mass. retains much of the charm of rural New England. On the corner of King and Main stands a handsome colonial revival structure, the regal Hotel Northampton. Exquisite paneling and Chippendale-style seating in the lobby suggest the ambience awaiting guests. Upholstery and drapery colors complement the hues of the Federal style carpet and reproduction of bouillotte lamps on the sofa table illuminating thriving greenery. A main feature is Wiggins Tavern, cleverly designed to emulate the former 18th century tavern. Sheathed in old timbers and decorated with period heirlooms, the tavern offers good food in a warm atmosphere.
>
> Conveniently situated near I-91, the hotel is an easy drive from both Historic Deerfield to the north and Old Sturbridge Village to the east. The city itself has interesting sights including the home of President Calvin Coolidge.

The Hotel Northampton was an independent property with no central reservations system. A franchise agreement was unlikely in the future, and General Manager Louis Bailey felt that the hotel could exceed the standards set by many chain operations. "We aren't as strict as a chain with our food or liquor cost," said Bailey, "and we aren't striving for an optimum percentage. As a result, we have the capability to provide a level of service which is superior to that offered by a chain organization. We market the hotel as a new product. We treat every customer as a new opportunity"

Rooms The renovation project had been comprehensive. The 85 rooms at the hotel were clean, comfortable, and pleasant, and most contained canopied beds, two wing chairs, a desk, table, and a rocking chair in addition to such modern conveniences as cable TV, modern spacious bathrooms, AM/FM radio, air conditioning, and direct-dial telephones. Sixteen of the rooms had steam baths. The hotel's brochure described the rooms as "modern elegance." Ten of the rooms, however, were only large enough for single occupancy, and some rooms had a poor view. The following was the 1988 room rate schedule:

Single/Twin Room	$48/56
Double/Double or Queen	52/60
King Bed or Special Queen	56/64
Oversized King or Specialty Room	60/68
Two Room Suite (5)	79/79

The rates for bus tour groups were $42 single and $49 double. For the commercial traveler, the rates were $45 and $52. The 1988 average room rate to date was $49.

Wiggins Wiggins Tavern was the focal point of the hotel. The stone walls, low ceilings, and dark wood remained unchanged from 1780. The food was good and the portions generous, and management continually worked on improving the food quality. The dinner menu is shown in Exhibit 4. Seating capacity was 125 and checks averaged $4.00 for breakfast, $5.00 for lunch, and $12.50 for dinner.

Wiggin's was generally slow for breakfast, mostly hotel guests, and moderately busy at lunch. Dinner covers averaged 70 to 80 Monday - Thursday, and 200 to 300 on Friday and Saturday nights.

Oak Room The Oak Room offered casual dining for a maximum of 60 customers in a room decorated with wood paneling, hanging ferns, and unusual ship's lights. The fare was primarily soups and sandwiches which were also available in the connecting lounge.

During the summer months, outdoor dining under the canopy was extremely popular. Management was considering enclosing the patio with glass to extend "outdoor" dining into the winter months. There was also an adjacent piano bar lounge.

EXHIBIT 4 Wiggin's Tavern Dinner Menu

Wiggins Tavern

APPETIZERS

Included with Entree, Choice of:
Chef's Fresh Paté of the Day
Supreme of Fresh Fruits & Walnuts
Fresh Soup of the Day

Fresh From The Sea

Freshly Shucked Oysters (5)
On the Half Shell $2.95
Topped with Sour Cream & Caviar $3.50
Ice Shrimp with Spicy Sauce $.90 each

Special Starters

Mesquite Smoked Turkey Breast
With Gherkins & Horseradish $3.25

Crab & Scallops Mornay
Baked in a Shell with Artichokes $3.95

Beef & Chicken Brochette
Tenderloin of Beef & Chicken Served with Sweet & Sour Sauce $3.50

Home-Made Pasta
Angel Hair Spaghetti, Tossed with Lobster Chunks & Cognac $4.50

Tavern-Made Sausage Cake
Baked Sour Dough Stuffed with Country Sausage & Havarti $2.95

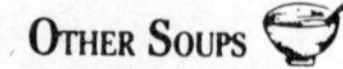

Other Soups

New England Clam Chowder $1.25
Onion Soup au Gratin $1.50

HOUSE WINES

Chablis, Rose, Burgundy, Lambrusco
By the Glass $1.50
1/2 Carafe $4.25
Full Carafe $7.25

Champagne
By the Glass $2.00
By the Bottle $9.00

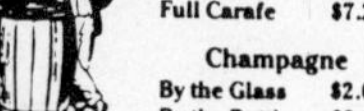

ENTREES

With Your Dinner...
Wiggins Salad Bowl
With Choice of Blue Cheese, Creamy Vinaigrette, or Green Herbal Walnut Dressing
Vegetable & Potato

Fresh Roast Turkey

Stuffed with Country Sausage, Onions & Celery. Served with Giblet Gravy & Cranberry Apple Garnish
$9.95

Wiggins Chicken Pot Pie

Tender Breast Sauteed with Vegetables & Potatoes, Baked in a Home-Made Crust
$9.95

Sauteed Chicken Marsala

Boneless Breasts Cooked in Marsala Wine with Mushrooms & Shallots
$10.25

Roast Fresh Native Lamb

Served Over Sauteed Sesame Spinach
$10.95

Country-Style Pork Chops

Center Cuts Stuffed with Mushrooms, Onions & Bacon. Corn Cake on the Side
$10.50

Roast Long Island Duckling

Topped with a Cointreau Mandarin Orange Sauce
$12.50

Broiled New York Sirloin

With Sauteed Mushrooms & Herb Butter
$14.95

Wiggins Filet Steak

The Most Tender Steak Available, Served with Bearnaise
$14.95

5% Mass. Tax Will Be Added to All Food Prices

Veal & Snow Crab Bearnaise

Sauteed Tenderloins with Crab Legs, Artichoke Hearts & Sauce Bearnaise
$14.95

Seafood Lasagna

Scallops, Shrimp, Lobster, Crabmeat & Ricotta Cheese, Baked en Casserole with a Sherried Cream Sauce
$11.95

Fresh New England Lobster

Boiled or Baked (Seasonal Price)

Baked Shrimp En Casserole

Baked Stuffed, or Sauteed with Sweet Butter & Herbs
$14.95

Fresh Sea Scallops

Baked, Fried, or Broiled. Lemon Garnish
$13.95

Swordfish Steak

Broiled Center-Cut, Seasonally Fresh, Topped with Our Special Tarragon Butter
$13.50

Fresh Boston Scrod

Baked with Seasoned Bread Crumbs
$9.95

Baked Sole Florentine

Stuffed with Spinach & Mushrooms, Topped with Our Fresh Lobster Sauce
$10.95

DESSERTS

For a Selection of Home-Made Sweets Please Consult Our Dessert Menu.

Function Rooms The main ballroom was located on the ground floor and accommodated between 125 and 300 guests, depending on the seating arrangement. The ballroom was booked mainly for wedding receptions and bus tour banquets. The Justin Morgan, Northampton, Currier & Ives, and Tavern rooms could handle 50 to 125 for dinner, 75 to 200 for receptions, and 40 to 150 for meetings, depending on the arrangement.

Wiggins Country Store In 1946, Lewis Wiggins dismantled the family store which was built in 1820, and reassembled the New North Salem structure on the grounds of the Hotel Northampton. In the summer of 1947 the store reopened for business. The store had been leased to a variety of tenants over the years. Currently, a local artist ran the store as a showcase for the works of local craftsmen. As one would expect, the country store was very popular with bus tour groups.

The District Attorney's Office In March of 1987, the District Attorney moved his office and staff of 35 into the annex section of the hotel. The annex was the original building constructed in 1927, now located at the back of the present structure.

To make room for the District Attorney, nine guest rooms, two smaller banquet rooms, and the executive offices were either relocated or taken out of service. In return, the hotel received a five year lease with a guaranteed square foot rate that was almost sufficient to pay the debt service for the entire hotel. There were thoughts of leasing another 10 rooms, perhaps to lawyers. The nine, or possibly 19, rooms lost were the least desirable in the hotel.

The Hotel's Image The General Manager said that he would like the facility to be perceived as a "small, old, classic hotel that would make the town's residents feel proud." Unfortunately, the problems of the past decade had left a negative reputation behind. There also seemed to be a gap in some people's perceptions as to what type of facilities were actually available. One of the managers noted that "90–95 percent of the people who come in say they didn't realize that the facilities were as nice as they are."

Louis Bailey did not mind the image of a senior citizen's hotel. Given the historic atmosphere and the lack of a swimming pool, he felt that senior citizens were the best market to pursue. Bailey also believed that the friendly staff provided good service on a consistent basis. It did not offer turndown service, but he was considering serving complimentary continental breakfast in the floor lobbies.

MANAGEMENT

George Page and Harry McColgan owned the Hotel Northampton jointly, although Page was certainly the more active partner. McColgan was a local resident who had first prospered in the real estate market. Page was a long time veteran of the hotel business. Page and his father currently owned the Northampton Hilton and had once owned as many as eight other hotels.

Louis Bailey stated that Mr. Page was receptive to new ideas, but then laughingly corrected himself, saying that Page felt that "there are no new ideas, it's just a matter of remembering the old ones."

The manager, Louis Bailey, had also been in the hotel business for most of his life. Bailey was responsible for overseeing Wiggins Tavern, the Oak Room and the bar, plus all other facets of the operation. Susan Bierly was the Director of Sales and handled all function arrangements as well as the booking of groups reserving 10 rooms or more. In describing the staff, Bierly said: "It's a family-oriented business from an employee relations point of view. Everyone gets along well and the lines of communication are open, which helps with customer relations. Mr. Page tells us that if a customer has a request that is within our capabilities, we should not ask but just do it."

MANAGEMENT OBJECTIVES

Mr. Page had stated that profits were the main objective, but the Hotel Northampton should not be considered a strictly bottom line-oriented company. "If a customer is dissatisfied," said Bailey, "we do everything possible to solve the problem. Rather than just apologize, we adjust bills quickly around here."

George Page did not expect any operation of this type to be profitable in its first year. As far as the second year was concerned, Page proposed the following steps to improve profitability:

DEVELOP A REPUTATION WITH BUS TOUR COMPANIES Of all bus travelers, 60 percent were senior citizens who were likely to be attracted to the old historic hotel, its traditional food, and the comparatively safe, downtown location. Seniors were also an ideal market segment since they were anxious to travel, had the time to do so, and frequently traveled during the normally slow midweek period. Management claimed that 50 percent of bus tour people either rebooked or recommended the tours to other groups. Tour Director Miller stated, "All the hotels in the area attempt to attract tours, but none as vigorously as us." Tour promotions had begun nine months ago and over 200 bus groups had come to the hotel since then.

Tours were booked anywhere from three months to eight months in advance. In March 1988, which was a slow month for bus tours, 55 buses of 40 people each visited the hotel. For $19.50 each, the tours enjoyed a luncheon while a three piece band played music from the '20s and '30s, and a tour of Smith College. The hotel grossed $42,900 from this during an off-peak period when the ballroom was generally free anyway. Usual peak periods for bus tours were, in order, fall, spring, and summer.

The most popular attractions for tours were Sturbridge Village, Historic Deerfield, and Tanglewood (an hour to the west), where the Boston Pops symphony orchestra played every summer. According to Miller, the greatest danger in promoting bus tours was that once tourists had seen the area, they would then seek other destinations. To counteract this, and to encourage overnight business, the hotel sponsored a dinner theatre. Cabaret shows were performed by a local cast and included song, dance, and audience participation. The breakeven point for these shows was 100 guests.

Bus tours comprised about 10 to 15 percent of the hotel's business. Page hoped that they would become a greater portion of the hotel's business in the future.

RESTORE THE QUALITY IMAGE OF WIGGINS TAVERN Page was convinced that the reputation of any hotel was based on its food and beverage operation.

INSTITUTE COST CONTAINMENT MEASURES For the first year, the owners did not spare the cost. "We had to put our best foot forward," said Page, "but now it's a different story. Our food and liquor costs are definitely inflated, and payroll is almost double what it should be. The second year these costs will be reduced in line with a normal hotel operation."

INVEST IN CAPITAL IMPROVEMENTS In an attempt to improve the quality of the service, $150,000 was spent on linen, china, glass and silver. Page also sunk an additional $400,000 in general improvements in the kitchen, the elevators, and the Justin Morgan room.

Other Thoughts Bierly thought that an outside salesperson would improve the profitability of the hotel, but Page was not so sure. "Eventually we may hire a salesperson for outside calls, but not right now. The problem is that the majority of calls would be to the corporate market whose biggest usage is for conferences and training seminars. We just don't have the small banquet space." Bierly and her secretaries concentrated mainly on booking wedding receptions and banquets. Bailey described their responsibilities as being *order takers*, "just taking the business that is being called in."

The Northampton Hilton employed an outside salesperson who sometimes mentioned the Hotel Northampton to her clients, but beyond that there was no joint selling effort. Naturally, the two hotels referred overflow business to one another.

According to Bailey, the key to a successful operation was a friendly staff that worked well together. Said Bailey,

> We need to please the customer so they will come back. We will work with the community so that the hotel will become the center of activity for weddings and banquets. We will also try to work up the room business the best we can. Our biggest drive for new business will be the bus tour market. This will be our first, main objective.

Bailey also stated that the previous owners, NHA, believed that after completing renovations they would run full occupancy. "That was not the case and still will not be the case. We will not run full occupancy," said Bailey. The manager believed that Page and McColgan were willing to wait a couple of years, to build the hotel's reputation by word of mouth, before profitability was expected.

PRICING

During the first year of operation, a survey was taken of competitive rates in the local area which showed that the Hotel Northampton was priced below the competition. The survey revealed that rooms at the hotel were 20 percent less expensive than their average competitor's, and that the food service facilities were priced 10 percent below the average competitive price for comparable items. The second year, room rates were raised 10 percent and food and beverage prices by five to eight percent. Bailey believed that a definite strength of the hotel was a strong price/value relationship.

The total revenue breakdown for the hotel was 60 percent food and beverage, 30 percent rooms, and 10 percent lease agreements. Whereas the leased space contributed 10 percent to gross revenue, it represented 50 percent of net profit. According to Page, "The present profit is in the leased space, but once that is leased out, the next best profit area is in the guest rooms. We need to push guest room sales as much as we can."

MARKET SEGMENTS

George Page identified the following market segments as significant or potentially significant to the hotel:

THE CASUAL DINER Given the size of the dining areas relative to the size of the hotel, Page felt that the restaurants should supply cash flow for the rest of the hotel.

BUS TOUR GROUPS

PLEASURE TRAVELERS Page was especially interested in senior citizens not traveling in a group. He wanted to attract people passing through the area with the image of Wiggins Tavern and the ambiance of the hotel itself.

COLLEGE RELATED BUSINESS

DOWNTOWN RELATED BUSINESS

THE SOCIAL FUNCTION MARKET

Page did not actively pursue the business traveler, although this market was considered important on a fill-in basis. The hotel was not set up for true seminar business because both the square footage and the number of function rooms were limited. According to Bailey, "We will only get corporate sales if the other guy makes a mistake." Some companies, however, such as *Coca-Cola,* used the hotel for small meetings. This had, in fact, resulted from a "mistake" at the Northampton Hilton, and *Coca-Cola* had continued to use the hotel.

According to Bierly, "We don't have a lot of seminars. The Hilton is tough competition. They have a solid reputation with businesses in the area. However, most of the businesses in Northampton are good. They spread their business around."

The Hotel Northampton was a member of the Pioneer Valley Convention and Visitors Bureau. Each week the Bureau sent leads to the hotel describing groups' facility needs, the number of rooms required, and the person to contact. Bierly answered these on a regular basis, but she did not have much spare time to call on local businesses as well.

The hotel had always had a close relationship with Smith College. Smith was a Signature Club member of the hotel which entitled the college to reduced rates. "Certain departments always call here," said Bierly.

ADVERTISING

Since Page believed that the reputation of any hotel was based on the food and beverage operation, advertising emphasized Wiggins Tavern. The majority of advertising dollars were spent in nearby Springfield, West Springfield, Longmeadow, and South Hadley since this was where most of the current customer base resided. Page did little advertising in Northampton because he thought that most residents preferred to drive out of town for dinner.

Management felt that word of mouth was most effective for promoting room sales. However, the hotel did receive free advertising space in the *New England Monthly* magazine in exchange for complimentary rooms.

COMPETITION

The main competition for the Hotel Northampton was seen as the 126-room Northampton Hilton. The Hilton was located away from the downtown area and was easily accessible by exit from Interstate 91. The Hilton offered many amenities including seven meeting rooms with a capacity of 10 to 300 people, plus an indoor and outdoor pool, whirlpool, saunas, and tennis.

During the week, the Hilton targeted the seminar and corporate market. On weekends, however, the market changed completely when package deals and the swimming pools attracted the pleasure market, and the hotel operated at nearly 100 percent occupancy. The Hilton's average occupancy for each of the past three years was 79.4 percent, 79.1 percent, and 79.5 percent, respectively, and its average room rate was nearly $10 higher than at the Hotel Northampton.

In addition to an outside sales representative, the Hilton employed an inside salesperson, a banquet salesperson, and a Director of Sales. Page thought that the social market was the same for both hotels, but that the overnight business was completely different because the Hilton did not accept bus tours.

The only other real competition in the Northampton area was the Autumn Inn. Located in a residential neighborhood near Smith College, the Autumn Inn had only 30 guest rooms and 2 meeting rooms with a maximum capacity of 35 people each. Bailey acknowledged that the Autumn Inn provided greater personalized service and had a loyal customer following.

At one time, the historic Lord Jeffrey Inn in Amherst had been in competition with the hotel for business related to the University of Massachusetts. The Lord Jeffrey had shut down in the fall of 1987 as a result of labor problems, but Page did not view this as an opportunity. "The Lord Jeff was not running a very high occupancy," said Page, "and all the hotels in the area get filled during peak times regardless of their status. During off-peak times, the Lord Jeff was not doing enough business so that its closing would significantly impact the competition." The Lord Jeff was due to reopen in May.

The remaining competition was not located in the immediate area. For the bus tour market, the major competition was felt to be the 23-room historic Deerfield Inn. There was also a 59-room Howard Johnson in the town of Hadley that was marginally competitive, although its only meeting room had a maximum capacity of 45.

Other possible competition included the 263-room Sheraton West Springfield whose rates were approximately $20 higher than those at the Hotel Northampton. The Sheraton had 13 meeting rooms plus a ballroom with a banquet capacity of 600. The 149-room Holiday Inn in Holyoke had three meeting rooms and a ballroom seating 350 guests. The Holiday Inn had also planned a 100-room addition in the near future. Rack rates in the area are shown in Exhibit 5.

EXHIBIT 5 Rack Rates of Area Hotels

	No.Rms	Rate
Autumn Inn	30	54/66
Deerfield Inn	23	60/74
Holiday Inn Holyoke	149	65/69
Howard Johnson's Hadley	59	52/62
Northampton Hilton	126	56/66
Sheraton West Springfield	263	76/86

THE FUTURE

When considering the future, George Page said, "I am not optimistic about 1988, either at the Hotel Northampton or at the Hilton. Hotel and restaurant business has been generally depressed across the country, and I don't think we will see any dramatic improvement in business until 1989. I expect that we will continue to lose money in 1988, but I hope it will not be as much as we lost in 1987." The revenue forecast for 1988 and the marketing budget, set at seven percent of revenue, are shown in Exhibit 6.

In November of 1988, occupancy for the year-to-date was 45 percent and food and beverage sales were 20 percent below forecast. Page and McColgan sold the Hotel Northampton for less than they had paid for it. The new owners had no qualms about a successful future. "This place is a gold mine," they said. "Its only problem has been that it hasn't been marketed properly."

EXHIBIT 7 1988 Revenue Forecast and Marketing Budget

Room revenue at 65% occupancy	$1,067,625
Food sales	668,100
Beverage sales	267,240
Function sales	500,000
Total revenue	2,502,965
Advertising	
Daily Hampshire Gazette	$ 6,054
Daily Collegian	5,485
Valley Advocate	3,600
Smith College Paper	5,565
Yellow Pages	660
WHMP Radio	576
Billboard on Route I-91	16,300
Horse and Buggy Magazine	10,000
Direct Mail	6,250
Scholarships	1,000
Donations	1,500
Sponsorships	1,000
Promotional Amenities	11,000
Sales Representative	19,500
Advertising Agency	24,200
Tour & Travel Agency	18,000
AHMA Membership	250
Promotional Food Cost	24,043
Promotional Beverage Cost	2,672
Promotional Room Night Cost	21,552
Total Marketing Expenses	$ 175,207

CASE 9

THE HARTFORD SUMMIT

Brian Fitzgerald, General Manager of the Summit Hotel in Hartford, Connecticut, got to his feet to welcome Scott Hermes, Director of Sales, into his office. Almost eleven months had passed since the hotel had joined the Summit Hotels franchise and Fitzgerald was eager to hear the most recent results of the sales efforts of Hermes and his staff. As the Summit lodging franchise was brand new, Fitzgerald was not confident that travelers were aware of the Summit and what it had to offer. The task of establishing an identity was made all the more difficult in that there was still much evidence of the preceding operators, Sonesta Hotels. Towels, ashtrays, brochures and signs still bore the Sonesta name and logo.

Apart from being updated on the progress made by the Summit sales staff, Fitzgerald also had some bad news to break to Hermes. The owners of the Summit Hotel property, Travelers Insurance Company, were building a company training center adjacent to the hotel. Since January, Fitzgerald had been meeting regularly with Travelers regarding the construction of a 700 seat ballroom and a health club in the training center for the use of hotel guests. As the existing meeting and exercise facilities in the Summit Hotel were quite limited, the ballroom and health club would have an important effect on the marketing of the Summit. Fitzgerald and Hermes had been counting on the facilities to enhance their marketing efforts. Fitzgerald was forced to tell Hermes that although the health club had been incorporated into the final plans, the ballroom had not. Fitzgerald knew that this decision called for adjustments in the marketing strategy.

HARTFORD

Hartford, Connecticut, renowned as the insurance capital of the world, was described by Mark Clements, manager of the Greater Hartford Convention and Visitors Bureau, as an "on the way to" or "passing through" destination. Located midway between New York City and Boston on the Northeast corridor and about 100 miles from each city, many travelers stopped in Hartford. Bradley International Airport, which served the central Connecticut and Massachusetts areas was, only 12 miles away halfway between the cities of Springfield and Hartford (Exhibit 1).

EXHIBIT 1 Map Locating Hartford (New York City is to the southwest, Boston is to the northeast)

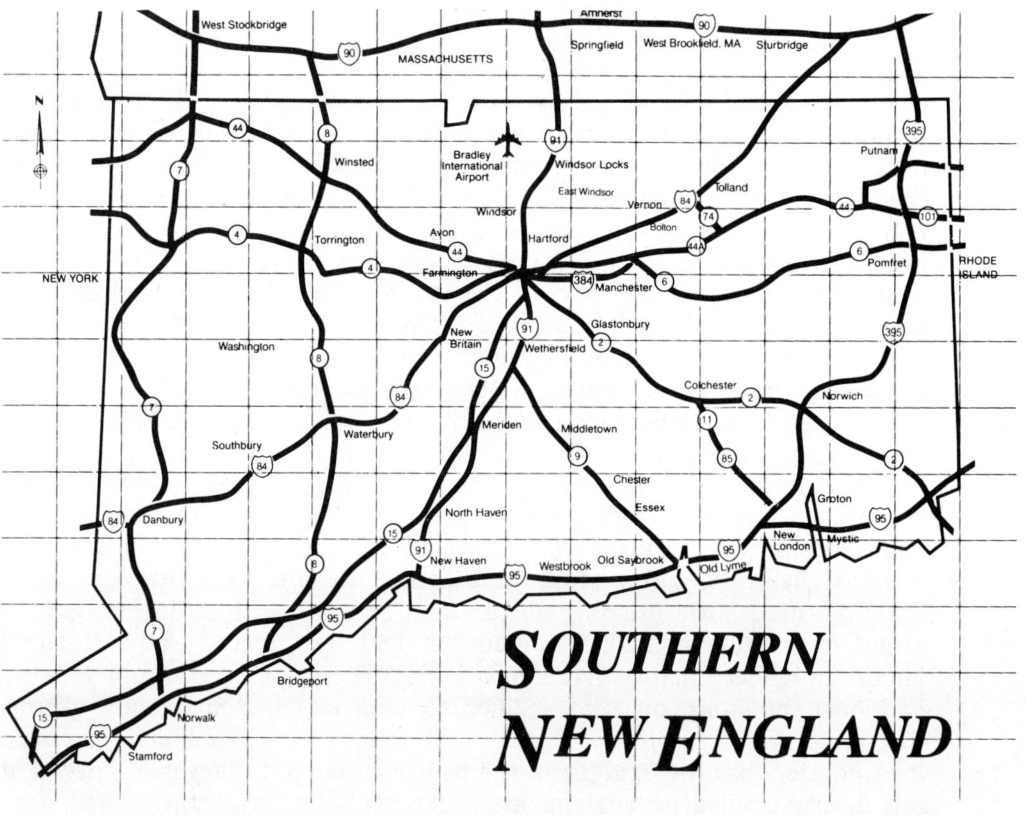

The city's economy was based on high-tech and aerospace industries as well as insurance companies. Large numbers of transient business people were drawn by Hartford's major businesses and its Civic Center. This convention center contained a coliseum seating 16,500, assembly and exhibition halls with 70,000 square feet of exhibition space and more than 60 shops and restaurants. It was a short walking distance from the Summit Hotel to the Civic Center (Exhibit 2).

EXHIBIT 2 Map Showing Hotels and Major Attractions in Hartford (The Marriott is about 12 miles to the west off Route I84)

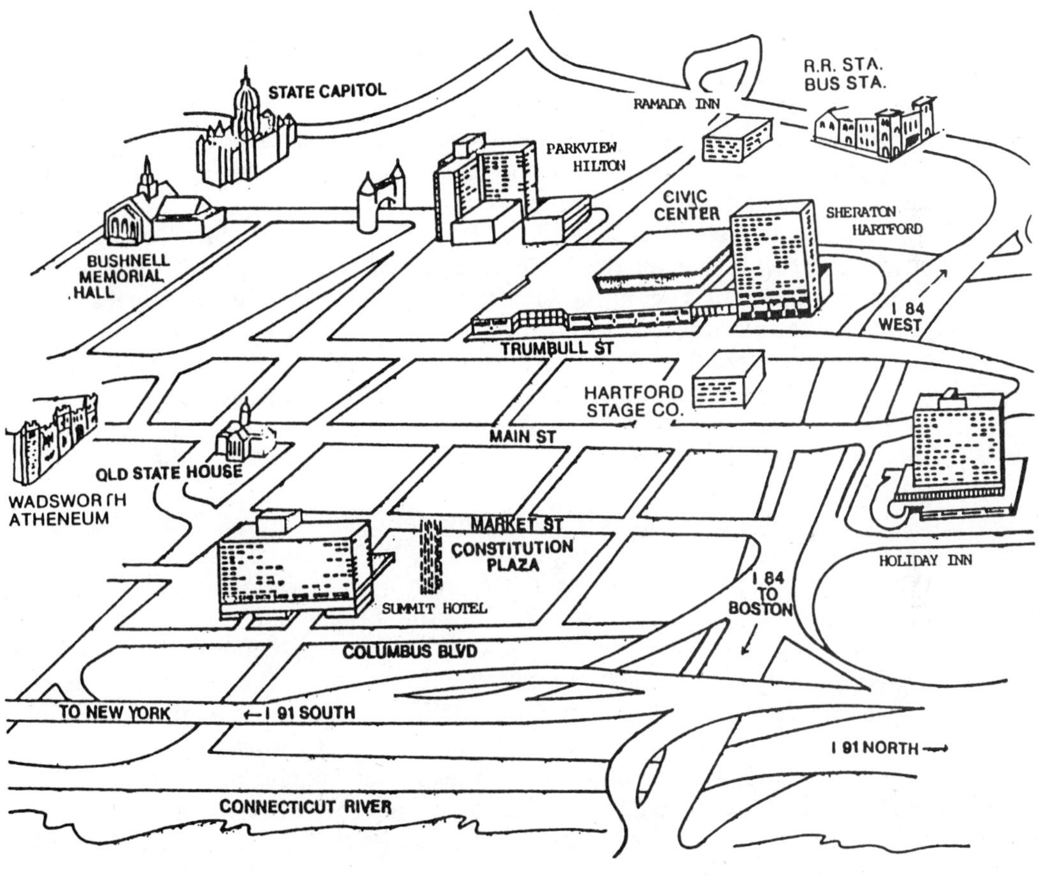

HISTORY OF THE HOTEL

The Summit Hotel was centrally located in Hartford, Connecticut near the junction of Interstate 91 and Interstate 84. A twelve-story structure of concrete and glass, the hotel was an integral part of Constitution Plaza, an office building complex that surrounded a paved area landscaped with trees and sculptures, and abounded by shops and boutiques. The Plaza was also owned by the Travelers Insurance Company which had its corporate headquarters in Hartford.

The hotel was built in 1964 by Travelers which leased the hotel at that time to Sonesta, a privately-owned hotel chain comprised of about eight properties. Sonesta operated the hotel for a few years until Travelers decided not to renew the lease. The hotel then came under the management of MHM Inc. which signed a management contract with Travelers. Together, they approached Summit Hotels International and became franchisees. Both MHM and Travelers signed the franchise agreement with Summit.

MHM Incorporated MHM Incorporated was an eight year old Dallas-based hotel management company responsible for the operation of approximately fifty two properties. Many of the hotels that the company managed were franchise operations including Holiday Inns, Rodeway Inns, Howard Johnsons, and Sheratons.

The arrangement between MHM and Travelers consisted of a five-year contract that specified that MHM receive 3 percent of the total revenue earned by the hotel as a management fee. All employees in the Summit Hotel were employed by MHM. Travelers paid for all capital expenditures including the renovations being carried out on the property.

As General Manager, Brian Fitzgerald was employed by and reported to the regional vice president of MHM Incorporated. He also worked closely with a Travelers vice president who was responsible for the real estate division.

Parkmount Summit Hotels International Summit Hotels International was a new lodging concept owned by Parkmount Hospitality Corporation which was also the owner of Rodeway Inns. Described as a "company on the go for people on the go" in the publication *Hotel and Resort Industry*, the original Summit Hotel in Dallas was "operated for the experienced, upper-level business traveler." Based on the success of its first property, Summit Hotels initiated a franchise development campaign (Exhibit 3). This was followed by the opening of a Summit resort property in Kona, Hawaii with the promise of other Summit Hotel franchise properties opening in Colorado, Texas, Oklahoma, California, and New Jersey.

In their mission statement, Summit Hotels International outlined the prerequisites for their hotels as follows:

> The minimum requirements for a Summit are 250-300 rooms with a high concentration of suites. Summit offers a luxury atmosphere at an affordable ($65-$85 ADR) rate. This concept of mid-luxury hotels will require a minimum of two dining rooms; one with continental cuisine and one upscale breakfast/lunch outlet, two lounges; one show lounge with top entertainment and one with a quiet, relaxed atmosphere. Public areas will have meeting, banquet, conference space, and an amphitheater accommodating from 10 to 750 persons in a variety of seating arrangements. Heavy emphasis is placed on ambience and high level of product/service in all areas of the hotel.

EXHIBIT 3 Excerpts from Summit Franchise Campaign Ad

As an independent hotelier, you value your autonomy. And you may hesitate to join a chain for fear of losing your independence. Yet in today's hotel industry, increasing competition and the limited financial resources of an independent hotel may make an affiliation particularly advantageous. Indeed, the market reach of a chain is almost essential to generate the consistently high occupancies necessary for success.

PROFIT FROM PRESTIGE. Summits are luxury commercial hotels offering all the services and amenities that the upscale corporate and leisure traveler demands.

PROFIT FROM EXPERTISE. Summit's staff can bring considerable design, marketing and operational experience to the table. Our assistance, from evaluating market studies to detailing renovation needs, is available at your request.

PROFIT FROM STRENGTH. At Summit Hotels International, we spend more than 50% of our on-going fees on marketing and the maintenance of our toll-free reservation system. Our marketing activities include national advertising and public relations.

Summit Hotels sought to position as a hotel chain concerned with a high level of service and value in terms of providing a luxury atmosphere at an affordable rate. Aiming for "the middle and upper market segments of the traveling public," Summit Hotels defined the target markets of their hotels as:

> The corporate traveler who is concerned with image; the meeting and convention planner looking for price-value; and the resort vacationer who wants all the amenities of a high quality hotel, but still has an eye on the budget. The Summit concept of fine dining, entertainment and full service meeting facilities will also cater to the needs of the local community.

Brian Fitzgerald described the Summit guest as the traveler who wanted to be pampered and taken care of and was willing to pay for it.

According to the contract between MHM, as management of the Hartford Summit Hotel; Travelers, as the owner of the property; and Parkmount Summit Hotels, Summit Hotels received a franchise fee equivalent to one percent of 60 percent of the room sales revenue. As Travelers

Insurance Company accounted for 40 percent of the room sales revenue of the Hartford Summit Hotel, the franchise fee was calculated solely on the business for which Summit Hotels could be credited. When a total of seven Summit Hotels had opened, franchisees would be charged an advertising fee in addition to the franchise fee. In the meantime, Parkmount Summit Hotels paid for national advertising.

THE HARTFORD SUMMIT

When MHM Incorporated became responsible for the Hartford property, Brian Fitzgerald was hired as the General Manager. He had previously been employed as General Manager of a Quality Inn in Columbus, Ohio. Earlier in his career, Fitzgerald was also a resident manager and a food and beverage manager.

The first task facing Fitzgerald was complete rehabilitation of the hotel. In his opinion, renovations were "about eight years overdue." In fact, after "nineteen years of bandaids," the problem had grown into a "big sore." Aiming to restore the reputation of the hotel to former levels and to raise the hotel to Summit standards, drastic renovations were carried out.

On the street level of the twelve-story building, the hotel lobby had been remodeled using marble and elegant furnishings in the public sitting area. Lighted by chandeliers, the lobby was furnished with a mahogany desk for the General Manager in order to provide him with high visibility to the guests. A concierge desk was also situated in the lobby.

On the second level which accessed Constitution Plaza, a new lounge was introduced. The Rendezvous lounge was decorated in green and beige with windows on two sides providing a view of the Plaza. With space for a band, a dance floor and a stand-up bar, the seating capacity was 139. During the week, the Rendezvous was popular with businesspeople employed in the surrounding office buildings. They were attracted by the buffet lunch and also the happy hour with reduced prices and complimentary hors d'oeuvres. The lively atmosphere was enhanced in the evenings by a three-piece band. Scott Hermes described the clientele as "sophisticated and middle-aged."

On the third floor, two dining facilities and a lounge were renovated. The Greenery was a bright and cheerful casual restaurant with a seating capacity of 104. Open for breakfast, lunch and dinner, it provided quick, friendly service to hotel guests and the employees of nearby companies.

However, it was Gabriel's, specializing in continental cuisine, that proved to be the real drawing card for Hartford residents. Gabriel's boasted the finest of European haute cuisine as well as traditional New England favorites, an extensive wine cellar, elegant decor and impeccable service. Decorated in rust and blue, there were tapestries hanging on the brick walls which added to the relaxed yet rich atmosphere. Tables and upholstered chairs were well spaced to allow for tableside cooking. Open for lunch and dinner with a seating capacity of 122, Gabriel's was frequented by an equal number of locals and hotel guests. In describing the clientele, Hermes noted that the restaurant was not geared toward the "average conventioneer" but was popular with "mid and upper management." During the week the patronage was largely business people who entertained clients at Gabriel's. On weekends it was a favorite choice of many Hartford residents for special occasion celebrations.

The Haypenny Lounge was situated next to Gabriel's and had a quiet, intimate atmosphere. Despite the two-for-one happy hour, complimentary hors d'oeuvres, and weekend entertainment, the Haypenny was largely frequented by hotel guests and served primarily as a holding room for Gabriel's. Exhibit 4 shows an advertisement for some of the hotel's featured attractions.

Rooms Approximately 50 percent of the 290 rooms had been redecorated as part of the overall renovation project. In keeping with Summit standards, the twelfth floor had been converted to a Concierge floor that included several amenities and special service. The remaining rooms were coordinated in blues and rusts and were equipped with televisions, direct dial telephones, individual climate control, and amenities.

Eighty of the hotel's rooms were called Plaza rooms. These accommodations were small rooms offering only a single size bed and a shower stall as opposed to a full bath. Hermes described the Plaza rooms as being "the size of broom closets." Summit management had arranged to use the rooms for students in training at Travelers Insurance and other companies. Fitzgerald stated that all of the rooms in the hotel were smaller than their counterparts in other hotels but he did not see this as a potential source of guest dissatisfaction. Hermes, however, felt differently. "The further reduction of our small guest rooms would enable us to begin to improve the poor image of the hotel guest rooms. This is a very real problem because one-third of our rooms are too small to efficiently compete with any other hotel in the area."

The Concierge Floor The twelfth floor had been converted into a VIP floor by adding a clubroom, combining every three rooms to form two, and by furnishing all rooms with either king or queen size beds. Hermes said that there were plans to convert the eleventh floor as well, due to the demand for the higher class accommodations. The redesigned eleventh floor would not include another clubroom but would involve the addition of a second presidential suite. The presidential suite on the twelfth floor was leased on an annual basis to a Hartford-based company, an arrangement that Fitzgerald found most agreeable. However, Fitzgerald felt the second presidential suite was desirable for marketing purposes. Plans to convert the eleventh floor would increase the total number of concierge rooms to approximately fifty. The Summit collateral proclaimed that:

EXHIBIT 4 **Featured Attractions of the Summit Hotel**

When asked what makes The Summit special, we couldn't come up with a single reason.

Enjoy service galore on the Concierge Floor.

Get carried away at the Rendezvous Room lunch buffet!

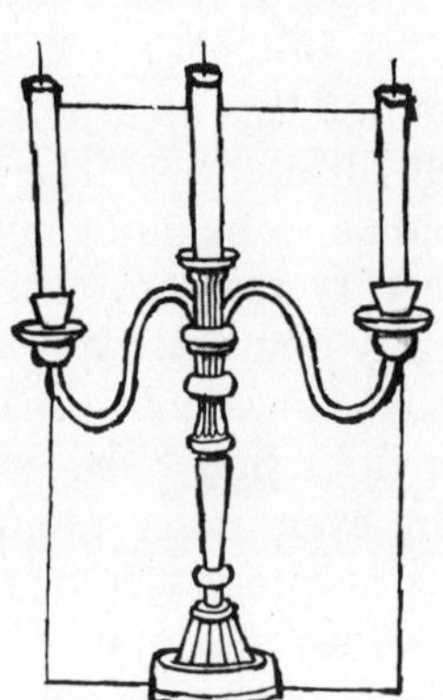

A Gabriel's dinner is always a winner.

To the Rendezvous Room back you go— just in time for this evening's show!

5 Constitution Plaza, Hartford, Connecticut 06103
(203) 278-2000

> The Concierge floor is the Summit's commitment to a level of service above and beyond the ordinary. It is designed for discriminating guests who appreciate elegant surroundings, superior service and unexpected amenities.

Concierge floor guests were given a limited access key that allowed them to enter the VIP area. A concierge was on duty from 6:30am to 11:00pm on the concierge floor to assist guests with problems. As well as being larger and uniquely decorated, each room was supplied with an electric shoe shine machine, a bathrobe, and fine soaps and shampoos. The maid who turned down the guests' beds in the evening left behind chocolates and small liqueurs.

Concierge floor guests had exclusive use of a clubroom equipped with a wide-screen television, pool table, card table, backgammon board, and stereo system. Guests were invited to a complimentary continental breakfast in the morning and a free bar between 5:00pm and 7:00pm in the clubroom.

Meeting Room Facilities Mark Clements of the Greater Hartford Convention and Visitors Bureau stated that the Summit was known for its exceptional food and beverage and efficient, friendly staff. He described the hotel as "upgrade, classy and European; a hotel with ambience." Its selling points were the Concierge floor and a high level of service and attention received at a competitive rate. For example, the Summit was the only hotel in Hartford that offered foreign currency exchange. The client best served by the Summit, in Clements' opinion, was the individual traveler and not the conventioneer.

Clements believed that the Summit had two major competitive disadvantages: meeting space that was "tight," and the fact that many of the guest rooms were simply too small for multiple occupancy. The Summit had eleven meeting rooms that had been renovated but Clements said there were problems handling larger break-out sessions, not to mention the lack of a formal ballroom. The largest meeting facility in the hotel had a capacity of 300 and its flexibility was limited by large support pillars in the middle of the room. Clements felt that "you need a ballroom to market competitively."

Occupancy Since the takeover, the occupancy of the Summit hotel has averaged 48 percent, while occupancy for other competitive Hartford hotels has been approximately 56 percent. Exhibit 5 compares the cyclical trends with Summit occupancies.

According to Scott Hermes, the Summit management was "starting to see a turnaround" and had set a goal of 54 percent average occupancy for the forthcoming year. He said that no comparison could be made with occupancy figures for the Sonesta property because conditions had changed considerably over the years. Three years before, Hartford had neither a Hilton nor a Marriott providing competition in the area. Further, the phys-

EXHIBIT 5 Hartford Cyclical Trends and Summit Occupancies

Month	Hartford	Summit (%)
July	Slow	33.5
August	Slow	69.4
September	Busy	58.0
October	Busy	66.1
November	Slows	49.9
December	Slow	25.4
January	Dead	34.8
February	Slow	45.1
March	Slow	50.5
April	Picks Up	53.6
May	Good	50.1
June	Good	52.2

ical deterioration of the hotel and the on-going construction in the surrounding blocks had negatively impacted occupancy. Hermes explained that there were other reasons for the relatively low occupancy figures during the last year. These included a lack of direct sales initiative by the Sonesta staff and the change of management in January. He also blamed unethical competition from certain employees at competing hotels who spread rumors that the hotel was being converted into a dormitory. Hermes also expressed the view that "weekend business kills you in Hartford." Occupancy percentages for a typical period by day of the week were: Sunday, 41.7; Monday, 60.9; Tuesday, 66.6; Wednesday, 65.4; Thursday, 52.9; Friday, 31.3; Saturday, 31.8.

Competition General Manager Brian Fitzgerald considered all hotels in the city to be competitors. He stated that "all I want is five rooms a night from every hotel in Hartford." In the strategic marketing plan developed by the sales staff, however, the Summit's competition was defined as the Ramada Inn, Holiday Inn, Parkview Hilton, Marriott Farmington, and the Sheraton Hartford. The sales staff narrowed the primary competition down to the last three. The locations of the various hotels can be seen in Exhibit 2. Exhibit 6 compares the strengths and weaknesses of the Summit Hotel to those of the competition.

Based upon the number of rooms in the Summit as a percentage of the total rooms in the six major hotels in the Hartford area, the Summit was allowed a 14.7 percent fair market share. In terms of the number of room

EXHIBIT 6 Competitive Analysis

	Summit	Marriott	Hilton	Sheraton	Holiday Inn	Ramada
Market Share (%)	12.2	18.1	17.7	24.5	16.8	10.2
Fair Market Share (%)	14.7	15.4	20.7	20.2	18.2	10.5
Occupancy (%)	48	66	50	69	55	55
Single Rates ($)	76–118*	85–105	83–103	75–105	60–69	62–69
Rooms	290	305	410	400	359	208
Suites	8	6	15	15	8	8
Meeting Rooms	11	22	10	14	12	12
Restaurants	2	4	2	2	1	1
Lounges	2	2	2	2	1	1
RmSvcHours	17	19	17	17	12	15
Pool	No	Yes (2)	No	Yes	Yes	Yes
Health Club	Not Yet	Yes	Yes	Yes	No	No
Distance (mi) from Airport	12	27	15	13	12	16
Facilities Rating (1–10)	5	10	6	8	4	4

* Does not include Plaza rooms at $55.00

nights sold by the Summit as a percentage of the total room nights sold by the major hotels in the city, the Summit had only a 12.2 percent market share including the rooms used by Travelers.

THE STRATEGIC MARKETING PLAN

The Summit sales staff had created a strategic marketing plan for the hotel. As part of their research, they evaluated Hartford in terms of the demand for hotel rooms by various market segments. They found that only the corporate segment was expected to increase in size, and this was not attributable to an influx of new companies but rather to expansion of the existing ones. The construction of a training center by Travelers Insurance was evidence of this trend.

Property Evaluation When the Summit sales staff conducted research prior to the preparation of their strategic plan, they determined the following:

1. We are best suited to the individual corporate traveler and the small corporate group.
2. The upscale renovations, location of the property, fine food and service, and Concierge level make us the ideal hotel for corporate business.
3. In addition to the corporate business, bus tours and special events are profitable segments to pursue. The addition of a ballroom would offer the option to target the weekend market of associations and city-wide conventions. Since Hartford is not a major destination, any new potential weekend markets would be welcome.

Target Markets Having analyzed the strengths and weaknesses of their property and those of the competition, the sales staff came to the following conclusions:

1. The two markets to whom we offer the most advantages are the individual corporate and the small corporate group.
2. We should pursue bus tours, special events, sports teams and small corporate groups more aggressively.
3. Our unique advantage is the quality of our renovations and the extremely good reputation of our food and our service.

Pricing Policy Regardless of occupancy level, all rooms had one rack rate. The double occupancy room rates were eliminated to reflect the fact that the Summit was "not a double occupancy hotel." Rack rates ranged from $55.00 for a Plaza room to $118.00 for a room on the Concierge floor. Suite rack rates ranged from $250 to $550 for the presidential suite.

Weekend Packages In order to bolster the low weekend occupancy, a Summit Send-Off package, which included transportation to and from the airport, and a Weekend for Married Lovers package were offered. However, both Fitzgerald and Hermes felt that it was better to optimize on potential business during the week. As far as weekend packages were concerned, they were satisfied to draw enough business "to cover the printing costs" of the brochures. Hermes doubted the packages would ever be successful because the Summit was not known as a chain and the hotel did not offer sport or health facilities. Regardless of the packages, the Summit offered a $49.00 rate for any room except a suite on weekend nights.

Positioning The outcome of the sales staff's research was the decision to position the Summit as "not the tallest hotel in Hartford, just the top." Fitzgerald was pleased to find that executives attending large meetings often preferred the Summit as their headquarter hotel. The Summit provided a place for them to "get away from the crazies."

In positioning, the sales staff held the view that:

- Realizing our function space limits us as to the markets we can pursue, we are still in the strongest position to capture the middle to upper level commercial traveler.
- Because of our fine reputation for service, cleanliness, and food, and with the upgrade renovation, we have maintained a distinctive product in keeping with the professionalism of the staff.

It was the sales staff's decision to use a "sophisticated" advertising style to project the updated image to those who had not yet experienced the new Summit. To date, the graphics had been completed but not yet approved by Fitzgerald.

In the spring, large illuminated "Summit" signage had been installed on the exterior of the building, but signs in the parking garage still bore the Sonesta name. Furthermore, towels, ashtrays, matchbooks, comment cards, room service menus, and hotel brochures continued to remind the guest of the hotel's past. In the summer, when the main restaurant had reopened as Gabriel's, a media blitz had announced the change, but little had been done to publicize the arrival of the Summit franchise to the area. As of November, only sparse advertising had been placed in trade journals for the corporate meeting planner.

CONCLUSION

In concluding the strategic marketing plan for the Summit Hotel, Scott Hermes emphasized the importance of approval of the 700 seat ballroom in the Travelers Insurance Company Training Center. Since the center was scheduled to open in the last quarter of the following year, Hermes and his staff needed to begin selling efforts immediately in order to book the ballroom and hotel space.

Now, as Fitzgerald welcomed Hermes into his office, he wondered what Hermes would say to the news that there would be no ballroom in the foreseeable future. More importantly, Fitzgerald was anxious to discuss what adjustments would need to be made in the hotel's marketing strategy.

CASE 10

ANDY'S BARBECUE

In May 1988, Andrew Johnston, president of Western Foods, Incorporated, commissioned a market research study to examine consumer attitudes toward Andy's Barbecue Restaurants, its restaurant division, and barbecue in general in order to determine the optimal type of restaurant for Andy's. According to Mr. Johnston, the focal question to be addressed in the research was: "Can Andy's appeal to more families to increase its dinner traffic for the purpose of generating $600,000 in sales per outlet, a 22 to 25 percent operating profit, and an ability to withstand intense competition?"

THE CORPORATION

Since 1962, Western Foods, Inc. had operated five restaurants in a major southwestern metropolitan area. Each restaurant specialized in barbecue sandwiches and barbecue plates as it main product, although some locations offered steaks. The price, cost, and gross margin of menu items are shown in Exhibit 1. The restaurants used a cafeteria style for food service; table service for dinner had been introduced at two restaurants on a limited experimental basis. Each restaurant also offered a take out service. In 1988, this service accounted for 25 to 30 percent of the total sales, which were about $500,000 per location.

Since 1974, Andy's had consciously moved away from the "barbecue joint-truck stop" image common among competitive outlets. Efforts to establish itself as a quality barbecue restaurant had resulted in an expanded menu, salad bars, and improved outlet decor. Concurrent with this move was a decline in lunch sales which had not been offset by increased dinner sales.

Andy's was the largest chain of barbecue restaurants in the metropolitan area. Andy's was also the only barbecue restaurant open seven days a week (11:00 am to 10:00 pm) for both lunch and dinner service. Competitive outlets were open five days a week from 11:00 am to 2:00 pm.

The five Andy's restaurants averaged a gross profit of 60 percent on sales with a 20 percent operating profit in 1988. It was Mr. Johnston's

---

This case was originally written by Roger Kerin, Professor of Marketing, Southern Methodist University, and is used with permission.

EXHIBIT 1 Price, Cost, and Gross Margin of Menu Items

	Price	Cost	Gross Margin	(%)
Sandwiches:				
Beef-regular	2.30	.70	1.60	(69.6)
jumbo	3.00	1.04	1.96	(65.3)
Ham-regular	2.30	.72	1.58	(68.7)
jumbo	3.00	1.08	1.92	(64.0)
Sausage-regular	2.30	.52	1.78	(77.4)
jumbo	3.00	.76	2.24	(74.7)
Beef Po Boy	3.10	1.00	2.10	(67.7)
Ham Po Boy	3.10	1.03	2.07	(66.8)
Big Tex (beef, ham, cheese, vegetables)	3.90	1.32	2.58	(66.2)
Dinners:				
Beef alone	5.90	1.85	4.05	(68.6)
w/salad	5.90	2.01	3.89	(65.9)
Ham alone	5.90	1.91	3.99	(67.6)
w/salad	5.90	1.93	3.97	(67.3)
Sausage alone	5.90	1.43	4.47	(75.8)
w/salad	5.90	1.45	4.45	(75.4)
Ribs alone	5.90	2.45	3.45	(58.5)
w/salad	5.90	2.47	3.43	(58.1)
Big Tex dinner	6.50	2.09	4.41	(67.8)
w/salad	6.50	2.11	4.39	(67.5)

Dinners include two vegetables, sauce and toast

policy to allocate 2.5 percent of sales to advertising and sales promotion annually. Promotion had typically included some radio advertising, complimentary dinners and direct mail to residents in the trade areas surrounding the restaurants.

In 1988, published statistics indicated that 1,246 restaurants were located in the metropolitan area served by Andy's Restaurants. Combined, the restaurants generated $924 million in sales annually. Dollar restaurant sales volume had increased at a rate of 10 percent annually.

There were 112 restaurants specializing in barbecue in the metropolitan area served by Andy's. Previous research commissioned by Western Foods indicated that barbecue as a separate food group accounted for five percent of restaurant dollar sales volume in the city or $46.2 million in 1988.

THE RESEARCH STUDY

In early August 1988, Mr. Johnston received the results of the commissioned research. Excerpts from the report are presented in the appendix.

REACTION TO THE STUDY

On August 19, 1988, after having reviewed the results of the study, Mr. Johnston prepared a statement of implications from the study results for his management team (Exhibit 2). At that time, he asked Dr. Oscar Miles, a Ph.D in Marketing and an independent marketing consultant, to work with Andy's on strategy development.

EXHIBIT 2 Andrew Johnston's Summary of Research Results

Date: August 19

To: Clark Tully, Director of Operations
Tom Smith, Director of Marketing
Oscar Miles, Marketing Consultant
From: Andrew Johnston

Subject: Research Report

I have had a chance to examine in greater depth the results from the research agency study. As I see it, the overall implications of the study are:

I. *Barbecue is not a particularLy favorite type of food; however, it is sufficient to build a successful restaurant business.*
   a. Compared with the general frequency of eating out at lunch and dinner where approximately 40% eat out twice or more per week, and another 40 to 50 % eat out once per month up to twice a week, only 28% eat barbecue five or more times a year. More precise figures on frequency are needed to get a fix on market potential!

II. *Barbecue is far more popular for lunch than dinner.*

III. *Reasons why barbecue in more popular at lunch than at dinner and how to change.*

   a. Women and children together are more influential than men, and they are the least favorable toward barbecue (support these two statements).

EXHIBIT 2 Research Summary (continued)

b. Barbecue is "filling" - report does not expand on the consequences of being "filling," but I would assume "hard to digest" may be the same as "filling," and no one likes this - particularly women and children at night when they don't have after-lunch activities to help digestion.

If the above is valid, perhaps some of the following would help to overcome the objection and expand the market - a market the Andy's is well ahead of the competition in capturing;

(1) Is steak any less filling or hard to digest? Is it just meat? Type of meat? Amount of smoke and its effects?
(2) Seek consul of doctors to determine how they might help.
(3) Are chicken and ham less difficult? If so, promote.
(4) Offer some variety, perhaps other than barbecue or meat.
(5) Barbecue considered tasty, build on it. Also reasonably priced, informal, friendly people, quick service at lunch.

c. Characteristics desired by dinner consumer differ from lunch consumer, which probably explains why restaurants have difficulties being successful at both. A number of dinner restaurants appear to be successful at both, perhaps Andy's can be also. The following suggestions might serve as a beginning; cafeteria for quick service at lunch; dinners at night with sandwiches offered; family style to be "leader" as it fits informal perception, and it fits Andy's and barbecue - different yet similar to "All You Can Eat." Also: add baked potato and steak at night, not at lunch; add a fish and shrimp at night (frozen); perhaps corn on the cob in husk at night and heated in a radar range. Special recruitment and training of waiter /waitress/hostess at night, as friendliness is important.

Keep working on "informal" interior decor that is barbecue but attractive and comfortable. Attempt to define what is informal. Similarly work on exterior.

Price evening food higher, particularly dinners, but sandwiches too if salad is included - one reason for calling "Plate" at lunch.

d. Continue to exploit take out. Andy's dollar sales of 25-30% far exceeds average barbecue of 10%. This is probably due to food packaging, separate take-out facility. More can be done.

I would like to schedule a meeting for September 4 to discuss the research report and consider strategic options. I have asked Oscar Miles of Miles and Friedman to consult with us on these matters.

The September 4 meeting brought together Andrew Johnston, Clark Tully, the director of outlet operations, Tom Smith, the director of marketing, and Oscar Miles, the marketing consultant. During the course of their meeting, the group reexamined the research results, outlined seven generalizations from the research, and stated a number of strategic considerations. The generalizations were:

1. Barbecue is a specialty food with a rather modest demand, yet a demand of sufficient magnitude to justify being in that business.
2. Barbecue is eaten significantly more at lunchtime than dinner.
3. Barbecue is significantly more popular with men than women and children.
4. The three primary characteristics at lunch are: quality of food, quick service, and waiting time. The three primary characteristics of dinner are: quality of food, friendly service, and table service.
5. Barbecue is perceived to be tasty, informal, moderately priced, middle-class, and pretty good for dinner.
6. Females make or influence where to eat 60 percent of the time.
7. At all times a balance must be maintained between marketing-production-finance.

The strategic considerations were:

1. Since desired sales volume requires more than a heavy lunch business, sales at night and weekends must be developed.
2. Since women find barbecue only moderately desirable, and since they are a major decision maker at selecting an evening and weekend restaurant, a special program needs to be developed to appeal to them, and it must be determined more precisely why they like barbecue less than other foods.
3. Special emphasis should be placed upon the primary characteristics that are desired by customers and that are different at lunch and dinner. At dinner they are quality food, friendly service, and table service.

After the meeting, Dr. Miles voiced several opinions on Andy's. He viewed the situation as one requiring rethinking the positioning of the restaurants. Dr. Miles commented that "Andy's has consciously moved away from the hard-core barbecue eaters who seek a barbecue joint. This alienation has resulted in a loss at lunch."

Having discussed Andy's communication efforts with the firms management group, Miles concluded that Andy's had been only moderately active in any communicative effort.

"What had been done, however, aimed primarily at communicating Andy's as offering quality barbecue," according to Miles. "Since the barbecue market is very thin, I suggested that further efforts in this direction would result in diminishing returns. Andy's should expand its market base by repositioning or repackaging in a manner that makes Andy's a logical alternative for evening and weekend dining."

"How should Andy's be positioned," noted Miles, "is the question to be answered. Should it be as a family dinner restaurant or as a barbecue lunch restaurant? Once a position is adopted, then a communication effort must be designed to convey the proper message."

On September 25, 1988, Mr Johnston and his management team met again with Oscar Miles. They addressed themselves to the following: (1) What should Andy's position be? (2) How do we package or get into that position? (3) How do we communicate this position to the potential customers? (4) How can we evaluate the effectiveness of the first three steps?

At the conclusion of the meeting, Mr Johnston summarized the opinions of those present:

> It is recognized that developing a different position at lunch and dinner requires very careful handling so as not to destroy both of them. The message communicated has to point up the fast food specialty food by cafeteria service while at the same time communicating the idea that Andy's is a logical alternative for evening dining—being informal, and offering friendly table service. Still further, the evening communication must include a strong message to women, since they are so influential in selecting the evening eating spot. A number of suggestions were made including the following: add chicken on the evening menu and keep the atmosphere warm and informal with such things as wooden floors, old chairs, checkered table cloths, and perhaps candles or lantern type lights. Special attention should be given to the menu with such additions as soup, cheese, sandwiches and wine being considered as well as fruit and salad. Also available should be one or two vegetables (such as asparagus) that particularly appeal to women.

The next day, Tom Smith, the director of marketing, contacted LaRouche, Markham and Smit, a local advertising agency. After briefing them about what had transpired in the meetings, he sent them a copy of the market study and requested a short advertising proposal.

On October 16, 1988, LaRoche, Markham, and Smit (LM&S) submitted both a review of the research as they saw it and a short advertising proposal. Both of these are shown in Exhibit 3.

EXHIBIT 3 LaRoche, Markham, and Smit Research Review and Advertising Proposal

1. Granted, Andy's appears to be the most popular barbecue restaurant. However, this preference is far from overwhelming-particularly since Andy's has more locations and thus exposure than direct competition; also the survey was conducted in the trading areas served by Andy's units.

	% Respondents for	
Where eat BBQ for:	Lunch	Dinner
No indication	37	51
No preference	22 (59)	17 (68)
Andy's	16	12
All others	25	20

Specifically, the major finding from this research is not that Andy's was apparently preferred by more respondents than any other barbecue establishment. In our judgement, the major finding is that around <u>two thirds of all respondents had no favorite whatever</u>. This indicates a low level of awareness overall, particularly in response to a guided question.

2. In barbecue, as in virtually every consumer marketing case, heavy user (12 times per year or more) emerge as the dominant force in the market. These users are conservatively estimated to account for 77 percent of all consumption occasions.

Criterion		#(%)	Proj. factor	Total Proj. occasions (%)
Heavy users	12+ /yr.	141 (47)	12X	1,692 (77)
Medium users	6-11/yr	26 (9)	8X	208 (9)
Light users	1-5/yr	100 (33)	3X	300 (14)
Nonusers	0	33 (11)	0	0
Totals				2,200 (100)

It is the attitudes toward trial and usage of Andy's by the heavy user segment that will be the most critical in successfully marketing the properties.

EXHIBIT 3 LM&S Review and Proposal (continued)

3. The attitudes of heavy users indicate that they are not necessarily convinced that Andy's offers "the best barbecue in the city." It suggests, though, that there is a basis for receptivity to this claim if effectively presented and if satisfactory trial ensues. Heavy user attitudes also indicate that they are quite satisfied with the current menu selection and do not think that Andy's should offer more than barbecue.

	Heavy Users	
Andy's:	Agree	Disagree
Has low quality food	9%	80%
Has sufficient variety	76%	11%
Should offer more than BBQ	15%	67%

Accordingly, a move to broaden the menu and change the basic character/appeal of Andy's would meet resistance from the most important market segment.

4. Further, research reveals that, while there may be some reluctance on the part of some family members to dine out on barbecue, there is a low incidence of their refusal to do so.

<u>Everyone</u> would eat barbecue	80%
Female would <u>not</u>	7%
Children would <u>not</u>	10%
Male would <u>not</u>	3%

5. While the wife plays an important role in dining-out decisions, it is hardly an overwhelming one, as the male is almost equally important.

Decision made by:	%
male, primarily	36 (47)
female, primarily	41 (52)
both, jointly	22

Thus, it has been noted that women play a role in 63 percent of decisions. But it should also be pointed out that men play a role in 58 percent of them.

EXHIBIT 3 LM&S Review and Proposal (continued)

6. Overall, then, it may be concluded from the research that: (a) Andy's offers a basically good product as is; (b) while relative preference versus direct competition is good, awareness is poor in the absolute; (c) a fundamental change in Andy's menu selection that would reposition the restaurants is not necessary and runs more risk of being harmful than being beneficial; (d) while barbecue may not be the most preferred food for dining out, neither would it be rejected out-of-hand as an alternative; and (e) men and women exhibit about equal sway in the dining out decision so that neither should be ignored in advertising planning (particularly when the men will tend to be more receptive).

7. Our proposal is consistent with the researcher's recommendations in the following areas: (a) communicate that barbecue is good for dinner; (b) communicate this proposition to women; and (c) develop carryout opportunity.

8. The LM&S proposal departs from the researcher's recommendation to "stress that barbecue need not be sloppy/too spicy." Rather than deal with a negative - removal of which is not viewed as a compelling motivation - we have chosen to accentuate the positive.

9. The objective of Andy's 1989 marketing program should be to increase traffic by: (a) gaining a larger share of the existing market for barbecue restaurants and (b) increasing the propensity among the current barbecue market to have barbecue when dining out at night. This would be accomplished by: (a) forcefully establishing Andy's positioning as a superior barbecue restaurant among barbecue users, preempting direct competition; (b) delivering the product (food, atmosphere, and service) to support this positioning; and (c) introducing the concept that Andy's is appropriate and good for nighttime dining ... an alternative to be considered.

POSITIONING

1. Clearly and firmly position Andy's as a barbecue restaurant of superior quality.
2. Exploit and develop existing favorable perceptions regarding barbecue - informal, hearty/masculine, tasty and friendly, quick service.

EXHIBIT 3 LM&S Review and Proposal (continued)

3. Accept those perceptions about barbecue which are not necessarily positive, and would be inactionable without compromising Andy's fundamental identity - spicy, somewhat downscale, moderately expensive, not "neat," limited selection.

OVERALL ADVERTISING AND PROMOTION STRATEGY

Invest all 1989 advertising and promotion expenditures toward current users of barbecue in order to: (a) stimulate new user trial of Andy's; (b) profitably increase frequency among current users; and (c) avoid short term price cutting that subsidizes current users without realizing any long-term benefits.
Insure that all efforts are consistent with Andy's positioning as a barbecue restaurant of superior quality.

CREATIVE STRATEGY

The primary objective of advertising for Andy's will be to convince the barbecue market that Andy's is a superior barbecue restaurant. This will be accomplished by distinctive, memorable advertising directed toward the quality of the barbecue from the standpoint of raw material selection and preparation. These product points will believably support the position that Andy's is the "Best Barbecue Restaurant in the City."

The secondary objective is to introduce the concept that Andy's is appropriate and good for nighttime dining. This will be accomplished by direct copy suggestion. It will be further supported by reference to the Family Platter. In addition, the opportunity to expand carryout business will be exploited.

Execution will strongly rely upon barbecue's inherent appetite appeal (among current barbecue users) and will be consistent with Andy's quality positioning.

MEDIA Andy's media objective should be to stimulate new users trial of Andy's and increase frequency among current users. This can be achieved as follows: (1) generate broad awareness of Andy's among the current barbecue market; (2) heighten introductory impact at the outset of the program; and (3) key message delivery to the most propitious time of day and day of week for dining-out decisions.

REACTION TO THE LM&S PROPOSAL

Receipt of the LM&S proposal produced a controversy among managers of Andy's management ranks. Tom Smith supported the proposal in it entirety, citing the reevaluation of research results as his major reason. Andrew Johnston was uneasy with the positioning aspect of the LM&S proposal. According to Johnston:

> Were we to accept the positioning of LM&S, we would be scrapping the positioning we worked out with Oscar Miles and returning to the positioning that previous advertising programs used and which were unsuccessful. The fact that we were to accept their positioning, the marketing, media, TV, strategy, and first quarter is attractive: however, since that positioning is unacceptable, makes what follows. It reminds me of the insurance salesman who asked if I was interested in a tax-free bond and although I said no, he continued to tell me how desirable it was.

Clark Tully displayed mixed feelings about the LM&S proposal and again raised the issues of outlet image and the lunch versus dinner patronage issue. His thoughts on these subjects were outlined in a memo to Andrew Johnston dated November 7, 1988 (Exhibit 4).

Oscar Miles impressions of the LM&S proposal were contained in a letter to Tom Smith on November 7. A summary of this letter is shown in Exhibit 5.

EXHIBIT 4 Clark Tully's Reaction to LM&S Proposal

To: Andrew Johnston
From: Clark Tully
Date: November 7, 1988
Subject: ANDY'S MARKETING & PROMOTIONAL STRATEGY

Perhaps beginning back in February, we have been wrestling with the question of exactly what kind of restaurant Andy's should be, to which market (or markets) it should be directed, and where we should go from there. Since then we have gone from the research report to the present LM&S proposal. All have been dealing with the same problem, namely how to market Andy's. During each phase, several important related questions have been raised, but all of the reports and memos share some similarities and common themes. I will try in this memo to pull my thoughts together on them and state how they may relate to any future action.

1. Image - What is Andy's "image" now in the minds of its customers? WHat has it been, and have we done anything to change it? This seems to be so important to us that we commissioned a marketing survey to find out. Its specific purpose, among others, was aimed at answering the question: "Can Andy's establish an identity that would separate it from the ordinary barbecue market and increase its nighttime and weekend patronage?" THe key word to me seems to be *identity or image*. Not surprisingly, the report confirmed that Andy's had a pretty good image or identity overall - not exactly great but good. To me, the problem is how to build on a good established image so that you can expand and grow. Also, what improvements can you make on along the way?

    From this report, the desirable improvements seemed to be table service, more variety, and more atmosphere so that we would attract more families and in particular, so that we would appeal to women and children. Certainly, maintaining consistent food quality was at the top of any list. The question of repackaging or repositioning Andy's was discussed. It was felt that in the past, Andy's had always been promoted as a good-great barbecue restaurant and that further efforts in this area would not produce any significant results. Based on limited experience, I would have to accept that premise since I so not know what has been done prior to 1986.

    But, in thinking of "repositioning," I believe we have to realize the fact that Andy's is a specialty barbecue restaurant and that people come to Andy's primarily because they want barbecue. Unless you completely change into another type of restaurant, this must be the basis for all action. In other words, I think for anyone to try Andy's, they must like barbecue since that is our specialty and that is what Andy's has been known for since it has been in business. I think sometimes we try to get away from this in attempting to find ways to appeal to everyone.

    I believe as long as we are a barbecue restaurant, we may just have to accept the fact that we are not going to appeal to everyone. Maybe doing $500-600,000 sales per year is excellent for a product with the limited appeal of barbecue. Therefore, I do not think you can "repackage" Andy's image into something other than a barbecue specialty restaurant - if you do, you might as well call it Andy's by pretending we are something we are not. Now certainly, you can appeal to people and attract new customers by offering things like better atmosphere and decor, a salad bar, and table service - if that's what they want - but *only* if they like barbecue or at least want to try it to begin with.

    My point remains, then, that we must build on Andy's established image and find ways to strengthen and improve it. Although I agree with the ideas of emphasizing table service and so on, I think that what we are really doing is improving and adding to what we do best and strengthening people's perceptions about Andy's.

2. Lunch versus Dinner - It has become obvious through all the discussions that one particular area in which Andy's has not been successful is the attracting of evening business. Perhaps we are trying to buck a fundamental trend of the market which is that barbecue is just not a type of meal people eat in the evenings. I believe that we raised this question before and still decided that we must find ways to attract more people in the evenings. *If* barbecue is not particulary attractive as an evening meal, then it would seem that the only way to attract customers is to offer other varieties of food, atmosphere, and so forth. However, I believe that as long as Andy's is a restaurant whose specialty is barbecue (and has been known as such for twenty-five years), then we should be careful about changing that image or perception in order not to drive away our primary customers who came specifically for barbecue.

   I have collected some data that gives a rough indication of our sales breakdown between lunch and dinner. This information was taken from sales records kept by various managers. (I believe the records are reasonably accurate.) On the average, we get about 50% of our business by 2 pm and about 40% after 5 pm. Although I do not have any data, I guess that most of the evening business is done between 5 pm and 7:30 pm. I think this information shows that obviously we do a great deal of our business at lunch, but we do now pick up a good bit in the evening. Perhaps the spread is not as lopsided toward lunch as you would have thought, but considering that we get half of our business in about three hours, it does leave room for much improvement the rest of the time we are open. Again, I do not think we want to lose our lunch business by getting away from the fact that we do specialize in barbecue.

   Relating all of this to the present marketing implications, I would say that it would be appropriate and consistent to promote Andy's as a good barbecue restaurant - still emphasizing barbecue - that is good for dinner. I do not think we want to get away from the face that we are a specialty restaurant. No matter how hard we try to get people in at any time, they will not come if they don't like barbecue; to go all out to please them at the expense of losing barbecue eaters would, in my opinion, be a mistake.

3. Finally, I must say something about advertising and promotion in general, relating to growth. Certainly, you must have a good operation in order of advertise to the public. You can never stop improving the operation, but, at the same time, you must keep your name in front of the public. This does not necessarily have to involve large amounts of money, but rather a consistent coordinated effort that lets people know about Andy's. I do not think that we have has such a consistent program since I have been here. I believe that the lack of long-term advertis-

ing program has contributed to the present problems. As the marketing survey showed, even in areas close to Andy's locations, there was a significant number of people who had not heard of or been in an Andy's, or who had not even tried barbecue. Thus, I believe that any reasonably constructed advertising program will, in the long run, benefit Andy's regardless of the exact message.

So, I am not necessarily disagreeing with LM&S Proposal because I think that any advertising or promotion help at this stage will be beneficial. Certainly, advertising is only a part of the overall strategy - the other more important part is the operation to provide the food and service on which to build business. Since it has been decided to concentrate on a message different from just "Andy's serves great barbecue," that seems simple enough to change. However, I say once again we should realize that Andy's is and is known by the public as, a specialty barbecue restaurant. We should thus orient all our efforts around the fact that customers come primarily because they like barbecue.

EXHIBIT 5 Oscar Miles Reaction to LM&S Proposal

Dear Tom:

The following remarks summarize my initial impressions of the LM&S proposal. These remarks are designed to stimulate discussion and should be interpreted accordingly.

<u>Positioning</u>
LM&S maintain that Andy's should position itself as "a BBQ restaurant of superior quality." Obviously, this position is almost directly opposite to the position we desire. I feel that Andy's has little to gain from this position because:

1. This is not a unique selling point for a BBQ restaurant - every one can say that!
2. I believe that the BBQ market is relatively narrow. Greater sales opportunities exist in expanding Andy's customer base.
3. Andy's must cultivate female/family dining. By emphasizing the "Best BBQ" position, we may further remove ourselves from this market.

Marketing Strategy
LM&S maintain Andy's can increase store traffic by:

1. Gaining a larger share of the existing market for BBQ restaurants
2. Increasing the propensity among the current BBQ market to have BBQ when dining out at night.

In terms of gaining a larger market share of BBQ restaurant users, I believe that the cost of converting Andy's noncustomers for BBQ to customers will be extremely high, relative to the opportunity cost of converting female/family evening dinning market. In other words, we will have greater success if we focus on the restaurant market. My feeling is that it will be easier to get a fraction of a percent market share from the restaurant market (which is obviously larger than the BBQ restaurant- a subset) than, let's say 1 percent of the BBQ restaurant market. Economics favor a larger customer base.

The second strategy concerning our increasing the propensity among BBQ users to consume at dinner seems more reasonable if the position is family dining rather than BBQ dining.

Overall Advertising and Promotion Strategy
LM&S maintain that all promotional expenditures should focus on current BBQ users to:

1. Stimulate new user trial of Andy's Pit BBQ;
2. Profitability increase frequency among current users;
3. Avoid short term price-cutting and so forth.

Media Strategy
Their strategy to "generate broad awareness of Andy's Pit BBQ among current barbecue market" is noteworthy. If previous research has any credibility, Andy already has broad awareness. That does not appear to be our problem. The remaining three strategies seem appropriate, providing the positioning controversy is resolved.

These remarks are based on my initial impressions of the LM&S proposal. I think we should discuss this proposal at greater length with you. In the meantime, I will try to schedule a meeting with Andrew.

APPENDIX Excerpts From Research Commissioned by Andy's Barbecue Restaurants

METHODOLOGY

STUDY SAMPLE AND DATA COLLECTION

A quota sampling technique was used to select households located within a two-mile radius of five Andy's Barbecue restaurants. Fifty households were selected from each trade area. Three hundred personal interviews were completed.

HOUSEHOLD CLASSIFICATION SCHEME

For purposes of analysis, households were classified according to the extent to which they (1) ate away from home generally, (2) ate barbecue, and (3) ate at Andy's. The classifications were Heavy, Medium, Light and Never. A definition of each category is shown in Table 1.

TABLE 1 Respondent Frequencies for Eating Out, Eating Barbecue, and Eating at Andy's

Number of Times Eat Lunch at a Restaurant

Frequency	n	Percent of Sample
Twice/week or more (heavy)	123	41.0
Once/month (medium)	119	39.7
Less than once/month (light)	40	13.3
Never	15	5.0
No response	3	1.0

Number of Times Eat Dinner at a Restaurant

Frequency	n	Percent of Sample
Twice/week or more (heavy)	118	39.3
Once/month (medium)	154	51.3
Less than once/month (light)	23	7.7
Never	5	1.7

Frequency of Eating Barbecue at Restaurant

Frequency	n	Percent of Sample
12 + /year (heavy)	141	47.0
6-11 /year (medium)	26	8.7
1-5 /year (light)	100	33.3
Never	30	10.0
No response	3	1.0

Frequency of Eating at Andy's

Frequency	n	Percent of Sample
5 + /year (heavy)	86	28.7
3-4 /year (medium)	29	9.7
1-2 /year (light)	86	28.7
Never	93	31.0
No response	6	2.0

RESULTS

RESTAURANT SELECTION CRITERIA (TABLE 2)

Reasons for selecting a restaurant for lunch and dinner vary considerably. For all households in the sample, the major reasons for selecting a restaurant for lunch were: (1) waiting time, (2) food quality, (3) friendly personnel, (4) quick service and (5) price. The major reasons for selecting a restaurant for dinner were: (1) food quality, (2) friendly personnel, (3) table service, (4) atmosphere, and (5) type of food. Some variation in selection criteria for lunch and dinner by type of use was also evident.

EATING OUT DECISION MAKING AND POPULARITY OF BARBECUE

Table 3 presents data on respondents decision making and eating habits. Respondents stated that in 36 percent of the cases, the male makes most of the decisions to eat out; 41 percent of the cases, the female makes most of the decisions; and 22 percent of the time, the decisions are made jointly (1 percent made no response).

Part two of table 3 shows that most people (80 percent) in the sample think that everyone would eat barbecue for dinner. Those most against barbecue for dinner are the children (10 percent) and the women (7 percent). In those households where women and children have a major influence in dining decisions, barbecue has less of a chance as an alternative for dinner. Overall, table 3 has implications for Andy's promotion activities. In almost 63 percent of the decisions on eating out, women are involved either as the major decision maker or as an equal decision maker. Women also are less fond of barbecue for dinner than men are. This suggests the need for some attitude change strategies directed at women to sway their perceptions of barbecue.

As a whole, the respondents perceive barbecue as being very filling, middle-class, moderately expensive, moderately sloppy, very tasty, rather spicy, somewhat for kids, and pretty good for dinner.

Table 2. Rankings of Restaurant Selection Criteria by Type of User for Lunch and DInner Patronage.

Selection Criteria	Lunch Heavy	Medium	Light	Total
Convenient Location	5	7	6	7
Quick Service	3	4	7	4
Waiting Time	2	1	1	1
Friendly Personnel	4	3	3.5	3
Price	6	6	3.5	5
Atmosphere	11	10	9	11
Liquor	14	15	14	14
Food Quality	1	2	2	2
Food/Serving	8	11	10	9.5
Food Variety	10	8	8	8
Table Service	7	5	5	6
Overall Decor	12	12	12	12
Type of Food	7	5	5	6
Cafeteria Service	13	13	13	13
Take out Service	15	14	15	15
Number of Households	123	119	40	282

Selection Criteria	Dinner Heavy	Medium	Light	Total
Convenient Location	13	13	13	13
Quick Service	12	11	11	11.5
Waiting Time	8	6	4	6
Friendly Personnel	2	2	2	2
Price	11	9	8	9.5
Atmosphere	4	5	5	4
Liquor	10	12	12	11.5
Food Quality	1	1	1	1
Food/Service	9	10	9	9.5
Food Variety	7	7	7	7
Table Service	3	3	3	3
Overall Decor	6	8	10	8
Type of Food	5	4	6	5
Cafeteria Service	14	14	14	14
Take out Service	15	15	15	15
Number of Households	118	154	23	295

Rankings based on average rating given to each selection: 1=mostimportant,15=least important

Table 3 Respondent Decision Making About Eating Habits

Decision Variable Who makes the most decisions (to dine out)	n	Percent of Sample
Male	109	36.3
Female	123	41.0
Joint Male/Female	65	21.7
No Response	3	1.0

Who in the household would not eat barbecue for dinner	n	Percent of Sample
Everyone would eat BBQ for dinner	240	80.0
Female of household would not	21	7.0
Children of household would not	30	10.0
Male of household would not	9	3.0

CONSUMER PERCEPTIONS OF BARBECUE RESTAURANTS

In addition to obtaining data on overall perceptions of barbecue, it was necessary to gather data about consumer perceptions of barbecue restaurants. Respondents think that barbecue restaurants are quite informal, moderately expensive, middle-class, rather clean, quite family oriented, with a good atmosphere. The data, when analyzed by type of user, indicate that the "heavy" user perceives the barbecue restaurant as being less clean than other user types perceive it. Although the differences are slight, the "light" user perceives the barbecue restaurant as more informal, less expensive, lower class, less clean, and less family-orientated with a poorer atmosphere than the "heavy" user perceives them. This pattern does not exist in the general perceptions of barbecue as food.

Table 4 reports the ratings for statements concerning Andy's. Respondents were asked to relate their degree of agreement or disagreement with each statement. The ratings in Table 4 suggest that respondents believe that Andy's is conveniently located, has quick service, does not have long lines, has friendly personnel, has a good atmosphere, does not have low quality food, has a sufficient variety of foods, and has a good interior and exterior appearance. Respondents are somewhat uncertain, however, as to the amount of food for the price, the reasonableness of the price, and whether or not Andy's should offer more than barbecue as the main food.

Focusing on dinner, the data shows that while Andy's is conveniently located, and has quick service and reasonable prices, these criteria are relatively unimportant for dinner. Thus, while Andy's is perceived quite well on these dimensions, consumers do not think them important for dinner restaurant selection.

The criteria perceived as being important, and in which Andy's is doing fine, are: length of waiting time, friendly personnel, good atmosphere, and quality of food. The criteria perceived as being important for dinner, and in which Andy's is not perceived as doing well are: the offering of sufficient variety of food (40% disagree that Andy's is offering such variety), having a good interior appearance (60% agree that Andy's does not have one), and having a good exterior appearance (21% agree that it does not have one)

Table 4 A Comparison of Andy's Ranks with General Selection Criteria.

Selection Criterion	Importance for Lunch or Dinner*		Likert Statement	Percent Responses**				
	Lunch	Dinner		SA	A	U	D	SD
Convenient Location	I	U	Andy's is conveniently located	49.2	35.4	9.8	4.7	.8
Quick Service	I	U	Andy's has quick service	29.6	46.6	20.2	3.2	.4
Waiting time to get in	I	I	Andy's waiting lines are too long	2.8	8.7	17.2	47.4	13.8
Friendly Personnel	I	I	Andy's personnel are unfriendly	1.6	11.1	30.0	43.5	13.6
Price	I	U	Andy's has reasonable prices	9.9	47.8	26.1	11.1	5.1
Atmosphere	I	U	Andy's has a good atmosphere	11.1	57.9	22.6	7.1	1.2
Quality of food	I	I	Andy's has low quality of food	6.7	6.7	24.9	45.1	16.6
Variety of food	U	I	Andy's offers a sufficient variety of foods	9.2	20.3	31.5	31.5	7.6
Overall Decor	U	I	Andy's does not have a good interior appearance	9.6	50.6	27.3	10.3	2.4
			Andy's does not have a good exterior appearance	5.5	14.6	21.3	45.8	12.6

*Based on Table 2 I - important, U - unimportant

**SA - strongly agree, A - agree, U - undecided, D - disagree, SD - strongly disagree

SECTION 4

THE MARKETING MIX

CASE 11

RAISE THE NUMBERS!

The Royal York Hotel in Toronto, Canada was built in 1929. Since that time it had been operated by CP Hotels, a division of the Canadian Pacific Railroad. The hotel had been successful as a top of the line property and over the years had developed a loyal clientele. In recent years, however, major competition had entered the market and was seriously threatening the hotel's market share. These new properties include those operated by Hilton International, Sheraton, and Four Seasons, among others. In the face of this competition, management recognized that the property had deteriorated and was in need of major refurbishing if it was going to maintain its market status.

In 1987, the company commenced a three year, $100 million renovation program that would completely refurbish all 1408 rooms as well as the lobby, food and beverage outlets, meeting rooms, and back of the house service areas. Rather than take the risk of losing customers, who might not return when the renovations were completed, to competitors, it was decided to keep open and in operation any rooms or portions of the hotel that did not have to be shut down for construction.

By 1989, 600 rooms would have been renovated but not without considerable difficulty. Customers were often forced to step over piles of lumber, around construction equipment, and through mazes of boxes, to get to their rooms. This had caused a considerable amount of dissatisfaction and numerous customer complaints. In fact, it was known that a number of regular customers had decided to go elsewhere, at least for the duration of the renovation period. Many, however, said they would return when it was finished.

At the same time, the economy in Toronto had taken a downturn. Hotel occupancies, citywide, had dropped. This caused even more intense competition among hotels for the existing business. With another one to two years to go with its renovation program, Royal York management was struggling to maintain its forecasts. Of particular concern was the corporate market, and the sales staff was working hard to maintain the hotel's share of this segment.

Corporate group room nights in 1988 were estimated to finish the year with 23,500. Corporate transient room nights would be about 60,000. Because of the renovation program and resultant periodic loss of meeting space, the 1989 forecast for corporate group room nights was lowered to

22,000. To compensate for this loss, the corporate transient forecast had been raised to 65,000 for 1989.

The sales department wasn't too sure just how it was going to meet the 1989 projections. The 1988 and 1989 projected corporate rate was $104 per night. This compared to a $99 rate at the Sheraton, and a $150 rate at the Four Seasons. Hilton's corporate rate ranged from $94 to $110, and it had vowed to keep these rates through the 1989 season, in view of the economy. These three hotels were perceived as the major competition for the corporate market in Toronto.

The Royal York sales staff had little difficulty competing with its $104 rate for the newly renovated rooms. In fact, the refurbishing was so successful that it felt it could probably obtain even higher rates for those rooms. However, there would be only 600 of them to sell for much of 1989 and they couldn't always guarantee them. Further, even though the rooms were very satisfying, customers still had the problem of ongoing construction in public areas and hallways, along with the attendant dust, confusion and noise.

For some customers, the quality rooms at $104 were worth the tradeoff of the renovation confusion. For others, it was not. Worse, however, was the situation when a customer was placed in an unrenovated room and still had to endure the renovation mess. These customers were becoming increasingly difficult to keep.

In November, 1988 the sales staff scheduled an all day meeting to plan its strategy for 1989; namely, how to maintain even 22,000 corporate group nights and how to increase corporate transient nights by 5,000. Also on the agenda was a longer term consideration: How to keep and/or get back the customers being lost because of the renovations, after the renovations were completed.

The Director of Sales began the meeting by reading a memo she had just received from the CP corporate office. They weren't very pleased, she read, about the forecast projecting a loss in corporate group nights, or the increase in corporate transient nights of only 5,000. However, they were somewhat persuaded that perhaps these figures were realistic in view of the renovations going on. To make up for the loss of revenue, however, they wanted the corporate rate for 1989 to be set at $118 per night.

CASE 12

THE MERRY WEEKEND PACKAGE

Richard Chambers, vice president of marketing for the Tara Hotel chain, had given careful thought to the proposed agenda for the upcoming general managers' meeting to discuss weekend packages at "non-traditional properties." The meeting had been planned following corporate research that revealed pertinent facts regarding the weekend customer. Chambers saw a need to develop a more appropriate and competitive weekend package plan other than the one presently offered at Tara's more "traditional" properties.

Since the purchase of some Dunfey owned and franchised hotels two years before, the need had grown for a more cohesive and uniform image for these properties that would better represent the Tara Hotel Company. Tara Hotels was the largest franchisee of the Sheraton Corporation in the New England area. They were positioned in the market place as up-scale properties, catering to higher rated groups and corporate travelers. The physical hotel product was above that of normal Sheraton standards.

Most of the former Dunfey properties were Sheraton franchise hotels, as were the original Tara hotels, but they had had no capital improvements for the past three years. It was planned to renovate and upgrade each facility to make it consistent with the present image of the original Tara properties. In the meanwhile, these hotels were more "inn-like" than "hotel-like" and presented some serious marketing problems.

One particular problem of the new acquisitions was the sale of Merry Weekend packages throughout the company. These packages had been developed for the traditional Tara properties and had proven to be very successful. They sold for $79.00 to $89.00 for two, per night, depending on the property, and are described in Exhibit 1. Exhibit 2 contains the welcoming letter for Merry Weekenders when they checked into the hotel.

It was suspected that loss of established Merry Weekend customers was beginning to take place within the company due to dissatisfaction with the product offering of the non-traditional properties. Merry Weekend customers were known to be loyal customers who went from property to property to enjoy their Merry Weekends. When they went to the new properties expecting the same facilities, they found that the same product

EXHIBIT 1 Brochure Description of the Merry Weekend Package

The Tara Merry Weekend

What royal memories are made of.

Your everyday routine is demanding. It's important to take a little time to get away.

Relax. We have the solution. A Tara Merry Weekend. It's a great way to get away and live like royalty for 3 days and 2 nights at one of 12 exciting locations.

Choose a castle, country or resort setting. From the romantic, rocky coast of Maine or the idyllic countryside of New Hampshire to the white-duned beaches on Cape Cod, or cosmopolitan ambience of Boston and beyond.

Your Tara Merry Weekend for two includes a sumptuous Saturday breakfast, complimentary fresh fruit basket, use of pool and health club facilities,* and a lavish Sunday brunch.

Join us for a Tara Merry Weekend and be treated like royalty. For reservations call the Tara Hotel of your choice.

*Additional charge for golf, tennis and racquetball. No indoor pool at Lexington.

A thoughtful treat for your favorite couple.

Tara Merry Weekend gift certificates are also available. Simply call the Tara Hotel of your choice for complete information.

EXHIBIT 2 Welcoming Letter for Merry Weekenders

Sheraton Tara Hotel FRAMINGHAM, MASSACHUSETTS 01701 • Tel. 617/879-7200

Welcome Merry Weekender,

This weekend your royal presence is requested to feast and romp royally while enjoying.....gourmet dining, lively entertainment, the Health Club and our Continental Pub. Remember our weekend continues on Sunday night. Check at the Front Desk or call Extension 2647 for details.

For your convenience, we offer some information and a schedule of our facilities that we hope you will use and enjoy. All facilities are located on the Lobby Level.

To begin your weekend in a relaxed manner, try a selection from our Room Service Menu, which offers a wide variety of food and beverage. Call Extension 2513 to place your order.

Our Health Club, complete with indoor/outdoor pools, exercise room, whirlpool, sauna and steam rooms, as well as a racquetball court, is open on Friday, Saturday and Sunday from 8:00 a.m. to 10:00 p.m. Due to limited space we ask that you change in your room. Towels are available at the pool. Call our Health Club for information at Extension 2188.

The Jester's Court Cafe serves some of your all-time favorite American entrees, as well as some delicious International specialties. The Jester's Court Cafe is open Friday and Saturday from 6:30 a.m. to 11:30 p.m. and on Sunday from 7:00 a.m. to 11:30 a.m. Reservations are accepted for Lunch and Dinner at Extension 2313.

The Upper Crust Restaurant has become one of the best known restaurants in the area, so by all means give it a try. Favorites from our Menu include Chateaubriand Bouquetiere, Filet of Lemon Sole Oscar, Veal Cutlet Saute Cordon Bleu, Roast Rack of Lamb Dijonnaise, Fresh Rainbow Trout Veronique.....too many more to mention. Our Specialty of the House consists of a crock of clam chowder, a bountiful platter of clams casino, schrod, fried scallops and baked stuffed shrimp. Leave room for dessert - our house specialty - the Tara Chocolate Cup, consisting of a cup of fine semi-sweet chocolate, a scoop of Haagen Dazs coffee ice cream, Kahlua, whipped cream and a cherry --- sinfully delicious!! Dine with us on Friday from 5:00 p.m. to 10:30 p.m., Saturday from 5:00 p.m. to 11:00 p.m. and on Sunday from 3:30 p.m. to 10:00 p.m. On Sunday the Upper Crust offers our fabulous Buffet Brunch from 9:30 a.m. to 2:00 p.m. Reservations are accepted on Friday for 5:00, 6:00 and 7:00 p.m. and on Saturday for 5:00 and 6:00 p.m. only. Call our Dining Room Manager at Extension 2413 after 4:30 p.m.

THE SHERATON TARA HOTELS ARE OWNED BY
TARA HOTELS – THE FLATLEY COMPANY AND OPERATED UNDER
A LICENSE ISSUED BY SHERATON INNS, INC.

EXHIBIT 2 Welcoming Letter (continued)

After dinner you will want to enjoy our Knaughty Knight Club with show entertainment on Friday from 9:00 p.m. to 2:00 a.m. and Saturday from 8:00 p.m. to 1:00 a.m. A $2.00 per person Entertainment Charge will be added to the checks of all guests who are in the Knaughty Knight Club from 9:00 p.m. on. Call our Knaughty Knight Club Hostess after 5:00 p.m. at Extension 2213 for information.

If you are in the mood for something a bit more quiet and casual, ZJ's Pub and Game Room may be your style. Watch the seasonal sport events and relax while having a drink or a snack. ZJ's is open Friday 11:00 a.m. to 2:00 a.m., Saturday from 11:00 a.m. to 1:00 a.m. and Sunday from Noon to 1:00 a.m. Dial Extension 2300 for information.

Please advise the Dining Room Manager or Hostess that you are a registered guest by showing your room key. You will then be placed on the Preferred Seating List.

Located in our Lobby, the Gift Shop is open daily from 7:00 a.m. to 11:00 p.m. and offers a wide variety of gifts, sundries, magazines and newspapers as well as our Avis Rent-a-Car service. Call Extension 2400 for information.

Hotel rates do not include gratuities. May we suggest a $1.00 per day gratuity for your maid service.

The entire Staff is ready to make this weekend merry for you.

Have a great time and return again soon!

Sincerely,

John Van Londen
General Manager

wasn't there. In fact, Tara reservationists were reporting irate phone calls after customers had been to the new properties.

This problem had occurred before in 1984 when the Danvers property was purchased from Radisson Hotels. At that time, three Tara hotels had the castle motif and there was a known 20,000 Merry Weekend customers. Advertisements and direct mail were aimed at these customers to lure them to the Danvers property before it was renovated. Many tried the property, taking business away from the other Taras. This also resulted in considerable dissatisfaction. Tara customers now had seven traditional Tara properties from which to choose, in addition to the five non-traditional properties (Exhibit 3), but the known Merry Weekend customer base had increased only to 23,000. Thus, the increase in hotels had not brought a proportionate increase in Merry Weekend customers.

EXHIBIT 3 Locations and Designations of Flatley Hotels in 1988

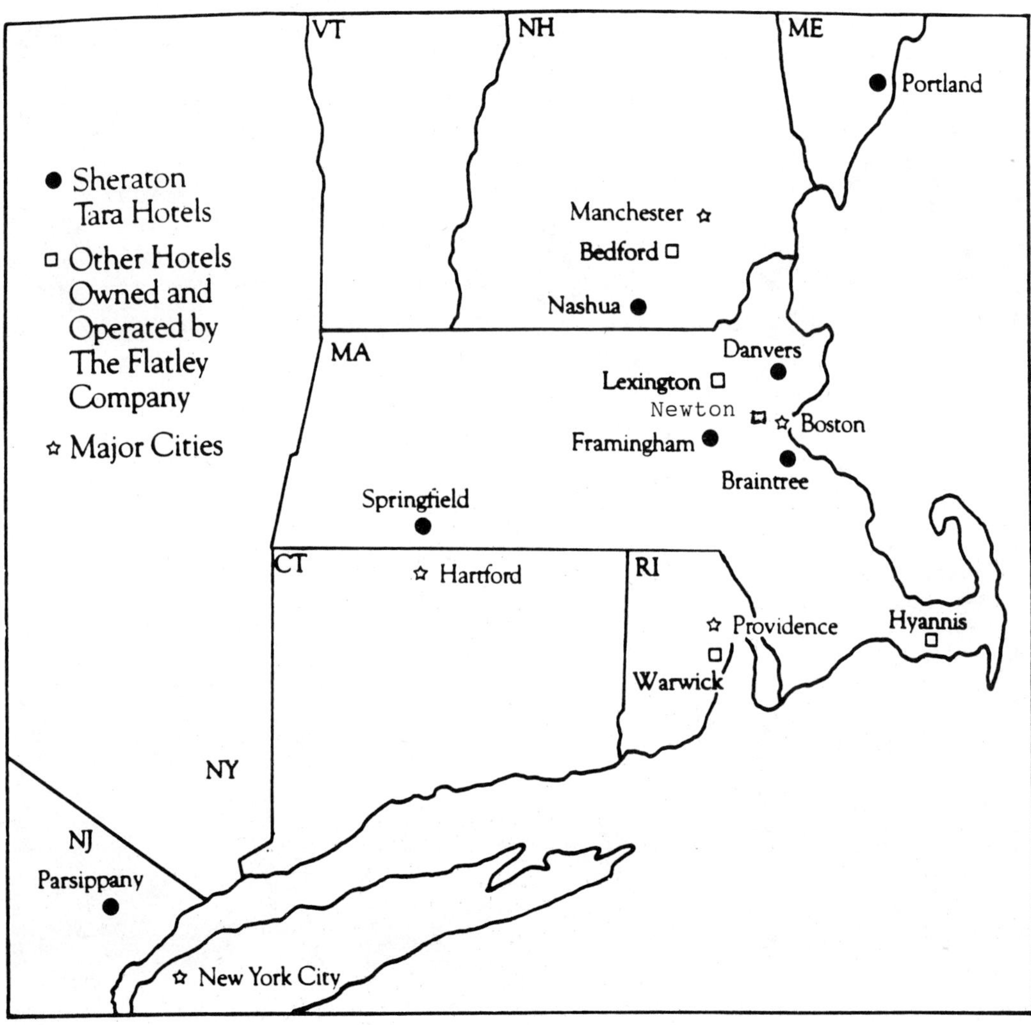

EXHIBIT 4 Descriptions of Tara Properties

Braintree, MA

The Sheraton Tara Hotel, Exit 6 off Route 93 (Route 128), Braintree, MA 617-848-0600. Just 12 miles south of downtown Boston, the 400-room Sheraton Tara in Braintree is a short drive from cultural, historical, and recreational attractions including the Museum of Fine Arts, The Aquarium and the Boston Garden, home of the Boston Celtics. Free shuttle to public transportation. Dine in the casual Jesters Court Cafe, the elegant Upper Crust Restaurant and the lively Tipperary Pub. The Laurels offers live, easy-listening entertainment. Complete health and fitness center with indoor and outdoor pools, and racquetball.

Danvers, MA

The Sheraton Tara Hotel at Ferncroft Village, Routes 95 and 1, Topsfield exit to Ferncroft Village, Danvers, MA, 617-777-2500. The 375-room Sheraton Tara, located 15 miles north of Boston on the scenic North Shore of Massachusetts, is only a short drive to "The Witch City" of Salem, and scenic Gloucester, Rockport and Marblehead. Dine in the casual Jesters Court Cafe, the elegant Upper Crust Restaurant, the lively Tipperary Pub and for live, easy-listening entertainment, The Laurels. Enjoy an 18-hole, Robert Trent Jones-designed golf course, outdoor tennis, indoor and outdoor swimming pools, and complete health & fitness center.

Framingham, MA

The Sheraton Tara Hotel, at Massachusetts Turnpike Exit 12 to Route 9 west, Framingham, MA 617-879-7200. Only 20 miles west of Boston, the Sheraton Tara Hotel offers 375 guest rooms and easy access to all of Boston sites and recreational activities. Old Sturbridge Village, a recreation of a New England town of the early 1800's, is minutes away. For dining, enjoy the casual Jesters Court Cafe, the elegant Upper Crust Restaurant, the lively Tipperary Pub and live, easy-listening entertainment in The Laurels. Complete health and fitness center with indoor and outdoor pools and racquetball.

Springfield, MA

Tara Hotel, Route 91 at State Street Exit, Springfield, MA. This 300-room deluxe hotel is centrally located to New York, Boston, Hartford and Worcester in the Berkshire Mountains. The Tara in Springfield is close to Symphony Hall, Stage West Theater, museums, the Springfield Civic Center and the Basketball Hall of Fame. Dine in the elegant Upper Crust Restaurant and the casual Jesters Court Cafe. Enjoy live entertainment in the Tipperary Pub. Complete health & fitness center, indoor pool and racquetball courts.

South Portland, ME

The Sheraton Tara Hotel, Maine Turnpike, Exit 7 to Maine Mall Road, South Portland, ME, 207-775-6161. Across from the Maine Mall this 220-room hotel is just minutes from Portland's Old Port and Cape Elizabeth's famous lighthouses, and 15 miles to Old Orchard Beach. Kennebunkport, Boothbay Harbor and Wiscasset are within an hour's drive. Dining and entertainment include The Season's Restaurant and Lounge and in-room movies. Recreational facilities include an indoor pool and saunas.

Bedford (Manchester), NH

The Sheraton Tara Wayfarer, Bedford Interchange, I-293, Bedford, NH, 603-622-3766. Situated by a mill stream with a pond and waterfalls, this 200-room hotel is just minutes from Manchester and the Mall of New Hampshire, yet also within an hour of the White Mountains, Lake Winnipesaukee, the seacoast, and Boston. For dining and entertainment, you'll find the Upper Crust and The Laurels; and for recreation, both indoor and outdoor swimming pools.

EXHIBIT 4 Descriptions of Properties (continued)

Cape Cod, MA

Tara Dunfey Hotel, Route 132 to Exit 6, North Street to West End Circle, Hyannis, MA, 617-775-7775. This 250-room resort hotel is located in the heart of scenic Cape Cod, famous for its sandy beaches, quaint villages and historic attractions. For dining and entertainment, visit the Silver Shell Restaurant and Tingles Lounge. Recreational amenities include indoor and outdoor pools, a Roman Bath, outdoor tennis, an 18-hole golf course and a health spa.

Lexington, MA

The Sheraton Tara Hotel, Marrett Road at Route 95, Exit 45B, Lexington, MA 617-862-8700. Located in the heart of historic Lexington near Minuteman National Park, the 115-room Sheraton Tara is only 15 miles west of Boston and a 40-minute drive to Cape Ann, Rockport, and Gloucester. Dining and entertainment include the Upper Crust Restaurant and The Laurels, as well as an outdoor pool.

Newton, MA

Howard Johnson's Hótel, Washington Street over the Massachusetts Turnpike at Exit 17, Newton, MA 617-969-3010. This 275-room hotel is just six miles west of downtown Boston. It is located near the cultural and historical attractions in Boston and Cambridge and is in close proximity to Harvard, Boston College, MIT and other colleges. Public transportation to Boston is available directly from the hotel. Indoor pool, saunas, a game room and HBO.

Nashua, NH

The Sheraton Tara Hotel, Tara Boulevard, Exit 1 off of Route 3, Nashua, NH 603-888-9970. The 350-room Sheraton Tara Hotel is located just over the Massachusetts border in southern New Hampshire. Close to cultural, historical and recreational attractions including Arts and Science Center, Fort Constitution and Benson's Wild Animal Park. Less than half an hour from Boston. Dine in the Upper Crust Restaurant and Z.J.'s Pub, enjoy live, easy-listening entertainment in The Laurels. Outdoor tennis and complete health and fitness center with indoor and outdoor swimming pools and racquetball.

Parsippany, NJ

Tara Hotel, intersection of Routes 287 and 80, Parsippany, NJ, 201-515-2000. This 400-room hotel is only 25 miles west of New York City and is located in historic Morris County, offering a wealth of local attractions including the Morris Museum, the Edison National Historic Site and Liberty State Park. Dine in the casual Jesters Court Cafe, the elegant Upper Crust Restaurant, or the lively Tipperary Pub. Enjoy The Laurels, for live, easy-listening entertainment. Complete health & fitness center with indoor and outdoor pools and racquetball.

Warwick, RI

The Sheraton Tara Airport Hotel, Route 1 at I-95, T.F. Green Airport Exit, Warwick, RI 401-738-4000. Located just minutes from Providence and Narragansett Bay and only 30 minutes from Newport's historic mansions. The 125-room hotel is near the Cliff Walk, Ocean Drive and one hour from Mystic Seaport and Fall River/New Bedford area. For your recreational and entertainment pleasure, there is HBO, an indoor pool and saunas.

BACKGROUND

Tara Hotel Company was owned by The Flatley Hotel Company of Braintree, Massachusetts, a diversified construction company with diversified real estate holdings. After constructing four traditional Tara hotels, built with an Irish castle motif, the Flatley Company purchased six other properties from Dunfey Hotels, the one from Radisson Hotels in Danvers, and constructed one contemporary atrium lobby hotel (Springfield). Descriptions of all the properties are given in Exhibit 4.

Since opening the first Sheraton Tara in 1971, the Tara Hotel division had developed a reputation for excellent physical products. The Sheraton Tara group of hotels offered its guests the finest in comfort with luxurious guest rooms, restaurants and coffee shops, ballrooms, meeting rooms, recreational facilities, indoor and outdoor swimming pools, saunas, steam baths, exercise rooms, and a PGA golf course, but not at all properties, as shown in Exhibit 5. Each hotel was designed with the business traveler in mind. In addition to the appropriate facilities, the nationwide Sheraton reservation line provided a strong system for confirming rooms to travelers outside New England.

EXHIBIT 5 Tara Hotels Inventory 1988

Location	Rooms	Dining and Entertainment	Swimming Pool Indoor	Swimming Pool Outdoor	Racquet-ball	Tennis	Golf	Saunas	Health Center
Nashua, NH	350	restaurant pub & lounge	Y	Y	Y	Y		Y	Y
Braintree, MA	400	2 restaurants pub and lounge	Y	Y	Y			Y	Y
Framingham, MA	375	2 restaurants pub & lounge	Y	Y	Y			Y	Y
Danvers, MA	367	2 restaurants & lounge	Y	Y	Y	Y	Y	Y	Y
Springfield, MA	300	2 restaurants & lounge	Y		Y			Y	Y
Parsippany, NJ	400	2 restaurants pub & lounge	Y	Y	Y			Y	Y
Hyannis, MA	224	restaurant & lounge	Y	Y		Y	Y	Y	Y
Bedford, NH	200	restaurant & lounge	Y	Y					
Lexington, MA	115	restaurant, pub & lounge		Y					
S. Portland, ME	220	restaurant, & lounge	Y					Y	
Newton, MA	261	restaurant, & lounge	Y					Y	
Warwick, RI	125	restaurant, & lounge	Y					Y	

CUSTOMER RESEARCH

Richard Warhola, director of market research for the Tara hotel group, had conducted a customer survey to learn the likes and dislikes of some of the Merry Weekend customers. The study was designed to determine customer satisfaction of Merry Weekend packages, to identify the most appealing promotional benefits, to assess competitors' package usage, and to develop a Merry Weekend customer profile. The study was conducted at the Nashua and Framingham properties. The survey questions, responses, and a summary of the findings can be found in an appendix to the case.

After completion of the survey, Chambers gathered data just prior to the general managers' meeting in an attempt to draw some conclusions from company sales information on the Merry Weekend packages. A comparison of the sales in the six traditional Tara hotels, plus Hyannis which was a semi-resort with Tara standards, versus the other five purchased properties, was revealed in this analysis (Exhibit 6).

Chambers distinguished between "Tara" and "non-Tara" hotels based on the current facilities offered at each property. The key difference between the two hotel groups was the offering of full or limited service. Merry Weekend customers didn't care whether the hotel looked like a castle; they wanted the health club, Upper Crust, and Jester's Court restaurants, and other full service amenities of the traditional Taras. Descriptions of typical outlets at these hotels are described in Exhibit 7.

Chambers also evaluated the strengths and weaknesses of the chain. Among the strengths he found were:

* the excellent location of all properties,
* the excellent services offered,
* the extensive marketing research being conducted,
* the competitive prices in the traditional Tara hotels,
* the positive image of the Tara properties,
* the good facilities provided in Tara properties, and
* the repeat customers, especially those with established brand loyalty to Tara hotels.

Among the weaknesses Chambers found were:

* the prices of the non-Taras being perhaps too high in respect to the facilities they offered,
* the poor facilities and small room sizes of the non-Taras,
* the confused image of the non-Taras because they were recently purchased from Dunfey,
* lack of customer awareness of ownership of non-Tara properties,
* the transition period while non-Taras upgraded to Tara levels with inconvenience and disservice to guests,

EXHIBIT 6 Summary Results of Merry Weekend Packages

TARA HOTELS MERRY WEEKEND ANALYSIS

	NOV		DEC		JAN		FEB		TOTALS	
HOTEL [# RMS]	1987	1986	1987	1986	1988	1987	1988	1987	87/88	86/87
"TARAS"										
Nashua	984	850	316	300	1067	1008	934	1629	3301	3787
Braintree	708	410	280	260	395	576	881	1065	2264	2311
Framingham	991	850	314	289	817	911	1087	1092	3209	3142
Danvers	198	150	73	70	228	200	405	350	904	770
Springfield	24	0	13	0	42	0	156	0	235	0
Parsippany	175	0	76	0	189	0	399	0	839	0
Hyannis	230	36	86	92	414	427	438	503	1168	1058
Total	3310	2296	1158	1011	3152	3122	4300	4639	11920	11068
"NON-TARAS"										
Bedford	146	34	45	42	84	137	98	273	373	486
Lexington	37	44	32	329	16	16	38	57	123	446
S. Portland	359	250	103	67	154	11	327	333	943	661
Newton	21	26	3	3	15	10	24	39	63	78
Warwick	0	0	0	0	0	0	0	0	0	0
Total	563	354	183	441	269	174	487	702	1502	1671
Grand Total									13422	12739
% Tara									88.8%	86.9%
% Non Tara									11.2%	13.1%

Inventory		
% Tara	72.3%	[2416 Rooms]
% Non Tara	27.7%	[921 Rooms]
Total		3337 Rooms

EXHIBIT 7 Descriptions of Tara Outlets

Because everything is here.

Restaurant

Our Haute Cuisine makes every dinner a festive event! Specialties include prime ribs, steaks and ocean-fresh lobster as well as veal, lamb, poultry and seafood dishes. Cheeses, relishes and hearth breads are included with your repast, and a dessert cart brings a selection of sweets to your table. Dinner served daily from 5 P.M. to 10:30 P.M., and reservations are available Sunday through Thursday. Also, a bountiful brunch is served each Sunday from 9:30 A.M. to 2 P.M.

Knightly Entertainment in a romantic setting of candlelight and arched ceilings. Complimentary hot hors d'oeuvres, cheese and fruit served Monday through Friday from 5 P.M. till 7 P.M. when the dancing begins. Popular cabaret groups (a new one every two weeks) provide live entertainment Monday through Saturday nights.

Regal Repasts cheerily served amid informal surroundings. Satisfying even the heartiest of appetites throughout the day, Monday through Saturday. Intriguing entrees such as Sole Oscar, Wiener Schnitzel and London Broil top the varied luncheon menu, served 11:30 AM - 5 PM. Dinner from 5 PM - 11:30 PM features international favorites, including veal marsala and scallopini, tournedos aux champignons, shrimp Mario. And exquisite desserts cap the evening.

Z.J.'s Pub

and Game Room

The Game's The Thing in a casual environment where you'll joust and jest amid dramatic archways and spectacular murals. Imbibe refreshment while you impress the joyous throng with your skills at backgammon and cribbage, checkers and chess. Open daily from 11 A.M. to 1 A.M., with complimentary hors d'oeuvres, cheese and fruit tray served Monday to Friday from 4 P.M. to 7 P.M.

Sheraton Tara Hotels

The Flatley Company

BRAINTREE • FRAMINGHAM • NASHUA, N.H.

* losing customers of the Tara hotels after they had patronized the non–Tara hotels, and
* offering Merry Weekenders seven traditional Taras instead of four.

Chambers saw the opportunities for the Tara Hotel Company to be:

* building on the existing reputation of the Tara image,
* maintaining existing repeat customers,
* identifying new markets through research, and
* capturing markets through price value in the non–Taras.

Chambers also saw threats in other hotels offering very competitive value packages, and the loss of Merry Weekend package customers within the Tara system because of disappointment at non–Taras and offering existing customers more products from which to choose.

The company used its current base of names and addresses from the traditional Tara properties to help promote the Merry Weekend packages at the new traditional Taras and at the non–Tara hotels. Some of these customers, after buying the package at a non–Tara, never came back to either a non–Tara or a Tara.

Without a distinction of services and facilities, Merry Weekend promotions continued to market the packages to known past customers. Little research, or even thought, had been given to the promotion of these packages and their consequences at the newly added properties.

THE GENERAL MANAGERS' MEETING

The meeting began promptly at 1:30 p.m. and was conducted by Chambers. Key corporate staff and general managers from the traditional and non–Tara properties were in attendance. The agenda read as follows:

1. Overview of the situation
2. Identification of problem
3. Analysis of competitive offerings
4. Product development
5. Marketing of product - advertising and direct mail

Each general manager and his director of sales spent 30 minutes discussing their situation. They identified the loss of their customers to new traditional Tara properties as well as the customer dissatisfaction with the non–traditional Tara product. Two additional hours were spent analyzing competitive offerings, discussing the product, the customers, and prices.

In addition to the survey results reported and discussed at the meeting, the round-table discussion about the customers who came to their properties indicated that a majority of their weekend guests loved to receive free in-room gifts, enjoyed shopping but liked to stay in the hotel for other activities (in fact, would sit in the lobby for hours feeling that the more time they spent in the hotel the more they received their money's worth), liked coupons for discounts in the restaurants and lounges, liked to have their picture taken with the Beefeater doorman (Exhibit 8), and arrived by automobile. Most managers suspected that most of their weekend customers belonged in the blue collar category.

Chambers' wanted to have a new package ready for sale throughout the Tara system by May 30 to insure customer awareness and support any opportunity for a strong pre-sale market for the upcoming summer season. Buy time, Chambers thought at the time, was averaging about two weeks out. It was later learned, however, that it was more like four to five weeks.

A basic problem discussed was that the Merry Weekend package was not working well at non-Taras because they had fewer facilities to offer the customers. Competition was also a major topic of discussion, centering around key competitors, especially the large chain affiliated hotels. These hotels recognized the contribution to revenues of weekend packages in their overall sales strategy, and courted the markets aggressively through advertising and very attractive prices. Some examples are given in Exhibit 9.

Chambers also wanted to use weekend packages to lure new customers, not just bring back or hold on to the old Merry Weekend customers who didn't want the unrenovated product. To accomplish this, Chambers felt a need to attract some different customers such as those who had once utilized the Dunfey "mini-vacation" concept of weekend packages.

Those at the meeting recognized that the company had to respond quickly and effectively if it was going to meet the competitive challenge. Management recognized the difficulties of competing in each hotel's respective market because of the varied degrees and methods of competition. If the non-Tara hotels were to remain competitive they would have to compensate somehow for their physical failings.

The meeting came to a close with optimistic enthusiasm regarding the new strategies that were to be put in place.

EXHIBIT 8 Merry Weekend Brochure Cover

Now You Can Enjoy Your Tara Merry Weekend at Even More Castles.

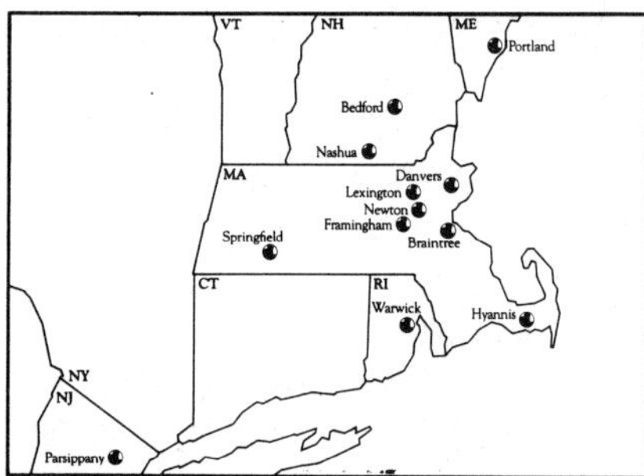

Tara Hotels is pleased to announce the addition of seven new properties. In Newton, Lexington and Hyannis, MA; Warwick, RI; Bedford, NH; South Portland, ME; and Parsippany, NJ. And coming soon to Springfield, MA.

Sheraton Tara Hotel
Braintree, MA 617-848-0600
Sheraton Tara Hotel
Danvers, MA 617-777-2500
Sheraton Tara Hotel
Framingham, MA 617-879-7200
Sheraton Tara Hotel
Lexington, MA 617-862-8700
Sheraton Tara Hotel
Springfield, MA 413-781-1010
Sheraton Tara Hotel
South Portland, ME 207-775-6161
Sheraton Tara Wayfarer Hotel
Bedford, NH 603-622-3766
Sheraton Tara Hotel
Nashua, NH 603-888-9970
Sheraton Tara Airport Hotel
Warwick, RI 401-738-4000
Tara Newton—A Howard Johnson's Hotel
Newton, MA 1-800-654-2000 or 617-969-3010
Tara Dunfey Hyannis Hotel
Hyannis, MA 1-800-THE TARA or 617-775-7775
Tara Hotel
Parsippany, NJ 201-515-2000

For Sheraton reservations: 1-800-325-3535

EXHIBIT 9 Competitive Weekend Packages

Stouffers, Bedford Glen

Four different weekend packages called "Breakations."

1. $59, one night, double, Friday or Saturday
2. $79, one night, double, Friday or Saturday, champagne on arrival, continental breakfast
3. $139, two nights, double, Friday & Saturday, champagne on arrival, continental breakfast on Saturday
4. $169, two nights, double, Friday & Saturday, champagne on arrival, continental breakfast on Saturday, Brunch on Sunday

* all packages based on availability

Days Inn, Burlington and Appleton Inn

No package. $65 rate for Friday or Saturday.

Marriott, Newton

Escape #1 - $169/$179 double, welcome champagne, dinner for two, breakfast or brunch or room service - one night
Escape $2 - $219 double, Friday/Saturday, dinner both nights, comp newspaper
$65 - super saver (room only)
$69 ($89 4/1) bed & breakfast

Marriott, Burlington

Escape #1 - $125, double, one night, 2 breakfasts, 2 dinners
Escape #2 - $149, double, two nights, 2 breakfasts, 2 dinners
$65 - super saver, room only
$69 - ($79 4/1) bed & breakfast

APPENDIX: Merry Weekender Customer Survey Results

PURPOSE OF RESEARCH

* Determine Customer satisfaction towards weekend package.
* Identify most appealing benefits of weekend packages.
* Assess competitor package usage.
* Develop Merry Weekend Customer profile.

METHODOLOGY

* Surveys distributed to all Merry Weekend customers on two weekends at the following properties:
  - -Nashua only on November 13-15, 1987
  - -Nashua and Framingham on November 20-22, 1987
* In total, 129 surveys were completed of the 273 distributed for a respectable response of 47%. The breakdown according to property and weekend is:

	Surveys Returned	Surveys Distrib.	Response Rate
Nashua, Nov. 13-15	45	104	43%
Nashua, Nov 20-22	58	95	61%
Framingham, Nov 20-22	26	74	35%
TOTALS	129	273	47%

Two properties with the most Merry Weekend business were selected. In April of 1988, a mail survey will be conducted with all Merry Weekend customers from January 1987 through March 1988. This later study will be representive of all Merry Weekend customers for all properties.

The present study developed from discussion concerning the January promotion to all Merry Weekend customers; specifically, we wanted to know if a third night free with a Merry Weekend package was an appealing benefit. This opportunity to survey customers allowed the capturing of additional information for directional purposes and also is the foundation for the mail survey to be conducted in April 1988.

Therefore, since this study does not represent all Merry Weekend customers, the results are directional only and should not be generalized to all Merry Weekend customers. However, the results which follow are very useful and give us a good idea and direction to follow.

1. How often have you used this Merry Weekend Package in the last TWO years (including this weekend)?

First Time today	52%
Two	9
Three	23
Four	7
Five	5
Six	1
Seven to nine	3
	100% (base = 129)

2. In the last two years, how often have you extended your Merry Weekend stay from 2 nights (Friday and Saturday) to 3 nights (Friday, Saturday and Sunday?)

Never	73%
Once	10
Twice	10
Three times	7
	100% (base = 60)

3. During your Merry Weekend stays, how often do you eat dinner in the hotel's restaurant?

Friday night only	25%
Saturday night only	52
Both Friday & Saturday	23
	100% (base = 60)

4. Please rate the following characteristics of the Merry Weekend packages with 5 being excellent and 1 being poor.

	%Very Good or Excellent	Average Rating
Cocktail Party	76%	4.1
Fruit Basket	68	4.0
Saturday Breakfast	81	4.1
Sunday Brunch	100	4.4
Value Overall	79	4.1
(base = 60)		

5. Which one factor was most important to you when selecting this Merry Weekend Package?

Location	41%
Price	23
Repeating	10
Friends	6
Other	9
Restaurant	4
Pool	4
Spa	3
	100% (base = 129)

6. How did you become aware of Merry Weekend Packages?

Repeat Customer	29%
Referral	26
Newspaper Ads	13
Gift Certificate	12
Called Hotel Directly	12
Friends	4
Other	4
	100% (base = 129)

7. Have you purchased any other weekend packages offered by a hotel other than Tara Hotels?

Yes	32%
No	68
	100 (base = 127)

8. Who were these packages offered by?

Marriott	37%
Sheraton	17
Hilton	17
Holiday Inn	12
Hyatt	10
Westin	5
Omni	2
Other	4 (base = 41)

9. Below is a list of benefits hotels have used in weekend packages. On a scale of 1 to 5, with 5 being very appealing, how appealing are these benefits to you?

	Percent appealing or very appealing		
	First Time MW Customers	Repeating MW Customers	All MWCustomers
Free Dinner for 2 in hotel's restaurant	96%	89%	93%
Free Tickets to local theatre, museum	38	33	34
Free Third night MW stay	42	59	50
Free use of pool and Health Spa	67	64	65
Free in-room movies	73	68	71
Free Brunch	96	94	95

	Average Rating		
	First Time MW Customers	Repeating MW Customers	All MWCustomers
Free Dinner for 2 in hotel's restaurant	4.7	4.7	4.7
Free Tickets to local theatre, museum	3.1	2.8	3.0
Free Third night MW stay	3.3	3.6	3.4
Free use of pool and Health Spa	4.0	4.0	4.0
Free in-room movies	4.1	3.9	4.0
Free Brunch	4.8	4.8	4.8

10. What one addition would you like to see to the Merry Weekend Package?

Addition	Willing to Pay (% yes)	
Dinner for two	43%	68%
Free Third night	6	83
Lounge Entertain.	5	100

Later Check out	4	25
Free HBO	4	0
Theatre Tickets	4	75
Better Service	2	100
Golf	2	100
Champagne on arrival	2	50
AM coffee in Lobby	2	50

Single Mentions:

Coed Steam Room, more activities, whirlpool for two, children's play area, all night room service, refrigerator in room, free massage (base = 95)

CUSTOMER PROFILE

11. In the last year, how often did your work require you to travel which included overnight stays in hotels?

Number of Overnights	
None	57%
one	6
two	12
three	4
four	2
five-nine	11
ten +	8
	100% (base = 115)
	average = 2.4 nights

12. Age

Under 30	16%	
30 to 39	26	
40 to 49	41	(avg.age = 41)
50 to 59	12	
60 to 69	4	
	100%	(base = 127)

13. Income

Under $35,000	17%	
35,000 to 49,999	41	(median income
50,000 to 69,999	27	= $47,682)
70,000 or more	15	
	100%	(base = 123)

RESULTS

Of the 129 survey respondents, 52% were on their first Merry Weekend. The 60 repeating Merry Weekend (MW) customers, on the average, had 2.6 MW trips in the past two years.

Characteristics of Repeating Customers

* The majority of MW (73%) have never extended their weekend trip to a third night.
* Three of every four (75%) repeating MW customers have at least one dinner in the hotel. Of the 60 repeating MW customers, eating dinner in the hotel is as follows:

Friday night only	25%
Saturday night only	52
Both Friday & Saturday	23

* Overall, repeating MW customers were very satisfied with the Weekend package. The most satisfing aspect of the package was the Sunday Brunch. The percentage of repeating customers who rated aspects of the Merry Weekend package as very good or excellent:

Cocktail Party	76%
Fruit Basket	68
Saturday Breakfast	81
Sunday Brunch	100
Value Overall	79

Awareness and Satisfaction

Respondents were asked to indicate how they became aware of the Merry Weekend package. Almost one in three (29%) customers indicated their awareness from being repeat customers.

* An important finding is that one of every four customers (26%) indicated that they were "referred" to the package from someone else.

This demonstrates the power of "positive word of mouth" advertising, but we must remember that the opposite is true as well — customers do not purchase the package because of hearing about bad experiences, which are usually customer orientated.

* Location and price are the two most cited factors for choosing a MW package.

Competitive Weekend Package Usage

Only one in every three (32%) MW customers have purchased competitive packages in the last year.

* Of those customers purchasing competitve packages, Marriott's weekend package was cited as being purchased the most often, followed by Sheraton and Hilton.
* Customers are purchasing these competitve packages for the same reasons that they purchased a MW package, price and location.

Promotional Benefits

In determining benefits that customers desire to receive in a weekend package, the following question was asked:

> "Below is a list of benefits hotels have used in weekend packages. On a scale of 1 to 5 with 5 being very appealing, how appealing are these benefits to you?"

Customers indicated that the free brunch was the most appealing benefit. The order of appeal for the six benefits is:

1. Free Brunch
2. Free Dinner for two in hotel's restaurant
3. Free in-house movies
4. Free use of the health spa and pool
5. Free third night on weekend package stay
6. Free tickets to local theatre and museums.

Suggested benefits for Merry Weekend Package

Customers were asked what one addition they would be willing to see to the MW package and would they be willing to pay a little extra for the package if this amenity was added.

* Dinner for two was cited by 68% of the respondents as the one addition they would like to see to the package. It is important to note that 68% of the respondants suggesting dinner for two would be willing to pay more for the weekend package. Dinner for two was the most widely suggested benefit by a wide margin.
* The "distant" second most appealing benefit was free third night with weekend package stay.

Customer Profile

The MW customer seems to be an infrequent traveler. In fact only 43% fo the respondants stayed in a hotel overnight in the past year for business. Even more, the average number of nights in a hotel for business for the last year is only 2.4 nights.

* the average age of a MW customer is 41 years
* The median HOUSEHOLD income for MW customers is $47,682.

Therefore the average MW customer is an infrequent traveler, who is a middle class and middle aged consumer living within driving distance of our hotels.

CONCLUSIONS

The customer profile of the MW customer is not surprising as this was very close to our educated guess. The percentage of first time (52%) MW customers strongly suggests that there is new business to be captured. Additionally, the 32% of the customers who have used competitor's weekend packages suggests that "brand loyalty" can be established either by adding amenities to the package or by simply reminding the customer of our package through direct mail or other forms of advertising.

"Third Night Free" is an appealing benefit as one of every two customers indicated this benefit to be appealing or very appealing, although this benefit did not appear as appealing as other benefits. One problem with assessing the appeal of this benefit is the actual description of a third night free without biasing the question for a positive response (for example, assigning a dollar value for the free night.) Also, one other problem is that benefits rated were also being offered, while a third night free is a new idea for a package.

With 75% of the customers already having one dinner meal in the hotel, the suggestion of having dinner for two included in the package, (even with a higher MW price per day) would "cut into" the food and beverage revenue. Since only 23% have both dinner meals at the hotel, our objective should be to increase this percentage.

CASE 13

MOVIANTE RESTAURANT

"I don't believe in advertising," John Quinn, co-owner of Moviante[1] stated. "You need lots of money to advertise and it's better to promote things in-house. Moviante has done the same amount of business since we stopped advertising. If I had the money to spend again, I would build a banquet room to increase our capacity to do business."

Moviante was a small, moderate price restaurant featuring northern Italian cuisine. It was located on a side street in the college town of Ithaca, New York. The decor was "simple, high tech, and New York chic."

Moviante had two storefronts: one featured a deli decor where passers-by could observe fresh pasta being made, and the other exposed the restaurant. As guests entered Moviante they passed the deli counter which displayed the artfully arranged antipasto ingredients and desserts. There was also a show kitchen that was separated from the dining room by a long white counter. A striped awning and white tile floor provided the visual division between the two areas. All final preparation of the food was done in the "show kitchen" to allow the customers to see for themselves "just how fresh the food is." The dining room was off to the left and down two steps. A very simple white decor gave the feeling of a modern, elegant restaurant.

BACKGROUND

Peter Schore, the other co-owner, held a Bachelors and a Master of Science degree in Hotel and Restaurant Management. Prior to opening Moviante, he was a Food and Beverage Manager of a major, international hotel chain and had been a teacher at a culinary school. Schore wanted to fulfill his dream of opening a restaurant. He purchased an inn outside Ithaca, New York where people would "take a Sunday drive to go and eat."

Schore wanted to start another more commercial venture in a city or large, suburban area. After vacationing in Italy for three months, he decided to open a restaurant featuring northern Italian cuisine. Schore chose Ithaca for three reasons: he resided there, he liked the town, and he wanted the restaurant to be a neighborhood place for fine food at moderate prices.

---

1 Names and locations have been disguised.

After weeks of searching, Schore discovered a location that was exactly what he wanted. He was most surprised when informed that a Mr. Quinn had recently approached the owner to discuss a similar proposition.

John Quinn had owned and operated a successful soup and salad style restaurant in Ithaca for the past seven years. He recognized that the latest trend in gourmet pasta restaurants was uniformly popular elsewhere in the country and believed that an ethnic restaurant of that type would also prosper in the Ithaca area.

Schore and Quinn agreed to join forces and combine their talents to develop Moviante. Quinn had also attracted seven investors who were interested in backing the venture. Italian Pasta, Inc. was formed since Moviante was envisioned as the prototype for a small chain in the New York/New England area. Schore and Quinn retained ownership of the trademark Moviante, while the restaurant itself was owned by Italian Pasta, Inc., a Subchapter S Corporation[2]. Schore and Quinn were the major stockholders of Italian Pasta, Inc., but were also employed as co-managers of Moviante for the first year of operation.

Since both of the principal partners recognized that a "co-manager" setup could be potentially problematic, they agreed to the following division of responsibilities:

1. Quinn would be in charge of all recordkeeping, advertising/promotion, cost control and maintenance, as well as the general supervision of the front of the house.
2. Schore would manage the back of the house to include food purchasing, storage, preparation and presentation.
3. Each of the co-managers would function as manager fifty percent of the time (20 to 30 hours a week).

GETTING OPEN

Moviante was started with a budget of $37,000. The white china was secondhand, the furniture was purchased at auction, and most of the equipment was also used merchandise. Plumbing, electrical and equipment hookup problems increased expenses to $98,000. Italian Pasta, Inc. provided $72,000 and $26,000 was financed by a local bank.

Quinn and Schore recognized that different meal periods would attract different customers, so they attempted to target their advertising to capture the appropriate markets. A brainstorming session produced the following consensus:

---

2 A Subchapter S corporation provides that, for tax purposes, income or losses flow directly to the stockholders.

Meal period	**Target Market**
Lunch	Intown and regional businesses
Dinner	Remote areas
Afternoon snack	Students, shoppers, locals
Brunch	Remote areas
Late night snack	Students, locals
Take out	Locals

Type of Media

13 local newspapers within a 30 mile radius
1 free valley newspaper
New York Times
New York Magazine
Local radio station

In October 1987, Moviante literally "just opened the doors." Two weeks prior to the opening, Quinn and Schore had placed advertisements in three surrounding newspapers with an ad simply stating "Moviante." One week before the opening the ad was amended to read "Moviante - Fine Italian Cuisine."

Arrangements had been made to host a press party and a grand opening party for Ithaca's Chamber of Commerce members, but the "endless hours" involved in opening the restaurant, as well as a cash shortage, necessitated that plans for these events be scrapped. The co-owners did visit the admissions offices of the surrounding colleges, the local conference center, and all of Ithaca's downtown merchants to familiarize them with Moviante and to invite them for a complimentary cocktail.

Moviante served much the same menu for lunch and dinner, although the luncheon portions were smaller and the prices lower. Beside the appetizer and full dinner menu (Exhibit 1), there was also a separate pasta menu (Exhibit 2). Both beer and wine, but not liquor, were available, with a rather extensive Italian wine list with selections ranging from $10.00 to $35.00 per bottle.

THE MOVIANTE CONCEPT

Moviante was conceived as an establishment which served only "the freshest possible food made from scratch." It was intended to be a moderately priced restaurant in a neighborhood setting. The owners insisted they were "not interested in making a fast buck or a tremendous return;" they just wanted "to do reasonably well."

EXHIBIT 1 Moviante Dinner Menu

• SPECIALTIES •

Served with bread & house salad.

EGGPLANT MASCARPONE ~ thick slices of roasted eggplant topped with mascarpone cheese, baked with tomatoes, spinach and marinara. $7.95

GIOBATTO ~ veal, hot sausage and chicken sautéed with tomatoes, mushrooms, fennel, Piedmonte red wine and veal stock ~ served over pasta. $9.25

SHRIMP FRA DIAVOLO ~ shrimp sautéed with pepperoncini, hot sausage, Sicilian olives in a fiery marinara sauce ~ served over egg linguine. $11.95

SHRIMP PICCANTE ~ shrimp sautéed with lemon, butter, garlic and capers in a wine sauce over pasta. $11.95

BAKED SHRIMP FLORENTINE ~ (3) jumbo shrimp stuffed with crabmeat, baked with spinach, mushrooms and marsala in a nutmeg-flavored cream sauce, topped with cheese. $13.95

CHICKEN GIOVANNI ~ breast of chicken sautéed with a gorgonzola cream sauce, sweet red peppers, a splash of brandy and enhanced by truffles. $12.95

CIOPPINO ~ a melange of seafood (clams, mussels, shrimp, fish and calamari) in a garlicky broth served over egg linguine. $12.95

LINGUINE ~ white clam sauce, fresh little-neck clams in a garlicky wine broth or red clam sauce. $10.95

SOLE ~ with shrimp and scallop mousse ~ baked with puff pastry and served on a mild pink peppercorn sauce. $11.95

VEAL ~ milk-fed provimi ~ preparation varies nightly.

Please inquire . . .

EXHIBIT 2 Moviante Pasta Menu

•PASTA•

Served with bread & house salad.

FETTUCINE/LINGUINE/SPAGHETTINI ~ marinara sauce ~ $5.95
meat sauce ~ $6.75

FETTUCINE/LINGUINE/SPAGHETTINI ~ alfredo $7.50 ~ additional items 50¢: bacon, sausage, prosciutto, peas, mushrooms, artichoke hearts, olives, broccoli.

FETTUCINE CARBONARA ~ prosciutto, bacon, parmesan, egg yolk, cream, fresh sage. $8.95

RIGATONI & BROCCOLI ~ a spicy sauté of olive oil, garlic, hot peppers, anchovie paste and broccoli, deglazed with marsala and topped with marinara. $6.95

PASTA POMIDORO ~ artichoke hearts, broccoli and prosciutto, sautéed in a fresh dill cream sauce over our tomato fettucine. $8.95

RASTA PASTA ~ pesto and fresh vegetables sautéed with alfredo sauce and tossed with herb fettucine. $8.95

TORTELLINI ROSÉ ~ meat filled pasta sautéed with sausage, tomatoes and spinach in a pink alfredo sauce. $8.95

PENNONI VAL D'OSTA ~ thin pasta tubes sautéed with porcini, roasted red peppers and artichoke hearts, sauced with cream, fontina val d'osta and campiociesa wine. $9.95

LASAGNE CLASSICO ~ egg noodles, sweet Italian sausage, herbs and ricotta, baked with marinara sauce. $7.25

LASAGNE VERDE ~ spinach noodles layered with mushrooms, tomatoes and spinach ~ sauce balsemedia. $7.95

MANICOTTI ~ spinach pasta crêpes stuffed with ricotta, pignoli and pesto, sauced with balsemedia and fontina. $8.95

BAKED STUFFED SHELLS ~ (3) jumbo shells stuffed with ricotta, served on a bed of pesto with a moat of marinara, balsemedia sauce and mozzarella on top. $9.95

OPERATIONS

In October 1988, Mark Jaslow became the manager of Moviante. He had been employed as a cook in New York City for the past six years and was just finishing his Hotel and Restaurant Management degree at Cornell University. Mark was originally hired as the cashier/assistant manager in March of that year. Upon his promotion, the co-owners retired from active management and assumed their new roles as "directors of investment and operations," and also restaurant consultants.

Mark described the business level in the spring and summer of 1988 as "booming." From November on, however, business began to decline. In an effort to improve the bottom line, manpower hours, laundry expenses, and advertising dollars were either decreased or, in the latter case, eliminated entirely. Lunch was eventually discontinued in December when advertisements for luncheon specials failed to significantly impact business. The owners decided that the amount of overhead simply exceeded the amount of sales revenue.

Jaslow staffed two to three waitpersons and no busperson on weekdays, and four waitpersons and one busperson on weekends. Moviante also employed a full-time chef and sous chef, and a part-time pasta maker and baker. All employees had been employed at Moviante's for over one year and all were very efficient, according to Jaslow.

Moviante's could accomodate 76 patrons at the 22 tables in the restaurant. Jaslow stated that in a good week the average turnover rate was below once on Sundays and weeknights, two times on Fridays, and three times on Saturdays. The average check for dinner was $15.00 per person and about 20 percent of the total was beer or wine.

According to Jaslow, close to ninety percent of the guests were repeat customers, and ten percent had been recommended by friends. The clientele was described as mostly upper middle class couples in the $30,000-$40,000 income bracket from the surrounding cities within half an hour of Ithaca. Based on the menu, clientele, and atmosphere, Mark classified the restaurant as "gourmet."

In 1988, the restaurant averaged $7500 per week in sales volume, with $4500 coming in on the weekend nights. Food, beverage and advertising costs are shown on the abbreviated income statement (Exhibit 3).

MARKETING

When asked his views on the marketing/advertising scenario, Quinn stated, "I feel our market is within a half hour drive of Ithaca. Because of easy accessibility to Route 80, we see Moviante as capturing the transient vacationer who might be enroute to ski, camp, or fish. People from the city heading to the country want to stop in a somewhat cosmopolitan, interesting town" (Exhibit 4).

EXHIBIT 3 **Abbreviated Income Statement 1988**

SALES			
Food			
Served	310,258		
Take Out	10,151		
Food Sales	320,409		
Wine & Beer	62,880		
TOTAL SALES			383,289
COST OF SALES			
Food	88,860		
Wine & Beer	25,844		
TOTAL COST OF SALES		114,704	
Advertising	8,985		
Promotion	1,890		
		10,875	
OTHER COSTS			
Total other operating costs		229,086	
TOTAL COSTS			354,665
PROFIT BEFORE OCCUPATION COST			28,624
OCCUPATION COSTS			31,832
PROFIT (LOSS) BEFORE DEPRECIATION			(3,208)

The major problem, according to Schore, was how to divert those travelers from the superhighway and into Ithaca. "We could never afford to construct a billboard on Route 80, so I decided to attend a Chamber of Commerce meeting to determine how Ithaca is promoting itself." At the meeting, Schore discussed his concerns with the members, and was instrumental in the creation of the Ithaca Publicity Committee.

This committee drafted a marketing proposal and designed a brochure to distribute to ski areas, campgrounds, tourist agencies, and other tourist spots. The committee members visited local merchants and sold $200 advertising blocks to finance the brochure. In return, the merchants were promised valuable exposure. An appendix shows the framework of the marketing plan.

EXHIBIT 4 Location of Moviante

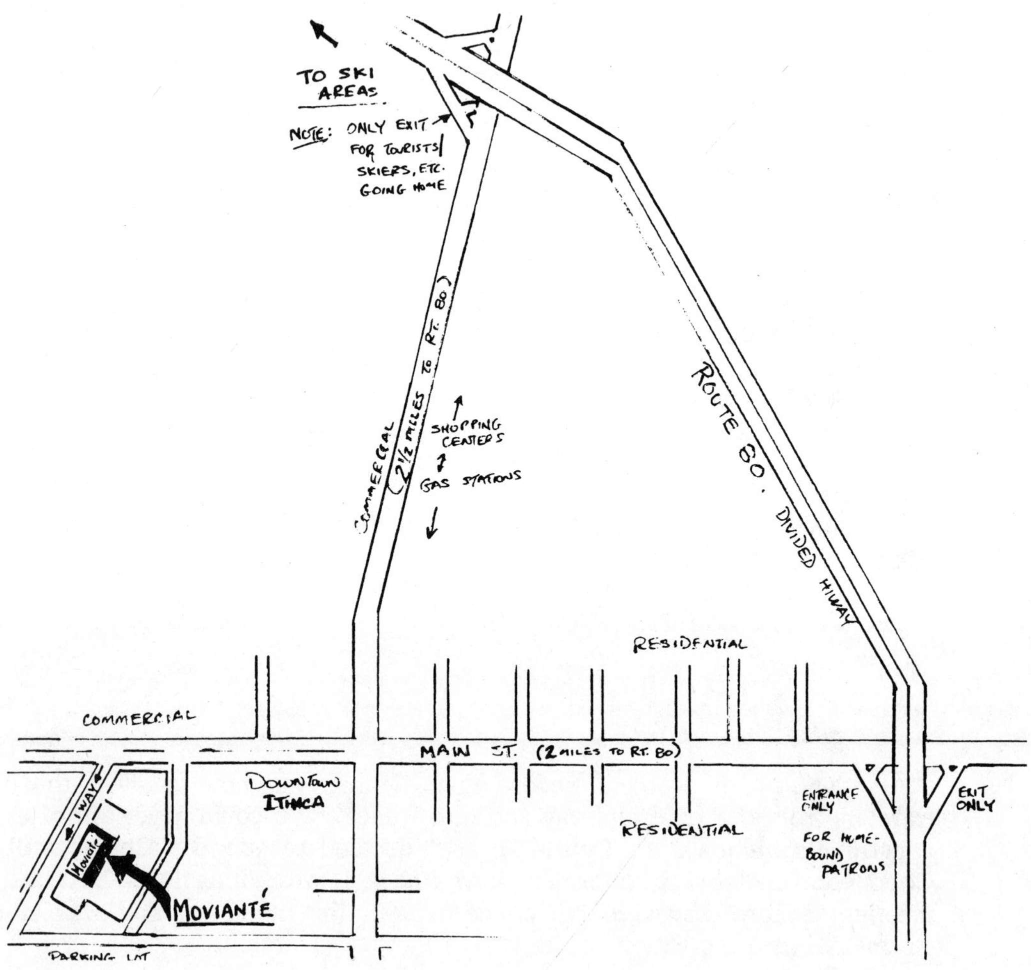

COMPETITION

There were 45 restaurants in Ithaca ranging from McDonald's to gourmet operations. Schore believed that the direct competition for Moviante were those which were medium priced and had a somewhat unique atmosphere. He identified seven restaurants in the area as competition:

Type of Menu	Atmosphere	Price
1. Vegetarian	cafe	low
2. Cheese raclette	traditional	medium
3. American-mixed	inn	medium-high
4. American-mixed	traditional	medium
5. Chinese	oriental	medium-high
6. Seafood	traditional	medium
7. Vegetarian	traditional	low-medium

Mark identified as competition three different restaurants which were within the Ithaca town lines:

Type of Menu	Atmosphere	Price
1. French	traditional	high
2. Italian	ethnic	medium
3. American	cafe	medium-high

ADVERTISING

Display advertising continued through most of 1988 until all ads were eventually cancelled in November. Seventy five percent of the ads simply stated "Moviante" and included a description of its food with the address and hours of operation. The remaining 25 percent of the ads were more informative with specific details about the food and often a unique gimmick to attract customers to the establishment. One example was a coupon ad that ran in the valley's free newspaper with a circulation of 29,000. Only ten coupons were redeemed.

An informal, unscientific study of twenty five residents within a ten mile radius of Ithaca conducted in February of 1989 revealed that none of the respondents recognized the name "Moviante" nor did they know what it was or where it was located.

APPENDIX Chamber of Commerce Marketing Plan

CAMPAIGN OBJECTIVES

To attract more people downtown for shopping, dining, and entertainment: **BY** Projecting "Main Street Ithaca" as a vibrant business community with traditional and contemporary elements which blend to give "Main Street Ithaca" broad appeal.

Target Markets
* Area residents
* Residents of major highway communities
* Colonial America buffs Shaker Community Historical New York
* Business Conference and Workshop Attendees
    Hotels and Motels Conference Centers Convention Bureaus
    Major Corporations University Centers
* Academic Travelers
    Prospective Students and Parents Visiting Parents
    Academic Conferences Returning Alumni
* Cultural Event Attendees
    Theatre at Colleges and University Chamber Concerts
    Regional Theatre, Orchestras, etc
* Summer Camp
    Staff Visiting Parents
* Antiques Buyers and Collectors
* Skiing area Patrons
* Craftspeople and Buyers
* Country Inn Devotees

PROMOTIONAL CAMPAIGN

Develop Identity throught consistantly used logo - "Main Street Ithaca"
Press Releases widely distributed to announce "Main Street Ithaca" Campaign and enumerate reasons to visit Ithaca.
Brochure/Business Directory distributed within two hour driving radius to:
* Other Chambers of Commerce * Tourist Booths
* College Visitors and Conferences * Hotels and Motels
* Culteral Events * Summer Camps
* Recreational Areas * Historical Areas
* Mailing to: Ad Respondants
    Area Resident Mailing List
    College Mailings
    Special Interest Lists

Advertising Campaign promoting "Main Street Ithaca" with brochure request element.

* Local Media — Large ads with elements of directory alternated with smaller institutional identification ads.
* New York, New England, and Northeast periodicals and newspapers and other media in 2 hour driving distance. Also special interest periodicals, general tourism guides and periodicals.

PRELIMANARY BUDGET

Brochure Development, Production and Mailing: Ad Layouts	$7,000
Local and Regional Media Advertising	9,000
National Travel and Special Interest Publications	10,000
Approximate First Year Budget:	26,000

UNDERWRITING THE CAMPAIGN

MIX OF

1. Directory Listing of Business on Main Street (Market to State Streets) and Side Streets (One block north and south of Main)

   Category
   Name Address Phone Number
   One line description
   100 participants @ $200 ($4.00 a week)

2. Corporate and Institutional Sponsers
   Listing under Sponsers
   $200 Minimum No Maximum

   Open to all business first year under sponshership of Downtown Business Association.

BREAKEVEN RETURN

$20,000 divided by 50 weeks = $400 per week or $80 per day

CASE 14

L'HOTEL DUPREE

Daniel Myette, Director of Marketing for L'Hotel DuPree[1] since its incorporation, sat at his desk one morning when a call came in from Jon Price, the hotel's controller. "Daniel, I think it's time for a change in our marketing strategy. I think it is time for a new direction. Do we really know who our customers are? Do we really know why they come to our hotel. Daniel, I think it's time we do some research; time to find out what our customers want from L'Hotel DuPree and how we can serve them better!"

"Jon," Daniel replied, "do you really think that's what this hotel needs? We're doing that now. Each year we look at the marketplace, define which markets L'Hotel DuPree can serve best, and plan our strategies accordingly. We just had our strategic planning meeting, and our goals are set. 1989 will be a big year for us. All renovations will be complete and L'Hotel DuPree will be comparable to the best hotels in the city!"

LAFAYETTE HOTELS INTERNATIONAL

L'Hotel DuPree was the flagship of the North American division of Lafayette Hotels Intn'l, an international hotel chain of 22 luxury hotels located in 15 countries throughout the world. Teamwork, qualified management, concern for the comfort of the traveler, and French flair were foundations of Lafayette's growth.

Because of the greatly varying geographical locations and clientele, each hotel of the chain catered to the needs of a particular market. Therefore, Lafayette favored a decentralized management system. Rather than establishing strict formulas and standards, Lafayette Hotels allowed the manager of each property the authority and flexibility to manage their property efficiently. This decentralization was key to achieving effective adaptation to the environment in which each hotel operates.

In addition to Chicago's L'Hotel DuPree, Lafayette operated hotels in San Francisco and New York. Lafayette's United States plans involved operating medium-sized properties rather than large, convention-type ones.

1 Names and places have been disguised.

The typical American Lafayette was to appeal to the affluent business and vacation traveler.

THE PHILLIP HASTING CORPORATION

The builder/owner of L'Hotel DuPree was Phillip Hastings, president and chairman of the board of the Phillip Hastings Corporation. He was one of the largest, most successful developers and managers of luxury residences and commercial properties in the United States.

L'Hotel DuPree was Phillip Hastings' first venture into the hospitality industry. When Hastings bought the building, he planned to build an apartment complex. Someone suggested he build a hotel, instead. Realizing other prosperous real estate developers had successfully entered the hotel industry, Hastings decided he also would make his mark in this industry. His plan was to create a hotel to rival big-name competitors in the Chicago area. He wanted the best in architectural design and beauty, and he wanted a five star, five diamond hotel.

Hastings took an active interest in the day to day operations of the hotel. Although managed by Lafayette Hotels Intn'l, the management contract gave Hastings the power to maintain full participation in the management of L'Hotel DuPree, and granted him the authority to appoint the General Manager, Director of Marketing, and Controller. With his office in the hotel, Hastings was frequently on the scene on a day-to-day basis.

THE HOTEL

L'Hotel DuPree was a 700 room hotel located near the financial and cultural district of Chicago, and close to the shore of Lake Michigan. It was also close to the major television, film, and recording studios. Advertised as the "hotel with the French flair," the hotel was the favorite of many television, film, and recording stars, as well as the top executives of many Fortune 500 companies.

Opened in 1984, L'Hotel DuPree was marketed as Chicago's first French hotel. The style for the hotel was based on the French art of living. One of the most distinguishing characteristics, specifically designed to enhance this French image, was the huge atrium lobby. Inspired by Gothic architecture, the lobby was a magnificient creation of brass and marble. Living plants, spacious public areas, marble floors, brass fixtures, columned walls, and a ceiling which soared in height, created a style and beauty which had earned the lobby of L'Hotel DuPree architectural design awards.

Also in keeping with the French theme was Le Restaurant Cheval Blanc, located off the lobby of L'Hotel DuPree. Le Restaurant Cheval Blanc served the finest Nouvelle cuisine. Famous chefs from around the world came to the restaurant to sample its fine food. It was known as one of the best French restaurants in the city of Chicago.

Le Fleur, located in the atrium, was a small cafe. Here breakfast, light lunches, snacks, and cocktails were served. In the adjoining Le Francais bar, reproductions of the works of impressionist painters decorated the interior.

Included in the 700 rooms of L'Hotel DuPree were 100 suites designed to be particularly attractive to corporations. These included studios, one and two bedroom accommodations, and a duplex penthouse. Some were rented on an annual basis.

All guests at L'Hotel DuPree received a complimentary membership in Le Centre Sportif, the hotel's health club, during their stay. Le Centre Sportif was a full service health club which included racquetball/handball and squash courts, Nautilus exercise equipment, daily aerobics classes, saunas, and a masseur. Other features of the club included a glass enclosed rooftop heated swimming pool overlooking Lake Michigan, indoor and outdoor suntanning decks, a rooftop jogging path, and a private sky-top lounge where guests could enjoy a drink and a breath-taking view of the city. Guests had full use of all facilities. A limited number of outside memberships were available to corporations and the general public.

Public space included Salle de Morell ballroom, which seated a maximum of 275 people; Salle de Lafayette room, used mostly for large seminars and major functions; and the Antoinette boardroom, equipped with a board of directors table and large comfortable chairs.

In designing L'Hotel DuPree, the owner attended to every detail. Even the graphics created for the directional and door signs were special. Everything at L'Hotel DuPree was planned to assure guests a memorable stay: the gracious flag-bedecked motor entrance, a multi-lingual concierge staff trained and dedicated to serving the needs of guests, living plants and trees, expert lighting, nightly turndown service, oversized beds, triple-draped windows for undisturbed sleep, underground parking, 24 hour room service, and the ultimate in French food, beverages, and service. As described by the general manager, the hotel was an expert blending of all things French the world had come to know and love - extraordinary style and ambience, impeccable service, and exquisite food - with American amiability, comfort, and technology.

CLIENTELE

As mentioned, L'Hotel DuPree was located near the major television, film, and recording studios, and attracted many East and West Coast film, television, and recording stars. The hotel was also located near Chicago's garment district. Management felt that, based on its location and physical facility, L'Hotel DuPree was an ideal business travelers hotel. The hotel's top corporate accounts included American Broadcasting Company, Central Broadcasting System, National Broadcasting Company, Warner Communications, and Federated and Allied Department Stores. Exhibit 1 is a list of L'Hotel Dupree's market segments and their primary reasons for staying at the hotel, according to management, and a breakdown of the market by geographic location.

EXHIBIT 1 Market Segments for L'Hotel DuPree

Purpose Segment	Rooms in 1987	Primary Buy Decision
Corporate Transient	40.8%	Price & Location
Pure Transient	40.2%	Location & Facility
Corporate Group	9.5%	Facility
Weekend Package	7.7%	Price & Location
Permanent	1.7%	Location & Price

Geographic Segments	
North America (85%)	
West Coast (L.A.)	18 - 24%
East Coast (N.Y.)	16 - 22%
Mid West (Chicago)	25 - 50%
North East	3 - 4 %
International (15%)	
France	7%
United Kingdom	5%
Other	3%

Management described its market as younger, sophisticated travelers. This segment was mainly 28-48 year olds, in mid-management positions, who had an average income of $50,000. Management estimated that repeat customers represented 30 to 40 percent of the hotel's business. However, no formal guest tracking method was used at L'Hotel DuPree. A computerized guest history system was installed, but not put into practice and as yet it remained under utilized. Guest comment cards, originally printed in both French and English, became difficult to interpret. They were in the process of being revised, to be printed only in English. Also, a market survey had been performed by the hotel's advertising agency in an effort to learn more about its customers. However, the agency never analyzed the data and the findings were unknown.

STRATEGY

When L'Hotel DuPree opened in 1984 it set out to accomplish three goals. The first was to introduce Lafayette Hotels International to North America; the second, to introduce L'Hotel DuPree to Chicago; the third, to position L'Hotel DuPree as one of the finest hotels in the city. Management felt it could do this by offering the market a hotel with the best product, product delivery (service), and location.

Achieving the first two objectives was not very difficult. Through advertising, promotion, and word of mouth, L'Hotel DuPree soon became a popular hotel in the marketplace. However, achieving the third objective required much more time and planning.

The management of L'Hotel DuPree perceived the hotel as being positioned in the mid-range segment of the highest priced luxury hotels in the area. This segment included the Fairmont Place, the Plaza, the Regal, and the Intercontinental. However, ownership was not satisfied with that position and wanted to position the hotel among the top priced hotels in the luxury category. These hotels include the Nelson Towers, the Ritz Carlton, and the Palace Royale. Exhibit 2 is a list of L'Hotel DuPree's direct competitors, and Exhibit 3 is a summary of the market share analysis of the hotels with which L'Hotel DuPree shared this information.

COMPETITIVE ANALYSIS

Each year the L'Hotel DuPree conducted a competitive analysis to determine how the hotel fared as compared to other city hotels in the same class. Representatives from the sales office checked into the competitor hotels and rated them on eight attributes - reservations, check-in and check-out procedures, lobby and public area appearance and impression, room decor, room service, housekeeping, bathroom amenities package, and average rate. Hotels were chosen either because their price, facilities, or location (or any combination of these) were comparable to L'Hotel DuPree. Competitor hotels were rated on these attributes as they compared to L'Hotel DuPree. The eight attributes were rated on a scale of +4 to -4 ("+" being better than that offered by L'Hotel DuPree, 0 being on par with that offered by L'Hotel DuPree, and "-" being poorer than that offered by L'Hotel DuPree), and the ratings for each of the attributes were tallied. The total net rating represented the overall impression of each hotel as compared to L'Hotel DuPree. This result was used to determine the price/value relationship for each hotel in the analysis. The results of the 1988 competitive survey are shown graphically on a twenty point scale in Exhibit 4. The purpose of the competitive analysis was twofold: (1) to identify those features of L' Hotel DuPree which distinguish it from other hotels in its class; (2) to develop pricing and positioning strategies for L'Hotel DuPree.

EXHIBIT 2 Hotels Competing Most Directly with L'Hotel DuPree

Name	Distance From DuPree	Rack Rate 1988 ($)	Advantages	Disadvantages
Ritz Carlton	4 Blocks	215 Lake View 185-235 City View 550-700 1 Bd Suite 700-950 2 Bd Suite	Excellent shore location Part of small exclusive chain, Restaurant Views of lake Spacious rooms	Very subdued atmosphere,Little rate flexibility
Fairmont Place	6 Blocks	155-200 Single 175-220 Double 250-550 Jr.Suite 450-640 Lg. Suite	Ex. midtown location Complimentary limo to financial district Lovely lobby and atrium	Some small rooms Service uneven Meeting space limited One restaurant only
Vista	20 min.	125-185 Single 145-220 Double 265-425 Suites	Location (downtown) Shuttle service to midtown Health Club Part of Hilton International chain	Location (downtown) Associated with Hilton International
Regency House	2 Blocks	150-195 Single 175-220 Double 425-625 Suite	Shore location Recently renovated rest Good banquet facilities Great price flexibilites	No parking Meeting room pillars First Japenese hotel Not widely known
Inter-Continental	1 mile	135-225 Single 155-245 Double 300 1 Bd. Suite	Positive chain affiliat. Large inviting lobby Old world charm Good restaurant	Old building Poor room service Small rooms Perceived not deluxe
Nelson Towers	3 Blocks	155-225 Single 175-245 Double 285-600 Suites	Shore views Large rooms Very well maintained Refigerator and bathrobe in every room	Expensive Can't negotiate rates Small rooms Limited banquet space
Palace Royale	8 Blocks	190-220 Single 240 Tower 210-260 Double 325-1600 Suites	Ex. midtown location Only hotel with AAA Five Diamond Award Magnificant restoration of building Heavy advertising campaign Bathrobe in every room	Service decreased Poor price/value reputation Limited function space Limited rate flexibility

Regal	7 Blocks	155-205 Single 175-225 Double 375-725 Suites	Excellent reputation Recent refurbishment New health Club Central east side location Bathrobe in every room	Limited meeting space Only one restaurant
Drake	3 Blocks	135-180 Single 155-200 Double 300-555 Suites 420 Honeymoon	East side location Refrigerator every room All telephones 2 lines Extremely rate flexible for corporate and groups	Furnishings are adequate Poor product reputation Poor F & B reputation
Plaza	2 miles	140-185 Single 160-210 Double 350-600 Suites	Facilities View from high rooms Proximity to major highway Complimentary limo to Financial District	Location (Chicago river) Limited meeting space
L'Hotel Dupree		135-195 Single 165-225 Double 275-750 Suites		

Note: Hotels chosen because either their price, facilities, or location, or any combination, are comparable to L'Hotel Dupree.

EXHIBIT 3 Competitive Market Share Analysis (Jan – Aug 1988)

Competitive Hotels	Rooms Available	Rooms Occupied	Percent Occupancy	Capacity Share	Market Share
L'Hotel Dupree 700	170,800	113,411	66.4%	13.9%	15.3%
Fairmont Place 417	101,748	71,325	70.1%	8.3%	9.6%
Inter-Continental 691	168,604	122,406	72.6%	13.7%	16.5%
Nelson Towers 627	152,988	88,886	58.1%	12.4%	12.0%
Palace Royale 949	231,556	118,788	51.3%	18.8%	16.0%
Regal 490	119,560	74,725	62.5%	9.7%	10.1%
Plaza 444	108,336	58,285	53.8%	8.8%	7.9%
Regency House 720	175,680	95,043	54.1%	14.3%	12.8%
Total	1,229,272	742,869	60.4%	100%	100%

EXHIBIT 4 Price/Value Relationships

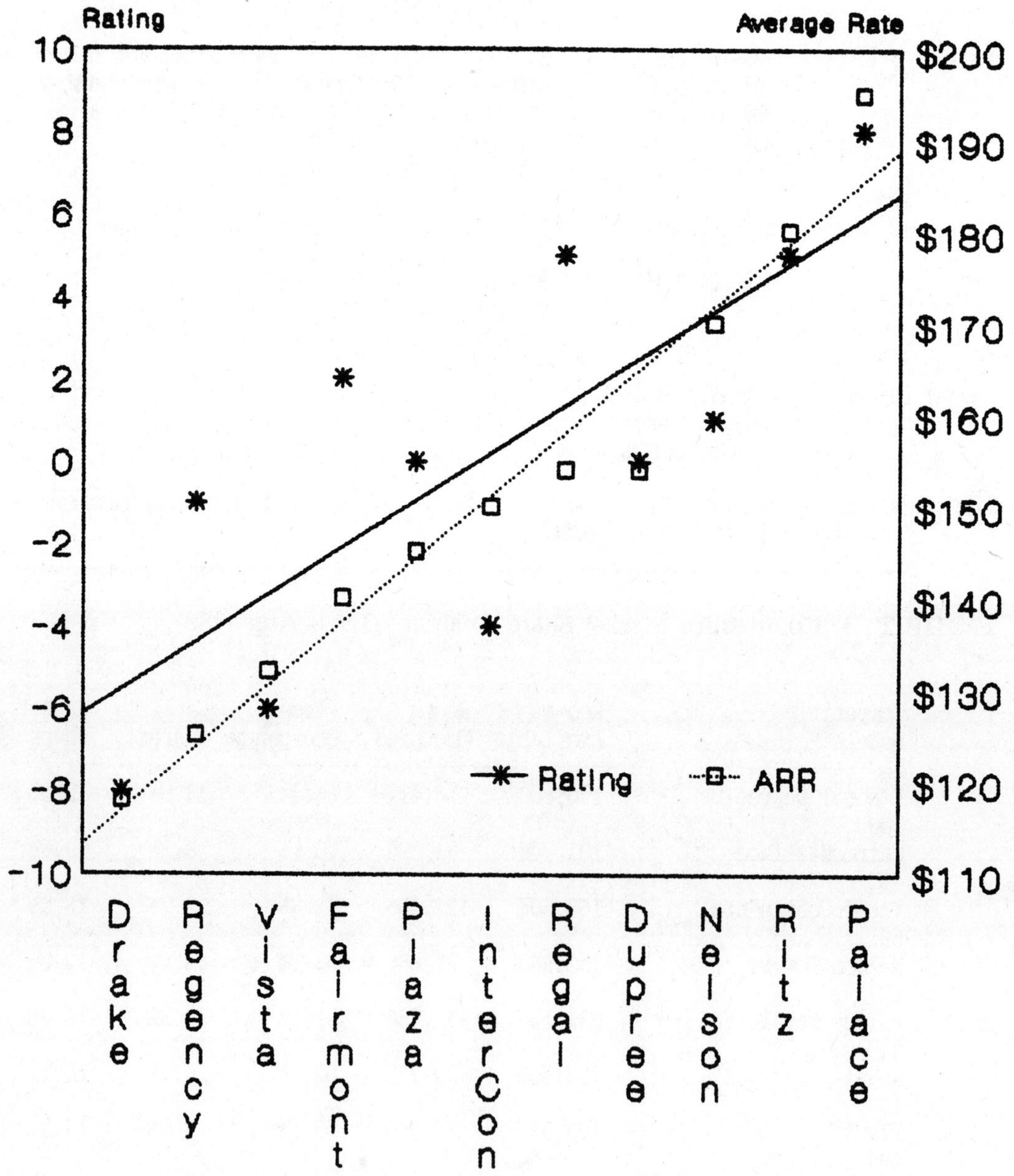

Four features of L'Hotel DuPree were found to positively distinguish it from competitor hotels. These features were location, lobby and atrium, restaurant (Le Restaurant Cheval Blanc), and health club and swimming pool.

Also included in the 1988 analysis was a review of the hotel by the American Automobile Association (AAA). Eleven negative aspects of the hotel were noted as preventing L'Hotel DuPree from receiving the coveted Five Diamond Award. It was determined that in order to position the hotel as one of the best hotels in the city, L'Hotel DuPree needed to overcome those deficiencies indicated by the AAA rating.

Until that was done, management felt that L'Hotel DuPree should be priced lower than the Palace Royale and the Ritz Carlton. It should be priced slightly lower than the Nelson Towers, and should be priced on line with the Regal, Plaza and Fairmont Place. A summary statement of the competitive and rating analysis is included as Exhibit 5.

Market Analysis The sales office also conducted a yearly market audit. This audit measured those factors which impact on the business climate. These factors included general economic factors, present and future economic factors, hotel industry supply, and rooms demand. Also measured were the available market segments, their demand periods and feasibility, as they relate to L'Hotel DuPree. Exhibit 6 summarizes this audit in the hotel's general positioning statement and includes the hotel's sales strategy.

L'Hotel DuPree had a fairly extensive media schedule in a variety of publications. The major goal of the advertising was to generate awareness of the hotel. Exhibit 7 is the projected 1988 media schedule.

CONCLUSION

"So Jon, we have compiled all the necessary information. Now all we have left to do is finish our 1988 renovation schedule. This includes refurbishing the guest rooms and other areas needing repair, and upgrading the amenities package and quality of our soft goods (linens, draperies, bedspreads, etc.). Like I said before, 1989 is going to be the big year for us! What do you think?"

EXHIBIT 5 Hotel Rating Summary Statement

Rating a hotel becomes a personal and subjective matter. Each hotel reviewer was given an eight page form listing one hundred fifteen particular questions for each hotel to keep the review as objective as possible.

While the true "value" of a hotel is based on all of the areas reviewed, the weight that each category carries does vary. An opulent lobby and guest corridors have little bearing on the attitude of a guest who is checked into a small dingy room facing an airshaft. Conversely, older, yet clean and well maintained facilities combined with caring and personalized service can overcome numerous physical faults.

The location of L'Hotel Dupree has been a distinct advantage. Other deluxe hotels it competes with are either on Lake Shore Drive or located in the more fashionable business district. While this hotel might be considered a pioneer by being located in the garment district, an area formerly inhabited only by conventional tourist class hotels, it indeed filled a void by providing a deluxe facility west of the financial district.

There are four distinct features that make L'Hotel Dupree unique and which directly contribute to its success. These features are its location, its lobby and atrium, the restaurant Cheval Blanc, and the health club and swimming pool.

Without these distinguishing amenities, the attractively appointed rooms would certainly place the hotel in a first class category. The addition of these features is the key to creating the hotel's deluxe status.

Also considered for this survey was a recent rating by Triple A, in which the hotel was awarded four diamonds. The following points were cited as preventing the hotel from receiving five diamond status:

1. Inadequate service elevators, e.g., service personnel on guest elevators
2. Chips and scars on toilet lids
3. Poor grouting in many bathrooms
4. Chipping paint from several areas in guest rooms, around doorways, and on window sills
5. Bedspreads and draperies of good, but not exceptional, quality
6. Jumble of exposed cable wiring behind television sets
7. No drawer stops on several dressers examined
8. No guest rooms equipped for the handicapped
9. Many of the green carpets spotted and worn
10. Bathroom plumbing of less than superior quality
11. Several desks and table tops marred with cigarette burns

EXHIBIT 5 Hotel Rating Summary Statement (continued)

Three times per year a representative from Triple A reserves a room and, unknown to management, spends two days in the hotel inspecting all aspects of a guest stay. The above 11 points were noted in our file as negative. Despite these negative aspects, the Triple A representative did point out that he and his associates have seen a marked improvement in housekeeping over the last twelve months. His interpretation of L'Hotel Dupree is that it is a very, very good hotel, but not yet a great hotel.

In overall comparison, five hotels rated higher than L'Hotel Dupree in providing quality in areas of service and facility. These five hotels are the Palace Royale, the Ritz Carlton, and the Regal, and to a lesser degree, the Nelson Towers and the Fairmont Place.

The Regency House and the Plaza scored closely on a par with L'Hotel Dupree. The Inter-Continental, Drake, and Vista finished anywhere from slightly to drastically behind L'Hotel Dupree in overall comparison.

The results of this study should enable management of the hotel to effectively position L'Hotel Dupree in a price structure with its competitors. At present, the hotel should be priced less than the Palace Royale and the Ritz Carlton. It should be slightly behind the Nelson Towers. The hotel should be priced on line with the Fairmont Place and the Regal and the Plaza, and should be positioned higher than the Drake, Inter-Continental, Regency and Vista.

In order to move up the scale, the hotel needs to overcome the physical deficiencies indicated in the Triple A rating. Many of these will be achieved through capital expenditures during the balance of 1988. Until such time that the management of L'Hotel Dupree is satisfied that the hotel can deliver a product offering on line with its top competitors, i.e., Palace Royale, Ritz Carlton, it will have to continue to position itself price-wise below these hotels.

By reviewing and comparing Chicago average room rate and rack rate, it is apparent that L'Hotel Dupree is successful in its rooms merchandising program. Other hotels which are either on line or slightly behind L'Hotel Dupree are still lagging behind the hotel in average rate by $10 - $35.

The hotel cannot continue to rely only on the market wave of supply and demand. Unless the hotel is able to provide a consistent level of price/value relationship, its success will be short lived. The only way to assure long term success is through product maintenance and improvement. At present, L'Hotel Dupree is teetering vicariously in several areas regarding product value. A careful assessment of the entire hotel is crucial to assure that the product being offered merits continual rate increases.

EXHIBIT 6 General Positioning Statement

The goal of L'Hotel Dupree is to position itself as one of the top three hotels in the city of Chicago. This can be achieved by assuring that the hotel has properly determined those markets which allow it to run at optimal occupancy with an optimal average rate and room sales efficiency.

For 1988, L'Hotel Dupree was budgeted to achieve an occupancy of 74.6 percent at an average rate of $171.67. This budget was based on previous years' actual figures as well as prevailing economic conditions. These figures have been revised to an annual occupancy of 68% at an average rate of $168.71.

The primary reason for this variance is a citywide drop in occupancies that began in January. In spite of an apparently healthy economy, transient travel into the city dropped to levels not seen since 1982. Nevertheless, L'Hotel Dupree has managed to maintain its share of the weakened market. It appears that the era of the free spending business executive is diminishing. The non-price sensitive transient market is decreasing. Corporations are consolidating their travel more than ever to insure the lowest possible rates for airlines, car rentals and hotels.

The Chicago hotels within our product class that have fared the best in 1988 have been the Inter-Continental and the Fairmont Place. These are also the hotels which negotiate corporate rates as low as $120.00 and $130.00, respectively.

Based on its location and physical facility, L'Hotel Dupree is an ideal business traveler's hotel. It is these individuals that comprise the corporate transient market - the backbone of the hotel's occupancy.

The transient market, while the most attractive dollar wise, is also the least reliable. The transient traveler is less likely to develop loyalty to a hotel than a corporate transient who uses a hotel because of company edict. The transient traveler is also the most likely to try a new hotel, or leave a past one due to dissatisfaction. Because he or she pays premium rates, the transient traveler rightfully expects the finest accommodations and service. The corporate traveler has a similar expectation level, but wants to have the sense of receiving some "deal" or concession on the rate being paid.

In questionable times the business traveler is the more reliable. In light of 1987 figures and those projected for 1988, the hotel must maintain and increase share in the corporate market. This may require offering corporate rates lower than rack and/or participating in promotional efforts to increase awareness and response.

The transient market should not, and will not, be diminished in its importance. Advertising and public relations efforts will continue to be directed to build this market. One conclusion to be drawn from this market

EXHIBIT 6 General Positioning Statement (continued)

audit is that transient travel is not likely to rebound tremendously for 1989. L'Hotel Dupree cannot rely greatly on this market for the coming year.

In 1989 the sales office will be more active and aggressive than ever in capturing new markets in the segments of corporate transient and corporate group.

Weekend packages will continue to remain very competitively priced. The strategy for this segment will be to offer a package five to ten dollars less than leading competitors to ensure occupancy during lower demand weekends, while maintaining availability for sales to higher rated segments during weekends of greater demand.

Finally, the hotel must make a commitment to provide a level of product and service that merits the prices charged. Management has recognized some shortcomings and has already begun a program to upgrade the room product, amenities package, and service levels. If these commitments are realized and sales strategies are executed, there is no reason that L'Hotel Dupree cannot gain its rightful position in the Chicago market and meet, or over-exceed, its 1988 budget.

SALES STRATEGY

Market Segment	Strategy
Corporate Transient	L'Hotel Dupree must maintain its foothold in the corporate market. This includes offering corporations lower than rack rate and participating in promotional efforts to increase awareness and response.
Pure Transient	Advertising/public relations will continue to be directed to build this market.
Corporate Group	The Sales office will be more active and aggressive than ever to capture new markets in the segments of corporate groups and corporate transient.
Weekend Package	Continue to remain competitively priced. Offer a package five to ten dollars less than leading competitors to ensure occupancy during lower demand weekends, while maintaining sales to higher rated segments during weekends of greater demand.

EXHIBIT 7 Projected Media Schedule

Publication	Total Cost
American Way (in flight magazine)	22,830.00
United (in flight magazine)	22,308.00
Wall Street Journal	117,573.13
Manhattan, Inc	11,358.00
New Yorker	54,234.00
Town & Country	13,740.00
New York Times Magazine	78,120.00
Travel & Leisure	10,880.00
European Travel & Leisure	1,935.00
New York Magazine	41,120.00
French/American Chamber of Commerce	823.53
Fortune	16,000.00
Business Week	100,331.51
PSA Magazine (in flight magazine)	7,300.00
California Business	7,965.00
Air Cal (in flight magazine)	9,020.00
Hollywood Reporter	11,975.70
Signiture (Diner's Club Magazine)	5,151.00
Grammy Awards Program	3,440.00
Bishop's Dinner Dance	117.65
Children's Medical Fund Journal	558.24
Master Chef	1,176.47
	537,957.23

CASE 15

ANTUN'S OF WESTCHESTER

In March 1988, John Antun, part owner and managing partner of Antun's of Westchester, was reviewing the financial performance of his operation for fiscal 1987. Sales and profits were up for the second straight year. John knew that these gains were due mainly to the yearly price increases for catering packages. What concerned John most was the fact that customer counts had continued to drop. The past two and half years had been costly to the restaurant with remodeling expenses and increased insurance rates. If the operation was to reach its full potential, then every customer counted.

A recent review of the competition by Antun's had shown a large variation between basic package prices charged for wedding functions. Even though Antun's had raised their package prices 44 percent over the last two years, John wondered if there was still room to go even higher. Since 42 percent of Antun's revenue had come from wedding functions in 1987, any increase in the standard package price would go a long way towards improving cash flow and profits.

HISTORY OF THE RESTAURANT

In 1980 John Antun, of the Antun Catering Company of Queensvillage and Hicksville, purchased a closed restaurant in Elmsford in central Westchester County (Exhibit 1). His objective was to renovate the structure and open a restaurant and catering facility. The building itself was unique. Originally designed as a carriage house, it had had several additions and gave the appearance of an old New England farmhouse.

In 1981, after almost a year of renovations, John and his partner opened a restaurant/nightclub called Razzberry's. The success of the establishment was short lived. Sales and profits dropped off by the third year and in 1985 Razzberry's was closed.

In July of 1985 John Antun and his new partner, an experienced chef, reopened the restaurant. Using his family's name for recognition, John named the new establishment Antun's of Westchester. The concept this time was more in line with his original objective – to be a restaurant/catering facility. Since the building was still in poor shape, John devised a three year remodeling plan with the strategy of changing the inside structure of the restaurant to better suit the objective of the company, group business. Initial volume was good while the catering business was slow with only low-end groups booking the establishment.

EXHIBIT 1 New York Area showing Antun's Three Operations

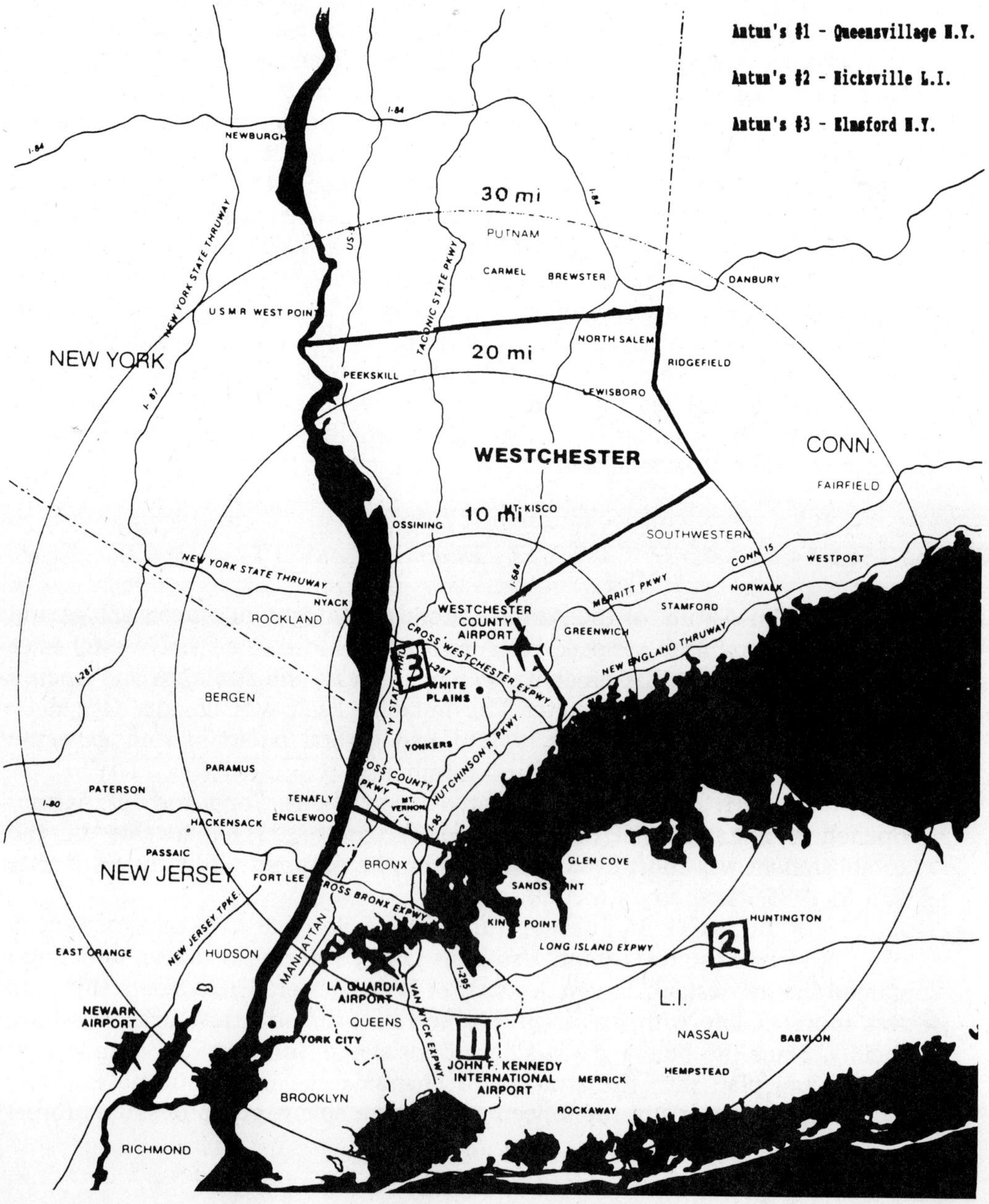

By 1986 John realized that the wedding function segment of the business was the most profitable. In order to take advantage of this opportunity, he started planning all aspects of the business around this segment. The planning done in 1986 paid off in 1987. Sales for wedding functions grew nearly 75 percent. Advanced bookings and sales estimates showed impressive gains for 1988 as well.

The pricing strategy that had developed for the wedding function business over the past two years was continued; each time the facility was remodeled the package price was raised 10 dollars per person. The increases were compared to others in a yearly competitive analysis to make sure that Antun's did not price itself out of the middle market.

Sales for the catering business continued to rise but John noticed that customer counts were starting to drop. As prices were being raised each year, the company felt that the decrease in customer counts would be offset by increased cash flow. Antun's objective was to keep raising package prices until it reached the upper middle segment of the market. The overall goal was to be a quality catering company with an outstanding reputation in Westchester County.

WESTCHESTER COUNTY

Westchester County, New York, nicknamed the "Golden Apple" to set it aside from the "Big Apple" title used for New York City, has been described as a county as "rich and interesting as a small country." County Executive Andrew O'Rourke described the county as:

> *... rich in history with a proud tradition as a cultivator of the arts. Our population provides an extensive skilled and white-collar labor force. Our residents enjoy high median incomes, easy access to mass transit and major transportation links, one of the busiest corporate airports and educational institutions second to none. . . . Just a few minutes from the financial, cultural and communications capital of the world -- New York City -- Westchester provides a hospitable climate for corporate development and is home to the headquarters of many corporate giants such as I.B.M., PepsiCo, General Foods, Readers Digest, Texaco, and the Nestle Company.*

Westchester is divided into three geographic sections - north, central, and southern (Exhibit 2). In 1987, the northern section had 60 percent of the county's area, with a variety of parks and lakes, and some of the most beautiful country homes in the state. This part of the county was generally rural and had very little commercial development. The central section was the smallest part of the county but had some of the largest square footage of office space, the county seat (White Plains), and the only east-west interstate highway in the county. The southern part of the county is divided

EXHIBT 2 Westchester County Showing Locations of Antun's and Competitors

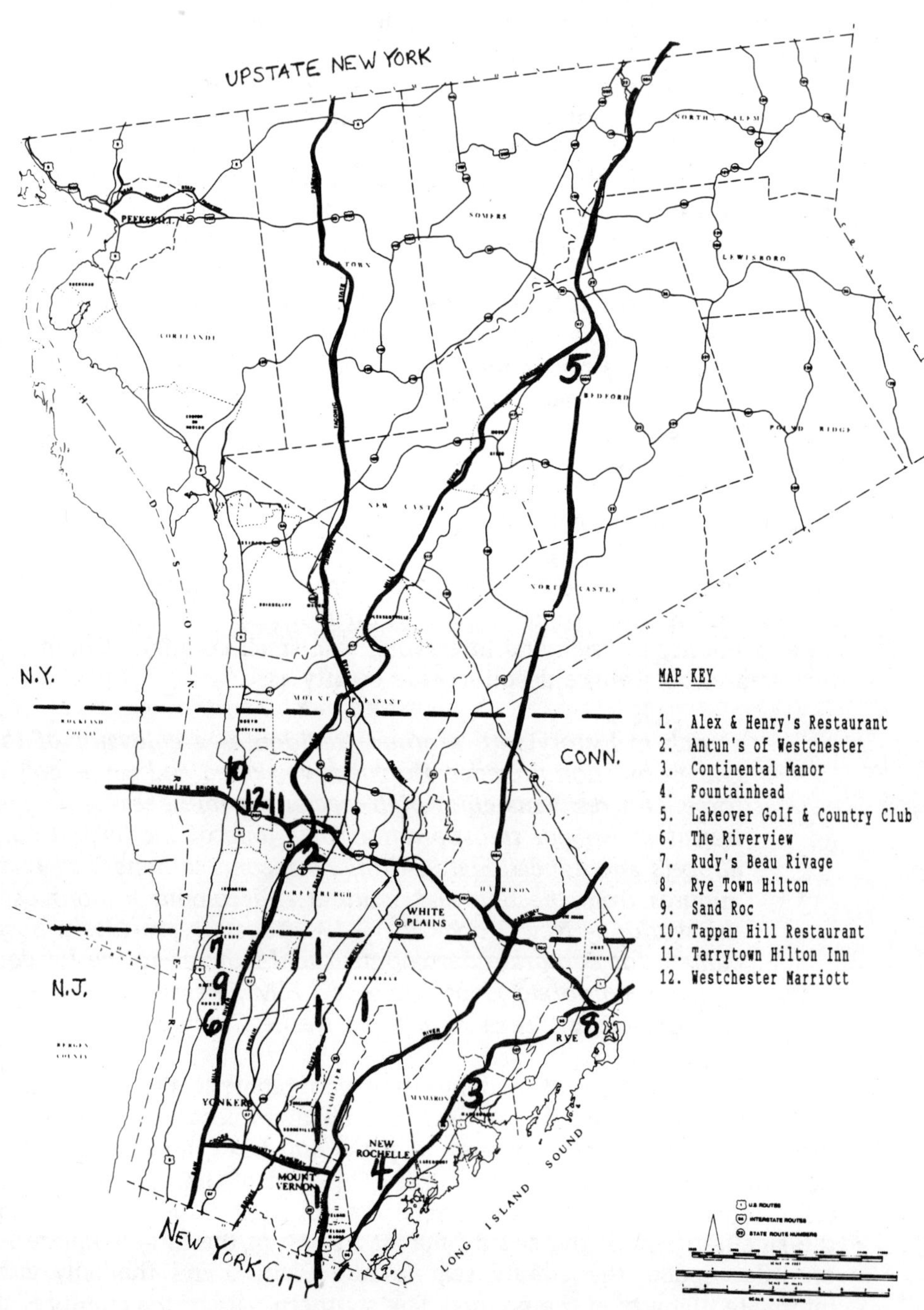

into east and west. The eastern part is located near Long Island Sound and is nicknamed the Gold Coast because it had some of the most expensive real estate in the county. The western section was the most urbanized and borders New York City. The county had ten major road systems, but only two ran east and west. General trends from 1980 to 1987 showed a 20 percent increase in the female population. The age group of 19 to 44 was at an all time high of 200,000 in 1987. Median family income had risen 42 percent since 1980 to $39,099. Overall, the county was expected to have a declining and aging population for the next twenty years.

RAZZBERRY'S

In 1981 John Antun opened Razzberry's with half of the building as a night club with dancing, and the other half as a restaurant. Live entertainment was offered five nights a week. The operation became an immediate success with the young single working person. The largest crowds were on Friday and Saturday nights which generated large profits, mainly from liquor sales.

By 1983, the owners started to see a drop in liquor sales even though patronage remained strong. Investigation showed that the decrease in liquor sales was due largely to the shift in the public's view of drinking, and the passage by state officials of stricter driving when intoxicated laws (DWI). At the same time, the company was facing a large increase in third party liability insurance. This was partly due to higher rates imposed by new Dram Shop laws[1], and partly because the restaurant's parking lot entered directly onto the Saw Mill River Parkway. The downward trend in liquor sales and the continuing tightening of government regulations forced the owners to rethink their business strategy.

ANTUN'S OF WESTCHESTER

In July of 1985, the company closed Razzberry's. The decor was changed and the restaurant was reopened under the new name of Antun's of West-chester. John's new partner, Ron Stytzer, was an executive chef with formal training and a GoldMedal in the 1980 Culinary Olympics. Ron gave the company the opportunity to change the direction of the operation from a lively night club with a limited menu, to one of an upscale dinner house with an expanded continental menu, and a relaxing atmosphere.

The live entertainment was phased out slowly over a two year period. To build restaurant awareness, the company advertised in local papers and in two local discount books with "two-fers" - two meals for the price of one. The twofers were offered on Tuesday, Wednesday, and Thursday

---

[1] Dram Shop laws place liability for damage caused by an intoxicated person on the establishment that served the intoxicating beverages.

evenings in hopes that they would boost low weekday restaurant sales. The program increased customer counts and sales volume, but did very little to improve profits. By October, the company realized that the operation could be more profitable if more time and money were spent on developing the catering business.

THE CATERING FACILITY

By late October 1985, the company began to close the restaurant on Mondays. In August of 1987, the restaurant closed for lunch. As restaurant hours decreased, the company moved to replace lost sales by booking any type of group catered business. The majority of these functions were inexpensive wedding receptions or last minute parties. The weddings were the most profitable because of their size and the higher per person prices. With the previous experience gained from his family operations, John and his partner set out to improve their product so that they could successfully compete in this market. The major priority was to remove the closed-in feeling of the individual dining rooms and expand their size. A renovation project was planned for each year 1986, 1987, and 1988. The early renovations involved mainly removing inner walls and replacing plumbing, electrical, and flooring.

The Tudor Room The first room to be remodeled was a rectangular shaped room located towards the back of the building. The room was redesigned as a traditional banquet room with neutral decor, a dance floor, and seating for average size functions up to 180 people. A unique feature of the room was that it had a door that opened onto a raised outside patio.

The Empire and Georgian Rooms In 1987 two smaller connecting dining rooms between the Tudor room and the lounge were remodeled. Each of these rooms had one whole side that overlooked the patio and garden area. The decor was light colors with wicker chairs, and tables with glass tops. Each room could seat 60 comfortably with added space for buffets or service bars.

The Crystal Garden Room Completed in March of 1988, the Crystal Garden Room was the show piece of the restaurant. The room was created from the old Garden Room, which had acted as the formal restaurant dining room. All dividing walls were removed, the ceiling raised at one end for a cathedral effect and a reinforced dance floor installed. The new space could seat 140 people comfortably. New tables and chairs were added and the floor and walls were covered with light pastel colors. The room was designed as the main reception area for weddings.

Other Banquet Space An additional L-shaped banquet room was located on the second floor of the restaurant. This room was not formally remodeled, but rather redecorated. The room could seat up to 80 people, and was used for business functions or parties that required more privacy.

Outdoor functions could be held in the garden/patio area next to the restaurant. The patio was raised and could hold 100 people for cocktails. The garden area was large enough for functions of up to 250 people and had an outside dance floor and bandstand.

Future Improvements An outside enclosed garden area adjacent to the Crystal Garden room was planned. This area would act as an outdoor reception area and it was estimated that it would hold 100 people. The main parking lot was also scheduled for repair since it had not been resurfaced for many years.

OPERATIONS

The Restaurant In March 1988, Antun's of Westchester operated the restaurant during the hours of:

4:30pm - 10:00pm Tuesday, Wednesday, Thursday
4:30pm - 11:00pm Friday and Saturday
11:30am - 3:00pm Sunday Brunch

Customers dining in the restaurant were served in the Georgian Room, which was part of the lounge and near the front entrance. The menu offered a variety of continental cuisine (Exhibit 3) with an average food check of $17.00. Service was American with waiters dressed conservatively. The restaurant also offered a variety of special holiday buffets.

Information on these buffets was posted in the lobby near the front door. The most popular buffets were Easter, Mothers Day, and Thanksgiving. The restaurant clientele described by management consisted of local people of middle age and income. If a catered function required the Georgian Room, then restaurant customers were moved to another part of the facility. If the entire operation was booked for a function, then a sign was posted in the lobby explaining the situation and inviting customers back at another time.

Catering The Banquet Office was open from 12:00 noon until 10:00 p.m., Tuesday through Sunday. The entire operation was closed on Monday. Wedding functions (showers, rehearsal dinners, wedding receptions, and anniversaries) were expected to account for 90 percent of Antun's catering business in 1988. Almost all wedding functions were held from April to October. The most popular days for wedding receptions were Friday, Saturday, or Sunday.

Customers could design their own functions or choose a wedding package. A wedding package included a cocktail reception with hot and cold hors d'oeuvres, followed by the customer's choice of a variety of sit down dinners. All gratuities and taxes were included (Exhibit 4). Prices for wedding packages varied by day and time. The most expensive package was offered Saturday evening, while the most inexpensive package was Sunday afternoon. The average time for a wedding reception was five hours.

EXHIBIT 3 Menu Entree Selection

Poultry

Chicken Pecan $11.95
Sauteed with crushed pecans, garnished with sliced peaches.

Chicken Calvados $11.95
A boneless breast stuffed with apples, raisins and herbed crumbs, served with a calvados sauce.

Chicken Americana $12.95
Sauteed with shrimps, shallots and mushrooms in a sauce cardinal with cognac and cream.

Chicken Queen Elizabeth $12.95
Breast of chicken with apple brandy, chestnuts, cranberries and cream.

Duckling a la Antun's $13.95
Crispy, roasted Long Island Duckling served with the chef's own combination of peaches and raspberries.

Duckling Orange $13.50
A Long Island Duckling roasted crispy and served with a grand marnier sauce.

Chestnut Duck $13.95
Crispy, roasted with a sauce of chestnuts and Frangelica Liqueur.

Breast of Duckling Vernon $14.50
Tender breast meat sauteed in a sauce of 3 peppercorns.

Beef

New Orleans Cajun Steak $13.95
Coated and blackened with cajun spices, accented with a piquant Louisiana sauce.

Steak and Shrimp $17.95
Our junior shell steak topped with jumbo shrimp, served scampi style, prepared in a butter, garlic and wine sauce.

New York Cut Shell Steak

Broiled to Perfection

Junior Cut $12.95

Large Cut $15.50

Veal

Veal la Epicure $14.95
Scallopine of veal sauteed with fresh melon and crabmeat in a lemon butter and wine sauce.

Veal Marsala $12.95
Medallions of veal, lightly sauteed with fresh mushrooms and marsala wine.

Veal Nouvelle $15.50
Scallopine of veal sauteed with shrimp, mushrooms, imported ham and shallots in a creamy wine sauce.

Veal St. Andrew $14.50
Sauteed scallopine of veal with artichoke hearts, prosciutto ham and mushrooms in a sauce demi glace.

Veal Parmigiana $12.95
A veal cutlet, lightly breaded, sauteed, topped with tomato and cheese, served with linguini.

Seafood

Sole Calypso $13.95
Filet of sole baked with sauterne wine and fresh fruit, topped with slivered almonds.

Broiled Lemon Sole $12.95
Broiled with wine, butter and lemon.

Shrimp Scampi $14.95
Prepared with garlic butter, white wine, served on a bed of rice.

Coconut Shrimp $15.50
Jumbo Shrimp in a batter covered with shredded coconut, deep fried golden brown, served with mango, chutney and an oriental dipping sauce.

Shrimp Martinique $15.50
Sauteed with fresh melon and proscuitto ham in a sauce cardinal flavored with cognac.

Seafood Possilippo $15.95
Shrimp, crabmeat, scallops and mussels served over a bed of linguini with a sauce of garlic, white wine and tomato.

Block Island Swordfish Provencale $14.95
Swordfish steak broiled, topped with a sauce of diced tomato, onion, garlic butter, lemon and wine.

Grilled Salmon Trout Pommeroy $13.95
Grilled baby salmon trout with a delectable sauce made from pommeroy mustard and cream.

Seafood Supreme al Pesto $14.95
Crabmeat, scallops and shrimp simmered in a supreme sauce, served over linguini aldente and laced with sauce pesto and pignoli nuts.

EXHIBIT 4 **Antun's Wedding Function Brochure**

EXHIBIT 4 Wedding Brochure (page 2)

To Begin... A SUMPTUOUS CONTINENTAL COCKTAIL PARTY AND INTERNATIONAL SMORGASBORD

One full hour of unlimited food and beverages served from beautiful, elaborately decorated tables, done in imported laces, ferns, flowers, centerpieces and candelabra and Sterling Silver trays.

UNLIMITED LIQUORS...

Served from stationary or rolling bars, by uniformed bartenders. Expertly mixed and properly served coctails to satisfy the most discriminating taste.

Manhattans * Martinis * Whiskey Sours * Daiquiries
Bacardis * Scotch Sours * Apricot Sours * Orange Blossoms
Pina Coladas * Bloody Marys * Strawberry Daiquiries

Generously poured straight liquors: – Popular, Name Brands

Rye * Scotch * Vodka * Gin * Bourbon * Rum
Budweiser Beer and Champagne

CHEESE AND WINE DISPLAY...

Many large wedges of imported cheeses:
Swiss * Gouda * Jarlsburg * Fontina * Provlone
Artfully displayed on a butcher block with fresh fruit,
French Bread and Italian Bread

Imported Portuguese Rose Wine * Italian Red Wine * French Chablis

COLD BUFFET...

Elaborately decorated and displayed by our own Garde Manger

CRUDITE... *Miniaturized raw vegetables served with a Savory Dip*

MELON CARVINGS filled with a Medley of Fresh Fruits

COLD CANAPES *consisting of...*

Filet of Anchovies * Red and Black Caviar * Smoked Salmon
Longostino * Chicken Liver Pate * Sweet Red Peppers
Sausage Pete * Ripe and Queen Olives * Artichoke Hearts * Sardines

COUNTRY FRENCH CHARCUTERIE...

Old country style basket trays, with tureens of cornichons, pommroy mustard, assorted sausages and salamis, dijon mustard served with special garnishes and seasonal fruits.

BREADS OF ALL NATIONS...

Unique and exotic breads from around the world displayed on a maple butcher block.

EXHIBIT 4 Wedding Brochure (page 3)

SERVED FROM SILVER TRAYS. . . BUTLER STYLE

Miniature Frankfurters wrapped in Puff Pastry

Swedish Meatballs in a Sauce Stockholm

Potato Skins with Cheddar Cheese and Bacon Bits

Crab Rangoon with a Plum Sauce

Thai Sate with Peanut Sauce

Rumacki

* * *

Hors d'Oeurve Mexicali

Icelandic fish Tid-Bits with tartare sauce

Old World Potato Pancakes with apple sauce

Louisiana Shrimp with cajun mayonnaise

Buffalo Wings with a blue cheese dip * Country Ka-Bobs

Oriental Egg Rolls with duck sauce * Mussels a la Maison

Vol au Vant de Mer * Oysters Rockefeller * Parmasean Toast

And After. . .

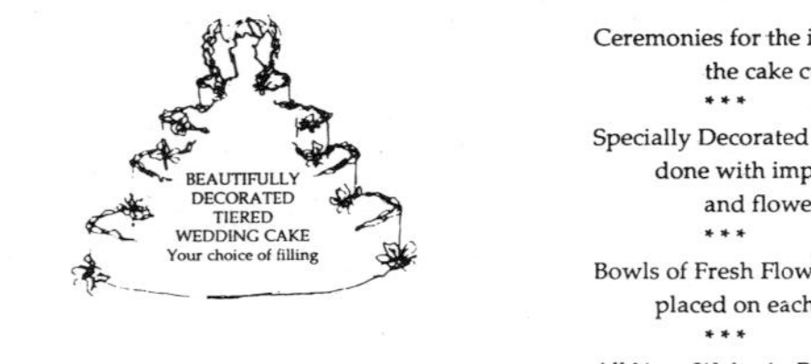

Ceremonies for the introductions and
the cake cutting

***

Specially Decorated Cake and Bridal Tables,
done with imported laces, candelabra, ferns
and flowers

***

Bowls of Fresh Flowers,
placed on each table, your choice of colors.

***

All Your Waiter's, Bartender's and
Captains Gratuities

***

Linens in your choice of colors

***

Personalized matches and stirrers with
Bride and Groom's name and date of wedding.

Liquor Service

ROLLING BARS, tended by uniformed bartenders serving
UNLIMITED Rye, Scotch, Gin, Vodka, Bourbon,
Manhattans, Martinis, Whiskey Sours, Daiquiries, Scotch Sours,
Apricot Sours, and Orange Blossoms, served for four hours.
Budweiser Beer, served unlimited throughout the reception
as requested.
Soft Drinks, served unlimited throughout the reception
as requested.

AFTER DINNER DRINKS
AND CORDIALS
served unlimited
Brandy, Sambucca,
Baily's Irish Cream,
Grand Marnier,
Amaretto

IMPORTED WINES
Unlimited imported Red, White and
Rose Wine served througout
the entire reception.

CHAMPAGNE Served throughout
the entire reception.

EXHIBIT 4 Wedding Brochure (page 4)

For Dinner. . .

The Toast to the Bride and Groom. . .

Traditional Bubbling Champagne

served Ice Cold

Appetizer. . . Fresh Fruit Princess, Adorned with Shaved

Coconut and miniature Marshmallows

served in Silver Supremes

– or –

A seasonal presentation of fresh fruits to include

a filled Hawaiian pineapple boats

– or –

Melon Crowns Garnished with Berries

Baskets of Oven Fresh Rolls and Bowls of Creamery Butter

Salad. . . Three Lettuce Salad with a wedge of tomato and served

with our Famous House Dressing and Seasoned Croutons

Entrees. . . ***–YOUR GUEST'S CHOICE OF THREE ENTREES –***

Breast of Chicken, Calvados

A Boneless Breast lightly stuffed with Apples, Raisins, Herbed Crumbs

and served with a Calvados Sauce

– or –

Roast Prime Ribs of Blue Ribbon Beef

au Jus

– or–

Grilled Alaskan Salmon Steak

with a lemon butter sauce

Vegetable. . . Fresh Seasonal Vegetable or Fresh Broccoli,

lightly steamed

Potatoes. . . Baked Idaho Potato

served with Sour Cream and Chives

Dessert. . . A Special Ceremony Presenting. . .

Flaming Cherries Jubilee

presented on French Vanilla Ice Cream

Beverages. . . Steaming Hot Coffee * Tea

Brewed Decaffeinated coffee

A variety of public and business functions accounted for the rest of Antun's catering business. These functions were usually smaller in size and held on weekdays. The strongest month for these packages was December. Two mini-packages were available:

Package #1 - NY Strip Steak or Filet of Sole
Tossed Salad
Baked Potato
Beverage and Dessert
Price: $18.95 each

Package #2 - Prime Rib or Grilled Salmon Steak
Tossed Salad
Baked Potato
Beverage and dessert
Price: $22.95 each

An additional $7.00 per person was charged for a cocktail hour. All taxes and gratuities were included in the prices.

Antun's owners had also tested a new catered "hot box lunch" concept for delivery to local corporate office buildings in White Plains. This program was designed to replace the loss of daytime sales when the restaurant closed for lunch. Introduction of this product was postponed until more help could be hired and trained.

Wedding Functions The wedding function market primarily consisted of one time users. According to Antun's management, important decisions about the catered function were shared between the bride and her parents. Location and facilities were more important to the bride, while price and services were more important to the parents. Management believed that 90 percent of the time the bride got her way. Antun's records showed that a majority of their wedding business came from Yonkers, a white middle class city in southern Westchester county. Other area markets were of less importance because of geographic and social boundaries. The market breakdown was as follows:

Yonkers 60%,
White Plains 30%
All Others 10% - Connecticut,New Jersey,Northern Westchester County, The Bronx

Other Functions Business meetings and other small functions came primarily from the local area which included White Plains.

Financial Performance First year sales for Antun's in 1985 were $1.25 million. The owners' figures for successive years showed annual sales increases of 21 to 22 percent. The percentage of catering to restaurant sales increased from 15 percent the first year to a projected 65 percent for the year 1988. Basic package prices also increased during the same period from $35 to $65. On the other hand, average customer counts showed annual

EXHIBIT 5 Wedding Function Statistics

	1985	1986	1987	1988
Basic Package Price/person	$35	$45	$55	$65
Catering as a % of Sales	15%	35%	50%	65%*
Catering Sales (000)	$188	$536	$935	$1469*
Wedding Function Customer Counts	4017	8917	12750	16950*
Number of Wedding Functions	35	80	120	165*
Avg. Size of Wedding Function	114	111	106	103*
Total Sales	1250**	1530	1870	2660*

* Based on two months sales, future bookings, budget estimates
** Includes sales of Razzberry's and Antun's, approximately six months each.

decreases both in the restaurant and package business (Exhibit 5).

THE MARKETING SITUATION

Competition Antun's reviewed the direct competition in Westchester county once a year (Exhibit 6). Direct competition was described as any company that had catering facilities and offered packages in the middle price segment of the market. The study showed the total number of seats available as:

Caterers with Facilities	1400
Hotels	1950
Restaurants	950
Public Clubs	300

(Private clubs are not included in the competition analysis because their state liquor licenses restrict their selling alcohol to non-members.)

Indirect competition described by management were public halls, religious centers, and specialty sites such as boats, museums, or historical buildings. These locations were excluded because they were not in the middle price segment of the market. Conference centers and resorts were not identified because it was believed that they served different markets.

Management used four factors in classifying the competition for the middle market segment. These factors were price of major packages (low,

EXHIBIT 6 Antun's Competition

Alex & Henry's Restaurant	
Location:	Scarsdale, NY. and Bronx NY.
Facility:	4 Banquet Rooms, maximum seating 400, New Italian decor.
Reputation:	30 Years Experience
Catering:	Variety of packages, Free Parking, T&T extra.
Package Price:	$90 - 100
Restaurant:	50 seats, Continental, average food, open 7 days for lunch or dinner.
Antun's of Westchester	
Location:	Elmsdale, NY. (Family has two other locations)
Facility:	5 Banquet rooms, Maximium seating, 300, (plus cocktail area), outdoor patio and garden area, local landmark, free parking.
Reputation:	6 years present location, 40 years in New York City.
Catering:	Variety of packages, Good food and service, T&T included.
Package Price:	$60, Dinner party packages, 18.95 to 22.95
Restaurant:	60 seats, Continental, good food, 5 days for dinner, Sunday brunch
Continental Manor	
Location:	Mamaroneck, NY.
Facility:	1 Banquet room, Maximum seating 300, Uninteresting building.
Reputation:	13 years experience
Catering:	Limited package, poor food, large portions.
Package price:	$45
Restaurant:	No.
Fountainhead	
Location:	New Rochelle, NY and 4 others in NY and NJ.
Facility:	Standard catering hall, 4 Banquet rooms with bars and checkrooms. Maximum seating 300.
Reputation:	15 years at present location
Catering:	Variety of packages, Kosher, good food
Package price:	$60-70
Restaurant:	No
Lakeover Golf and Country Club Inc.	
Location:	Bedford Hills NY.
Facility:	Seperate catering facilities from club house. 4 private banquet rooms, maximum seating 300. Overlooking lake.
Reputation:	8 years
Catering:	Variety of packages, upscale service
Package price:	$60
Restaurant:	Club house restaurant for members and guests.

EXHIBIT 6 Antun's Competition (page 2)

The Riverview

Location:	Hastings-on-Hudson, NY
Facility:	2 Banquet rooms overlooking Hudson River, Maximum seating - 300, Outdoor patio, free parking.
Reputation:	12 years
Catering:	Limited packages, poor food
Package prices:	$50
Restaurant:	no

Rudy's Beau Rivage

Location:	Dobbs Ferry, NY
Facility:	2 Banquet rooms overlooking Hudson River
Reputation:	15 years
Catering:	Variety of packages, Good food
Package price:	$50
Restaurant:	no

Rye Town Hilton Inn

Location:	Rye Brook NY
Facility:	Excellent, pool, saunas, tennis courts, variety of banquet rooms, maximum seating 400
Reputation:	15 years
Catering:	Variety of packages, excellent food and service
Package price:	$100-125, plus add-ons. Weekend packages available.
Restaurant:	yes, average food

Sand Roc

Location:	Hastings-on-Hudson
Facility:	Large ballrooms, Maximum seating 500, outdoor patio, Italien decor
Reputation:	14 years
Catering:	Variety of packages, good food
Package price:	$65
Restaurant:	No

Tappan Hill Restaurant

Location:	Tarrytown, NY
Facility:	The Old Mark Twain house overlooking the Hudson river, Several banquet rooms, maximum seating 250.
Reputation:	15 years
Catering:	Several packages
Package price:	$100
Restaurant:	yes, very good food

EXHIBIT 6 Antun's Competition (page 3)

Tarrytown Hilton Inn	
Location:	Tarrytown, NY
Facility:	Excellent, Indoor/outdoor pool, Exercise room, tennis, saunas, meeting room, Maximum seating 350.
Reputation:	15 years
Catering:	Variety of packages, average food
Package price:	$100-125 with add-ons, weekend packages available.
Restaurant:	yes, average food

Westchester Marriott	
Location:	Tarrytown, NY
Facility:	Variety of rooms, maximum seating 500, pool, night club, spa, lounge.
Reputation:	8 years
Catering:	Variety of packages, Average food and excellent service.
Package price:	$100-125 with add-ons, weekend packages available.
Restaurant:	yes, good food.

middle, high), location (ease of access to parts of the county and surroundings), reputation, and facilities. The overall determining factor, according to management, was price. Management identified reputation as a major buying influence for customers in the upper end of the market segment. Antun's analysis of the competition and where John Antun thought the restaurant should be positioned is shown in Exhibit 7.

Marketing Objectives In March 1988, Antun's owners' major marketing objective was to reposition their product by price to the upper middle segment of the wedding function market. A secondary objective was to develop other types (brands) of catering products in order to diversify revenue sources.

Marketing Strategies In order to reach their first objective, Antun's had developed these strategies:

1. Develop a positive image in Westchester county.
2. Offer a stronger price/value product to the customer.
3. Review the competition yearly to determine new opportunities.
4. Raise prices slowly each year in conjunction with the completion of a renovation project.

Advertising Antun's advertising consisted primarily of ads for specialty events in local papers, and yearly ads in the *New York Wedding Planner* and the Westchester Telephone Yellow Pages. In-house advertising was also done with signs in the lobby and promotional information printed on the menu. The owners believed that the majority of their wedding function business was referred by members of previous wedding parties or guests of past functions.

Marketing Environment The wedding function market in the United States was showing signs of continued expansion. Marriage rates per 1000 population had risen almost continuously since 1960. The number of second marriages was at an all time high. The average age of first-marriage brides and grooms had increased since 1963. In this older, more educated market couples had the resources to allow for more flexibility and creativity in planning their weddings. One example of this was the rise in weekend long "renaissance weddings" where married couples had a second, later ceremony and invited their friends to participate in a gala weekend. Other wedding trends are shown in Exhibit 8.

John Antun figured the time was ripe to tap this lucrative market.

EXHIBIT 7 Competitive Analysis Matrices

BASIC WEDDING PACKAGE PRICE RANGE

FACILITIES

	Low $50 & Under	Medium $60-70	Target $75-85	High $90-125
Above Avg.		Lakeview Country Club		Hilton.T.Inn Hilton R.Inn Marriott
Avg	Riverview	Fountainhead Sand Roc Antun's	Desired Postion	Alex & Henry Restaurant Tappan Hill Resturant
Below Avg.	Continental Manor Rudy's Beau Rivage			

REPUTATION

	Low $50 & Under	Medium $60-70	Target $75-85	High $90-125
Very Good				Alex & Henry Tappan Hill Hilton T.Inn Hilton R.Inn Marriott
Good	Rudy's Beau Rivage	Fountainhead Sand Roc Antun's Lakeover CC.	Desired Position	
Poor	Continental Manor Riverview			

LOCATION

	Low $50 & Under	Medium $60-70	Target $75-85	High $90-125
Above Avg.		Antun's	Desired Position	Tappan Hill Hilton T.Inn Marriott
Avg.	Riverview Rudy Beau Rivage	Sand Roc		Alex & Henry
Below Avg.	Continental Manor	Fountainhead Lakeview CC.		Hilton R.Inn

EXHIBIT 8 Wedding Market Trends

In 1986, *Bride's Magazine* sent 3500 questionnaires to a national sample of newstand buyers and subscribers who had requested information from the magazine. The purpose was to provide current information on the formal wedding market. 1469 replies were received and indicated the following:

* 95% had a formal wedding
* More ceremonies took place in the afternoon (60%) than the evening (26%), or morning (14%)
* 19% said weddings were combined with other family celebrations
* 100% had a wedding reception
* 91% had a rehearsal dinner
* 76% of rehearsal dinners were hosted by groom's parents
* 43% had receptions at either a club or catering facility, 10% at a hotel or restaurant, 15% at a religious center, 12% at a community hall, and 10% at miscellaneous locations
* Average number of guests attending weddings was 207. The largest percentage group was 150 - 200 (23%). Median number of guests attending was 184.
* 53% chose a buffet reception. 37% chose a sit-down dinner. 10% had miscellaneous choices.

In 1988, *Bride's* reported the following "Wedding Planning Secrets:"

* More couples are paying for their own wedding expenses.
* Grooms are becoming more involved in planning weddings and are particularly interested in the areas of menu, music, and liquor.
* Couples are having larger weddings and larger receptions, with all the traditional trimmings, regardless of age or if they ahve been married before.
* Menus are becoming lighter (pastas, salads, crepes, and seafood) to accommodate the nutrition conscious; more varied (tapas, pasta, sushi, Cajun creoles, special coffees) to please eclectic palates.
* Buffets are the norm instead of sit-down dinners.
* Weekend-long "Renaissance" weddings with unlimited entertainment possibilities are becoming more common.
* More couples are using wedding consultants or party planners to assist in wedding arrangements.

In 1988, the New York State Department of Health reported the following statistics:

* The New York metropolitan area had experienced a 33% increase in the issuance of marriage licenses since 1980, a 9% increase over the national average.
* Marriage licenses issued in Westchester County were increasing at a rate of 12% a year. 8073 were issued in 1986.

SECTION 5

RESEARCH

AND

MARKETING

INFORMATION

CASE 16

WAS IT WORTH IT?

The Americana Canyon Hotel in Palm Springs, California suffered, as did all Palm Springs hotels, during the summer off-season. To a lesser degree, occupancy was also low during the shoulder seasons of spring and fall. Unlike many Palm Springs hotels, the Americana Canyon stayed open during these periods and did the best it could with the market it could draw. Management, however, felt that the hotel had more to offer if it could find the market to which to offer it, and could offer it at a very affordable price during this time of the year.

The marketing department was assigned the task of developing a package that would draw a new market during, to start, the spring shoulder season. The hotel had the usual amenities of Palm Springs resorts including a golf course and multiple tennis courts. It also had a proportionately high number of suites. The marketing department felt that these were the facilities to feature, but it needed something extra. The extra turned out to be a Lincoln Town car for customers who were flying in to the Los Angeles airport and would have to make the commute to Palm Springs, over 100 miles away. The package developed is shown in Exhibit 1 and had the additional attraction for the Canadian market of offering to convert Canadian dollars at par with U.S. dollars, a savings of about 12 cents a dollar.

The ad in Exhibit 1 was primarily aimed at the travel agent. It ran for four weeks in all major travel agent trade publications. Additionally, it ran in Sunday sections of Chicago and Vancouver, British Columbia newspapers. The response was excellent. Spring weeks quickly filled up increasing the normal 40 to 50 percent occupancy to 70 percent occupancy or better.

Management and the marketing department were pleased with the results, but thought that further evaluation was needed. The promotion had not been inexpensive. First, there was the advertising expense; on top of this were the travel agents' commissions on an already low rate. A further additional cost were the Lincoln Town cars. Management's first question was: Was all this worth it, or could we have done as well with normal off-season discount rates and without the extra expenses?

The second question was: What made the promotion a success? Was it the total package, or individual parts of it? If the latter, which parts?

Management didn't have the answers to these questions and decided that the only way to get them was to commission some research.

EXHIBIT 1 Travel Agent Ad for the Americana Canyon Promotion

CASE 17

BON AMI RESTAURANT

"Something is wrong, Phil," said Joe Smith, the manager of Bon Ami Restaurant[1] in June, 1989. "It just doesn't make sense. Our customers tell us they love us. In fact, we hear nothing but compliments. Read the comments in the guest book that people sign on the way out; they indicate nothing but praise. Newspaper reviews have also been excellent. One writer in Baltimore has stated that we are one of the best restaurants in the state. Yet business is going nowhere but down. Slowly, to be sure, but surely. Look at the graphs I ran on the PC (Exhibits 1 and 2). Customer counts are down. And worse, we're losing from $12,000 to $15,000 a month."

"Okay, Joe," replied Phil Jones, the backer and principal owner of Bon Ami, "I'm well aware of the figures and its my pocket the money is coming out of. We've gone over the costs item by item and they're certainly not out of line compared to national operating figures. Our food cost stays constant around 31 percent and our bar cost at 19 percent. What's killing us of course is our labor cost at 35 percent. But we can't cut labor unless we reduce the service level we're trying to provide. And that would defeat our whole purpose of being here. Clearly we have to find a way to do more volume."

"Well, we've certainly advertised enough," replied Joe."Just look at the figures of what we've spent. I'm begining to think there just aren't enough people in this meat and potatoes town who appreciate good food. Maybe we'll have to change our concept. But how do we know? And how do we know what to change it to? And how do we know if it will work? Do we really know why people come or don't come here? If they don't come here, where do they go? After all, there's only one other French restaurant in the area that competes with us and they can't all go there. Maybe we're just not meeting the demands of the market. I think we had better learn something about the market before we go off half-cocked again. I suggest we do a market research study. What do you think?"

---

1 Names and locations have been disguised.

EXHIBIT 1 Weekly Lunch Sales ($'000) 1987 – 1989

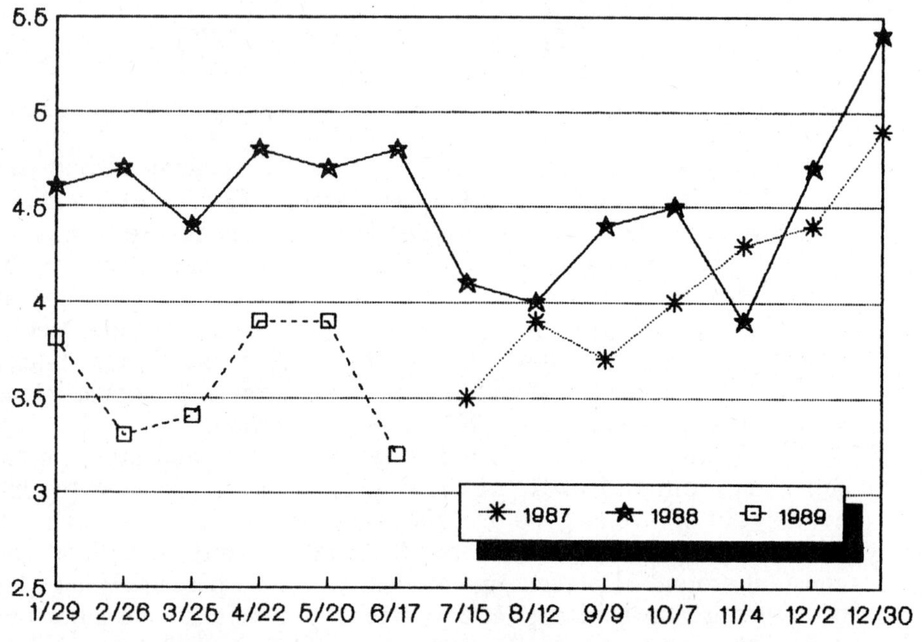

EXHIBIT 2 Weekly Dinner Sales ($'000) 1987 – 1989

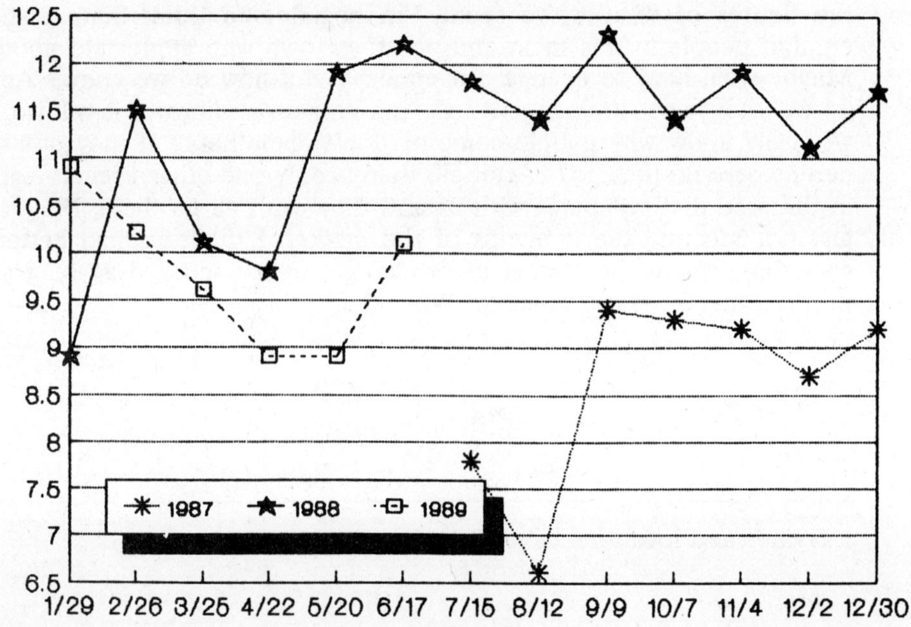

HISTORY OF BON AMI

Bon Ami Restaurant opened in July of 1987. It had been well planned and well executed and almost no expense had been spared. Almost everyone would agree that it was an elegant restaurant. The owners were especially proud of the elegant bathrooms with their gold fixtures.

Phil Jones was the principal owner of Bon Ami. Joe Smith and his wife were minor partners and managers of the restaurant. Phil Jones was in his sixties and essentially retired from business. He had accumulated a small fortune as one of the original McDonald's franchisees. After he sold his franchise back to McDonald's he decided he would like to own a truly different type of restaurant for more upscale tastes, but he did not want to be involved in active management. His search for an active and managing partner eventually led him to Joe Smith and his wife.

Joe Smith was 36 years old. He was the graduate of a four year university hotel program. After college, Joe had worked for awhile for Radisson hotels in food and beverage. He subsequently went to work for T.G.I. Friday's restaurants and opened three of their new units. Along the way he had obtained substantial cooking experience as well as management knowhow. At the age of 27 he decided he wanted to operate his own restaurant.

The Smith's first attempt at their own operation was a restaurant on the Maryland coast that they leased on a year-to-year basis in 1976. The realistic operating season, however, was only four months. They ended the first season $50,000 in debt. Two years later they had paid off the debt and were making a profit. By 1980, the Smiths felt they had outgrown the location. They were looking for an expansion location in Baltimore when they heard of Phil Jones's search for a partner. The partners shared a common dream - to establish a top class French restaurant.

Phil Jones had lived in this same Delaware community all his life and had many friends there. When he decided to open an upscale restaurant he conducted his own survey among his friends. This told him that what people in the area wanted was a French restaurant. Money was no obstacle and Phil was willing to spend what it took. On the other hand, he was not inclined to build an ego monument either. A man of humble origin, he had never had a financial failure and he was determined that his new restaurant would also be profitable.

THE RESTAURANT

Under construction, the new restaurant grew from an original 1500 square feet to about 8000 square feet with two dining rooms that seated a total of 135 people. There was also a sizeable kitchen, office and storage space, and room in the basement for later conversion to small banquet rooms. A nationally known food and wine consultant was retained at a sizeable fee to advise on the name, the menu, the layout, the style, the decor, and the promotion of the restaurant. A continental chef with an excellent reputation was hired.

As one entered Bon Ami, he or she first passed through a massive double door under an eye-catching kiosk roof. The only external identification of the restaurant was a highly polished brass plate with the name Bon Ami on it. Immediately inside was a wide entrance hall with a maitre d's desk at the end. In back of this desk were floor-to-ceiling wine racks. To the right was a room seating 40. This room had banquettes along the front of the building. Behind the banquettes and in the center of the wall, there was a small cut-glass window to the outside. Across the room was an elegant polished rosewood bar with eight stools.

On the other side of the entrance way was a dining room seating 95 persons on two levels. The front of the room was again banquettes, but there was no window to the outside. Both rooms were furnished with French provincial tables, chairs and other decor. Joe Smith was quoted in an interview as saying, "We designed the restaurant to be like a French chateau, with one dining room for casual meals and another room for formal dining." The formal room to the left had linen table cloths; the informal room had no cloths or placemats. Both rooms had fine crystal, silver and china, and fresh flowers on every table.

The restaurant property itself was part of a small strip shopping center in the wealthiest suburb of Wilmington, built and owned by Mr. Jones. On one end of the strip and next to Bon Ami was a bank. On the other end was an inexpensive but quality family restaurant, and a branch of an upscale area department store. In-between were small exclusive shops. Bon Ami was indistinguishable from its neighbors in this strip except for the front brick facade in place of windows, the kiosk, and the brass name plate. It was not readily recognizable as a restaurant. In fact, some had said that it looks more like a funeral parlor.

THE AREA

The suburb of Newport in which Bon Ami was located had one of the highest per capita incomes in the state. It was about five miles from the center of Wilmington and was a bedroom community for a blend of corporate executives and small business owners.

The life style, however, was very conservative. The remainder of the greater Wilmington area (population about 150,000) was a changing scene but one that clung to tradition. Almost on the Maryland state line, 8 miles to the southwest, was the well-to-do community of Newark, many residents of which commuted to Baltimore, 50 miles away, as well as to Wilmington. Other areas of Wilmington were more middle class and some were strictly working class. Across the Delaware River, about six miles from Newport, were a number of other communities in Salem County, New Jersey. Many of the residents of this area worked in the Wilmington area. Exhibit 3 shows a map of the area.

EXHIBIT 3 Map of the Wilmington Area

According to *Restaurant Business' Restaurant Growth Index* (RGI), eating and drinking sales in the Wilmington area were $249 million in 1988, but the population was somewhat less likely to eat out than the national average. The RGI index of 106, where 100 means that supply exactly equals demand, indicated that the market growth potential was slightly higher than the average American city.

THE DEVELOPMENT

When Bon Ami first opened, for dinner only in May 1987, they did no advertising. This was because the consultant had said that her name was so famous that people would come from the publicity alone. When very few came in the first two months, the partners decided that they had better do something. According to Joe Smith, a rumor started soon after opening that Bon Ami was so elegant, dinner cost $100 per person. Actually, meals with beverage averaged just under $30 per person at dinner.

Creative advertising was commenced with a decidedly French flavor. For example, when a brunch was introduced on Sunday it was advertised as Le Bon Brunch. Buffets were called Le Bon Buffet. The restaurant was described as "Bon Elegant" versus "Bon Stuffy" to dispel the $100 check rumor. Area newspapers were the primary media used.

Business at Bon Ami picked up after advertising was commenced. Average dinner covers reached 60 per night, partly due to an average of 125 on Saturdays. Subsequently, Bon Ami opened for luncheon with menu items priced from $2.95 to $6.95 and business was excellent almost from the start. Check averages at luncheon eventually grew to $12.00 per person.

Other changes took place as time progressed. Management discovered that the local definition of French food was Caesar salad, quiche, crepes, and so forth - not nouvelle or classical cuisine. Adaptations were made without sacrificing the integrity of the food. A prime rib buffet was introduced on Sundays. An eight item early bird dinner menu for those who arrived before 6:30 pm, with all entrees priced at $9.95, was added to meet the demands of customers who wanted lower priced meals. Originally it was planned to serve this menu in the casual (bar) dining room, but it was found that status conscious customers didn't want to sit in the "discount" room. Early-bird check averages were constant at around $10.00 per person; business was brisk at this time and eventually became 60 percent of the total dinner covers during the week, with a $15.00 check average. Exhibit 4 shows various menus of the restaurant at the time of the case writing.

The menu was accompanied by an excellent wine list starting at $17.50 per bottle for Muscadet, Alsace riesling, Entre deux Mers, Rose d'Anjou, white Zinfandel, and a Cotes du Ventoux from the Rhone valley. For around $20.00, one could obtain Vouvray, Macon, California Chenin Blanc, Sauvignon Blanc, Fume Blanc and Gewurtztraminer, Tavel rose, or a red Graves, Medoc, or Beaujolais Villages. Other listings ranged from California Chardonnay, Pouilly Fuisse, Grand Cru Chablis, Santenay and Chateau Talbot for $25 to $30.00 to Chateau Latour 1976 at $140.00. No half bottles were offered.

As business developed at Bon Ami, a number of customers became regulars. Others never returned or did so only on special occasions. Business stabilized for a short period at about $70,000 per month. About 10 percent of this was from off-premise catering, 11 percent was liquor sales, and 13 percent was wine sales. The casual or bar dining room was seldom used, for meals or for drinking.

In 1989 business began to slip. Some tie-in direct mail coupon campaigns were initiated with little effect. Two-for-one dinners were very popular for a six week period with those who "seemed to come out of the woods" but did not fit Bon Ami's clientel image. Business resumed its slide when they were discontinued. Customer comments continued to be good but customer counts fell at both lunch and dinner. Management tried various new approaches but none seemed to have any more than initial impact, if that. Revenue dropped to an average of $60,000 a month, including outside catering, with about two-thirds of this at dinner and one-third at lunch.

CONCLUSION

"Well Joe," said Phil in response to the question about doing a research study, "we are a one-of-a-kind restaurant in this area, that is for sure. All of our competition is lower priced, less formal, and more casual, and none of them have food or service that reaches our level. This certainly defines for us a unique niche in the market place. We have made some accommodations to the meat and potato crowd by taking the tuxedos off our waiters and by introducing buffets, brunch, early-bird specials, and so forth. We have a loyal clientel; we just don't have enough of it. Comments on our food and service continue to be excellent. Yet, obviously, business is slipping and we are losing money, so we must be doing something wrong. I'm not opposed to change and I'm not opposed to a research study. But I am opposed to throwing good money after bad. What is this study going to tell us? What do we expect to learn? The table top study conducted by our advertising agency a few weeks ago told us that we're doing everything right and nothing about what we should change (Exhibit 5). As a result, the agency thinks we have to put even more emphasis in our advertising on the quality of our food and our French ambience. We've thought this all along. How is this study going to be any different?

EXHIBIT 4 Bon Ami Menus

Our Philosophy

We pride ourselves on being a restaurant dedicated to quality. Certainly, by today's standards, any experienced traveler knows our offerings are more than affordable. Bon Ami is for those who appreciate the finer things in life. It is a restaurant built upon attention to detail. With rare exceptions, we make everything on premise. Many of our items are now available for you to take home. Our palmier cookies have been served at a wide variety of functions, from recitals in Baltimore to a meeting with the Governor at the State House. The legend of our rolls has been covered numerous times by the Baltimore papers. Our pride continues...Our fresh herbs are cultivated in our own greenhouse.

Christine's soups are now available by the quart, and we now do regular off-premise catering.

For those of you who are looking for that "special" place for your next private party, consider Bon Ami. We do have certain size restrictions. However, our specialities include executive and business breakfasts, cocktail receptions, luncheons, and small dinner parties.

Thank you for welcoming us into this community. We are proud to be here.

Your Hosts

Active Members of: National Restaurant Association
Chaine de Rotisseurs
Les Amis d' Escoffier
Maryland Restaurant Association
Greater Baltimore Ch. of Commerce
American Culinary Federation, Inc.

LUNCHEON MENU

SIDE DISHES

Onion Soup	*3.25*
Bon Ami Salad	*2.75*
Soup of the Day	*3.75*

ENTREES
**All hot entrees include a Bon Ami salad*

Jumbo Shrimp and Orange Salad	*8.75*
Chicken Livers Madeira with Spaetzle	*7.45*
Fluffy Omelettes with Sauteed Potatoes	*6.45*
An Assortment of French Terrines, Pates, and Gallantines served with a glass of wine	*8.45*
Charcoal Broiled Norwegian Salmon with Summer Vegetables	*9.45*
Fresh Maine Shrimp and Pasta Salad with Avocados	*8.45*
Oysters and Scallops on Spinach Fettucine with Pernod Cream Sauce	*10.45*
A Ragout of Tender Braised Meats with a Bouquet of Vegetables in a Savory Sauce	*7.45*
Baked Stuffed Sole with Nantua Sauce	*8.45*
Chicken and Mushroom Crepe	*8.45*
The Boss' Lunch (Low in sodium, cholesterol & calories)	*Price Varies*
Caesar Salad with Croissant	*8.25*

SUNDAY BRUNCH

BUFFET $14.95

Enjoy a complimentary Bloody Mary, Glass of Champagne, or Orange Juice, and sample our Award Winning Cuisine.

In April of 1989, our Chefs received numerous awards from the American Culinary Federation at the Baltimore Restaurant Show, including our Executive Chef, Christine Buchholz, who won a Gold Medal. Each week Bon Ami Chefs will demonstrate these skills in the food items we present on our Sunday Buffet.

The presentation will offer a variety of hot and cold foods, with many items changing each week. Our Buffet will be committed to the quality and artistry we have been recognized for both regionally and nationally.

BRUNCH a la CARTE

Entrees include complimentary Baker's Basket, coffee, tea or milk

Sauteed Chicken Livers with Spaetzle	*8.95*
Grilled Fresh Norwegian Salmon (compound butter)	*11.45*
The Classic - Eggs Benedict	*10.45*
French Style Herb Omelette with Hash Browns	*7.95*

EARLY BIRD MENU

AMERICAN FARE WITH A FRENCH FLAIR !

Appetizers

A Slice of Country Terrine	*3.50*
Mushroom Caps - Seafood Stuffing & Gruyere Cheese	*3.95*
Shrimp Cocktail	*4.95*
Pasta Primavera	*4.50*

Entrees

Grilled Cod Steaks - Basted with a savory sauce. Served with vegetables of the day and Bliss Potatoes

Prime Rib with Watercress & Potato Puree and braised carrots and leeks LIMITED AVAILABILITY

American Cassoulet - Great Northern Beans with Pork Tenderloin, grilled Duck, and Sausage

Baked Stuffed Shrimp

Creole Fried Chicken - accompanied by Potato Gratin and Green Beans

Seafood Kabob - Skewered grilled Scallops, Shrimp, Halibut, and Salmon

California Veal Birds - Medallions of Stuffed Veal with Herbs, Olives, and Cornichons

Baked Stuffed Sole with Nantua sauce

Deep Fried Cape Scallops - Served with Creole Tartar Sauce and Cole Slaw

All entrees are only $12.95 and include a choice of soup of the day or Bon Ami Salad and Freshly Baked Rolls!

This Menu is available 5:00 - 6:30 Monday through Saturday
3:00 - 6:30 Sunday

Early dining guests are requested to arrive before 6:30 p.m. to receive the special pricing.

DINNER MENU

APPETIZERS

Fried Stuffed Mushroom Caps with Watercress Sauce	*4.50*
Wellfleet Oysters wrapped in Canadian Bacon, Broiled and served with Hollandaise Sauce	*7.25*
Escargots, Raisins and Hazelnuts in a Nest of Filo Dough	*5.50*
Shrimp and Maine Crab in an Orange Thyme Cream	*8.75*
Scotch Smoked Salmon with Golden Caviar and Lemon-Pepper Vodka	*6.50*
Assortment of French Terrines, Pates, and Gallantines	*5.75*
Soups - Several Selections Available	*2.95 - 4.50*

Fresh herbs from our garden is another reason why Bon Ami is the untypical French Restaurant.

ENTREES

Each evening our chefs have several signature items available. They represent Classic French, Nouvelle and American Cuisines.

Bon Appetit!

Charcoal Grilled Norwegian Salmon	*15.50*
Chicken in Clementine Sauce on a Crispy Noodle Pillow with Snow Peas and Almonds	*13.50*
Duck Breast Grilled Rare, Native Corn Souffle, Fresh Raspberries	*16.50*
Veal and Lobster in Champagne Sauce	*18.75*
Shrimp and Scallop de Jonghe, baked with Fines Herbes, Shallots, and Sherry	*14.50*
Veal Medallions Sauteed with Melon, Mushrooms, Capers	*17.50*
Veal Oscar - Plume Veal with Chunks of Lobster and Shrimp in a Bearnaise Sauce, Fresh brocoli	*18.50*
Charcoal Grilled Pork Tenderloin with Sweet Potato Fettuccini, Cranberry-Nut Compote	*13.50*
Braised Bay Scallops and Oysters on Spinach Pasta Sauced with a light Pernod Cream	*14.75*
Fusilli (Curly Pasta) with Prosciutto, Leeks, and an Asiago Cream Sauce	*11.50*
Skillet Steak Diane - Medallions of Tenderloin with a Classic Sauce of Cognac, Dijon Mustard, and Demi-Glaze	*15.00*

EXHIBIT 5 Table Top Questionnaire

We'd like to make Bon Ami even better for you and your guests.
If you'd be good enough to answer the questions below, we'd appreciate it very much. It's totally confidential of course.

ABOUT BON AMI

Did you consider your meal___excellent___good___fair___poor
Do you find the service___excellent___good___fair___poor
Do you dine here___once a week___once a month
___less frequent___first time
Compared to other fine restaurants, do you think our prices are
___too high___just right___lower than most
Your favorite entree at Bon Ami is:________________________

ABOUT YOU

Where you reside(town,zip)___________________________________
Occupation____
Approximate household income____less than $25,000
____$25,000 – $50,000 ____over $50,000
Favorite type of restaurant_____French_____American_____Italian
_____Mexican_____Other
Dine out__________________times per week
Business meals per week________________
Are they primarily_____lunch_____dinner

MERCI!
You can drop this card in the convenient box near the door or mail it to us.

Table Top Questionnaire Results

Survey conducted 11/23/88 to 12/31/88; 836 covers, 292 returned

Considered meal: excellent 176, good 97, fair 17, poor 2
Considered service: excellent 235, good 55, fair 3, poor 0
Dine here: once a week 15, once a month 53, less frequently 111, first time 106
Think prices are: too high 61, just right 195, lower than most 20
Household income: <$25,000 9, $25,000 – $50,000 69, >$50,000 138
Favorite type of restaurant: French 168, American 42, Italian 57, Mexican 10, Chinese 13, German 1
Number of times dine out per week: 456, business 390, lunch 211, dinner 119

Favorite entree at Bon Ami: veal 29, lamb 28, duck 15, fish 13, seafood 9, chicken 8, veal & lobster 7, steak 7, sole 6, schrod 4

Occupation: businessman 32, doctor 17, executive 14, teacher or self-employed 12, vice-president or retired 7, administrator, attorney, accountant or consultant 5, psychologist, sales rep, insurance, advertising or waiter 4, secretary, district manager, professor, investor, marketing, or real estate 3, engineer, psycotherapist, homemaker, entrepreneur, nurse, stockbroker, artist, public relations, salesman, contractor, designer, florist, or restaurant manager 2, retail manager, lawn service, manufacturer, union rep, computer analyst, economist, barber, tennis pro, fashion designer, dentist, machine operator, book dealer, or auto dealer 1

Specific comments:

Excellent service – will definitely return.
First time ever I didn't get change from gift certificate. Will use credit for my last time at Bon Ami. Pure parsimoniousness.
Waitress very nice. Too much hovering and speediness by waiters.
For every entree in a French restaurant there should be an intermezzo course and place plates used.
Heat your coffee (2), warm your bread.
L'Escargot's prices are lower.
Only wrinkled tablecloths were less than excellent.
Portions too small (4).
Suggest less chocolate on dessert menu.
Veal Oscar not up to expectation, chocolate mousse too small.
Keep early bird special!
Mousse in the cake not good, all else superb.
Carla great waitress (3).
Quality was superb (5)!
Yellow pages advertising deceiving as far as attire and atmosphere.
Have dined here many times and always found excellent but disappointed in early bird special.
Prices too high for liquor (2).
An elegant restaurant must offer the courtesy to take guests' coats and bring them upon leaving.
Needs fresh flowers. Too noisy.
Enjoyed the evening, will return.
Miss the country room menu.
People should be well-dressed in main dining room.
Enjoyed our first experience, look forward to returning.
Choice of menu is excellent.
Enjoy early diners' specials.
Charles is the greatest (3)!
Reinstate Caesar salad and croissants at lunch.
More veal dishes for dinner.
Croissants disappointing, cold and overdone.
Roast of lamb should be carved at table.

Table Top Questionnaire Summary

The purpose of this questionnaire was to ascertain certain demographic and lifestyle characteristics of Bon Ami's customer base, as well as to develop a benchmark for customer satisfaction, dining habits, etc.

Customer satisfaction levels at Bon Ami are very high in terms of food, service and price. It appears that no substantive changes are indicated. The high "just right" answer to the pricing question, however, deserves some notice in that customers ordinarily feel that most restaurant prices are too high. Combined with the high household income scores, Bon Ami should not be reluctant to inch its prices higher. People tend to equate quality with price -- prices that are too low (or even "just right") may be perceived as indicating a lower quality.

In analyzing the residence information provided by respondents, it is readily apparent that the bulk of Bon Ami's business comes from the Wilmington area. However, given that Bon Ami has been in this market for two years, and has been a fairly steady advertiser, it must be assumed that awareness is as high as can be expected in the Wilmington market, based on dollar expenditures to date. In other words, Bon Ami's message has reached nearly as many people as affordable within budgetary constraints.

The resultant traffic levels are the product of this awareness level. Therefore, raising the traffic level will require raising the awareness level within the Wilmington market. This will in part be accomplished via word-of-mouth. However, it can be assumed that lower advertising levels will result in lower traffic levels and conversely. Only by experimenting with increased ad levels will it be know whether there is a wider market in Wilmington.

It is possible that increased ad levels may not draw the increase in traffic necessary to offset the additional expenditure. In other words, it is possible that Bon Ami has already drawn as much as it will from Wilmington.

This assumption is somewhat supported by the high percentage of out-of-state customers. According to the figures, there were 46% as many out-of-staters as there were Wilmington residents, 41% as many as there were Wilmington area residents. Bon Ami, in other words, has a strong pulling power from the demographically and psychographically different markets of nearby Maryland. This may indicate a strength that Bon Ami has not tapped; a potential reservoir of business that is more accustomed to and receptive to the Bon Ami dining experience.

The occupational information offers some support to this hypothesis. From the figures derived in the study, occupations were categorized into three major groupings: business people (129), professionals (53), and others (19).

The business/professional marketplace, while widely varied and diverse, represents a major strength to Bon Ami. This data strongly suggests that future marketing plans be aimed at maximizing Bon Ami's impact upon this market. Interestingly, the northern Maryland region represents a strong bastion of business/professional people, certainly much stronger than does the Wilmington market.

In general, these people tend to be more mobile, more adventuresome, and more discriminating in their choices of food, eating and entertainment.

With its strong out-of-town pulling power and an apparent softness in its "home-town" markets, it may behoove Bon Ami to consider making a strong push for attracting this more affluent and receptive out-of-town customer. Considering the truly unique nature of the establishment, this suggests that Bon Ami make a conscious decision to become a "regional" restaurant rather than a local one. It must be understood, however, that such a decision would require a substantial advertising and public relations effort at first.

SECTION 6

STRATEGY AND THE MARKETING PLAN

CASE 18

THE WEEKEND MARKET

By 1988 Le Meridien, a 300 room hotel in Boston, Massachusetts had well turned the corner but it had been a tough struggle. The hotel had opened In 1983, the worse of times to open a hotel in Boston. In the early 1980s, the number of hotel rooms in Boston had increased by 50 percent. Almost all of these new rooms were at the deluxe end of the market. The result had been a glut of rooms on the market and a fierce fight for market share. Additionally, the Hynes Auditorium, the only major large convention center and exhibit hall in Boston, was closed for renovation and enlargement and would not reopen until 1988. This forced large groups to shun Boston and put further pressure on the excess room supply.

In addition to these problems, Le Meridien had problems of its own. It was built within an historic landmark, the old Federal Reserve Building of Boston. Retaining the integrity of the landmark made construction both difficult and expensive. Further, although the hotel was located in the financial district, it was not the most desirable location. It was difficult to find for strangers and even some who lived in the Boston area, a city noted for its unfathomable maze of streets, as well as "crazy" Boston drivers. Traffic was intense and parking was difficult, at best. This area would soon see some major construction and renovation projects. In the meantime, however, Le Meridien was in the middle of nowhere, so to speak, and the construction would only aggravate the situation until it was completed.

All, however, was not lost. The building was beautifully restored and the hotel, once inside, was elegant. Further, the hotel was located within walking distance of the famous stores of Boston such as Filene's and Jordan Marsh. It was also close to Faneuil Market, a major shopping and eating attraction on the harbor front for both Bostonians and visitors alike. Le Meridien also had a health and sports center, unique in Boston.

Occupancy built slowly as awareness was created, but the major marketing effort went into positioning the hotel's classic French restaurant, Julien. Management was determined to make this restaurant the best in the city, a city not known for good French restaurants. The effort was successful and through the restaurant the hotel gained awareness and attention and attracted more room customers. Eventually, both the city and Le Meridien recovered demand to meet the supply and the hotel developed its own market segment.

The weekday business market was the major market segment for Le Meridien. For this market, in 1988, the hotel competed against similar quality properties such as the Ritz Carlton and the Four Seasons, both located on the Boston Common in the center of the city. Weekday rates at Le Meridien were $160 to $210, which were competitive with the other two properties, and occupancy ran at 70 to 80 percent.

Weekends, however, were a different story. At these times, the competition was different. Three new hotels located next door to Faneuil Market, and on or close to the waterfront, ran close to 100 percent occupancy on weekends. These hotels were the 400 room Marriott Long Wharf, the highest occupancy hotel in the Marriott system, and the smaller (under 200 rooms), more elegant Bostonian and Boston Harbor hotels. The Marriott Long Wharf could not compete, product-wise, with Le Meridien but its choice location and strong Marriott affiliation, placed it in high demand.

The Bostonian and Boston Harbor hotels were independent properties but their high quality product, plus also choice locations, made them highly desirable. All three of these hotels drew heavy weekend business from the New York City market, barely an hour's flight away.

Le Meridien, in contrast, ran 45 percent occupancy on Friday and 50 to 60 percent on Saturday. Special weekend packages (the weekend rate was $105), advertisements in the *New York Times, New York, and New Yorker* magazines, and special arrangements with travel agents, seemed to have little effect on the occupancy rate. Essentially, management wondered how it could effectively compete for this market against the locations of the other properties.

CASE 19

HOWARD JOHNSON HOTEL

In 1988, the Howard Johnson Hotel in Colorado Springs, Colorado[1] achieved an average occupancy rate of 67.6 percent, 2.1 percentage points above the average for area competitors, with an average room rate of $55.05. Exhibits 1 and 2 show occupancy and average rate comparisons. Kurt Schwoebel, General Manager of the property, was pleased with this statistic but was striving to increase his profit in 1989 by improving on both occupancy levels and average room rates. Schwoebel was convinced that broadening the customer base was the means to achieving his goal.

Strong repeat business from a loyal clientele made it clear that past guests were satisfied, but non-users needed to be attracted. The hotel's advertising budget was controlled by Prime Motor Inns and was severely limited. As a result, Schwoebel feared that the restrictive budget would hinder his advertising efforts and prevent him from achieving his 1989 goals.

BACKGROUND

The first Howard Johnson's[2] was established in 1925 as a soda fountain shop in Quincy, Massachusetts. Howard Johnson later anticipated the impact the automobile would have on American eating habits, and responded by opening the country's first turnpike restaurant in 1940. In 1954, Johnson built a motor lodge "wherever there were roads." Howard Johnson Sr. relinquished the presidency to his son in 1959 with instructions to "make it grow."

Skyrocketing gasoline prices in the 1970's affected the entire hospitality industry, but the Howard Johnson's chain was particularly hard hit. Glaring deficiencies developed as the chain turned to a heavy profit orientation - service slowed, prices increased, and the quality of the rooms and restaurants dropped to a level below the standards of competitors Holiday Inn and Marriott. As Howard Johnson Jr. described the operation: "We run

---

1 Names and location have been disguised.

2 The original name was Howard Johnson's. In the 1980's the apostrophe s was dropped.

EXHIBIT 1 1988 Occupancy vs. Average Room Rate

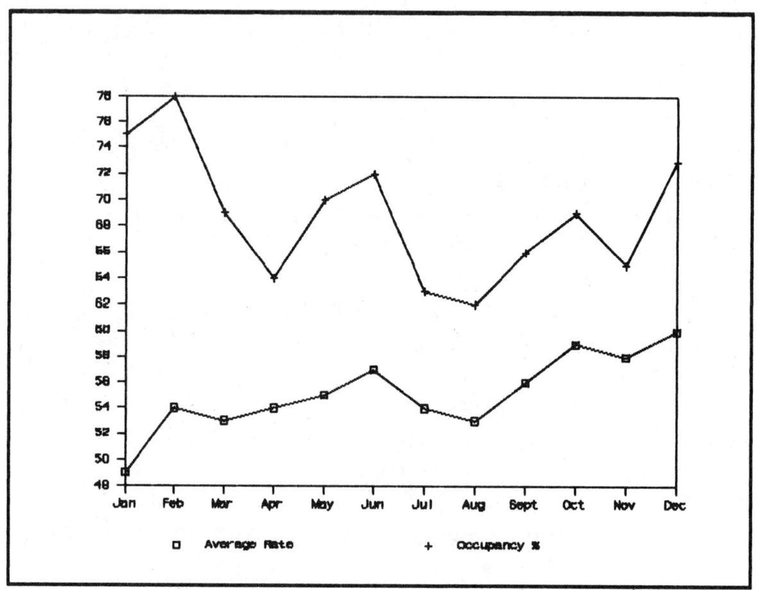

EXHIBIT 2 Weekday Occupancy vs. Average Room Rate

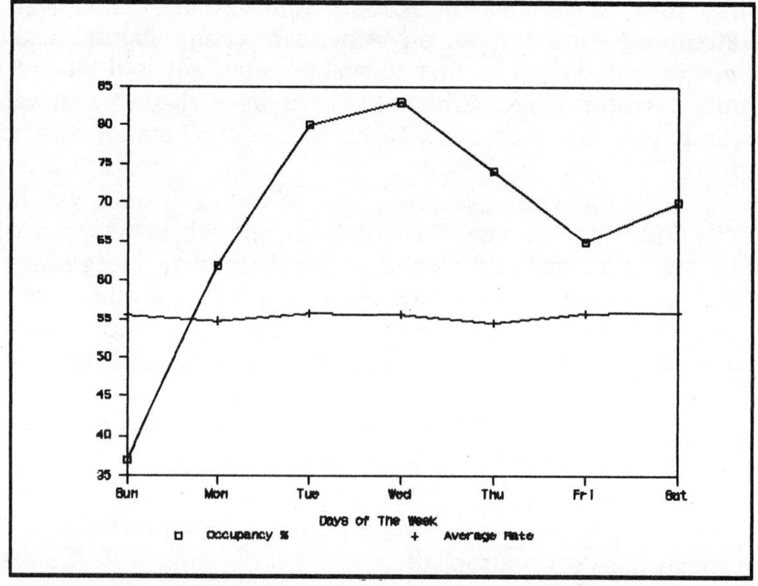

a very tight ship. We keep our expenses low. We are on top of the numbers daily." By this point in time, the traveler had begun to expect something extra from hotels. Rivals such as Holiday Inn, Best Western, and Ramada were in the process of upgrading many of their facilities, while Howard Johnson's retained its 1950's turnpike image and poor reputation.

A British company, Imperial Group PLC., purchased Howard Johnson's in 1980. After five disappointing years, and without improving the image, Imperial sold everything to Marriott Corp. which immediately sold 125 hotels and motor lodges, 190 franchised restaurants, and 375 franchised lodges to Prime Motor Inns. Marriott retained 418 restaurants.

PRIME MOTOR INNS

Prime Motor Inns was formed in 1968 as a public franchise company which owned and/or managed many Ramada Inns, Sheratons, Holiday Inns, and Howard Johnsons. It was one of the fastest growing companies in the lodging industry, and Melvin Taub, CEO, credited the company's organizational structure as the key to its success. Every business function was handled in-house, and a price mark-up to cover third party expenses was not necessary. Cost reduction and strict control over its profitability and earnings contributed greatly to Prime's success.

Ninety percent of Prime's business derived from the commercial traveler, and inns were constructed with this market segment in mind. Dollars were concentrated in guest rooms rather than fancy lobbies, and the hotels were staffed and priced to communicate value to the corporate guest.

In regard to the September 1985 purchase of Howard Johnson, Taub stated: "It's a prized possession. It's kind of like mother, apple pie and maybe Coca-Cola." Taub felt that the Howard Johnson name was a major asset of the corporation. Intentions were to retain the name and capitalize on its familiarity and recognition among American travelers. However, despite Prime's efforts in that direction, the customer base of the Colorado Springs property had remained constant since Imperial days.

The Howard Johnson Hotel and Lodge Division of Prime Motor Inns, Inc., was charged with delivering the public professionally run, clean, and well-maintained hotels, lodges, and restaurants, in a friendly, courteous environment while optimizing profits and aggressively pursuing sales and marketing opportunities. The divison's specific goals were stated as follows:

> *Goal #1: The Optimization of Profits*
> *Profits are the result of all activities, but they must be handled with proper balance of short-term profitability and long-term profit potential. Critical success factors: increased sales volume, effective house profit/cost controls, superior guest orientation/services, high quality F & B operations.*

Goal #2: Sales and Marketing
Provide a product that meets the needs of targeted markets in the broadest sense. Convey timely information and support to the Vice President of Sales and Regional Director of Sales, allowing them to maximize marketing efforts, and in this way meet the company's sales and profit objectives. Critical success factors: maximize targeted market share, consistent guest perception/satisfaction, effective marketing and sales information systems, periodic sales personnel training.

Goal #3: Quality of Operation
Strongly influence the company's effective pursuit of excellence by delivering service, quality, cleanliness, and value to all guests. Critical success factors: develop best moderately priced lodging and food service accommodations in industry, maintain preventive maintenance philosophy, develop guest perception of positive price/value relationship of quality.

Goal #4: Organizational Climate
Develop an organization which produces an environment in which individuals are: a) highly responsive to the guests, employees, market conditions, and the needs of the company; and b) personally responsible for profits, sales and the training and development of people. Critical success factors: employee training and relations, personnel development, management development.

HOWARD JOHNSON OF COLORADO SPRINGS

The Colorado Springs Howard Johnson property was a company-owned hotel which was visible from Interstate 25, a major route running from Montana to the Mexican border. The hotel was easily accessible from both I-25 and Route 83 and its immediate surroundings included "mom and pop" type restaurants, motels, and stores. A Sheraton hotel was located next door with a sign which was also visible from I-25.

Colorado Springs was a city of 215,000 population, and contained the U.S. Air Force Academy, two colleges, the Eisenhower Medical Center, and the famous Broadmoor Resort Hotel. The city's primary airport service was at the Denver airport, 70 miles to the north.

Colorado Springs was a stop-over as well as a destination city. The downtown area was four miles away from the Howard Johnson hotel. Pikes Peak and the Garden of the Gods were in the immediate vicinity. Fine dining and fast food restaurants, lounges, cinemas, and a public health club were located within a mile of the hotel.

Kurt Schwoebel, the General Manager, had been with the Howard Johnson Company for 13 years, nine years in the restaurant division and four years in lodging. He began his career as a dishwasher, and progressed to cook, head cook, assistant manager, manager, and finally General Manager. He had been the General Manager of the Colorado Springs property for the past six months. Schwoebel reported to a district manager who reported to the Vice President-Rocky Mountain Region, who, in turn reported to the Vice President of the Howard Johnson Motor Lodge Division of Prime Motor Inns.

GUEST ROOMS

The Howard Johnson Hotel included 112 guest rooms and five suites. All been redecorated within the past two years. Each room featured a panel switch at bedside, touch-tone telephone, a well-lighted desk area, and sliding glass doors to a private balcony. Thirty four rooms had one queen size bed, 26 rooms had two, eight had a king size bed, and 44 rooms having either one king size or two queen size beds were in the Executive Section.

Rates were determined based on room type and season of the year. In an attempt to maximize revenue, the Sales Director kept track of area events and adjusted the rate structure during peak periods. These changes were entered into the national reservation system to facilitate the processing of 800 telephone number requests. Executive Section and corporate rates were fixed for each calendar year period, and did not fluctuate according to availability. Average posted rates were as follows:

Category	Sgl	Dbl
Executive Section	64	78
Rack	62	72
Corporate/Government	52	62
Tour/Travel/Group	49	55
Athletic	44	44

The Executive Section was a Prime Motor Inn nationally advertised "Businessman's Hospitality Package", but was not available in all lodge and hotel properties (Exhibit 3). The Colorado Springs Howard Johnson hotel participated in the Executive Section campaign and offered it from Monday through Thursday nights. The fourth and fifth floors of the hotel comprised the Executive Section, and guests were greeted by a brass sign when alighting from the elevator on these two floors.

Mr. Schwoebel had created an optional "Captain's Table" for dinner each Monday through Thursday night (Exhibit 4). A private dining room was reserved for Executive Section guests who preferred the alternative of table companions rather than dining alone in the restaurant. Two entrees were offered each evening with prices ranging from $12 to $15 per meal.

EXHIBIT 3 **Nationally Advertised Howard Johnson Executive Section**

HOWARD JOHNSON

Businessman's Hospitality Package

WE WANT YOUR BUSINESS!

Here's a special package
For the Frequent Business Traveler

$ 58 Single Occupancy
Executive Section
INCLUDES:

- Complimentary Cocktail Party
  5:30 to 8:00 p.m. Monday thru Thursday
- Complimentary Breakfast (from the menu)

Plus
THE EXECUTIVE SECTION

Try these new features of our Executive Section

- Complimentary coffee, sanka or tea each morning delivered to your room
- Complimentary Wall Street Journal or USA Today delivered to your room each morning
- Complimentary wine and mints await your arrival
- Special amenities package
- Year round single commercial rates apply

ALL OF THE EXECUTIVE SECTION FEATURES PLUS

- Special Gold Key guest courtesies
- Restaurant and Lounge on premises

AND OTHER EXTRAS FOR THE FREQUENT
BUSINESS TRAVELER!

EXHIBIT 4 Captain's Table Invitation

Indulge Yourself in The Executive Section

*Introducing ..... **"Captain's Table"***

Through guest suggestions and a survey among our business travelers, we have found that many of you would enjoy dining with other guests who are, like you would enjoy dining with other guests who are, like yourself, traveling alone on business.

*Therefore, We are proud to announce .... our **"Captain's Table"***

In a private dining room, with your personal waitress, you will be served your choice of the two featured entrees of the night. All meals include appetizer, vegtable, rolls and butter and beverage.

*Joining you for dinner will be other guests in the Executive Section wishing to dine at the **"Captain's Table"**.*

All you need to do is to contact our Hotel Customer Representative by dialing "0" to make your reservation. Should you forget to do so and make a last minute decision to join us, please do so. We will be more than happy to accommodate you.

I will be looking forward to having you join us and have attached daily menus for this week.

We appreciate your patronage as our corporate travelers are among our most valused guests. We are continually striving to meet the needs of our guests and your comfort is our greatest concern.

Sincerly,

Kurt Schwoebel
General Manager

THE RESTAURANT

A Howard Johnson restaurant was located within the confines of the property and was owned and operated by the Marriott Corporation. Because the restaurant retained the Howard Johnson name, guests understandably assumed that the General Manager of the hotel oversaw the food service operation as well. As a result, a bad experience in the restaurant often reflected negatively on the lodging experience. Also, normal room service was not offered.

Service in the restaurant was slow and unprofessional, and prices were high relative to the quality of the food and the level of service. The lounge was generally inactive and hotel guests often frequented neighborhood restaurants and lounges rather than patronize the in-house facilities.

The hotel received only 10 percent of the food and beverage revenue, although it assumed all advertising and printing costs for the outlets. The lodging Sales Director was hesitant to book food service business since the return to the hotel was low and the quality of the offering could not be guaranteed. Conference groups planning a meeting usually expected free function space in return for the food and beverage business, and the lodging side was expected to provide it. Needless to say, a moderate degree of tension existed between Schwoebel and the manager of the restaurant.

The Captain's Table option was one of the few areas of agreement between the lodging and food service managers. A substantial amount of revenue was generated by the Captain's Table, thus pleasing the restaurant manager. From the lodging point of view, the heightened satisfaction of Executive Section guests clearly warranted continuation of the program, although Schwoebel was forced to contribute a great deal of his own time to the Captain's Table.

ADDITIONAL FEATURES

The lobby of the Howard Johnson Colorado Springs was small but tastefully furnished with a contemporary flair. The General Manager's office was located next to the Front Desk in order to increase managerial visibility and to encourage guest interaction. The restaurant and lounge were adjacent to the lobby, and an indoor swimming pool was accessible from the ground level.

There were also three break-out meeting rooms on the first floor which opened into one room with a capacity of 110 people. The property was surrounded by a large parking lot which provided free parking. Handicapped facilities as well as overnight weekday valet service were also available.

COMPETITION

Schwoebel perceived his competition to be the following:

Name	Distance from Howard Johnson
Sheraton	next door
Ramada Inn	3 miles
Quality Inn	3 miles
Marriott	5 miles
Harley Hotel	20 miles

Characteristics of these properties are given in Exhibit 5.

Schwoebel was on friendly terms with the General Managers of each of these properties and exchanged quarterly rate and occupancy data with them. He believed that his lack of cable television placed him at an extreme disadvantage since all his competitors offered this amenity. Schwoebel priced his facility in such a way as to overcome this disadvantage and remain competitive within the area. He did not want to attract the clientele which frequented the "Mom and Pop" type motels adjacent to the hotel, many of which offered hourly rates.

MARKETING PLAN 1989

The overall customer mix of the Howard Johnson Colorado Springs was 60 percent corporate, 30 percent tour and travel, and 10 percent athletic or government. Fifty percent of the corporate business was repeat, and 47 percent of these guests chose the Executive Section over a standard room if the option was available.

During the winter months, ski-oriented tours comprised the majority of the business. The month of June was also positively impacted by the influx of parents and guests attending the Air Force Academy graduation festivities.

The marketing objective for the year 1989 was to increase the annual occupancy three percentage points, and to improve the average rate by $3.00. The achievement of the higher occupancy percentage and the improved average rate would result in the targeted $150,000 improvement in room sales.

The 1989 marketing plan called for the following tactics:

* tighter control of reservations
* fill in slow periods (July and August) and slow weekends
* encourage upgrade from standard to Executive Section

* perform a monthly source of business analysis to target market segments and surface potential leads
* compile a list of major employers in the area and personally visit each one
* contact the Air Force Academy and all area schools and organizations to promote the group rate
* continue to monitor customer feedback through guest interaction in the Executive Lounge and at the Captain's Table and the Front Desk

Schwoebel had initiated new advertising campaigns in an attempt to broaden his customer base. Rooms were exchanged for radio time on Pueblo station WIZZ, and two different ads promoting the Executive Section were currently being aired. The Executive Section was offered at half price to new customers, and the Captain's Table was also featured. Rolodex cards listing basic information about the hotel were printed and mailed to local secretaries. New athletic rates had been established and a motorcoach package was being created in an attempt to generate weekend business. Advertisements were placed in local newspapers as part of an active effort to draw from these markets.

The most widely used selling tool continued to be a one-on-one approach. Schwoebel spent an inordinate amount of time with present customers and attended the Captain's Table each night. He was in favor of additional advertising, but his budget was set by Prime and did not permit it.

CONCLUSION

Schwoebel believed he had a superior product as compared to other Howard Johnson Lodges and Hotels. His standards for cleanliness and quality of service were well above corporate standards, and his Executive Section offered more value for less money than any Howard Johnsons or other competitor. He believed that he was conveying the image that Prime desired (see memorandum in Exhibit 6), yet it was not recognized because visits from corporate executives were infrequent.

If Prime executives were aware of the high quality level of the property, Schwoebel felt that they would increase his advertising budget. Present occupancy and profit levels were acceptable, but Schwoebel was encountering difficulties in attracting new customers. Once new customers experienced his product, Schwoebel was confident that they would return. However, he was stymied as to how to entice a first visit without increasing his advertising budget which confined his efforts to the local area and local markets.

EXHIBIT 5 Howard Johnson Competition

SHERATON, Colorado Springs

Rooms/Suites:	263/5
Features:	15 Function rooms, 6500 sq. ft. Ballroom, 1 restaurant, 2 lounges, entertainment, popular Sunday Brunch, indoor-outdoor pool, room service, valet service, health club, free parking, concierge floor.
Rack Rate:	S - $84, D - $94
Corp. Rate:	S - 72, D - 82
Exec. Pack. Rate:	S - 94, D - 104
Exec. Pack. Features:	Concierge floor, jacuzzis, concierge lounge, turndown service, free newspaper, complimentary buffet and bar, complimentary breakfast, receptionist.
Major Source of Business:	Corporate and weddings.

RAMADA INN, Chapel Hill

Rooms/Suites:	120/1
Features:	4 function rooms, capacity 200, 1 restaurant, 1 lounge, heated outdoor pool, Businessman special, free parking
Rack Rate:	S - $55, D - $63
Corp. Rate:	S - 49, D - 55
Exec. Pack. Rate:	S - 60, D - 71
Exec. Pack. Features:	Businessman's special, wine amenities, newspaper, coffee, breakfast.
Major Source of Business:	Tour and Travel.

MARRIOTT, Colorado Springs

Rooms/Suites:	265/9
Features:	11 function rooms, 6000 sq. ft. ballroom, 4 star restaurant, 1 lounge, dancing, room service, valet service, indoor pool, health club.
Rack Rate:	S - $90, D - $100
Corp. Rate:	S - 85, D - 95
Exec. Pack. Rate:	None
Exec. Pack. Features:	None
Major Source of Business:	Corporate

EXHIBIT 5 Competition (page 2)

QUALITY INN, Chapel Hill

Rooms/Suites:	185
Features:	13 function rooms, capacity 900, 1 restaurant, 1 lounge, outdoor pool, free parking.
Rack Rate:	S - $47, D - 52
Corp. Rate:	S - 44, D - 50
Exec. Pack. Rate:	None
Exec. Pack. Features:	None
Major Source of Business:	Groups.

HARLEY HOTEL, Monument

Rooms/Suites:	181
Features:	17 function rooms, 1 ballroom, 1 restaurant, 1 lounge, entertainment, room service, valet service, babysitting services, indoor-outdoor pool, saunas, tennis courts, 50 miles from Denver, Ambassadors Row, free parking, deluxe amenities.
Rack Rate:	S - $78, D - $88
Corp. Rate:	S - 63, D - 83
Exec. Pack. Rate:	S - 91, D - 101
Exec. Pack. Features:	Ambassador's Row, private entrance, library lounge, conference room, shoe shine, aide, complimentary breakfast and newspaper.

EXHIBIT 6 Memorandum from Prime Headquarters

TO: District General Managers
General Managers
Lodge Managers

FROM: Joe Kane

DATE: March 14, 1988

RE: Image

During the past several weeks, I have had an opportunity to visit over 50 locations throughout the various Regions. We feel that it is imperative that, to remain competitive, our lodges must be totally well maintained and clean. Unfortunately, this has not been the case in many of the locations that I have visited.

We have been stressing the importance of getting out and selling, offering competitive rates; Billboard snips; etc., to capture or recapture lost market share. If we don't keep our house in order it won't work.

I find that rooms are not being checked daily; our Quick Check program is not in use or being used wrong, no mattress rotation program, not practicing our Standard of Excellence, etc. There are no excuses for this and none will be tolerated by this office.

We all have a major opportunity to impact our industry in rebuilding our business base and image as a company. We want commitments, not excuses. How about you? Are you a part of this renaissance? Can your property be a Prime representative? We think so, but we don't have a lot of time for excuses. Let's get the job done and give it your all. Let's make Hospitality Industry history.

CASE 20

THE CASE OF THE DWINDLING BOXCARS

In 1969, Richard Bradley, a former investment broker, Robert Freeman, a former in-flight service supervisor for Pan Am, and Peter Lee, a former Sky Chef cost analyst, had two things in common: they were 1963 graduates of the Cornell Hotel School and they wanted to organize a quality operating business enterprise where operations were critical to success. Bradley, Lee and Freeman felt they had the ability to operate nearly any type of business, but wanted to obtain maximum leverage. The restaurant opportunity presented itself first. They finally decided on a limited menu, theme restaurant in the mid-priced market. After much discussion the concept of Victoria Station was agreed upon, based on the elements they considered crucial for success: concept uniqueness, quality control, and financial control.

Concept Uniqueness Victoria Station was designed for the growing number of singles, couples, and families who liked to eat out but who could not afford high prices. Victoria Station featured prime rib of beef served in a unique railroad atmosphere of boxcars converted into restaurants. The interiors of the boxcars were refurbished to retain as much authenticity as possible including railroad equipment and memorabilia. Old baggage carts were used as room dividers and tables. Prime rib was displayed in large glass front refrigerators in the central bar area.

Gas lights, a red English telephone booth, and a London taxi were placed in front of the restaurants, which depended largely on the unique exteriors to draw customers. Prime rib was the major menu drawing card. At the time, it was usually sold only in expensive restaurants whereas steak and lobster restaurants were plentiful.

The first restaurants seated about 150 persons. Male college students were used as waiters while young women provided cocktail service. The atmosphere at a Victoria Station was very relaxed. It was possible for a couple to enjoy prime rib dinner, which represented approximately 70 percent of orders, with salad and wine for approximately $15.00, including tip. The average lunch check was $4.00, without tip.

No advertising or paid promotion was utilized and the restaurants relied entirely on initial publicity before opening, and word-of-mouth advertising for its marketing success. Simply being open for lunch, particularly in downton areas, was considered by management as a form of advertising for couple or family dinner business.

Quality Control Management felt that its first job was to ensure uniformly high quality at all locations. Beef was cut to specification and Victoria Station used controlled portion filets and top sirloin butts. Produce and most service items and accessories were purchased locally from an approved purveyor list. A computerized checking system verified that unapproved vendors would be brought to management's attention.

Execution was a matter of strong management supervision to ensure strict adherence to standards, which were defined in a comprehensive operations manual. Appearance, food preparation and service, beverage preparation and service, atmosphere, equipment maintenance, safety, inventory control, and other matters were set down in detail, together with complete job descriptions for all managers. A checklist was the basis for determining whether the manager and his two assistants would be eligible for a semi-annual performance bonus. Failure to qualify for the performance bonus eliminated an individual from participation in the profitability bonus.

Financial Control Financial control was maintained through detailed reports. Daily meal counts, sales receipts and expenditure reports, and sales breakdowns for food, wine and other beverages were tallied for each waiter at both lunch and dinner. Daily inventories were taken. A profit and loss statement was prepared monthly for each restaurant. Computer operations provided financial analysis of similar-sized restaurants by region, budget and actual variance, man-hours, revenues per seat, and revenues per square foot.

Meat costs represented 70 percent of food costs and management constantly monitored meat prices. Prices were on an upward trend and it was felt that there would be an increase of 12 to 18 percent over the next 12 months. This emphasized the need for a well-executed cost control program.

1973

By late 1973, the initial phases of the development strategy had been completed. Bradley, President, and Freeman and Lee, Vice Presidents, were preparing for the next growth phase by developing operating controls and reporting procedures to maintain profits, while continuing to open new units. Victoria Stations numbered 17, with an additional five under construction, and 10 more committed to or being designed. The financial community described the Victoria Station growth record as most impressive. The stock was selling at about $18.00 a share with a price/earnings ratio of approximately 59 times 1972 earnings. Analysts felt that the price was justified based on past and anticipated growth, but was dependent on a continued record of growth in the number of units and profitability. The annual report for the year ending March 31, 1973 contained the following statements:

> It is gratifying to report that fiscal year 1973 was unquestionably the most successful in the history of Victoria Station. In many ways 1973 was truly a spectacular year, particularly for so young a corporation. Challenges, often severe and frequently beyond our control or that of any lone corporation, also abounded during fiscal 1973. Sharply rising costs in virtually all areas, frequent frustrating construction delays, and significantly increased competition, often from vastly larger organizations, were major problems we faced most of the year. Nevertheless, we close out 1973 by all standards a far stronger company than we were 12 months ago. Perhaps the true measure of 1973 is the height of our achievements, given our rapid rate of growth and the challenges created by it and a host of other factors...

At a meeting of the company's officers, the following remarks were made in regard to the future.

> We have built the foundations for a much larger company. The cost controls, quality controls, and organization we have installed are intended for the future. If we were planning to stay at our present size, these expenditures would not be necessary. The financial community has high expectations for Victoria Station. They expect fast, steady, profitable growth. How fast does growth have to be to satisfy them and our investors? The real question, however, is how fast does it have to be to satisfy ourselves? How much should we sacrifice day-to-day operations to maintain growth just to please others? Should we be concerned that we are losing our objective?

1976

In June 1976 the company operated 46 Victoria Station restaurants. Prime rib was 51 percent of sales and the restaurants were a popular rendezvous for dinner, cocktails, and lunch. Three other restaurants with diversified themes in the San Francisco Bay Area were additions to the company's business: Thomas Lord's was designed after an English sporting tavern; The Royal Exchange in the financial district had an English stock exchange atmosphere; Quinn's Lighthouse was located in a renovated Coast Guard lighthouse and featured seafood as well as beef entrees. The company also operated the Plantation Gardens restaurant on the Island of Kauai, Hawaii.

Atlanta, Georgia was the location of the most radical diversification. Quinn's Mill restaurant resembled an old grist mill and featured an expanded menu including appetizers, which no other Victoria Station property served. The restaurant had a spectacular lakeshore location.

Victoria Station had gained national recognition. A TV network special cited the restaurants, of all so-called theme restaurants, as a model of effective execution. *Business Week* featured Richard Bradley in a two-page article. Bradley was also named "Man of the Year" by the Multi-Unit Food Service Operators Association at its annual convention.

Marketing With competition increasing, management was determining the necessary strategy that would enable it to dominate the industry in the years to come. The company established a marketing department to increase sales growth in existing properties. The present director of human resources, Harlow White, also took on the job of director of marketing. He felt that the company was not using its marketing information to best advantage and that restaurants were losing marketing opportunities because they didn't know how to generate additional business. White's view of the reasons for the company's success was,

> It was product definition that made us do so well. We concluded that we were selling a product that was more than a piece of meat on a plate, more than an ounce and a quarter shot in a 13 ounce glass. It was a total experience. The general ambience of the restaurant, the quality of the product, the size of the portions, and the architecture of the place all contributed.

Success had been attained without paid advertising except for direct mail announcements at the time of each restaurant's opening. While the restaurants were under construction management sought TV and press coverage for free publicity. Prior to opening, lists of prospective customers were obtained from country clubs, banking contacts, and the American Express mailing list for a direct mailing to some 20,000 persons. Management felt that the food, service, and atmosphere offered was the best advertising by word-of-mouth.

It was also felt, however, that some primary research should be conducted to determine the market segments attracted to the restaurants. A market research firm was engaged and used in-house interviews to establish a consumer profile and geographic target markets. Additionally, awareness and trial levels, and customer perceptions were obtained from telephone interviews. It was found that customers tended to be under 35, college educated, married, and had annual incomes of $20,000 or more.

Customers most often mentioned food (71%), atmosphere (65%), and service (24%) as what they liked about Victoria Station. Over two-thirds saw the restaurants as specializing in red meat, and one-third mentioned prime rib as the specialty. Total awareness of Victoria Station was found to range from 71 to 84 percent of the sample in the three cities surveyed, while unaided awareness ranged from five to 16 percent. From 38 to 51 percent of the sample had patronized Victoria Station, while 32 to 41 percent listed themselves as current patrons. Five to eight percent named Victoria Station as their most patronized restaurant. These figures were all considerably below the leading competitors in each city, showing that there was considerable potential for improvement.

Management was most surprised that atmosphere was so frequently mentioned by respondents, as they had put so much emphasis on the quality of the food product. They felt that success could not be based on atmosphere because this attribute was vulnerable to erosion from competition. They decided that advertising emphasis should stress the food and a billboard campaign was developed featuring "Perhaps the Finest Prime Rib Ever." Brochures were printed with food pictures and the same tag line. Radio advertising emphasized the food, and then the atmosphere. Local managers were not involved in advertising policy decisions.

COMPETITION AND STRATEGY

The limited menu theme restaurant was highly in vogue by 1976, much of it targeting the singles market. Victoria Station, however, concentrated on the dinner business of couples and families. There were a number of imitators, as well, using the boxcar dining concept. Large companies also joined the theme restaurant fray. Pillsbury acquired Steak & Ale, a 100 unit English pub concept. General Mills bought the 180 unit Red Lobster seafood chain, and planned other concepts. Far West Services operated theme restaurants under the names of Reuben's, The Plankhouse, Moonraker, and Reuben E. Lee. Saga was operating Velvet Turtle, Black Angus, and The Refectory. All of these concepts competed broadly in the Victoria Station market segment.

Victoria Station's policy had been to build only in areas of one million population or more, as this was considered the necessary level to maintain consistent volume. In 1976 - 1977 management changed this policy and started building in areas of lower population in places like Virginia, Maryland, and Canada.

Management also recognized that, on any given night, customers' desires in food type would vary. To capture the same market in these cases, it was decided that a second, but different, restaurant was appropriate for expansion in selected market areas.

Other multi-unit operators were beginning to build larger units that enabled them to produce higher volume levels with lower fixed cost percentages. Accordingly, Victoria Station increased the size of their new units to 300 seats wherever possible. It was found, however, that after the inital opening rush that sales tended to slacken. Advertising was planned to counteract this.

Pricing of menu items was changed from the previous one price policy throughout the country to one of regional pricing based on perceived value in local markets. The company strongly fought any price increases as management's strategy included a high price/value offering. At some locations, both prices and portion sizes were reduced.

By the end of 1976, management's future plans envisioned at least 150 Victoria Stations in North America. They were still unsure how large a population was required to support a Victoria Station. As costs of construction increased, plans were made to put more emphasis on the food product and less on the decor. The threat of competition from sophisticated, large operators was omnipresent; management's challenge was to be prepared to meet it.

1978/1979

In 1978, almost 100 Victoria Stations throughout the country were grossing up to $1.5 million a year. However, beef prices had started to rise in 1976 and were continuing an upward trend. Nevertheless, 1978 fiscal year revenues had increased 32 percent over 1977 to $101.2 million, and earnings had risen 20 percent to almost $5 million.

In 1979, sales increased 18.5 percent to $120 million, but income declined 30 percent to $3.3 million. The profit slide was attributed to decline in customer counts, partly due to the 1979 gasoline crunch and general economic malaise.

1980

In fiscal 1980, Victoria Station experienced the first loss in its 10 year history, accumulating sales of $128 million while losing $1.2 million. Average unit volume slipped to $1.3 million. The year 1980 also marked the beginning of a series of turnaround efforts.

Brunch In 1979 the chain offered brunch in 34 units across the country, but the concept didn't catch on in the southwest so it was discontinued in that area. In January 1980 the chain started to add brunch to carefully selected restaurants in the east, midwest, and west where management believed customers would be predisposed to accept it. It was expected to have brunch in one-third of the 103 units by September and, ultimately, in about 60 units. Senior vice president - marketing, Paul Sheppard, said that brunch would be added only in those units with above average performance and discontinued if the unit failed to sell 125 - 150 brunches per Sunday. Besides a fruit bar, there was also a *Station Master's Counter* where eggs Benedict, quiche, scrambled eggs, eggs Florentine, lox and bagels, sauteed mushrooms, and prime rib carved to order were available. "All you can eat" was $7.95 for adults, $3.95 for children under 12, and free for children under five. Food costs were higher than the chain's standard 40 percent, but the company looked to build high margins on items like dessert.

Price Reductions In July, after a quarter of even revenues but a loss of $663,000 compared to net earnings of $876,000 the year before, Victoria Station began changing menu prices, instituting new promotions, and converting some of its less profitable units to new concepts. The company implemented price reductions in many of its units to improve traffic. Plans were to gradually increase them again while concurrently upgrading the product offerings to reflect a proper price/value relationship. Menu offerings were reevaluated as was the total Victoria Station dining experience.

Barbeque Ribs To broaden its traditional customer base, the company promoted all-you-can-eat barbecue beef ribs for $6.95 in a special heavily advertised summer campaign. The eight week "Have I Got a Barbecue for You" campaign raised the customer count about 30 percent, according to executives, after customer counts had been down 15 percent. The rib promotion gave people a good reason to come back, according to Sheppard.

New Concepts Three units were closed for renovations and repositioning. According to President Bradley, each was in a good restaurant market but it had become inappropriate for the standard Victoria Station concept. One unit was reopened as *Mules*, featuring sandwiches in a pub atmosphere. Another was reborn as a limited menu, medium priced French Cafe and bar called Bistrot Les Halles. The third reopened in Toronto as an east side New York style saloon called *The Temperance Grill at Yorkville*. Bradley said that other marginal units might be converted to one of the new concepts in the future.

Game Hen In the fall of 1980, Victoria Station rolled out a promotion to introduce a "gourmet" game hen entree. Similar to a Cornish hen, it had been pretested in 16 cities. Sheppard, now executive vice president, said that while Victoria Station would probably not attempt to shed its image as a prime rib house, there would be a subtle de-emphasis of prime rib on the menu. The game hen promotion was designed to draw new customers into the restaurants without actually shedding the prime rib image. The promotions were also calculated to allow the company to restructure its menu while broadening the base of its traditional customer demographics.

Personnel Changes The chain reduced its regional manager team from 19 to 14. It also hired a new advertising agency, Bozell and Jacobs, and established a network of 12 public relations companies across the country. Jon Rose, formerly with Bozell and Jacobs, was named marketing director; Laura Phillips, formerly with the National Restaurant Association, was named public relations director; and Victoria Victory, formerly field marketing manager, was named director of advertising. Peter Lee, executive vice president and one of the founders, resigned for personal reasons. The position of vice president for corporate development was eliminated and its occupant also resigned. Also eliminated were the positions of director of corporate projects, director of architecture, and director of engineering and construction.

Despite the personnel changes, Sheppard said there was a new enthusiasm among the company's employees, a good deal of which was due to the success of the barbecued rib promotion. Sheppard wouldn't predict the financial future of the company, only saying that he was optimistic and that the year was one of transition and rebuilding.

In December, Richard Bradley, president, CEO, and one of the founders, announced his resignation as soon as a successor could be found. He continued as chairman. No reason was given. Also in December, Victoria Station suspended its quarterly dividend. Sheppard, who was now spearheading the turnaround and was a candidate for the president's slot, stated, "I am looking for other significant [personnel] cuts, both in the field and at headquarters, to expedite specific fourth quarter goals."

The Menu The menu was quietly expanded from seven to 15 items. "By January, we will have a new format menu with 20 plus items," Sheppard said. The items were to include fish, shellfish, and some sort of casserole dishes. Sheppard said that the new menu emphasis away from red meats, combined with the decreased cost of red meats, could speed a possible turnaround.

An outside observer visited a Victoria Station restaurant in December 1980 and made the comments contained in Exhibit 1.

1981

By 1981, it appeared that Victoria Station was getting back on track. An article in *Restaurant Business* outlined the past problems:

> It was inevitable. Victoria Station followed a story line all too familiar to developing restaurant chains. Its mis-steps included:
>
> * Over-expansion - opening too many new units in too many new markets in too short a time span.
> * An inflexible approach to interior and exterior design.
> * An over-reliance on a red meat-based menu.
> * An insufficient reservoir of trained, competent unit management.
>
> At the same time, these internal mistakes were compounded by such external factors as skyrocketing food, energy and labor costs and a rapid shift in the tastes of the dining-out public.
>
> ... Losses have continued through the first two quarters of fiscal 1981, but the chain's current management believes the downward trend, while continuing through the third quarter, will be arrested in the fourth quarter and reversed in the first quarter of fiscal 1982. According to Paul Sheppard, "We'll break even at the end of fiscal

EXHIBIT 1 An Observer's Comments on One Particular Victoria Station

Victoria Station is a theme restaurant, serving American food and offering a unique fun dining experience. Though this location is superb, the setting is unattractive. The restaurant is situated in a large, bare parking lot with little landscaping. Improvements such as plusher surroundings could help stress its theme.

The theme of Victoria Station is a British railroad station, which is reflected in both the indoor and outdoor decor of the restaurant, which consists of British railway artifacts. From the time reservations are made to the time of departure, the mood is effectively set for an exciting dining experience in a railroad boxcar.

Upon arrival, one can see several adjoining train cars which form Victoria Station. They look like old fashioned train cars. They are muddy red in color and sit on steel railroad tracks. There is even a red caboose! At the foot of the entrance is an old fashioned red telephone booth.Along the outside of the train cars are black steel railroad traffic lamps.

One enters the restaurant through the caboose and is greeted by a friendly hostess. Above her head is a small scale model of the restaurant protruding from the wall. The hostess suggests a seat at one the cocktail tables while waiting for a dinner table. On the cocktail tables are jars of cheddar cheese and baskets of crackers. Friendly waitresses quickly return with the cocktail of choice.

There are two flaws with the cocktail system. One is the television at the bar which takes away from the restaurant's atmosphere. The other is that waitresses bombard the customer too frequently, a bit too eager to take an order, which becomes annoying.

As one awaits a seat for dinner, everywhere he looks are different sections, or "depots," all having signs, decorations or contraptions dealing with train schedules, passengers, or train cars. Also noticeable is the steel of the outside decor continuing inside, which gives the feeling of continuity and realism and the feeling that you are really in a train station. Placing the cocktail tables in the center of activity gives the customer a chance to get into the mood of the place. One feels like he is people-watching at a train station.

Looking up, a busy decor prevails. There are two large skylights. Large steel beams support the ceiling. A ladder leads to a high loft where trunks, duffle bags and beer drums are loosely scattered under a sign reading "Baggage Claim." Plants hang from the barnboard rafters. Even the bar is involved in this decor; there are screened box compartments filled with wines and connected to the rafters.

The kitchen's food pickup window also resembles a train stop, as it is decorated with copper lamps and headed with a depot name. The cooks are dressed as train conductors in blue and white overalls and caps.

A customer sits in one of the dining cars to have dinner. Each dining car has separate compartments which are individual tables made of barnboard. Before sitting down, you can hang your coat on a steel spike coat rack. The tables are set with a simple red tablecloth and traditional silverware, dishes and glasses. Each dining compartment has its own small traffic light, which is dim enough to set a romantic atmosphere for two. On the wall is a picture of an old train or a train schedule. At the end of the car is a framed layout design of a train.

Busboys, waiters and waitresses are dressed in simple street clothes and employ typical American service. The menu is a piece of paper burned around the edges, shellacked onto a slim, rectangular piece of wood, headed "NOTICE." All foods are listed under "Tracks" or "Platforms." Track One is a choice of "Engineman's soup" or "Baggage Cart Salad Bar." Platform Two is the entree list, Platform Three is vegetables, and Platform Four is desserts and beverages. The bottom of the menu states management's goal: To provide the customer with the best food and service available. Management urges complaints if the customer is not satisfied.

Victoria Station has some good points as well as some flaws. The aisles in each dining car are very narrow. There is no room for the waiter or waitress to put the meals down before putting them on the customer's table. A greater problem is that parties on one side of the car are very close to those on the other side, limiting the privacy of the experience. Another fault is the limitation of the menu; it is geared toward the American steak and potato customer. The limited menu and the high prices make the restaurant dependent on its unique atmosphere.

Victoria Station is not a typical family restaurant. One would not want to bring children here, since prices are high and there are no children's portions. The restaurant is geared toward the night-out group, specifically couples, who want a high class atmosphere, food and service. The entire property is dimly lighted, which sets a romantic mood. Dress ranges from smart casual to three-piece suits.

Victoria Station has the usual promotional items such as matchbooks, postcards and napkins, all headed with the restaurant's trade mark. They also have items such as gift certificates, food coupons, and promotion material for private parties, conventions, and birthday parties.

The atmosphere of Victoria Station is busy like a train station, yet it is unrushed for the customer. There is a comfortable amount of time between courses so one can relax, chat and digest. Management seems to attempt to play on the imaginative, fun side of the customer, while still maintaining high quality standards of good food and service.

Victoria Station is as close to a railway station as a restaurant could be. Although there are several flaws in the layout and service, the restaurant is a most enjoyable one. The facilities are clean and well-tended, the staff is well trained, well-mannered and hospitable, the food is superb, and the atmosphere is unusually delightful.

> 1981 and be much better positioned for 1982, when we'll be up again. It's not a matter of *wanting* to be up, we *have* to be up.'
>
> Today, Victoria Station is in the hardest phase - the turn around - of the so-called "chain restaurant life-cycle." Management has attacked a variety of problem areas and devised a program to return the chain to its past successes, with these key elements:
>
> * A halt in unit expansion.
> * Reorganization of the management structure at every level.
> * Increased cost controls at each level, watched on a daily basis.
> * The addition of new menu items.
> * Changes in its menu pricing strategy.
> * New marketing and promotional techniques to hold the traditional customer base while expanding the chain's appeal.
> * The closing of some units, remodeling and conversion of others.
>
> A sense of urgency exists in the chain's headquarters as well as in the field; public optimism and private worry characterize chain employees; the entire corporate staff is aware that decisions they make now will determine whether the chain continues to exist.[1]

The departure of Bradley was believed to signal the beginning of a change from "entrepreneurial" to "professional" management. Sheppard was the front running candidate for president and the current direction of the chain came primarily from him. Sheppard stated, "There will be absolutely no new units built until we see concrete, on-going evidence that the numbers have changed."

The major problem seen to be facing the company was falling customer counts caused by a declining price/value perception of Victoria Station. Bradley, however, defended the chain's history.

> ... we were also caught in some other binds not of our making. First of all, the economy was getting squeamish. Our segment was impacted first, and the results have hung on longer. We were in a rising cost environment which we couldn't control and were unable to pass on those costs through increased menu prices because of customer resistance. Also, customer spending habits and tastes were changing. We may have made tactical errors, but I disagree with

---

[1] "Getting back on track," *Restaurant Business*, January 1, 1981, p.23. Other parts of this section also draw from this article.

> critics who claim our theme is outdated. Decor is not the determining factor - price, food quality and service are all more important than decor.

Sheppard agreed, "After 10 years, I think it is safe to say that the decor concept has withstood the test of time."

An all-out attempt was made to bring customers back into the restaurants. Better cost controls, improved communications, and a cut in support service expenses were instituted in addition to attempts to make the company more responsive both from the bottom up and from the top down.

To attract more customers and adjust the poor consumer price/value perception, the company inaugurated "Operation Rollback," during which prices in two-thirds of the restaurants were decreased anywhere from 11 to 22 percent. This caused some additional problems, however. Victoria Station had cut prices to the point where they further eroded profit margins. According to Sheppard,

> Operation Rollback created some problems in that we established a new base from which we had to raise prices. Although we brought the customers in because of the program, it did have some long-lasting unfortunate consequences. We're still trying to get to where we should have been in relationship to the price of beef.

However, the company also saw positive effects in preparing the chain for a return to higher customer counts. Accoring to Bradley, "Rollback made us return to the basics - service, food, quality, and attitude. Today we can go after more customers with the confidence that we can handle them."

The new emphasis could be seen at Victoria Station headquarters where a second floor office was emblazoned with a large sign reading, "War Room." Walls were covered with performance charts for each unit. The room had a large conference table at which department heads met regularly. If a unit was in good shape, it was left alone but the wall charts highlighted any apparent difficulties so that they could be addressed promptly. The focus was on results. Said Sheppard,

> Each manager reports weekly. That includes sales and food and labor costs for both the current week and the next week's objectives. By keeping an eye on those figures and comparing them to objectives almost daily, we can see where the problems are and move on them immediately. We have already succeeded in lowering our food costs six point in 60 days through unit level controls coupled with our changed price strategy. Our purchasing is better, our pricing is more equitable on our new menu items, and labor hours are scheduled more tightly. We are managing the company on a daily basis.

Menu changes were made to reduce the image of a "prime rib palace" which more or less excluded from the customer base those persons who didn't eat beef. Shrimp Victoria or teriyaki chicken with prime rib or top sirloin, and shrimp Victoria with teriyaki chicken replaced the 23 ounce "Owner's Cut" of prime rib with its high food cost. "The response has been excellent," said Sheppard, "and we anticipate more additions to the menu along those lines - items we haven't been known for in the past which the customer is looking for today.

Other additions included an "Inflation-fighter's Special" at lunch for $2.95, a teriyaki chicken breast with rice or an artichoke, and spinach quiche with salad. A children's menu was also introduced. "The door is open," said Sheppard, we're not locked in to anything." Added Sheppard, "Today, we're looking for a wider customer base, and I feel we're succeeding. We're less skewed toward one customer and attracting more families, seniors and non-red meat eaters."

In referring to the recent game hen promotion, an item which remained on the regular menu, Jon Rose, vice president of marketing, said, "It's a good new product with a good food cost. And the message is, 'Victoria Station has something different, good and inexpensive, and it's not red meat.'" According to Rose, the hen promotion didn't generate customer count increases, but it wasn't expected to. "We just wanted to get across the message that we're changing. Our new-item promotions are designed to communicate to the public that Victoria Station is diversified and affordable."

Sheppard decentralized marketing and promotional activities and hired six public relations firms across the country to help create less of a chain-like image. Some units were closed and others remodeled or repositioned. According to one corporate executive, "I think all we need is time. If the lenders are willing to give us that time, we'll make it. If not, I just don't know what will happen."

Sheppard was generally seen as the man to get most of the credit if the company made a turn-around. In January, the board of directors named Sheppard chief operating officer, reporting only to the board with all divisions reporting to him. His rise was seen as meteoric in the nine months since he had left Marriott Corporation as vice president of international operations.

THE GUARD CHANGES

Nation's Restaurant News of March 16, 1981 carried the following news item.

COLLINS NEW CEO AT VICTORIA STATION

Larkspur, Calif. - Terrance A. Collins has joined financially troubled Victoria Station as president and executive officer. He was president of General Foods Burger Chef chain for four years. Collins, 39, replaces Richard Bradley who resigned last October. Bradley was the last of the 90-unit specialty dinnerhouse chains's founders to leave the company. But he remains board chairman.

Collins makes the transition from the fast food segment to a dinner house chain with this switch. He has 13 years experience in the fast food business, first as western regional vice-president for McDonald's and, since 1977, as head of the 900 unit Burger Chef hamburger chain.

Paul Sheppard continues at Victoria Station as executive vice-president and chief operating officer. Sheppard joined Victoria Station early last year from Marriott Corp., where he was vice-president of international operations. He joined as senior vice-president of markleting and subsequently became executive vice-president and chief operating officer as well.

Collins task as the new president will be to pull the ailing restaurant chain into full financial recovery. However, company officials pointed out that for the month of December, the company showed its first operating profit in 15 months.

The March 28 issue of *Nation's Restaurant News* carried these items.

VICTORIA STATION REORGANIZES

Larkspur, Calif. - A tremendous reorganization of Victoria Station is underway along with extensive menu testing and marketing programs.

Currently, four new menu programs are ongoing at various Victoria Stations throughout the country. All the menu changes are designed to appeal to a large segment of the population.

Victoria Station had been recognized mostly as a roast beef and red meat dining facility. "Because of the limited appeal menu, people weren't coming as frequently," a spokeswoman said, adding that the trend in dining is toward a lighter diet and less red meat. An extensive selection including lighter fares and many "stack-type" items is being pilot tested for use in other Victoria Stations. Among the items featured are, "It's a Crock" (soup), "There's No Tamale" (chile nachos, quesadillas, Mexican pizza), "Quiche Me Quick" (artichoke and spinach or crab quiche), "Network" (seafood).

To date, the new menu has been "extremely successful" in so far as cocktail and dinner business has improved greatly, the spokeswoman said.

The second ongoing promotion features Dungeness crab from Oregon. When first introduced last month in Dallas, the item went over so well that an additional 40,000 pounds had to be shipped to the restaurant the first week. The number of units in which this promotion will be featured will depend on the supply of the crab.

The third promotion, "All you can eat B-B-Q chicken and ribs," will be featured in southern California. A fourth promotion, "the inflation-fighters luncheon," will be used in most of the Victoria Stations in the western region of the country, and on a limited basis in the east. It offers a choice of a cheeseburger with french fries, an artichoke and spinach quiche with soup of the day, or teriyaki chicken breast with rice pilaf for $2.95. For an additional $1.25, the customer has unlimited use of the salad bar.

The pilot programs are in the initial stages, the spokeswoman said, explaining that it is too early to know how extensive their use will be throughout the chain.

VICTORIA STATION TESTING ALL-DAY MENUS IN 3 UNITS

Larkspur, Calif. - In its latest effort to improve customer counts and stimulate repeat business, Victoria Station has introduced experimental all-day menus in three of the chain's 99 units. The chain traditionally has used separate lunch and dinner menus.

The new menus offer a wide variety of items at price points that appeal to a larger segment of customers, marketing vice president Jon Rose said.

... "Preliminary results are very positive," Rose said. He said the test would run for at least three months before the company would judge the success of the experiment.

The new menus are printed on a huge role of butcher shop brown paper and are left on the role and handed to customers as they enter the restaurant.

COLLINS - VICTORIA STATION'S MYSTERY MAN

Larkspur, Calif. - ...Although sources say he appeared to be happy at Burger Chef, Collins decided it was the right time for a change. "Aside from the fact that he was well compensated, Terry apparently felt that he could make a real contribution at Victoria Station," a high level source said. "It was a challenge. I'm not a safe player," Collins said, in a 1977 interview for the Burger Chef publication, Scene.

... Collins is currently involved in a period of assessment at the chain and is scheduled for a two week cross-country trip to visit many of the company's 99 units. "He's a very one-on-one person," Victoria Station vice president of marketing Jon Rose says... "He wants to make sure he's fully aware of everything before making any major decisions."

What those major decisions may be is still unclear. And chain officials note that many of the "hard decisions" have already been made. "He's [Collins] joining a company that is fairly on its way to recovery," Rose says.

Many of those decisions have been made by executive vice president and COO Paul G. Sheppard... Under Sheppard, management ranks have been pared at both headquarters and in the field. His turnaround strategy, centered around decreasing the operational expenses while increasing customer counts through menu expansion and heavy promotion, appears to be showing some signs of success... Overall customer counts are reportedly up over last year and sources say the chain stands a good chance of showing a profit in the final quarter.

Despite the modest improvements, some analysts maintain that very serious problems remain. "Efforts have been made to change the format and the menu, and they've done some good creative advertising, but nothing seems to stick," says Edward M. Tavlin, an analyst with Prescott, Bull and Turben.

"They've got a very heavy capital expenditure in each unit requiring high unit volumes and they have been impacted in a large part by circumstances beyond their control [rising red meat prices]," he said. "The unit itself is more of a novelty type," he continued, "and the big question is whether it can stand the test of time."

... Collins is the lead role in a play that is still being written. The play is about survival. Whether that drama turns into a triumph or a tragedy is yet to be determined.

By June, 1981, Victoria Station's menu had a completely new look both in format and in menu offerings. The changes were rolled out nationally this month and were aimed at broadening the chain's market appeal by offering more variety and lower-priced items. The menu was leather bound with a printed insert instead of the boards that had been used in the past, but still had a train motif and theme. It contained new appetizers, a wine list, special house drinks, and a half dozen more entrees. The changes had been tested in 10 markets.

Appetizers, which had not generally been on previous menus, included potato skins, nachos and zucchini. New entrees were boneless filet of salmon, stuffed shrimp, an eight ounce cut of prime rib, teriyaki beef kabob, and Shrimp Diana, shrimp baked in wine, cheese, garlic, and bread crumbs. The new entrees included a starch accompaniment, which previously had to be ordered separately.

Although the new items had lower prices, management expected the check average to remain the same at about $14.00 because there were more items to choose from, such as appetizers and drinks. These were expected to offset the lower-priced entrees in the total check. The company also was testing all-day menus in three of its units. These menus included such items as soup, salad, chili, nachos, quesdillas, artichoke and spinach quiche, crab quiche, and seafood. The new menu quickly improved food cost figures, according to Rose.

Also introduced in 1981 was a new wine program. After careful study over a year's time, three core wine lists were designed for various sections of the U.S. and Canada. A special feature was a carefully selected group of California and imported wines available by the glass as well as by the bottle. An extensive training program in wine identification, appreciation, and service was initiated. A special handbook was developed for employees that included a description of of the basic elements of wine and the steps in the production of wine from the vine to the bottle. Also included were a glossary of wine terms, features of wine service, suggestive selling and merchandising techniques. "Wine of the Month," and "Manager's Selection" were also featured. "From the patron's point of view," said Rose, "the opportunity to try before you buy and sampling a wine or two by the glass before ordering a bottle, provided an easy and inexpensive way to compare wines and develop a certain expertise."

In the fiscal quarter ending June 1981, the chain reported a net profit of $703,000 on sales of $30.1 million, as opposed to a net loss for the first quarter of $1.2 million on the same amount of sales. According to Collins, the positive results were due to a continued cost control program, the new expanded menu, and elimination of several marginal properties. He also stated that the results provided firm evidence that the strategies initiated over the last year were moving the company toward a gradual, planned return to long-term profitability.

Thousands of dollars were invested in capital improvements to upgrade units. Banquet facilities were being added and, in some locations, windows were put in to give a lighter, more open appearance.

NEW MARKETS

In October 1981, Victoria Station announced that it was making a major push to obtain group business. Ken Bracken, manager of field marketing, stated, "We are going after the tour and travel, corporate and local group business as a major project. It's a lucrative market and in many areas we see a great shortage of rooms where meals and liquor service are available for groups of 20 to 80 persons." A new "tour and travel menu package" was put together to be sold at major travel shows such as that of the American Bus Association. The move was accompanied by the creation of a new national group sales staff. According to Bracken, "We hope to add several million dollars a year in sales." Group business was solicited in off-hours when the restaurant was not normally open with a "Rent a Restaurant Rent-Free" program. The chain also worked with various local attractions such as the Boston Children's Museum and the Museum of Transportation. "Working with local attractions," said Bracken, "helps build business for us and for them."

Advertising was commenced in major sports events programs with discount coupons. Local sports teams were asked to select their favorite charity and sponsor fund-raising dinners at Victoria Station restaurants. The following year it was planned to take part in the Jerry Lewis Muscular Dystrophy fund-raising appeal. "Now that we have turned around, we can do these things," said Bracken.

END OF THE TUNNEL

By the end of 1981, Victoria Station was seeing an end to its financial woes. In the quarter ended September 13, it reported profits of $391,000 on sales of $30.4 million, compared to a loss of $1.6 million for the same period a year earlier. Sheppard explained the turn-around:

> The target was brought into range primarily through far better controls in food and beverage and attention to detail at the unit level. We've cut our costs by hedging beef requirements, and by better short and long range negotiating in our purchasing. Being able to broaden the menu, offering an expanded dinner selection and a broader price structure has also helped. [However, customer counts are] probably close to even with last year's [19 percent

> below what they were the last profitable year, 1979].
>
> It's not something that happens overnight. We're hoping that with the changes we're making we'll answers that question [of not bringing more people in through the front door]. [The intention now is to] appeal to every market from the secretary to the businessman and local family business.

Collins stated it this way:

> Victoria Station is now competing in a tougher marketplace, but we are successfully competing. The basic concept on which our system was built has now withstood the test of over a decade of operation and two years of adversity. We have turned the corner back to profitability, expanded our demographic appeal, and tightened our management and control mechanisms where necessary. We cannot promise miracles. Our return to prosperity will be gradual, but it will be steady - and planned.

1982

1982 saw Victoria Station double the size of its lunch menu and revise the dinner menu once again, after a year of testing in markets from Cincinnati to Portland. The company went from a limited lunch menu to a much broader menu that included lower-priced items, an "Express Lunch" section promising complete service within 30 minutes, and other special sections including Mexican dishes, appetizers, soups, and meals for the calorie conscious.

"Historically," Rose said, Victoria Station has not drawn "clerical workers and non-executives. The lunch changes are an effort to bring in all types of people and expand the chain's demographic base. Four more "inflation-fighter" items were added, as well as rainbow trout and an item called "Stuff a Wild Potato" which was a baked potato, split and loaded with a Mexican, Italian, or California style filling.

The soup selection was expanded to seven to include such items as tomato florentine, Golden Gate mushroom, and southern style chicken gumbo. The salad bar now had four ways in which it could be ordered. Appetizers from the dinner menu were also added to the lunch menu.

The dinner menu was also revised. The salmon dish was dropped in favor of Alaskan King Crab, and a shellfish sampler was added. Shrimp Victoria was reinstated in place of Shrimp Diana.

Rose said the changes would be reflected in a small increase in the average check, but the purpose was primarily to increase meal counts. "We want to expand the customer's perception of Victoria Station," he said.

THE GUARD CHANGES AGAIN

In May 1982, the board of directors eliminated the positions held by Paul Sheppard and Jon Rose, in a tightening-up process. Collins, in addition to retaining his titles of chairman, president, and CEO, also took on Sheppard's position of COO. It was reported that he was anxious to take more direct control in his greatest area of expertise, operations. Victoria Victory continued as marketing director.

In July 1982, Collins resigned from the company in a dispute with the board of directors over the company's future course. Richard Niglio, vice president and general manager of the fast-food and restaurant division of International Multifoods, who had started with that company as president of the Mr. Donut division, was named as his replacement. He was a 1964 Yale graduate with a degree in economics who had started his career with the J. Walter Thompson advertising agency. From there he became director of national advertising and the vice president of marketing for Kentucky Fried Chicken. At age 26 he had taken over as president and CEO of KFC's troubled H.Salt fish and chips division, and took it from a loss to a profit.

Fiscal 1982, for the year ending March 28, showed a $7 million turnaround from 1981's $6.3 million loss to 1982's net earnings of $1.2 million. Although Collins had rolled out a broader menu, the improvement was due to "totally improved" operational controls, according to a company spokesman.

Niglio, 39, commenting on his appointment, said that most likely what Victoria Station needs is a simpler "repositioning from a marketing point of view," to include greater menu development. Niglio's reputation was that of a "fixer." With strengths in marketing, advertising, and franchising, he had helped patch up a number of troubled operations in a 15 year career as a foodservice executive. Collins, the trade press noted, had a similar reputation.

1983

Nation's Restaurant News of January 3, 1983 reported the following:

DISCOUNTING STRATEGY BACKFIRES

Larkspur, Calif. - Victoria Station, wounded by a now-abandoned discounting strategy and suffering from an on-going decline in meal counts, has posted a $1.2 million loss for the second quarter ended September 12. Revenues were $25.5 million, compared to $30.4 million a year ago.

For the first 24 weeks of fiscal 1983, the loss was $1.1 million vs. earnings of $1.1 million for the previous year. Revenues

> were $52.4 million compared to $60.4 million.
>
> Along with the probability of damage to its image from discounting, president and CEO Richard Niglio pointed to the slump in customer counts as the basis for the troubles.
>
> Niglio's strategy for both short- and long-term recovery is based on revamping the company's marketing structure and philosophy. Included in the short-term moves are the replacement of some dinner items with more fresh fish; the elimination of the company's field marketing staff, which had been heavily involved with discount and coupon promotions, and creation of a broadcast-oriented media campaign to boost seafood sales.
>
> For long-term reversal of the meal count decline, the company is constructing an entirely revamped menu which will feature a wider selection of entrees with a greater range of prices.
>
> Other changes, which Niglio characterized as "a significant change in strategic direction for the company," include an overhaul and repositioning of the Victoria Station concept and format and its reintroduction to the marketplace through a high-impact television advertising effort. Niglio declined to give any further details of his newly conceived battleplan.

In July, Victoria Station reported a net loss of $8.3 million for the fiscal year ended April 3, compared to net earnings of $1.21 million in fiscal 1982. Revenue declined to $112.3 million from $123.9 million the year before. The company reported that it was testing various menu modifications in hopes of reversing a drastic decline in customer counts. "We're very hopeful the economy will improve, and that we will experience some of that improvement," said a spokesman. He indicated the chain was concentrating on test markets in the southeast, where broader menu offerings had been introduced and eventually would be deployed in other major markets.

The menu changes were "not necessarily a de-emphasis of beef, or an emphasis on seafood, but involve a realignment of items to offer broader appeal with something for everyone." Victoria Station was proceeding cautiously in rolling out new menus, "not from financial restraints, but because of efforts to maintain quality as it shifts to new concepts."

In November, Victoria Station reported a net loss of $1.06 million for its second quarter ended September 18th on revenues of $23.09 million. The company also said that it had reached an agreement in principle with its lenders that would allow for a restructuring of loan payments, and a plan to sell off up to 35 of its restaurants over a three year period. The plan to sell off up to one-third of its units was part of a corporate strategy to achieve greater market penetration through more effective allocation of company resources. Proceeds from the sale would be used to support the introduction of a new menu and new merchandising concepts for working capital purposes and to repay debt.

1984

Nation's Restaurant News of March 27, 1984 reported the following:

> **VIC STATION LOOKS TO BONKERS TO HELP CUT STAGGERING LOSSES**
>
> Larkspur, Calif. - Victoria Station is opting to trade boxcars for burgers in its newest strategy to overcome staggering, ongoing losses. While reporting a $1.95 million net loss on revenue of $30 million for the third quarter ending January 8, the 97 unit chain disclosed plans to jump on the upscale burger bandwagon with conversion to a new concept, Bonkers.
>
> The company said it anticipated conversion of a significant number of its restaurants to the fast-growing segment, starting with two units. Bonkers will feature a new exterior and interior design, while the traditional railcar concept will continue in non-converted units. ...[The announcement] came one day after American Values, a Bermuda-based investment company and Victoria Station's biggest stockholder, sold most of its interest in the company.

Richard Niglio said that converting the company's restaurants to a new concept may "substantially impact long-term profitability." The concept included a retail bakery, and self-serve format. Burgers, hot dogs, soups, salad bar, and other items comprised its menu. "The Victoria Station concept, as originally conceived, was outmoded," declared Niglio, "but we have breathed some life into it." Results were being felt. Customer counts were up in the last half of fiscal 1984. Now a revolution was rising in the form of Bonkers.

Niglio felt that the new concept was the key element in a long-term solution that would return the company to profitability. Said Niglio,

> We are very enthusiastic about Bonkers, and may convert a significant number of units to the concept. We were looking for a home run concept. We considered the fern bar concept, but there is too much capital investment involved and the segment is too mature. Upscale, adult fast food is a new segment. Customers are trading up from fast food; there's erosion from the dinner house segment. I see long-term growth.
>
> The baby boom has grown up on fast food. A big bulge of the population is growing older and, though they still enjoy fast food, the baby boomers want more ambience and a higher quality product. There has been a lot of banter about this, but I believe it is true.
>
> The check average at Victoria Station is $15; fast food checks average a few dollars. There is a hole of $4 to $6 between

> these two ranges that is yet to be filled. Bonkers is an adult fast food hamburger restaurant. It is a fun food place. Alcoholic beverage sales are under 20 percent. We can get that up four or five points, and we will, but we want to keep it fun. It's an unstructured dining experience, very informal. There are no rules. It's self-serve like fast food.

The Bonkers theme combined the nostalgia of the 50s with the flair of the 80s. The exterior was reminiscent of an east coast diner of the 50s era with stainless steel trim and neon highlighting. The concept was aimed at appealing to a broad range of customers. Baby boomers were the main target, but it was expected to appeal to their kids as well. For parents, it was a change from fast food, and they could order a drink if they wanted. Niglio felt that Bonkers' prices and good value would attract seniors as well. The half-pound "ultimate hamburger," ground fresh from quality raw product, complete with on-premise made buns, and "add-it-yourself" trimmings, was priced at $3.75.

The company planned to open 10 to 15 Bonkers in 1984. All units would be conversions of Victoria Stations, and would disguise the boxcars, at a conversion cost of under $300,000. The check average was $5 to $6. The company expected a unit to do over $2 million annually. Food costs were lower (about 30 percent) than a Victoria Station, as were labor costs, largely due to the self-service aspect.

Niglio's summation of his attack against Victoria Station's problems was three-pronged: First, changes to the Victoria Station concept; second, the roll-out of Bonkers as a long-term solution; and third, the disposal of unprofitable operations. "We've come with a long-term solution and the financing to do it," he said. "We are excited about the future." Exhibit 2 describes the Bonkers concept.

The future, however, did not bear out the promise. Cash-strapped, and unable to nail down a crucial $5 million loan it needed to appease its banks and to carry out more Bonkers conversions, Victoria Stations tried to formulate a new survival strategy. The prospect of bankruptcy had pervaded the company, as evidenced by Niglio's golden parachute move to guarantee his minimum $200,000 annual salary through 1987 if the company succumbed to its financial ailments, or his contract was otherwise breached.

The company had been able to sell only a few of its restaurants that it had put on the block, and was facing lower than anticipated sales. The reportedly high-grossing Bonkers units were facing reluctance by outsiders to finance the conversions. For fiscal 1984, net losses were $6 million on sales of $101.5 million, a revenue decline of 9.6 percent from 1983.

EXHIBIT 2 The Bonkers Concept

Victoria Station Customers Go Bonkers!

Bonkers for burgers

As the kids of the McDonald's generation have grown up and become more sophisticated, their food tastes and eating-out preferences have been changing. They have become young adults, and they are no longer content with the plastic decor and prepackaged fast food that they happily consumed as children. While very value-conscious, they are seeking more interesting eating-out experiences and, most importantly, fresher, higher quality food. However, they have not lost their taste for hamburgers. Thus, an entirely new market segment of the foodservice industry is emerging—the "adult gourmet hamburger" market. The potential size of this new business promises to be substantial, and it seems to appeal to a much broader segment of the population than the young adults for whom it was originated. The concept seems attractive to just about everyone—from budget-conscious single parents and retirees, to vested businessmen looking for a quick lunch, and trendy young pacesetters out for an evening of fun.

Bonkers for the future

During the past fiscal year, the Company developed "Bonkers Burger Grill & Bar" to enter this emerging adult hamburger business. The first unit was converted from a former Victoria Station restaurant and opened in Southern California in March of 1984. Bonkers was conceived as a contemporary, hamburger-specialty establi·hment which offers simple, top quality foods and beverages at readily perceived low prices in a casual, fun atmosphere. The results of the initial restaurant have exceeded projections by a wide margin, and the Company plans to convert several additional locations to the new Bonkers concept over the next two to three years.

Bonkers for a new look

In the transition to Bonkers, both the interior and exterior of the original train-themed Victoria Station restaurant are completely remodeled so that the boxcars and other railroad elements virtually disappear. An entirely new facia is built completely around the boxcars and caboose which comprise the existing structure. Windows and

skylights are added, and most interior walls are removed to provide an open and airy feeling. The new atmosphere has a contemporary feel, yet it is reminiscent of the fifties decade and evokes nostalgia for that simple, popular period in our history. Bold architectural elements have been added to call attention to all the changes, including the use of neon, curved hard surfaces, gleaming metallics, bright graphics, and colors. Night or day, it is truly difficult to pass by a Bonkers restaurant without looking and stopping.

Bonkers for fresh food and fun

The Bonkers menu, served all day, is relatively simple to prepare and offers the high quality and level of variety that are expected by today's discerning customers at reasonable, attractive prices. The Bonkers specialty is a half-pound, freshly ground pure beef hamburger, grilled to order in the open kitchen, and served on a large sesame-seed bun that is baked fresh every hour in Bonkers' own bakery. Customers garnish their own burger with a variety of dressings and fresh produce which are laden on convenient condiment bars. Other items on the menu include the popular and abundant 59-item salad bar, a hefty New York-style hot dog, a marinated teriyaki chicken sandwich, and a New York steak sandwich—all served on home-baked Bonkers buns. Beef ribs, a smaller children's burger, and side orders such as chili, special fries, and thick homemade milkshakes and malts complete the Bonkers menu. Oversized, freshly-baked cookies and brownies are available to take out from the bakery in addition to ice cream cones. The fun atmosphere at Bonkers is enhanced by a friendly, lively young staff, an attractive, open bar specializing in beer by the bucket, blended drinks and fruit-based cocktails, and a fifties-style jukebox playing beloved oldies.

Bonkers for success

Bonkers is designed to be fun, exciting, memorable, highly recommendable, and priced right for the frequent restaurant-goer of today and tomorrow. It has an obvious appeal to contemporary casual lifestyles and delivers the high levels of quality and freshness which consumers are demanding. In short, Bonkers is the restaurant with a hint of the 50's, which is styled for the 80's and 90's—styled for success.

1985

Nation's Restaurant News:

JULY 22: VICTORIA STATION NARROWS NET LOSS

Larkspur, Calif. - Victoria Stations Inc. said it narrowed its annual net loss to $5.26 million for the year ended March 31 from $5.76 million from 1984. Revenue declined 8%, to $93.8 million. The company is retrofitting some of its steak houses into Bonkers dinnerhouses and closing others.

NOVEMBER 4: VICTORIA STATION FACES NEW HITCH

Larkspur, Calif. - Victoria Station Inc., facing a $3 million operating loss for its second quarter because of disappointing sales in its dinnerhouses and new Bonkers hamburger restaurants, said a complex plan to renegotiate leaseholds and restructure its debt load is vital to the company's continued viability.

The company completed a balance sheet restructuring last April amid hopes that the Bonkers concept would boost sales and profits while it exited from the steakhouse business.

NOVEMBER 11: VICTORIA STATION LOSSES MOUNT

Larkspur, Calif. - Victoria Station Inc., hobbled by poor sales in both its old dinnerhouses and its new Bonkers restaurants, lost $3.21 million in the second quarter ended Sept. 15, almost twce as deep a loss as that of the year-ago quarter, $1.65 million. Revenue slumped 12%, to $20.1 million.

1986

Nation's Restaurant News

MARCH 10: RESTAURANT UNSURE OF NEGOTIATION OUTCOME

Larkspur, Calif. - Victoria Station said that current negotiations with lessors, lenders and other parties over lease and debt restructuring are "vital to the continuing viability" of the company. But, it added, it can offer "no assurances" about the outcome of the negotiations.

Once a leading theme dinnerhouse chain, Victoria Station has been buffeted in recent years by huge losses, the latest coming in the third quarter ended Jan. 5, when the beleaguered chain posted a net loss of $19.1 million on revenues of $22.3 million.

Victoria Station has shuttered 34 of its 91 restaurants since last May. It took a $17.6 million charge for closing 29 of the units in the most recent quarter. The ongoing closings and sales of restaurants, including four of its seven of its Bonkers burger outlets, put Victoria Station in violation of its loan agreements.

Victoria Station's nine-month losses totaled $24.3 million, compared with a $3.7 million loss for the same period a year ago.

JUNE 2: VICTORIA STATION FILES CHAPTER 11 PETITION

SAN FRANCISCO - No longer confident it could keep creditors at bay and pressed to find additional capital after losing more than $40 million in four years, Victoria Station, Inc. has filed for protection under Chapter 11...

... officials of the company said they had taken the unusual step of filing a reorganization plan with a petition for protection, a step that could substantially shorten the reorganization process... The 45-unit railroad themed chain, which closed 46 of its restaurants and laid off about 2000 of its employees during the past year... list company assets of $36.4 million and liabilities of $34.2 million.

The small mountain of paperwork...covered the parent Delaware corporation and 11 subsidiaries, including eight doing business as Victoria Station in as many states; Euston Station in New York; Railhead Restaurants in Texas; and Bonkers, of California, the company's ill-fated `gourmet' burger concept.

Founded in San Francisco in 1969, the steak, prime rib and seafood chain by the mid-70s was considered by many to be on the fast track to success... However, skyrocketing red-meat prices, a drop in the consumption of such meat by most Americans in recent years and an aging concept has left the company fighting for its life. It lost $19 million between April 1983 and March 1985 and reported $23 million in losses during the first nine months of fiscal 1986.

Victoria Station officials have amazed industry observers for years with their ability to come up with new funding and fight off creditors... Much of the miracle workers' efforts were wasted.

The snake-bitten company plowed a good deal of its new resources into the development of Bonkers Burger Grill and Bar. The 50's-themed burger restaurant seemed just the ticket for the clean conversion of Victoria Station units, but like many other concepts born during `gourmet' burger mania, it fell by the wayside, taking much of the chain's future with it.

1987

RETROSPECTIVE

The following is excerpted from comments in *Restaurant Business* printed in its July 20, 1987 issue.

> For six long and painful years, the troubled publicly owned company struggled with various strategies and schemes to stage a turnaround. In the end, all efforts proved futile. Victoria Station just took a long time to die.
>
> "In retrospect, I think Victoria Station needed a priest, not a doctor," says former president Richard Niglio. "I think it is a miracle the company didn't go into bankruptcy before it did."
>
> Victoria Station has closed all but 12 or 14 of its units. Remaining units have been located on the east coast, so headquarters have been moved to the premises of a unit in Darien, CN. Mike Colonna, for years a regional manager, has taken the reins as president. Niglio left at the end of April to become chief executive of Darien-based Child Care Centers of America, a chain of day-care centers.
>
> According to Niglio and to several observers, what happened to Victoria Station could easily happen to another company. Like the stories other failed chains have to tell, this is the tale of a company that expanded too fast, was too heavily leveraged, and was too closely tied to a single very identifiable theme.
>
> Niglio was convinced that the long-term solution to Victoria Station's problems was to allocate funds from the mature dinnerhouse market to a segment with growth potential. Thus Bonkers, an upscale fast food restaurant was born. As late as June 1985, Victoria Station was planning aggressive franchising of Bonkers. A vice president of franchising was named and an additional $5 million in new financing was arranged.
>
> A lot of other companies saw potential in the idea of adult fast food, and the so-called gourmet burger niche turned out to bew too small for all the players jostling to get in. Six Bonkers were opened in all.
>
> The question is, why did all Victoria Station's attempts at repositioning fail? Other companies have made the transition from one concept to another without going into bankruptcy.
>
> Today, Freeman is president of San Francisco-based California Restaurants. Bradley operates Mexican restaurants in Hawaii, and Lee is a business man in the San Francisco area, assembling and distributing laser-disc video jukeboxes.

CASE 21

CROWNE PLAZA/AMSTERDAM

Based in Memphis, Tennessee, the Holiday Corporation operated the largest hotel chain in the world. This included over 300,000 rooms in over 1750 hotels in over 60 countries worldwide. In 1982, President and CEO Mike Rose had stated:

> The mission of the hotel group is to increase Holiday Inn's leadership position in the broad midscale segments of the lodging industry. This mission will be achieved by producing superior consumer satisfaction through increased emphasis on the quality of our product and further capitalization on our significant distributional advantages over all other competitors. We also intend to increase our consumer recognition as the preferred brand in the lodging industry.

Holiday's hotels were divided into two groups: company owned and operated, and franchisee owned and operated. Over 80 percent of the system was operated by franchisees, although management cited the following advantages from operating its own hotels: "It provides a basis for innovation and leadership in the marketplace, e.g., company operated hotels provide an extensive research base for the development of marketing information, operating procedures, and marketing techniques."

COMPANY HISTORY

In spite of this belief the number of company operated hotels had decreased steadily from 1974 to 1981, because management wanted to phase aging properties out of the system, and Holiday had become largely a franchise organization. The company carefully screened all franchise applicants. Franchise agreements, which were for a 20 year period, set standards for service and the quality of the accommodations. The company trained franchise management at Holiday Inn University near Memphis, conducted inspections three times a year, and provided detailed operations manuals, training films, and instructional aids for franchisee personnel.

Territorial constraints and ensuing legal problems placed limitations on Holiday's growth in the United States. This led Holiday to begin a program of rapid expansion abroad. Their strategy called for building strong national chains within the countries in which Holiday operated, as well as to gradually expand into new markets, rather than to have one location in major overseas cities as some competitors had done. Only apparent politically stable locations were chosen. By 1981, the number of non U.S. locations was 226. By 1988, Holiday had five properties in The Netherlands and five in the other Benelux countries of Belgium and Luxembourg. The mission statement for Holiday Inn International stated:

> Recognizing the value of distribution in enhancing customer flow among all regions, the Holiday Inn International mission is to become the world's largest hotel company outside the United States. The European Division will seek rapid growth through 1994, with mid and upscale distribution in all major gateway and destination cities and in secondary cities. Customer satisfaction will be consistent with Hotel Group goals and will be equal or superior to the competition.

In the United States, however, Holiday's competitive position had begun to weaken. Many three and four star hotels were badly in need of refurbishment and there was increased competition from new, innovative hotel companies. Quality Inns and Days Inn were hurting Holiday in the lower tier segments; Hyatt and Marriott were hurting in the upper segments. Occupancy and image suffered. Holiday perceived the major growth markets to be the upper luxury, suite, and budget segments. With its "middle of the road" three and four star properties, it was losing market share.

In response to its deteriorating image, Holiday introduced in 1981 a "no excuses" room guarantee program for all its U.S. hotels. This program guaranteed guests' satisfaction or their money refunded. This tactical response proved to be inadequate for changing market conditions. Holiday was forced to rethink its strategy.

One strategy was to enter the perceived major growth market segments and directly challenge the competition in those markets. The result was an emphasis on Crowne Plaza, Embassy Suites, and Hampton Inns in developing the extended product line. A distributional advantage was the Holidex reservation system, the largest of its kind in the industry and one which linked thousands of terminals throughout the world. Holidex II added room inventory and marketing data base capabilities. Holidex III, to be introduced in 1988, would represent further state of the art capabilities.

Holiday also had a distributional advantage in its travel agent program. This program paid commissions within 30 days of booking in the agent's local currency. Other hotel companies were noted for paying in 60 days or more. Holiday also paid with just one monthly check and included a computerized listing of all monthly booking activity. The success of this program was attested to by a 50 percent increase in agents' bookings over a three year period.

Holiday also had made a successful entry into casino gaming operations in 1979. In a joint venture with Harrah's of Nevada, Holiday became the largest U.S. gaming company. By 1986 casino gaming would represent over 30 percent of overall company profit. With this success under their belt, Holiday entered the luxury, suite, and budget segments of the market in the early 1980s so that the product line included:

Hampton Inns - two star budget (called Garden Inn in Europe)
Holiday Inn - three and four star middle tier
Harrah's - casinos in Las Vegas, Reno, Tahoe, Atlantic City
Embassy Suites - an all-suite product
Holiday Inn Crowne Plaza - five star, upscale, luxury

Except for Crowne Plaza, Holiday chose not to use the Holiday name for its new products. Some industry observers believed that this was a deliberate attempt to create a new brand image separate from the old, tarnished Holiday Inn image of aging, mediocre hotels. Some also doubted if Holiday, entrenched in a three or four star mentality, could operate and compete at a five star level. In fact, in the United States, very few of all properties had ever reached four star status and none ever received five star designation. Abroad, however, the Holiday Inn image was considerably stonger than it was in the United States. This was largely due to better quality and better managed properties.

AMSTERDAM

Between 1983 and 1985, hotel occupancies in Amsterdam were near 70 percent and profit levels were high. Amsterdam, a city of 750,000 and an airport (Schiphol) reputed to be the best in the world, was a major cultural and business city, but few international hotel chains had located there. Holiday, as well as Meridien, SAS, and others, conducted feasibilty studies and, based on the positive findings, decided to operate new properties there. These decisions, however, preceded an actual opening by three to six years.

In 1986 a combination of the Chernoble nuclear disaster in Russia, terrorist bombings in Europe, and the declining value of the American dollar caused the bottom to drop out of the tourism market. Although Amsterdam itself was not affected by the disasters, its primary foreign market, Americans, chose to spend its holidays elsewhere. Amsterdam was not a major tourist destination city, but it was on many tour itineraries. Thus, the decline in European vacations in general in 1986 also affected Amsterdam.

Hotel companies developing in Amsterdam, faced with this situation, decided that this was an isolated occurrence and pressed ahead with their building plans. 1987 also turned out to be a disaster year in terms of the American tourist. Coinciding with the opening of the Holiday Inn Amsterdam Crowne Palace, was a decline in the American tourist market from 23.5 percent of all five star room nights in 1985 to 14 percent in 1987. Amsterdam was also suffering from accessibilty, crime, and image problems which had been internationally reported in the press.

Also contributing to the hotel marketing problem in Amsterdam was the general product level. What was considered a five star product in the Benelux countries was not equal to a five star product in the United States.

Historic Centre City Centre City was the historic heart of Amsterdam and the main tourist attraction in The Netherlands. Much of the country's business was located there. It served as a gateway to the rest of the country, as well as to several European countries.

Domestic business in Centre City had grown slightly over the past years, while foreign travel had experienced a definite decrease. The decrease was attributed to the lower value of the American dollar, an increase in crime and pollution, and negative publicity during the previous two to three years. For some tourists, Centre City was the place to be. For many others, it was the place to avoid. Exhibit 1 provides some statistics for Amsterdam hotels in general, and Centre City hotels in particular.

CROWNE PLAZA/AMSTERDAM

The first Crowne Plaza in Europe was opened in Amsterdam in March, 1987. The Crowne Plaza concept had been heavily researched in the U.S., but not at all in Europe. Initial expectations were optimistic but first year losses exceeded one million guilders (approx. USD 500,000). Occupancy levels ranged between 55 and 60 percent. The Crowne Plaza's problems were not unique. Amsterdam hotels in general, especially the five star category, had suffered from a supply of hotel rooms that had increased steadily while demand was decreasing, as shown in Exhibit 1.

Management and Personnel The Crowne Plaza management team reported to Holiday Inn International Headquarters in London. Although the management structure was initially decentralized, headquarters became increasingly involved in the operation as actual operating results did not meet the optimistic projections. The personnel turnover rate was high.

Target Markets and Positioning As the first Crowne Plaza in Europe, Holiday Inn International was anxious that this hotel be positioned at the 5 star level, but slightly below the Amstel. Some industry observers, however, felt that the hotel was not optimally positioned in the market. They believed that the upscale traveler was discouraged from trying the Crowne Plaza because it was associated with the traditional Holiday Inn.

EXHIBIT 1 Amsterdam Hotel Statistics

A. Hotel Supply in Amsterdam

	5 star	4 star	3 star	1-2 star	Total
1980					
Hotels	22	17	33	191	263
Rooms	4481	1436	1123	3126	10166
1985					
Hotel	22	17	31	176	246
Rooms	4578	1469	1111	2832	9990

B. Expansion in Amsterdam Since 1985

Hotel	Category	Location	Rooms	Date Completed
Expansion of Existing Properties				
Eden	3 star	Centre	36	Apr `87
de L'Europe	5 star	Centre	35	Jul `87
GT Barb Centre	5 star	Centre	121	Nov `86
GT Barb Airport	4 star	Airport	82	Jun `87
Pulitzer	5 star	Centre	40	Jan `88
Hilton Schiphol	5 star	Airport	78	May `86
Ibis	3 star	Badhoeved	108	Jun `87
Victoria	4 star	Centre	160	Apr `89
Subtotal			660	
New Properties				
Acca	4 star	Suburb	25	`85
Ascot	4 star	Centre	110	Aug `86
Bastion	3 star	Suburb	40	Feb `85
Borgmann	3 star	Suburb	15	Apr `86
Pullman	4 star	Centre	148	Mar `86
Cok 1st Class	4 star	Suburb	40	`86
GT Barb Palace	5 star	Centre	266	May `88
HI Crowne Plaza	5 star	Centre	270	Mar `87
Meridien	5 star	Centre	200	`90
SAS Hotel	5 star	Centre	230	`89
Subtotal			1344	
Total New Rooms	3 star		199	
Total New Rooms	4 star		565	
Total New Rooms	5 star		1240	
Grand Total			2004	

EXHIBIT 1 Amsterdam Statistics (continued)

C. Percentage Change in Hotel Demand in Amsterdam by Room Nights Sold in 1986 vs. 1985

5 star	4 star	3 star	1-2 star	Total
-14.05	-4.28	20.21	-3.67	-6.51

Occupancy 1980

68.6%	69.7%	64.1%

Occupancy 1987

59.1%	65.8%	65.1%

D. Rooms Available in Centre City Area

1980	1985	1987
5066	5900	6800

E. Sources of Guests 1987

	All Hotels	Centre City Area
Domestic	39.4%	11.1%
Foreign	60.6%	88.9%

F. Guest Types 1987

	All Hotels	Centre City Area
Government	3.2%	11.1%
Business	48.0	39.7
Tourists	31.7	32.2
Conferences	10.1	9.0
Others	7.0	15.9
Dutch	39.4	
German	12.7	
British	10.3	
French	4.2	
Scandinavian	5.4	
Other European	7.2	
American	8.7	
Japanese	3.1	

The primary target market was the individual business traveler who payed full rates, but there were also many corporate clients who enjoyed discounted rates. The total business market represented about 65 percent of total room nights. The other 35 percent was composed of tourists, many of them associated with groups. Americans represented 19 percent of total occupancy, the British 15 percent, and the Dutch nine percent.

Management also attempted to attract incentive group business, but was unable to create the proper packages and had little success. It was suggested that incentive organizers were used to dealing with sophisticated organizations and Holiday Inn "did not speak their language."

The Marketing Department The Director of Marketing handled major corporate clients such as IBM, Shell Oil, and Unilever and also coordinated with the public relations and advertising agencies. The sales manager was responsible for the leisure market, and two sales reps handled the other corporate clients. The budget was about average for a 5 star property, approximately five percent of estimated sales. No expenditures were made in the American market and no sales trips were planned to the United States.

The Product The Crowne Plaza's physical product was considered excellent and the 270 guest rooms were attractively furnished (Exhibit 2). The hotel's strategy was to offer a superior product at competitive prices. A unique selling point was the fact that part of the hotel was built behind the facades of 17th century buildings. The Crowne Plaza also contained the only hotel swimming pool in Amsterdam, a whirlpool, two saunas, solariums, and a fitness center.

The hotel's location in historic Centre City, however, was not optimal. Parking, small crime, and proximity to the Dam (a well known gathering point for drug users) were problems. Located in the same area were the hotels Sonesta, Krasnapolski, and the soon to be opened Golden Tulip Barbizon Palace.

Food and beverage outlets at the Crowne Plaza were not consistent with the hotel's desired positioning. Czar Peter's was a 100 seat pancake house that was successful during the day but had been closed at night. The Seven Seas, an 80 seat seafood restaurant, was successful during dinner but was closed for lunch. There was also a 50 seat pub (De Amsterdammer), a 50 seat bar (The Flagship), a 40 seat coffee shop (De Patio), and 24 hour room service.

The Crowne Plaza had experimented with various themes but sometimes waited only six months or less to see if they were successful. Concepts were changed monthly, weekly, even daily. Customers suffered from this disruption and it was believed that the hotel's image had suffered accordingly. Food and beverage revenues accounted for 35 percent of total revenue.

A food and beverage expert from The Hague Hotel School stated, "As a tourist I would love to stay in the rooms but I would never eat in the restaurants." This person believed that there was an opportunity in the

EXHIBIT 2 **The Crowne Plaza Advertised Product**

A JEWEL OF CHARACTER IN THE HEART OF AMSTERDAM.

Crowne Plaza Hotels - the distinctive group within Holiday Inn - raising service to an art. The opening of Holiday Inn Crowne Plaza Amsterdam on the 2nd of March 1987 marked the European arrival of supreme sophistication for the discerning traveller.

- Situated near Central Station.
- 270 elegantly decorated rooms and suites.
- Swimming-pool, whirlpool, sauna, solariums and fitness-room.
- "The Seven Seas" fish-speciality-restaurant.
- "Czaar Peter's" coffeeshop in "Zaanse" style.
- "De Amsterdammer" brown-café (local pub).
- "Flagship Bar" for international cocktails.
- Meeting and banquet accommodation for up to 300 persons.
- Parking garage.

Holiday Inn®
CROWNE PLAZA

N.Z. Voorburgwal 5, P.O. Box 2216, 1000 CE Amsterdam.
Tel. 31-20-200 500, telex 15183 Hicpa NL.
For reservations in the US/Canada call 1-800 Holiday or see your local travel agent.

area for high quality dining, but none presently existed. The Sonesta Hotel, located down the street, had employed the same chef for 20 years. Apparently, he had not made many changes during that period and Sonesta's food service did not enjoy a good reputation.

Pricing The Crowne Plaza utilized a penetration pricing strategy for the first month of operation. By charging only 100 guilders per night, they were able to achieve reasonable occupancies, especially in the March off-season. After this, pricing was based on a competitive analysis. As management desired a position in the middle of the 5 star category, they priced about 10 percent below the Sonesta and the Marriott. Variable room costs were about 25 guilders a night.

Distribution Distribution was considered a problem in spite of the fact that the Crowne Plaza was connected to the largest, most advanced reservation system in the industry. The difficulty was perceived as one of trying to reach full rate customers who normally did not book through travel agents. It was also assumed that many potential customers would come from the United States and locating this market was problematic.

It was expected that it would take at least a year before the new reservations system became fully effective. In the meantime, corporate customers tended to individually call the central reservation number. Apparently, many were unaware of the hotel's existence. This resulted in failure to maximize this business.

Advertising Advertising for the Crowne Plaza was handled by the same London firm that also handled traditional Holiday Inn advertising for Europe. This was a problem for two reasons.

The agency was experienced with advertising for a 3 or 4 star hotel, and seemed to lack the expertise to promote a 5 star property. Second, messages were created for the English market, then used for the Dutch market. For example, a successful champagne promotion in England was less than successful in The Netherlands. There was a feeling that the agency did not understand the Dutch market, and messages and media utilized were not appropriate.

No effort was made at improving advertising effectiveness. If a campaign failed to meet its objectives after three months or so, another campaign was inaugurated.

COMPETITION

Analysis of the competition revealed some diverse strategies. The Amstel hotel, managed by Inter-Continental and also bearing its name, was the top-of-the-line hotel in Amsterdam with a superb reputation for product quality. Its location, however, was not the most favorable. Located away from Centre City, the Amstel's accessibility was difficult and the parking situation was poor.

The Sonesta hotel had been hurt by adopting a short-run profit maximization strategy in the high occupancy years of 1982 - 1985. The hotel maximized its average rate by targeting full rate tourists and saying, "Sorry," to corporate clients who called when the hotel was fully booked. Occupancy levels fell fast in 1986 when the tourists stopped coming.

Marriott used a long range strategy. This hotel targeted the business segment even if sacrificing short-term revenues. Marriott set aside and held a block of rooms for its corporate discount customers during the peak tourist season. When the tourists stopped coming, Marriott had a loyal and stable business segment relationship. Marriott also had a superior location on the Leidseplein with convenient access to both business and tourist attractions such as restaurants and night clubs, without the disadvantages of Centre City. The Crowne Plaza considered the Marriott to be its toughest competitor.

The Krasnapolsky and the Victoria hotels developed unique segmentation strategies during the 1982 - 1985 boom period. Instead of relying on the traditional British and American markets, these hotels concentrated on the fast growing markets of the Far East, South America, and Australia. This helped develop a loyal foreign market for these hotels.

The Golden Tulip hotel chain, owned by Royal Dutch Airlines (KLM), was to operate two Barbizon hotels within the city of Amsterdam. The Barbizon Centre was a relatively new, small hotel located near the Marriott. It was not considered a major threat by Crowne Plaza management. The Barbizon Palace was scheduled to open in May, 1988. This hotel was intended to be the flagship property for KLM.

The Barbizon Palace was also being built behind the facades of historical 17th century buildings at its location in Centre City, across from the railroad station. The hotel's objective was to be the best FIT hotel in town. Primary target markets were the transient and corporate business customers, but marketing efforts were also directed at tourist individuals, small groups, and the incentive market. North America, Britain, Scandinavia, Germany, France, Italy, and the Far East were all targeted markets, as well as The Netherlands.

The Barbizon Palace was not expected to add room nights to the market, but would surely take its fair share. KLM ownership was seen as a distinctive advantage because the airline could channel business to the Palace that it had previously sent elsewhere.

The Hilton Amsterdam was located in an Amsterdam suburb and was felt to cater to different markets than those which preferred Centre City.

Rate and occupancy comparisons for selected Amsterdam hotels are shown in Exhibits 3 and 4. Crowne Plaza management also conducted a strength and weakness comparative analysis with hotels perceived as their major competitors. Results of the analysis are shown in Exhibit 5.

EXHIBIT 3 Published 1988 Hotel Rate Comparisons

	Low Season Sgl/Dbl	High Season Sgl/Dbl
Barbizon Palace	335-415/450-525	385-415/495-525
Barbizon Centre	320-365/390-435	370-400/440-470
Amstel	325-440/430-540	same
de L'Europe	315-365/415-465	365-415/465-515
Marriott	365-440/435-510	same
Sonesta	340-450/405-515	same
Hilton Amsterdam	350-410/430-510	same
Crowne Plaza	310-395/395-480	335-420/425-495
Okura	320-365/410-455	370-420/460-510
Apollo	290-330/365-410	320-390/415-465
Krasnapolsky	290-375/345-395	same
Pulitzer	290-330/355-400	320-370/410-455

Prices quoted are in Dutch guilders ($1 = +/- 2 guilders)

EXHIBIT 4 Selected 1987 Hotel Occupancy Comparisons

	Rooms	Occupancy%	ARR	FMS	AMS
Amstel	111	58.7	335	5.1%	5.0%
de L'Europe	100	64.0	325	4.6	4.9
Marriott	400	70.5	243	18.3	21.7
Sonesta	425	58.4	238	19.4	19.1
Hilton	274	53.5	234	12.5	11.3
Okura	370	58.9	200	16.9	16.8
Barbizon Ctr	242	51.7	256	11.0	9.6
Crowne Plaza	270	56.2	235	12.3	11.9
Totals	2192	59.4		100.0	100.0

EXHIBIT 5 **Strength and Weakness Competitive Analysis**

Transient Market

	AMS	BP	EUR	HIL	CP	MAR	SON
Location	1	2	2	1	2	3	2
Service	2	2	2	1	1	1	1
Rooms	2	2	2	2	2	1	1
F & B	3	2	3	1	1	2	1
FreqTravPr	3	2	1	3	3	3	1

Meetings Market

	BP	KRA	HIL	CP	MAR	SON
Location	2	2	3	2	3	2
Parking	2	3	3	2	3	3
Facilities	2	1	2	2	2	2
Room sizes	2	3	2	2	3	3
Banquet capacity	2	3	2	2	3	3

Key: 1 = inferior to the competition
2 = comparable to the competition
3 = superior to the competition

CONCLUSION

As of March 1988, tourist demand for Europe in general was returning to 1985 levels. Management of the Crowne Plaza faced a number of strategic questions, the answers to which would greatly impact the future of the hotel. Should the hotel be positioned as a 5 star property, or something else? Could anything be done about the Amsterdam Centre City image? How was the hotel being impacted by the stereotypical Holiday Inn image? If negatively, how should it be combated? Would the American tourist market bounce back? If so, should this be the target market? Or should Crowne Plaza follow its competitors and "spread the risk?" What should be done about food and beverage, advertising and distribution? How should they meet the threat of the new Barbizon Palace?

These and many other questions were on the agenda as management, representatives from Holiday Inn International, representatives from Holiday Corporation/Memphis, lenders, and developers of the hotel sat down for an all day strategic planning meeting.

SECTION 7

COMPREHENSIVE

CASE

CASE 22

THE OMNI PARK CENTRAL HOTEL

Richard Chambers sat back from his desk at the Omni Park Central Hotel and stared out his office window onto New York City's congested Seventh Avenue. He had just received the month end figures for the hotel for October, 1985. Although occupancy looked much better than it had, he knew that October was always the best month of the year and there was no hope of reaching the budgeted $10.6 million in gross operating profit set by the Omni/Dunfey Corporation for 1985. Food and beverage revenues were also low and would certainly end the year deep in the red. The hotel was consistently the last in the city to sell out. In addition, customer feedback continued to be negative. The situation looked pretty grim, at best.

As Director of Marketing at the Omni Park Central Hotel, Rich had been brought in as part of a management team whose purpose it was to implement a turn-around strategy to save the ailing hotel. Yet no improvement appeared in sight. What's more, the 1986 budget had just gone in to corporate and Rich knew some changes had to take place if there was to be any chance of making it.

BACKGROUND

The Omni Park Central Hotel was located on Manhattan's west side. It was across from Carnegie Hall, two blocks from Central Park, and near museums, Lincoln Center for the Performing Arts, Broadway theatres, the Rockefeller Center tourist attraction, and fashionable Fifth Avenue shopping (Exhibit 1). The hotel had 1240 rooms including 179 suites. Due to the number of multi-room suites, the actual number of bedrooms was 1450.

The Omni Park Central was owned by VMS Realty, a Chicago based real estate company. It was operated by Omni International Hotels under a management contract. Omni International was a division of Dunfey Hotels Corporation, itself a wholely owned subsidiary of Aer Lingus/Dunfey Corporation. As shown in Exhibit 2, Omni Hotels was a chain of 50 or so properties although only 28 of these did, or soon would, carry the Omni name. The other properties carried the Dunfey name or the name of the franchisor. These included Sheraton, Ramada, and Howard Johnson. Omni was also a member of the Supranational reservations network.

EXHIBIT 1 Location of Hotels and Major Attractions in Midtown Manhattan

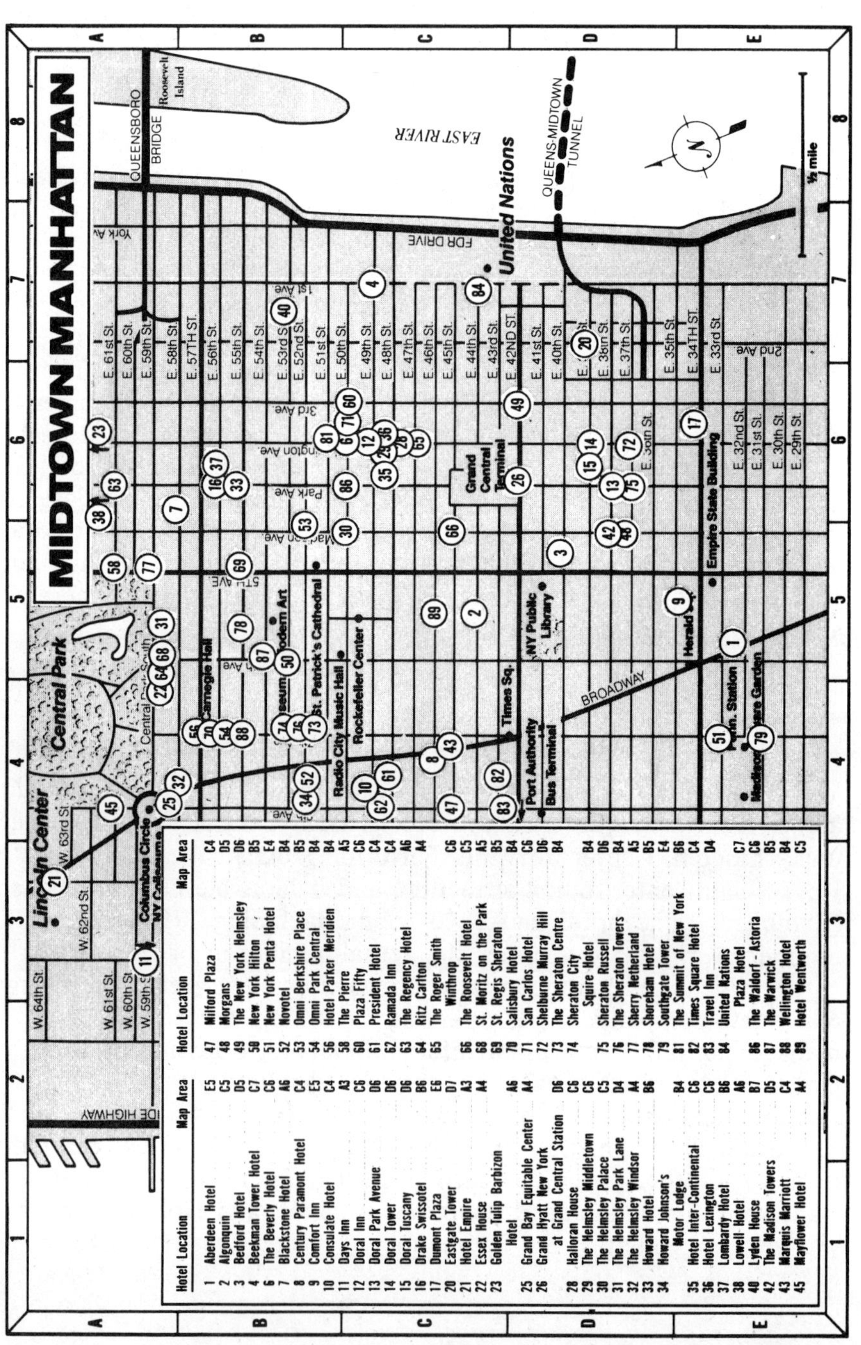

	Hotel Location	Map Area
1	Aberdeen Hotel	E5
2	Algonquin	C5
3	Bedford Hotel	D5
4	Beekman Tower Hotel	C7
6	The Beverly Hotel	C6
7	Blackstone Hotel	A6
8	Century Paramont Hotel	C4
9	Comfort Inn	E5
10	Consulate Hotel	C4
11	Days Inn	A3
12	Doral Inn	C6
13	Doral Park Avenue	D6
14	Doral Tower	D6
15	Doral Tuscany	D6
16	Drake Swissotel	B6
17	Dumont Plaza	E6
20	Eastgate Tower	D7
21	Hotel Empire	A3
22	Essex House	A4
23	Golden Tulip Barbizon Hotel	A6
25	Grand Bay Equitable Center	A4
26	Grand Hyatt New York at Grand Central Station	D6
28	Halloran House	C6
29	The Helmsley Middletown	C6
30	The Helmsley Palace	C5
31	The Helmsley Park Lane	D4
32	The Helmsley Windsor	A4
33	Howard Hotel	B6
34	Howard Johnson's Motor Lodge	B4
35	Hotel Inter-Continental	C6
36	Hotel Lexington	C6
37	Lombardy Hotel	B6
38	Lowell Hotel	A6
40	Lyden House	B7
42	The Madison Towers	D5
43	Marquis Marriott	C4
45	Mayflower Hotel	A4
47	Milford Plaza	C4
48	Morgans	D5
49	The New York Helmsley	D6
50	New York Hilton	B5
51	New York Penta Hotel	E4
52	Novotel	B4
53	Omni Berkshire Place	B5
54	Omni Park Central	B4
56	Hotel Parker Meridien	B4
58	The Pierre	A5
60	Plaza Fifty	C6
61	President Hotel	C4
62	Ramada Inn	C4
63	The Regency Hotel	A6
64	Ritz Carlton	A4
65	The Roger Smith Winthrop	C6
66	The Roosevelt Hotel	C5
68	St. Moritz on the Park	A5
69	St. Regis Sheraton	B5
70	Salisbury Hotel	B4
71	San Carlos Hotel	C6
72	Shelburne Murray Hill	D6
73	The Sheraton Centre	B4
74	Sheraton City Squire Hotel	B4
75	Sheraton Russell	D6
76	The Sheraton Towers	B4
77	Sherry Netherland	A5
78	Shoreham Hotel	B5
79	Southgate Tower	E4
81	The Summit of New York	B6
82	Times Square Hotel	C4
83	Travel Inn	D4
84	United Nations Plaza Hotel	C7
86	The Waldorf - Astoria	C6
87	The Warwick	B5
88	Wellington Hotel	B4
89	Hotel Wentworth	C5

EXHIBIT 2 The Omni Hotels International Network in 1985

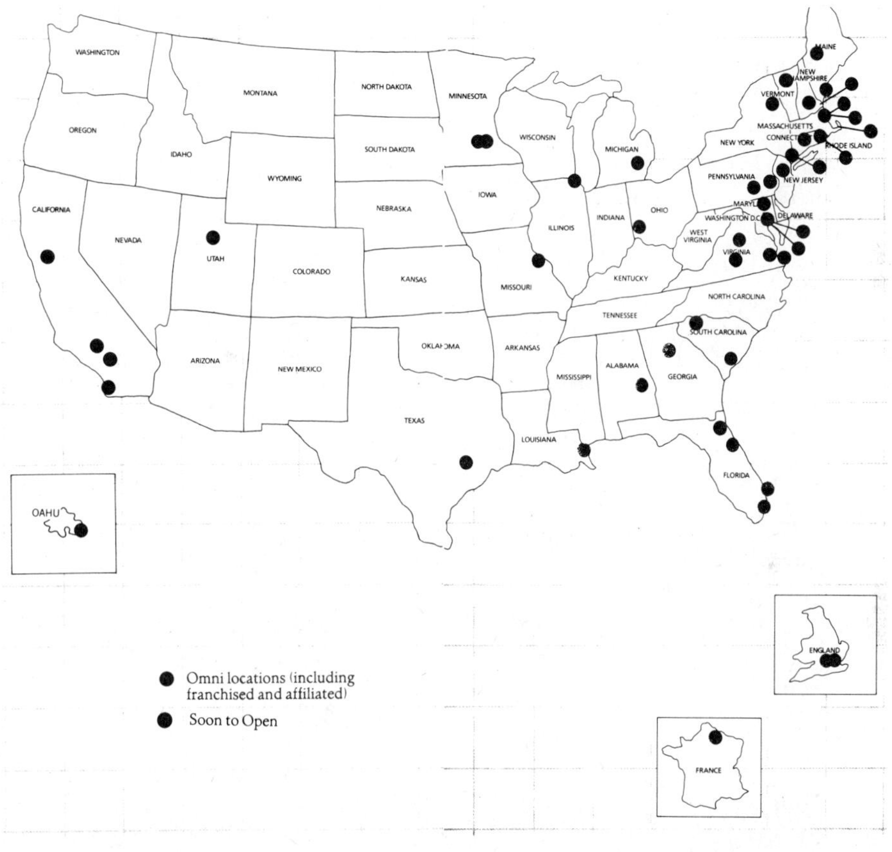

Omni was a strong, group-based hotel company with three hotels, and two others building, when Dunfey, primarily a transient hotel company, bought it in 1983. The Omni Park Central not only marked the merger of the two companies, but also Dunfey's entrance into the upper middle-class range of the New York hotel market. Dunfey replaced its name in many of its hotels with the name Omni after its research showed that Omni was a more widely recognized and respected name.

The Omni Park Central was the second Omni Dunfey hotel in New York City. The first was Berkshire Place which had been positioned in the middle-tier market but discovered that it could succeed admirably in the up-scale market. This success led Dunfey to warrant the acquisition of a second New York City hotel.

EXHIBIT 2 Omni International Network (continued)

OMNI INTERNATIONAL HOTELS

1985–86 DIRECTORY

HOW TO MAKE A RESERVATION

Contact your Travel Agent, or. . . Omni Supranational Worldwide Toll-Free Reservations:

1-800-THE-OMNI

(For affiliated or Franchise Hotel Reservations, see toll-free numbers listed on page 36 in this directory.)

Reservations can also be made through our toll-free number, 800-THE-OMNI, for more than 400 hotels around the world by taking advantage of Omni Hotels' affiliation in the Supranational Reservation System. This system consists of deluxe, first-class and standard-class hotels located in the main business centers of 260 cities around the world.

The following services are part of the Supranational System:

- Individual reservations are accepted.
- Immediate confirmation of bookings.
- Official rates, as published by the hotel, are quoted.
- Close cooperation with all travel agents and airlines guarantees full commission and identity.

SUPRANATIONAL MEMBER HOTELS:

AUSTRIA
Austria Hotels

AUSTRALIA/NEW ZEALAND/SO. PACIFIC
Southern Pacific Hotel Corporation

BRAZIL
Horsa Hotels

CANADA/ISRAEL/CARIBBEAN
Canadian Pacific Hotels

FAR EAST
Orient Hotels

DENMARK
The Grand Hotels

FED. REPUBLIC OF GERMANY
Associated Supra-National Hotels

FINLAND
Sokos Hotels

FRANCE/BELGIUM/EGYPT
Hotels Concorde

GERMAN DEM. REPUBLIC
Vereinigung Interhotel

GREAT BRITAIN
Thistle Hotels

HUNGARY
Hungar Hotels

ITALY
Space Hotels

SOUTH KOREA
Seoul Plaza Hotel

SPAIN/PORTUGAL PUERTO RICO
Hotels Unidos SA

SWEDEN
Reso Hotels

SWITZERLAND/ECUADOR
CEM Hotels

UNITED STATES
Omni International Hotels

The Berkshire Place received about 70 percent of its business from the individual business traveler. Many of these guests were part of Omni Dunfey's Executive Service Plan, or ESP. Omni Dunfey aggressively solicited ESP guests and, as a result, was one of the stronger hotel companies in this market. One reason for this emphasis was because the company recognized the weakness of its toll-free reservation system relative to the larger chains, and saw the need for an alternative marketing tool. ESP details and those of other Omni marketing tools are shown in Exhibit 3.

Omni's current advertising campaign was developed by the well-known, in hotel circles, Spiro Agency. The campaign sought to promote a uniform and high class level of accommodations and service for all Omni

EXHIBIT 3 Omni Marketing Tools

For the Corporate Traveler:

ESP®, EXECUTIVE SERVICE PLAN®

Our exclusive Corporate Service Program, ESP, EXECUTIVE SERVICE PLAN, offers some very special privileges for the busy executive. ESP is offered at all Omni and most affiliated hotels, and offers participants in this program *guaranteed* privileges like:

- Exclusive Toll-Free Private ESP Reservation Number
- Guaranteed Availability
- Guaranteed Rate
- Guaranteed No-Walk Policy
- Express Check-In and Check-Out
- Double Occupancy at Single Rate when traveling with your Spouse
- Increased Personal Check-Cashing Privileges
- Discounted Auto Rental Rates
- Complimentary Newspaper and Coffee

For more detailed information on ESP and how to qualify for this exclusive program, contact an ESP Representative at any participating Omni or affiliated hotel.

For the Frequent Traveler:

SELECT GUEST™ PROGRAM

Our SELECT GUEST PROGRAM is a great way to make each and every visit to participating Omni and affiliated hotels even more rewarding and enjoyable. You can earn up to a week's complimentary accommodations for two at all participating Omni or affiliated hotels. So start earning credits now and ask about a SELECT GUEST PASSBOOK™ the next time you stay at any participating Omni or affiliated hotel in the U.S.

For the Discriminating Traveler:

OMNI CLASSIC SERVICE™

We are delighted to offer OMNI CLASSIC SERVICE. . . an innovation in hospitality. Each Omni International Hotel has set aside specially appointed OMNI CLASSIC rooms, where guests are assured of a high level of quality, elegant accommodations, VIP amenities, special registration and touches beyond expectations.

OMNI CLASSIC rooms are designed with your comfort and convenience in mind, from non-smokers' guest rooms, padded hangers, makeup/shaving mirrors, luxurious terry bathrobes and plush oversized towels, to refreshments and beautiful plants in your room upon arrival.

For a truly memorable experience at any Omni International Hotel, simply call toll-free:

1-800-THE-OMNI

and request an Omni Classic room Reservation.

For the Meeting Planner:

GOOD MEETING GUARANTEE®

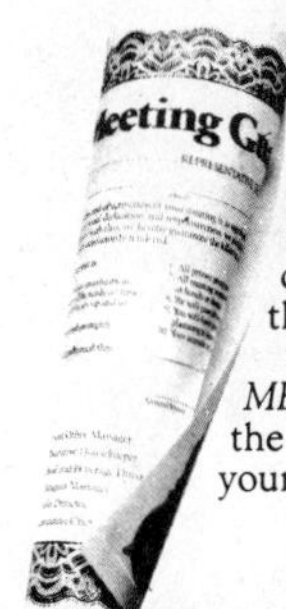

At Omni Hotels, we not only do our best to make your meeting smooth-running and trouble-free, we *guarantee* it. Of course, we want the chance to rectify the situation first. But if we fail to satisfy you, we'll adjust your bill accordingly. What you don't like, *you simply don't pay for.* When you think about it, that's quite a guarantee!

For more information on our *10-Point GOOD MEETING GUARANTEE PROGRAM*, contact the Sales Office at any of the hotels listed, or your nearest Omni Regional Sales Office.

hotels. Architecturally, however, the hotels were quite different. In fact, Dunfey prided itself on buying landmark, traditional hotels like the Parker House in Boston, renovating them, and applying the Dunfey (Omni) "Classic" touch. An example of the advertising designed to give a uniform image is shown in Exhibit 4.

Prior to June, 1983 the Omni Park Central was the New York Sheraton. Under Sheraton management the hotel had experienced an 85 percent occupancy rate with a $65 – $85 single rate range. Between 350 and 450 rooms were sold nightly by Sheraton's strong toll-free reservations system. Another 200 rooms were booked nightly by airlines for their crew members. In addition, almost all the professional baseball and football teams

EXHIBIT 4 Omni Classic Advertising

were regular guests of the hotel when in New York City. This had the added bonus of attracting local clientele to the hotel's restaurants and bar in hopes of catching a glimpse of favorite players.

Reluctantly, Sheraton decided to sell the property. Sheraton had four other hotels in Manhattan with over 4000 rooms and had recently sold the Sheraton Centre to a group of investors. As part of an agreement with owners of the other Sheraton properties in New York City, the New York Sheraton was eliminated from the Sheraton system. Thus, the New York Sheraton came under Dunfey management in June of 1983.

THE HOTEL UNDER OMNI DUNFEY MANAGEMENT

Until January of 1984 Dunfey operated the hotel as a Sheraton franchise. During this period occupancy and room rates remained pretty much as they had been under Sheraton ownership. In January 1984, the name was changed from the New York Sheraton to the Omni Park Central and major renovations were begun on the lobby, function rooms, restaurants, and hallways. In addition, 770 of the guest rooms which had not recently been renovated by Sheraton were refurbished. The intent was to position the hotel as an Omni Classic aimed at the upper end of the market.

During renovations, occupancy rates fell relative to New York City occupancies in the same rate range. This continued throughout 1985 as shown in Exhibit 5. Customers became irritated as they literally had to step between piles of lumber to get through the lobby. Furthermore, Dunfey was not as inclined to be as cozy with the union as was Sheraton. This caused service quality to decline as employees were unhappy with the management change.

The physical changes that the hotel was undergoing were also disturbing to the employees. For example, the hotel's major restaurant had previously been a casual family-style eating place. Omni's vice president of food and beverage felt that more class was needed in keeping with the new tone of the hotel. The result was Nicole, Brasserie de Paris, intended to be an elegant French restaurant. These types of changes increased management turnover below the top level and resulted in line employees developing a negative attitude toward serving the needs of the guests.

Dunfey compensated for declining occupancies by cutting costs to the bone. The first to go were all the bathroom amenities and valet service that Dunfey had instituted when the hotel became an Omni. Payroll was cut wherever possible. Employees saw Dunfey as a strictly cost-oriented company. Guests also complained as can be seen from the guest comment card summaries in Exhibit 6.

EXHIBIT 5 1985 New York City Occupancies in the $75 - $100 Rate-Range vs. Omni Park Central Occupancies

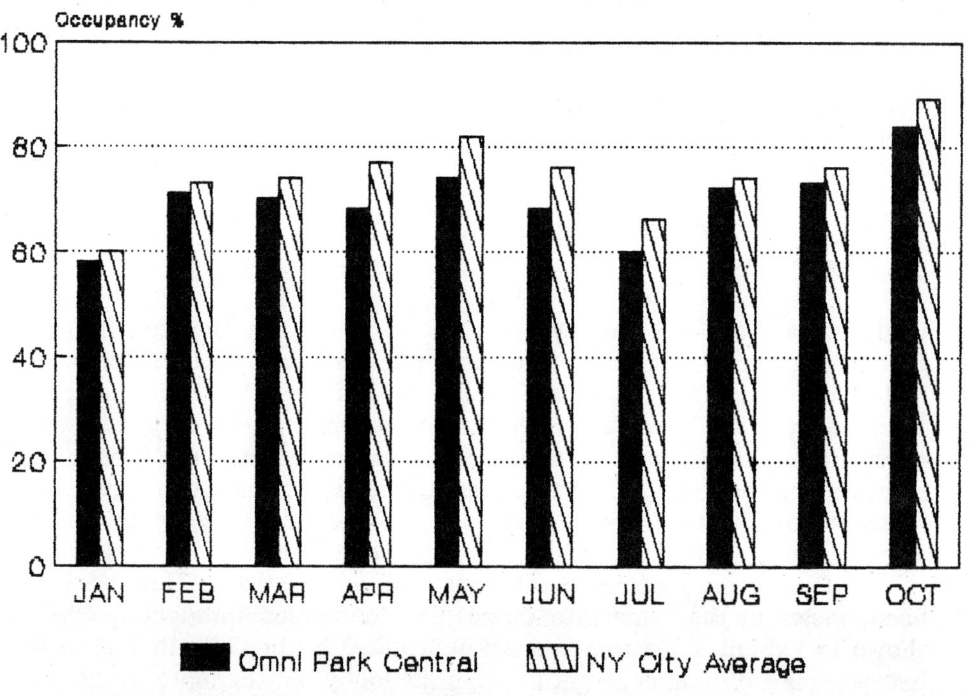

THE RENOVATED HOTEL

In March 1985, renovations were completed. The lobby was beautifully decorated in gold and beige. A marble inlaid floor was installed along with a unique island reception desk in the center of the lobby. The circular reception desk had multiple check-in and check-out points around its entire circumference. An open Cafe seating 64 and located to the rear of the lobby, served a buffet breakfast as well as light meals and beverages throughout the day and evening. From 7:00 am to 9:00 am there was usually a waiting line to get seats for breakfast. Two Seventh Avenue entrances to Nicole and to the Parallel Bar were located on either side of the front entrance to the lobby.

Nicole, Brasserie de Paris, was tastefully decorated in coral and black marble. An authentic antique French bar was located to the left of the entrance way. The restaurant seated 129 and offered a fine selection of French cuisine (Exhibit 7) and wines. Breakfast was no longer served in Nicole after May.

EXHIBIT 6 Guest Comment Card Summary February – May, 1985

Grn–Favorable/Neutral; Red–Unfavorable (Some have more than one comment)

	February		March		April		May		Year to Date	
	Grn	Red	Grn	Red	Grn	Red	Grn	Red	Grn	Red
ROOMS DIVISION										
Reservations	1	2		1	1	10		4	2	11
Doormen	1	1	1	1	1	1			4	3
Bellmen	2		3	3	1	4	2	5	9	12
Check-in	5	6	5	12	3	17	4	26	18	66
Check-out		2	1		1	3			2	14
Concierge/Ass't. Manager	1	3			1	1	2	3	4	7
Telephone/Messages	1	7	1	2		8		2	2	20
Service- General			2	1	1		2	1	6	2
Housekeeping										
Cleanliness-room		8	3	13	4	17	1	5	8	49
Cleanliness-bathroom		4		5		11		8		28
Supplies	2	9	2	11	2	10	3	12	10	53
Room Condition	6	27	13	14	9	15	5	25	37	85
Service General			1	4	2	10	6	4	10	18
Engineering										
Heating/Cooling		9		10		10		7		46
Lights		6		4		6		3		22
Plumbing		14		14		26	1	12	1	68
Television		10	1	8		11	1	13	2	44
Other		10	1	10		16		8	1	53
Parking		1								4
Price/Value Comments	1	8	3	9		14	1	15	21	50
General Hotel Comments	21	2	28	2	31	17	17	12	97	33
Subtotal	41	129	65	124	57	207	45	173	234	688
FOOD AND BEVERAGE										
Food Quality		1	5	3	3	4	5	8	15	16
Food/Bev. Service	2	3	1	7	3	8	2	5	10	26
Beverage Service			1	1					1	2
Cleanliness								1		1
Menu Price-Value	1	1	1			2		1	2	5
Subtotal	3	5	8	11	6	15	7	15	28	50
GRAND TOTAL	44	134	73	135	63	222	52	188	262	738
Rooms % per night	0.16	0.52	0.24	0.46	0.22	0.02	0.15	0.60	0.16	0.53
F & B % per cover	0.01	0.03	0.04	0.05	0.03	0.07	0.03	0.07	0.03	0.05
Room Nights sold		24590		26943		25458		28780		127864
% Occupancy		71.47		70.09		68.44		74.9		68.3
Covers served		16275		30642		21542		23255		93817
Total Cards Return		93		106		142		108		496
% of Rooms sold		0.37		0.39		0.56		0.37		0.39

EXHIBIT 7 Menu of Nicole, Brasserie de Paris

Nicole

BRASSERIE DE PARIS

EXHIBIT 7 Menu of Nicole (continued)

LES APÉRITIFS

KIR ROYALE	5.00
DUBONNET	4.00
RICARD	4.00
LILLET	4.00

LES EAUX MINÉRALES

POLAND SPRING *(Maine)*	2.75
PERRIER *(France)*	2.75
SARATOGA *(New York)*	2.75
SAN PELLEGRINO *(Italy)*	2.75

LES BIÈRES

Bouteilles

BECK'S, LIGHT OR DARK *(Germany)*	3.75
BRASSEURS BIÈRE DE PARIS MALT *(France)*	3.75
SAMUEL SMITH'S STOUT *(England)*	4.50
HEINEKEN *(Holland)*	3.75
AMSTEL LIGHT *(Holland)*	3.75
KRONENBOURG *(France)*	3.75
DUVEL *(Belgium)*	4.00
NEW AMSTERDAM *(New York)*	3.75
BUDWEISER *(USA)*	3.50
MILLER LITE *(USA)*	3.50

LES HORS D'OEUVRES

All Hors d'Oeuvres $1.00 less with Entree.

HUÎTRES EN SAISON, DRESSÉES SUR GLACE
Oysters in Season
Market Price

PALOURDES DE L'OCÉAN
Clams on the Half Shell
Market Price

COCKTAIL DE CREVETTES
Jumbo Shrimp Cocktail
11.50

ESCARGOTS, JAMBON DE PARME ET TOMATES SUR UN LIT DE CHEVEUX D'ANGE
Snails with Prosciutto and Tomato served on Angel Hair Pasta
10.00

ASSORTIMENT DE TERRINES MAISON
Assorted House Pâtés
6.75

TERRINE DE LÉGUMES, COULIS DE TOMATE
Vegetable Terrine, Coulis of Fresh Tomato
7.00

TORTELLINI AUX ÉPINARDS ET FROMAGE DE CHÈVRE, COULIS DE POIVRON ROUGE
Tortellini of Spinach and Goat Cheese, Puree of Sweet Red Bell Pepper
8.25

ROULADES D'ASPERGES AU SAUMON FUMÉ
Fresh Asparagus rolled in Smoked Salmon, Herbed Vinaigrette Dressing
7.75

PÂTES FRAÎCHES AUX PALOURDES
Linguini with Clams and Fresh Tomatoes
8.75

LES POTAGES

GRATINÉE SAVOYARDE "LES HALLES"
French Onion Soup Gratinee
4.75

SOUPE DU JOUR
Soup of the Day
4.75

CRÈME DE MOULES "BILLI BI"
Cream of Mussels, Saffron, and Shallots
4.75

EXHIBIT 7 Menu of Nicole (continued)

LES SPÉCIALITÉS MAISON

BOUCHEÉ DE FRUITS DE MER, SAUCE SAFRAN
Melange of Seafood in Puff Pastry with Saffron Sauce
21.00

CASSOULET "CHEZ NICOLE"
Lamb, Duck, Garlic Sausage, stewed with White Beans and Tomatoes
17.50

ENTRECÔTE CAFÉ DE PARIS
Grilled Sirloin Steak with Herb Butter
22.50

LES ENTRÉES POISSONS

SOLE MEUNIÈRE OU GRILLÉE
Dover Sole, Sauteed or Grilled, Meuniere Butter
19.00

SAUMON GRILLÉ, SAUCE BASILIC
Grilled Salmon, Fresh Basil Sauce
19.75

COQUILLE ST. JACQUES GRATINÉE
Sea Scallops, Shrimp, Mussels, and Mushrooms Gratinee
17.00

GÂTEAUX DE CRABE, SAUCE POIVRADE
Crabcakes, Tomato and Sweet Red Bell Pepper Sauce
17.25

CREVETTES POÊLÉES, SAUCE HOMARD À L'ESTRAGON
Sauteed Jumbo Shrimp, Lobster Tarragon Sauce served on Pasta
22.00

ESPADON GRILLÉ, AU BEURRE CIBOULETTE
Grilled Swordfish with Chive Butter
21.50

CHAMPAGNES

DOMAINE CHANDON, BLANC DE NOIRS — 28.00

MOËT & CHANDON, BRUT IMPÉRIAL — 60.00

DOM PÉRIGNON, VINTAGE — 140.00

LA SÉLECTION DE NOTRE CAVE

(Complete Wine List also Available)

CHARDONNAY, FETZER SUNDIAL
Bottle 19.50 *Glass* 5.25

MUSCADET DE SÈVRE ET MAINE SUR LIE, DOMAINE DE L'HYVERNIÈRE
Bottle 15.50 *Glass* 4.00

RIESLING, TRIMBACH
Bottle 16.00 *Glass* 4.25

MÂCON - LUGNY "LES CHARMES"
Bottle 15.00 *Glass* 4.50

CABERNET SAUVIGNON, BEAULIEU VINEYARDS, RUTHERFORD
Bottle 20.00 *Glass* 5.25

BEAUJOLAIS-VILLAGES
Bottle 15.50 *Glass* 4.00

LES DIGESTIFS

F. E. TRIMBACH EAUX DE VIE, FRAMBOISE, MIRABELLE, KIRSCH, POIRE WILLIAM
4.50

RÉMY MARTIN V.S.O.P
6.50

RÉMY MARTIN NAPOLÉON
8.50

MARTELL CORDON BLEU
8.50

MANDARINE NAPOLÉON
5.00

CORDIALS AND PORTS

MARIE BRIZARD
4.50

SANDEMAN FOUNDERS RESERVE
5.00

TAYLOR FLADGATE, VINTAGE
8.50

EXHIBIT 7 Menu of Nicole (continued)

VIANDES & VOLAILLES

POULET MARINÉ AU ROMARIN, ACCOMPAGNÉ D'UNE SALADE
Rosemary Marinated Chicken, Fresh Vegetable Salad
15.75

CANARD RÔTI AU CASSIS ET GINGEMBRE
Roast Duckling, Cassis and Ginger Sauce
17.25

NOISETTES D'AGNEAU RÔTIES
Sliced Medallions of Lamb, Shallot and Herb Sauce
19.50

CÔTE DE VEAU AUX CHAMPIGNONS SAUVAGES
Sauteed Veal Chop with Wild Mushrooms
22.50

CÔTE DE BOEUF RÔTIE, SAUCE BÉARNAISE
Roast Prime Rib with Bearnaise Sauce
21.00

LES SALADES

SALAD VERTE
Mixed Green Salad
5.00

SALADE NIÇOISE
Salad of Tuna, Potatoes, and Vegetables, Mustard Vinaigrette
9.75

SALADE DE LENTILLES AU CERVELAT
Lentil Salad with Cervelat Sausage
8.25

SALADE DU CHEF
Chef's Salad
9.75

SALADE VERTE, CROUTONS AU FROMAGE DE CHÈVRE
Mixed Green Salad, Warm Goat Cheese Croutons
6.50

SALADE DE FRUITS FRAIS
Fresh Fruit Plate with choice of Yogurt, Cottage Cheese or Sherbet
10.75

ASSORTIMENT DE POISSONS FUMÉS
Smoked Fish Plate
11.25

LES DÉSSERTS

MOUSSE AU CHOCOLAT BLANC, SAUCE FRAMBOISE
White Chocolate Mousse with Raspberry Sauce 5.00

CRÈME CARAMEL
Creme Caramel 4.50

CRÈME GLACÉE
Ice Cream 4.00

CHARIOT DE PÂTISSERIES
Assorted Pastries from the Cart 4.75

TERRINE AU CHOCOLAT
Chocolate Pâté, Hazelnut Sauce 5.25

GÂTEAU AU FROMAGE BLANC
New York Cheesecake 5.25

ASSORTIMENT DE FROMAGES
Cheese Plate 6.25

The Parallel Bar was built around a turn-of-the-century gymnasium theme. The entrance way was built like a locker room with lockers and benches on either side. A large bar was located to the rear of the room. Beyond the bar was a spacious dance floor surrounded by mirrored walls. A disc jockey played contemporary, 50's and 60's, and big band ballads.

The food and beverage outlets were expected to contribute only a small percentage of total revenues. Management believed that the majority of guests do not frequent in-house restaurants, preferring instead to visit any number of the hundreds of restaurants available in New York City.

All of the hotel's 12 conference and private dining rooms were renovated along with its two major ballrooms. The largest ballroom accommodated up to 1000 people, small for a hotel of this size. Conventioneers staying at the hotel were usually attending conventions held at the Coliseum, only two blocks away. All in all, $16 million was spent on renovations; two-thirds of this was spent on public space. VMS gave Omni a blank check for renovations but Omni didn't want to carry any more debt burden.

The 770 renovated rooms were done comfortably, but inexpensively. The remaining rooms had either been renovated recently by Sheraton or were in desperate need of refurbishing. These rooms were scheduled for renovation in 1986, to be paid for out of earnings.

MARKETING THE NEWLY RENOVATED PRODUCT

Upon completion of the renovations, the hotel was presumed ready to market partially as an Omni Classic hotel. Amenities went back into the bathrooms including more "upscale" shampoo, soap, bath gel, shoe horns and bath robes in the higher priced rooms. Remote TV and plants were also added to the rooms. Rack rates were increased on March 30, 1985 to $100/110 single, $120/130 double for unrenovated rooms; $139 single, $149 double for regular rooms; $149 single and $159 double for Omni Classic rooms; and $169 for most suites. Corporate rates were $139 single and $149 double. Omni Dunfey management was bullish on prices and assessed the city as having room for even higher rates (Exhibit 8).

Sales people were instructed along with the regional sales offices, that the Omni would accept only rack rated bookings. Actual rack rate sales, however, ranged from five percent of occupancy in the summer months to 10 to 20 percent in other months. Rack rate sales were largely dependent on city-wide sell-outs (about 100 nights a year), i.e., if the city was fully booked, remaining rooms were sold only at rack rates. Management anticipated a strong transient demand, much like the Berkshire Place property. Airline crews, sports teams, and most previously accommodated group market segments were regarded as downscale and no longer solicited. Other groups were discouraged except for VIP, corporate, and other high rate groups. The toll free 800 number brought about 20 reservations a night.

EXHIBIT 8 1985 New York City Monthly Average Rates in the $75 - $100 Rate Range vs. Omni Park Central Average Rates

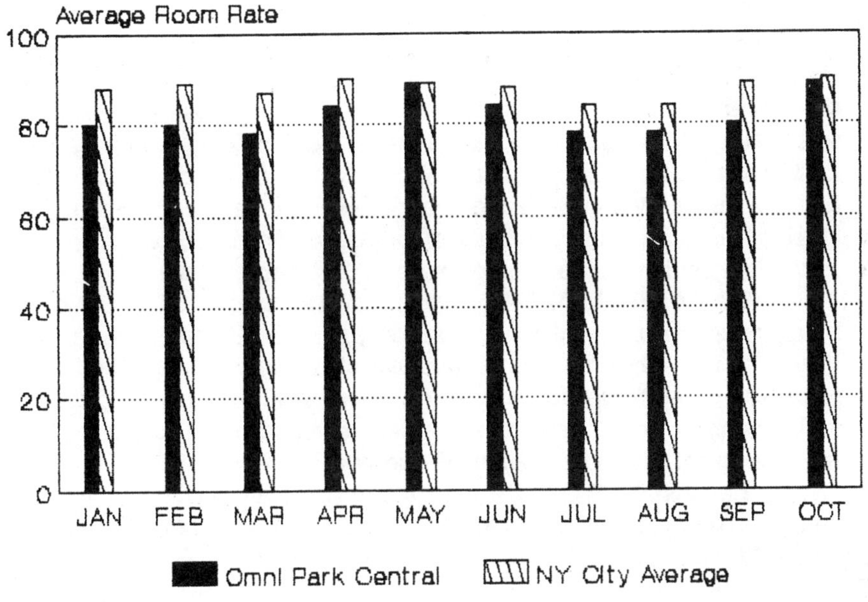

A new five-tiered marketing plan developed by the corporate office was instituted in early April. Corporate management believed that this plan would be a sure success and would quickly put the hotel back on target. The marketing plan divided the hotel into five different hotels based on available room types. Each "hotel" was to be positioned to a different market segment, with different check-in points at the circular front desk. The newly renovated rooms were to be positioned to the high-rated guests. The rooms renovated by Sheraton and the unrenovated rooms were to be sold to low-rated guests at more attractive rates. This strategy and the market position statements for each tier are detailed in Exhibit 9. Exhibit 10 details the 1985 mission statement for the remainder of the year.

A completely new management team was sent in to implement this new turn-around strategy. This team included Philip Georgas as General Manager and Richard Chambers as Director of Marketing, a team that had worked together at the Parker House in Boston. Of the old crew, only line-level unionized employees remained. Once again, they were forced to adapt to changes imposed by a new management. This time they were ready to fight. As city-wide union contract negotiations were to begin in a few weeks, there was talk of striking.

EXHIBIT 9 The 1985 Market Position Statement

The OMNI PARK CENTRAL is a 1450 room (1243 key) first class commercial hotel which enjoys an excellent location in mid-town Manhattan at 56th Street and 7th Avenue. The location is most advantageous in that it is in the commercial center of New York City, it is in close proximity to nearly all of the city cultural offerings and primary shopping areas, it is a short distance from Central Park, and it is in the West Side area that is currently experiencing a high level of physical renovation activity. These location advantages appeal to the multiple market segments served by the hotel's positive image in the marketplace.

The OMNI PARK CENTRAL, as a renovated product offering dramatically improved service, enters the market in 1985 with the task of establishing its new identity. The unique and strikingly attractive lobby, 770 renovated guest rooms and corridors, three new exciting food and beverage outlets, and a bold new facade that makes an identity statement, support and complement the positioning of the hotel.

The OMNI PARK CENTRAL will serve multiple markets with a multi-tiered product line. This product line in 1985 will be approached as five different hotels:

The Omni Suite Hotel
The Omni Classic Service Hotel
The Omni Executive Hotel
The Standard Commercial Hotel
The Airline Hotel

... each with its own identity, market segment to satisfy, marketing strategy and operating mode.

The **Omni Suite Hotel** is a 164 key, all-suite hotel comprised of family units, deluxe suites and two-bedroom suites. Product and service approaches Omni Classic Service, with appeal to the sophisticated guest. Omni Suites are attractively priced for a traditional suite, typically well below market value. However, its uniqueness is in offering a suite at a rate on par with the top rated rooms of the competition.

The targeted markets for the Omni Suite Hotel are the non-price sensitive pure transient, non-price sensitive corporate transient, corporate group, retail travel agent, long-term relocation, and the Deluxe Weekend Package User. This hotel, ideally, will not have a competitor, but will compete with and is priced below the New York Hilton, Sheraton Centre, Parker Meridien, Essex House, and the Marriott Marquis, all of which are offering normal suite rates.

EXHIBIT 9 Market Position Statement (page 2)

The **Omni Classic Service Hotel** is a 130 key, luxury hotel offering a level of service and product which will further differentiate the Omni Park Central from the competition. Omni Classic Service is designed to cater to the discriminating non-price sensitive traveler in all markets.

The targeted markets for the Omni Classic Service Hotel are the non-price sensitive pure transient and corporate transient, deluxe ESP user, corporate group, retail travel agent, social/leisure traveler, and the weekend package user. This hotel competes with and is priced below the Tower sections of the Parker Meridien, Essex House, Hilton Towers, Sheraton Towers and the Marriott Marquis, but in line with the top corporate rate offered at each of these hotels.

The **Omni Executive Hotel** is a 460 key, corporate transient hotel, dedicated to the loyal corporate Executive Service Plan guest. The rooms are a mix of early Sheraton renovated rooms and newly renovated Omni rooms. They are attractively priced to promote repeat use by frequent travelers.

The targeted markets for the Omni Executive Hotel are the pure transient, ESP user, association and corporate groups, trade shows, deluxe buyer users, retail travel agents, mini vacation user, weekend package user. The Omni Executive Hotel competes with and is priced above the St. Moritz, Sheraton Centre, Sheraton City Squire, Barbizon Plaza, Summit and Halloran House; equal to the Warwick, and below Essex House, Parker Meridien, New York Hilton, Novotel, and the Marriott Marquis.

The **Standard Commercial Hotel** consists of 239 keys, comprised of 27 economy and 212 standard unrenovated rooms. These rooms are clean and nicely appointed, however somewhat old and tired. The rooms have Murphy Beds and furnishings and soft goods are of lesser quality than in better hotels. However, a consistent standard of quality will enable this hotel to be perceived as the best value in the city.

The targeted markets for the Standard Commercial Hotel are the price-sensitive pure transient, buyers, special transient, FIT's, tours, association group, trade shows, other group, and price sensitive corporate group. This hotel competes with and is priced equal to the Sheraton Centre, Sheraton City Squire; below the Summit and Novotel; and above the Barbizon, Roosevelt, Penta and Holiday Inn.

The **Airline Hotel** is a 250 key hotel dedicated to 100 percent annual occupancy. The rooms are all renovated, a mix of earlier Sheraton renovated and newly renovated Omni rooms. The rooms are on floors dedicated to privacy and quiet. As this market is critical for a strong guaranteed business base covering overhead expenses, the product is of very high quality although reasonably priced. Everything is done to provide guests with a residential environment consisting of gracious hospitality and comfort. These amenities combined make this the city's best airline hotel.

EXHIBIT 9 Market Position Statement (page 3)

The airline hotel competes with and is priced above the Summit, Doral, Lexington, Roosevelt, Penta, and Milford Plaza; equal to the Sheraton Centre, City Squire and Novotel.

FOOD AND BEVERAGE

The new food and beverage offerings of the Omni Park Central in 1985 are integral to the repositioning and success of the hotel. The improved product and service combine with the new outlet concepts to satisfy all desired in-house and local markets, thereby strengthening the perception of the hotel as a product which is attractive and dynamic ... a hotel where people want to be.

THE CAFE is a new outlet located in the lobby behind the unique island front desk. It is open to the lobby allowing guests to enjoy the hotel activity. Although it is a light and open concept, the design is still sensitive enough to allow a degree of privacy. The Cafe will primarily satisfy the in-house guest for breakfast, light lunch, light foods throughout the day, and full beverage service complemented by live piano entertainment. Afternoon tea is also offered appealing to afternoon shoppers, theatre crowd, and in-house guest.

NICOLE is an exciting and bustling Parisienne Brasserie appealing to the cosmopolitan customer. Nicole satisfies in-house breakfast demand, and for lunch and dinner is positioned as a free-standing restaurant capable of catering to the cosmopolitan element in greater New York. As a brasserie, its product strength is its product consistency and simplicity. With the immigration to the West Side of young, upwardly mobile professionals, Nicole is a very popular restaurant. Nicole will also be a favorite for the theatre crowd, as it has a very congenial atmosphere. Both pre and post theatre menus are available.

The **PARALLEL BAR** is designed to appeal to the surrounding business and residential community, the trendy element of greater Manhattan, and the in-house guest. It will be positioned as a free-standing lounge which offers a high energy atmosphere achieved through the gymnasium design, state of the art lighting, special effects, sound equipment and programmed music.

EXHIBIT 10 The 1985 Mission Statement

FORWARD

This yearly mission represents a broad set of directions of "marching orders" for the hotel's EOC to use its resources now to maintain the hotel at the approved level of market position, or significantly move it toward such a position. It represents a delicate balance among the sometimes conflicting short and long term objectives related to owners, employees, and customers. The Vice President - Operations has the responsibility to keep the hotel's EOC team on the proper short term objectives. This should be done with the spirit of the mission. The moment this is no longer feasible, the matter should be directed to the Office of the President.

I. ROOMS DIVISION

A. Elements of Rooms Merchandising

The primary objective of the Omni Park Central in 1985 is to effectively reposition the hotel in the market by shifting from low-rated group, tour and airline segments to desirable high-rated transient and corporate segments. The newly renovated product will have an immediate consequent impact in this effort.

The key element, therefore, is to measure and capitalize on the demand available and created by these factors, and channel them into the hotel in the most effective manner, in order to both position the hotel correctly in the market and to be as profitable as possible. The vehicle chosen to do this is the unique approach to the concept of ideal business mix, controlled by selective sell targets. The unique approach is to merchandise the hotel as five separate hotels, each with a different product, each targeted to a different market segment.

The selective sell targets will direct the merchandising and operating strategies. Mid-week demand, particularly in high-demand months will emphasize only the highest rated market segments; weekend and low demand will be satisfied by packages, tours and other low-rated market segments.

EXHIBIT 10 Mission Statement (page 2)

The integrity of the concept is affected by measure of demand, and this will result in some deliberate cross-utilization of the product lines and defined market segments. The first quarter experience has been a transition period from low to higher segments, since this period immediately followed the completion of the major renovation.

As the AIRLINE HOTEL is currently 100% full and the STANDARD COMMERCIAL HOTEL will fill itself due to the already negotiated contracts for 1985 in the F.I.T. and Tour segments, very little marketing effort will be necessary to fill these hotels. The OMNI SUITE HOTEL, OMNI CLASSIC SERVICE HOTEL, and the OMNI EXECUTIVE HOTEL are the hotels that will require a substantial marketing effort and commitment to be successful in 1985. Following are the key strategies:

1. The selective sell targets will direct the merchandising and operating strategies. Mid-week demand, particularly in high-demand markets, will emphasize only the highest-rated market segments; weekends and low-demand will be satisfied by packages, tours, and low rated market segments.

2. The advertising program will concentrate on increasing the awareness of the SUITE, CLASSIC SERVICE, and EXECUTIVE HOTELS and impacting the weekend package market. Advertising will emphasize the value and uniquness of this product offering.

3. Public relations has an opportunity to create excitement and interest in this new "product" with special attention given to the SUITE and CLASSIC SERVICE Hotels.

4. Direct sales will concentrate on the corporate market for both ESP and group to impact the three primary hotels. This includes an aggressive solicitation and direct mail effort.

5. Direct sales has the responsiblility to insure that the STANDARD COMMERCIAL and AIRLINE Hotels are committed to the appropriate markets.

B. Operating Mode

The Omni Park Central will be substantially a new hotel in which the guest experience will be given the highest priority in order to support the product offering and assure the market repositioning of the hotel.

Significant emphasis will be placed on training for service. The Rooms Division will be managed in a highly cost efficient manner, resulting in a very profitable business. Most importantly, each of the five hotels will have management accountablility for the service and product rendered. From a housekeeping and mechanical persepctive, great attention must be given to maintaining the newly renovated guest rooms and public areas.

EXHIBIT 10 Mission Statement page 3)

As the Omni Park Central moves into the five hotel concept, the key hotels for success are the OMNI SUITE HOTEL, the OMNI CLASSIC SERVICE HOTEL, and the OMNI EXECUTIVE HOTEL.

Each hotel will operate independently of each other and success will be determined by the consistency of service and product as implemented by the employee and experienced by the guest. If the guest experience is positive, and they return for a future stay, then that is success.

1. OMNI SUITE HOTEL

The OMNI SUITE HOTEL has great potential for profitability and must be maintained as a quality product, as well as providing spacious accommodations. To insure this consistency, an Assistant Executive Housekeeper and an Assistant Front Office Manager have been assigned to this hotel. The bathroom amenities will be the same as in the Omni Classic Service Hotel. Additionally, a full concept may be developed for this hotel which may include a refrigerator, and other select features, which will create a more residential and comfortable environment for the guest.

2. OMNI CLASSIC SERVICE HOTEL

The OMNI CLASSIC SERVICE HOTEL must provide the standard amenities as outlined for Omni Classic Service throughout the Omni International Hotels. In order to do so, an Assistant Front Office Manager and an Assistant Housekeeper have been assigned to this hotel. Amenities and special services are basic to this luxury hotel. Attention to detail and service are throughly inspected for housekeeping and maintainence several times a week. To create further preferential treatment, a separate check-in area has been assigned at the Front Desk, designated by signage.

3. OMNI EXECUTIVE HOTEL

All ESP Standards are fully expected in this hotel and on par with the standards of Omni International Hotels. Although unable to offer guaranteed availability, the hotel is careful to measure demand accurately and thus attempts to always be able to satisfy demand from this market.

A complimentary morning paper and coffee is offered as part of the package for ESP guest, as well as express check-out. Pre-registration goals have also been set for the hotel in order to speed up the check-in process.

To insure consistency, an Assistant Front Office Manager and an Assistant Housekeeper have been assigned responsiblity for this hotel.

EXHIBIT 10 Mission Statement (page 4)

4. STANDARD COMMERCIAL HOTEL

This hotel contains almost all of the non-renovated rooms. The operating mode is to return to the basics ... insure cleanliness, everything works, no major objections and "no surprises." In order to accomplish this, the hotel will undergo a cosmetic in-house renovation to fix everything and provide a basic, clean, working room at a reasonable rate, the best value in the city. A detailed plan has been developed to define the objectionable rooms and to gradually move these rooms to the desirable, unobjectionable status.

5. AIRLINE HOTEL

This hotel has great potential, particularly for the new Omni Park Central. It is a determined strategy, however, to substantially limit the capacity of this hotel to provide the ideal mix for the total hotel in 1985. The hotel will limit itself to a select few airlines, preferably major domestic carriers, and price these airlines slightly above market due not only to the product and service, but also to supply and demand dynamics for this market in the City. The hotel will, without sacrificing rentable space, provide laundry facilities for the airlines without compromising the cost efficiency of the island Front Desk, and provide a seperate registration area for the airlines crews. In essence, this hotel will be in the highest demand by this segment, and will be the finest Airline Hotel in the City. The demand will then allow the hotel to be selective about the airlines contracted with, and will allow greater leverage in the pricing strategy.

II FOOD AND BEVERAGE

The objective of the Food and Beverage Division will be the successful commencement of the new product outlet concepts. achievement of the desired level of product and service on a consistent basis, and sufficiently high volumes to result in a profitable operation. All outlets will be supported by in-house collateral.

A. BANQUET/CATERING

The hotel will offer much improved Banquet product and service that will appeal to the small to medium size, high level corporate meeting market to include breakfast, luncheon, dinner and receptions. The social market is of limited demand for the hotel, but will nonetheless be aggressively pursued through the cross reference and usage of The Cafe and Nicole.

EXHIBIT 10 Mission Statement (page 5)

B. ROOM SERVICE

Room Service will be provided 16 hours a day according to established Omni standards. In-room dining will be a satisfying experience, with courteous and efficient order-taking, a creative menu offering, exceptionally high-quality product, expeditious delivery, and meticulous preparation. In addition, a daily Plate du Jour Program featuring a touch of Nicole will be offered.

C. THE CAFE

The Cafe will offer relaxed Food and Beverage service in a comfortable and open-design scheme. The menu offering is light foods, with emphasis on baked goods, cheese, pates, fresh fruits, and afternoon tea. The Cafe is removed from, but offers an interesting perspective of the activity in the Lobby. Live piano music as a backdrop enhances the overall experience and ambiance. The Cafe will be supported by its visual perception from the Lobby by in-house collateral.

D. NICOLE

The thrust of Nicole, a Parisienne Brasserie, will be its ambience. The environment is relaxed, unpretentious, convivial, and appealing. This is carried through from the design scheme to the menu, to the food preparation and service. The food offering features assorted pates, entrecote, cassoulet, choucroute, coq au vin, couscous royale. Nicole will be supported by a very significant public relations and advertising commitment as well as in-house promotional collateral.

E. PARALLEL BAR

The Parallel Bar will function as the beverage entertainment center offering beverage service only in a high energy atmosphere. The concept is that of a "sports bar" with a turn-of-the-century gymnasium effect. Service will be casual but efficient. Entertainment will be offered via programmed music and an emcee, with a mix of contemporary, 50's and 60's and big band ballads. The Parallel Bar will be supported by public relations, advertising, and in-house promotional collateral.

The new management team spent the month of May preparing for the strike which came in June and lasted almost the entire month. Because of the strike, it was impossible to tell how the hotel was doing business-wise. While most hotels had difficulty controlling their employees during this period, striking workers at the Omni Park Central were particularly violent and offensive to both managemenmt and hotel guests. Business slowed in the city for the remainder of the summer as people with flexibility in their schedules went elsewhere.

Once the city had begun to recover from the effects of the strike, management at the Omni Park Central began to realize how serious their problems were. Although occupancy went over 70 percent in August, the hotel was the last hotel in the city to sell out. The anticipated demand for ESP guests wasn't occurring. Management concluded that the individual business traveler must be going to smaller, more personalized hotels.

THE COMPETITIVE SITUATION

Competition was getting stiffer. A Novotel opened right around the corner with rates of $89 and $99 and completely took away the Omni's symphony business. Rubbing salt into their wounds, Novotel guests were walking around and past the Omni to get to Carnegie Hall. A major analysis of the competition was undertaken by management in an effort to learn what competitive advantages could be achieved.

A list of the rates and facilities of many Manhattan hotels appears in Exhibit 11. Exhibit 12 shows market share figures that were tracked. Management began to consider the New York Penta, the Sheraton City Squire, and the Sheraton Centre, to be its major competitors.

In keeping with the industry trend, the demand for hotel rooms in New York City softened between 1984 and 1985 (Exhibit 13). However, the overall health of the market was considered to be very good as New York City was one of the strongest rate markets in the country. According to the hotel accounting firm Pannell Kerr Forster's (PKF) "Trends in the Hospitality Industry," the largest increase in occupancy rate in NYC (62.7 percent to 69.4 percent) occurred for hotels with an average room rate of less than $45. At the same time, occupancy rates at the city's luxury properties remained steady at about 75 percent.

In July of 1985, the Marriott Marquis opened on Times Square. This was the first major convention hotel to be built in the city in over two decades. The Jacob K. Javits Convention Center was scheduled to open nearby in April of 1986. This Center would span five square blocks and would replace the Coliseum as New York City's major convention center.

All this boded well for New York City as a hotel town. Furthermore, in spite of the occupancy decline, average room rates in 1985 were up 7.8 percent according to PKF. However, PKF also noted that there was nothing portending an upward trend in occupancy in 1986.

The marketing department also undertook a study comparing the Park Central with 15 hotels in terms of product, location, service history, rack rate, corporate rate, and group facilities. Hotels that had either deluxe or first class accommodations were selected, since the Omni had rooms in both categories. Each hotel was rated as to whether it was superior, inferior or equal to the Omni Park Central. A critical factor in judging location was management's view that East side hotels were preferable to West side hotels. The results of this comparative study appear in Exhibit 14.

WHAT TO DO?

Richard Chambers turned away from the window and began to rethink the hotel's position, starting from square one. First, he reviewed the 1985 figures to date and November/December forecasts (Exhibit 15) and analyzed the market segments. He noted also that less than 5 percent of reservations were coming through the Omni 800 number. Fewer customers than that were walk-ins, which meant that over 90 percent of the hotel's business was direct.

From the 1985 figures, Chambers noted that the Park Central would be lucky to have a gross operating profit (GOP) of $6.6 million, never mind the $10.6 million wanted by corporate. He went back over the five year supply/demand outlook and questionnaire answers he had recently submitted to corporate (Exhibit 16), along with the 1986 mission and market position statements shown in Exhibit 17. And here was the 1986 GOP forecasted at $10.5 million. Pretty aggressive, he thought, as he reviewed the 1986 forecast (Exhibit 18) and compared it to sales figures of 1984 and 1985 (Exhibit 19). Chambers than reviewed the competition that he had asked Brenda Fields in the ESP sales office to especially investigate in what he considered to be an especially vulnerable market (Exhibit 20).

Unfortunately, there was no simple or apparent answer and the repercussions of the Omni Park Central situation were being felt throughout the company. The corporate plan of "five hotels" might have been an innovative idea but the execution of it didn't work. Even when business was good, it was "bad" like when attempts to change the market mix caused more problems such as walking three buses of 150 people with New York City dinner reservations and theatre tickets, back to Baltimore.

As a matter of fact, thought Chambers, the Omni brand name doesn't seem to be helping us a bit in this market. I wonder how strongly we should identify with it? And with Omni Classic? Are we an Omni Classic, or are we something unique? Do we position by our name or by what we are? Somehow, he thought, we need to rethink our strategy.

Chambers was about to pick up the phone and call corporate to see what they had to say about it, when Phillip Georgas, the General Manager of the Omni Park Central Hotel, walked into his office. Rich looked squarely at Mr. Georgas with the frustration of the past six months showing in his appearance.

"I just had a call from corporate," said Georgas." They say we have to identify the correct positioning for this hotel once and for all and implement the solution. Do you think our rate structure is off? Could we be losers because of our location? Is it our product? Or the quality of our service? Or, is it because Omni Dunfey lacks the brand recognition of a Sheraton or a Hilton? Rich, what do you think we should do?

EXHIBIT 11 Rates and Facilities of Manhattan Hotels

Hotel	# of Guest Rooms	Facilities	Sg Rate	Db Rate	Corp Sg. Rate	Corp Db. Rate	Week end Rate	# of Airline Room/night
The Berkshire Place	414	Atrium Lobby, Restaurant Bar, Facilities for small meetings only.	165-210	185-230	no corporate rates		133 Sg. 150 Dbl	
Days Inn	596	Restaurant, Lounge, Meeting and Banquet Facilities for up to 900, Bathroom Amenities Include Soap, Shampoo, and Toothpaste, Outdoor Pool.	86-109	96-119	79	89		150
Essex House	700	Older, Traditional New York Hotel, Elegant parkside restaurant, Lounge, Function space for 15-600 people, Press Conference Center, Beautiful Rooms, Anyone can get a corporate rate, Other rates based on volume, Basket of goodies in the Bathroom	160-210	185-235	175	200	249 One Night inc. meals.	
The Grand Hyatt	1347	Two Restaurants, and Lounges Meeting Facilities for 12 to 2,000. Array of Bathroom Amenities.	145-205	170-235	155	180	98	
The Harley	790	New Very Modern Hotel,a touch feminine, Marble Bathrooms with full amenities.	145	145	115	115		
The Helmsley Palace	1050	Two Restaurants and Four Lounges, Refrigerator in rooms, Some rooms have fireplaces and Terraces, Deluxe Bathroom Amenities.	185-245	185-265			80 per night	

EXHIBIT 11 Rates and Facilities (page 2)

Hotel	# of Guest Rooms	Facilities	Sg Rate	Db Rate	Corp Sg. Rate	Corp Db. Rate	Week end Rate	# of Airline Room/night
Howard Johnson's	300	Restaurant and Lounge, Free Parking, Safety Deposit Box in Room, Rooms are musty, in poor condition, located in poor, not very nice section of the city.	75-115	87-127	75	75		
The Marriott Marquis	1877	Opened July 1985, New York's Tallest Hotel with World's Highest Atrium, Five Restaurants four lounges, 80,000 sq. feet Meeting and Exhibition Space Largest Grand Ballroom in city.	200	225	175	200	150	
The Mayflower	700	Restaurant and Cafe, Most rooms have Kitchenettes	107-137	122-157	85-100	85-100		
The Milford Plaza	1310	Two Restaurants and Lobby Bar, all featuring Live Entertainment, Meeting Facilities for 15-550.	71-110	85-115	75	85		350
The New York Hilton	2200	Newly Renovated, Two Restaurants, Discotheque, Excellent Convention and Meeting Facilities.	140-200	165-225	150	175	215 Sg. 240 Dbl Two nights	
The New York Penta	1700	Nicely renovated rooms Only soap in Bathrooms. Excellent Meeting and Convention Facilities for all types of functions. Variety of Bars and Restaurants.	89	110			60/night	300

EXHIBIT 11 Rates and Facilities (page 3)

Hotel	# of Guest Rooms	Facilities	Sg Rate	Db Rate	Corp Sg. Rate	Corp Db. Rate	Week end Rate	# of Airline Room/night
Novotel	470	Opened October 1984 Two Restaurants, one Bar	115-150	125-160	110			
The Parker Meridan	700	Two Restaurants, Bar, Pool, Track, Squash, Racquetball, Nautilus, Sauna, Jacuzzi, Conference Facilities for 10-250	165	185	155	175	260 two/nights	
The Ramada Inn	366	Restaurant, Lounge, Pool One meeting room for 40, Safety Box in Room, Rooms are musty, in poor condition, located in poor, not very nice section of the city.	95-115	107-127	75	75		
Sheraton Centre	1850	Atrium Lobby, Restaurant Cafe, Show Lounge	130-175	155-200	140	165	95/night	200
Sheraton City Squire	720	Restaurant, Pastry Shop, Lobby Bar, Glass Enclosed Pool and Health Club, Indoor Parking, Functions Rooms for 25-300, Good, Typical Sheraton rooms.	99-150	124-175	125	150	87	200
The St. Moritz	600	Restaurant, Sidewalk Cafe, Lounge,Home of Rumpelmayer's Famous Ice Cream and Pastry Shop, Meeting and Banquet for 10-300, Rooms are musty, overcrowded, and need repair.	125-165	145-185	100-125	100-125	90-115 per/night	
The Vista International	829	Two Restaurants, two lounges, Meetings for 14-950, In Heart of Financial District, Fitness Center, Indoor Pool, Sauna, Gymnasium, Sauna, Steam Baths, Racquetball Courts, Jogging Tracks.	140-210	170-230	No Corporate Rates			

EXHIBIT 12 Tracked Market Share Figures

Hotel	Jan		Feb		Mar	Apr		May	
	%Occ	Rank	%Occ	Rank		%Occ	Rank	%Occ	Rank
City Squire	68.56	1	81.49	1	n	86.38	1	81.22	3
Essex House	64.35	2	75.61	2	o	80.14	3	83.78	1
Milford Plaza	62.19	3	71.71	4	t	83.35	2	82.71	2
Berkshire Place	61.73	4	69.30	7		71.01	6	79.23	4
Vista	61.54	5	66.81	8	a	71.08	5	74.54	8
Parker Meridien	59.60	6	71.42	6	v	66.82	8	76.87	5
Omni Park Central	57.47	7	71.47	5	a	68.44	7	74.95	7
Sheraton Centre	56.57	8	75.16	3	i	75.88	4	73.19	9
N.Y. Penta	49.93	9	56.54	11	b	63.27	9	66.28	10
Palace	49.50	10	58.93	10	l	68.45	11	65.47	11
Novotel	43.13	11	62.15	9	e	66.80	10	75.71	6
Avg. % Occ	57.69		69.14			72.07		75.81	

Hotel	Jun		Jul		Aug		Y-T-D	
	%Occ	Rank	%Occ	Rank	%Occ	Rank	%Occ	Rank
City Squire	84.18	2	79.92	1	88.01	2	81.39	1
Essex House	82.55	3	54.96	10	68.76	7	72.88	3
Milford Plaza	87.01	1	76.60	2	90.00	1	79.88	2
Berkshire Place	72.47	8	62.32	5	63.23	9	68.47	5
Vista	77.33	4	61.83	6	58.40	10	67.36	9
Parker Meridien	73.53	7	60.09	7	70.15	5	68.35	6
Omni Park Central	68.20	9	59.45	8	72.68	4	67.52	8
Sheraton Centre	75.76	5	67.88	4	68.32	8	70.28	4
N.Y. Penta	62.83	10	57.64	9	70.12	6	60.88	10
Palace	56.68	11	46.64	11	47.33	11	54.91	11
Novotel	74.41	6	70.16	3	80.95	3	67.62	7
	74.05		64.08		70.72		68.98	

EXHIBIT 12 Market Share (continued)

Hotels	Rooms	Percentage of Market	September Occ. Rate	September Mkt. Share	October Occ. Rate	October Mkt. Share	YTD Occ. Rate	YTD Mkt. Share
Omni Park Central	1240	15.08%	73.55%	15.75%	80.27%	15.29%	69.61%	15.03%
Penta	1753	21.32	63.49	19.21	72.92	19.64	62.51	19.08
Novotel	430	5.23	74.79	5.55	81.97	5.41	70.01	5.24
Parker Meridan	700	8.51	73.00	8.82	85.00	9.14	70.07	8.62
Vista	829	10.08	68.75	9.84	77.81	9.91	68.66	9.91
Sheraton Centre	1850	22.50	72.33	23.10	79.61	22.62	71.54	23.04
Essex House	700	8.51	65.01	7.86	76.39	8.21	72.39	8.82
City Squire	720	8.76	79.40	9.87	88.40	9.78	81.95	10.27
Total	8222	100.0%	71.29%	100.0%	80.30%	100.0%	70.93%	100.0%

EXHIBIT 13 New York City Monthly Occupancies, 1984 vs. 1985

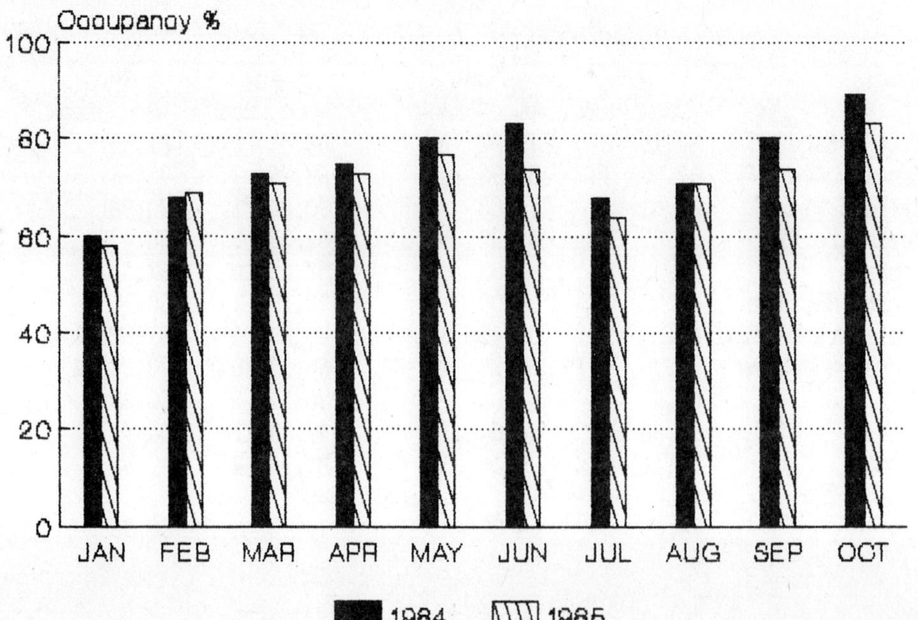

EXHIBIT 14 Comparative Study of Competitive Hotels

+ Superior to Omni Park Central (Rate Higher)
- Inferior to Omni Park Central (Rate Lower)
= Equal to Omni Park Central
? Unknown
Del Deluxe
Fc First Class

	Product		Location		Service History		Rack Rate		Corporate Rate	
	Del	Fc	Del	Fc	Del	Fc	Del	Fc.	Del	Fc
Parker Meridien	+		+		+		+16		+16	
Essex House	+		+		+		+ 1		+16	
Sheraton Centre	+		=		+		-10		=	
Sheraton Squire		+		=		+		-20		+18
St. Moritz	-		+		+		-30		-30	
Penta		+		-		+		-10		-18
Milford Plaza		=		-		+		-27		-32
Hilton	+		+		+		-24		+15	
Warwick	+		+		+		-24		-15	
Days Inn		=		-		+		-35		-27
Harley	+		+		+		-24		- 5	
Mayflower		+		+		+		-15		- 2
Ramada Inn		-		-		+		-25		-22
Novotel		+		-		+		=		- 2
Marriott	+		-		+		+51		+45	

RESULTS OF THE COMPARATIVE HOTEL STUDY

	Superior	Inferior	Equal
Product	11	2	2
Location	7	6	2
Service History	14	one is unknown	
Group Facilities	5	1	
Rate Differentials	More $	Less $	Equal $
Rack Rate	3	11	1
Coporate Rate	5	9	1
Lunch Average Check	6		

EXHIBIT 15 1985 Operating Figures and Projections (a) Income Statement

		Jan	Feb	Mar	Apr	May	Jun
REVENUES	Rooms	1773384	1988393	2105078	2127317	2553605	2103470
	Food	109411	142488	207281	280702	255115	125239
	Beverage	54347	68122	95350	104538	138290	40867
	F & B Misc	16070	39302	36556	32861	44863	27593
	Telephone	70779	76614	96674	73139	97531	99190
	Laundry/Valet	8183	14724	8545	11979	13891	6936
	Other Income	35536	-15929	23579	-11128	15567	22677
	Comm. Rents	32022	33005	30512	35843	42033	94298
Total Revenues		2099732	2346719	2603575	2655251	3160895	2520270
PROFIT/LOSS	Rooms	1041332	1243578	1307063	1361865	1700853	1563736
	Food/Beverage	-166144	-213315	-201849	-166553	-102387	-38265
	Telephone	-57576	-48393	-38742	-44628	-38494	-36129
	Laundry/Valet	2145	2443	2314	3886	1980	3226
	Comm. Rents	32822	33005	30512	35843	42033	94298
	Other Income	35536	-15929	23579	-11128	15567	22677
Operating Income		888115	1001389	1122877	1179285	1619552	1609543
DEDUCTIONS	Fees	63164	70489	77848	82500	91961	75990
	A & G	194597	197691	206978	234358	225467	217325
	Marketing	110228	184482	285156	191138	159593	158057
	Energy	142529	142369	179755	147912	137959	129215
	Prop. Opers.	189116	128834	147869	161566	183785	79339
Total Deductions		699634	723865	897606	817474	798765	659926
GOP		188481	277524	225271	361811	820787	949617
		8.94%	11.83%	8.65%	13.57%	25.96%	38.00%
	Taxes	113200	113200	170200	151200	151200	132200
	Insurance	25598	25545	44076	31587	31507	34859
OPERATING PROFIT		49683	138779	10995	638000	638008	790558
	Interest	878625	875606	883230	900745	900745	891406
	Depreciation	692500	692500	692500	721612	721612	711656
	Other Costs	152187	154862	153811	158464	158464	154852
EARNINGS		-1673629	-1584189	-1718546	-1142821	-1142813	-967356
	Rooms Avail.	38595	34860	38595	37200	38533	37200
	Rooms Sold	22105	24814	26943	25449	28780	25189
	Occ %	57.3%	71.2%	69.8%	68.1%	74.7%	67.7%
	Avg Rm Rate	$80.23	$80.13	$78.13	$83.59	$88.73	$83.51
	Payroll $	674984	724030	892791	875725	850372	531648
	Payroll %	32.1%	30.9%	34.3%	33.0%	26.9%	21.1%
	RoomProfit %	58.7%	62.5%	62.1%	64.0%	66.6%	74.3%
	FB Profit %	-92.4%	-85.4%	-59.5%	-39.8%	-23.4%	-15.6%
	Food Cost %	39.1%	35.2%	34.5%	30.7%	23.8%	34.8%
	Bev Cost %	13.6%	19.5%	15.6%	18.8%	12.1%	22.0%

EXHIBIT 15 (a)Income Statement (continued)

	Jul	Aug	Sept	Oct	Nov	Dec	Total
Rooms	1794968	2198910	2193640	2831262	2615475	2390477	26675979
Food	151646	171857	288141	321922	250968	395582	2700352
Beverage	51594	74111	83853	123723	116179	154710	1105684
F & B Misc	2093	14671	52658	65048	38610	41168	411493
Telephone	84754	96528	94944	139031	124161	109242	1162587
Laundry/Valet	6546	8296	14082	10976	10814	5239	120211
Other Income	12421	-8650	-15401	12856	11791	28842	112161
Comm. Rents	39380	37616	40910	39961	37963	35294	498837
Total Revenues	2143402	2593339	2752827	3544779	3205961	3160554	32787304
Rooms	1881925	1455544	1423641	2004324	1744238	1506038	17434107
Food/Beverage	-214359	-180962	-85131	1683	-123334	-15616	-1506232
Telephone	-47961	-29042	-25218	-3264	-13084	-19118	-401649
Laundry/Valet	827	2042	986	2478	835	-10988	12174
Comm. Rents	39380	37616	40910	39961	37963	35294	499637
Other Income	12421	-8650	-15401	12856	11791	28842	112161
Operating Income	1672233	1276548	1339787	2058038	1658409	1524452	16150198
Fees	64500	77718	82244	108163	94382	94817	983776
A & G	203490	208586	206666	229063	276592	284489	2685302
Marketing	175769	127756	202560	133995	138488	206833	2074055
Energy	125409	145986	164315	133835	131420	98671	1679375
Prop. Opers.	152388	171489	197361	199613	242706	222922	2076988
Total Deduction	801556	821535	853146	804669	883588	907732	9499496
	870677	455013	486641	1253369	774821	616720	6650702
	7.83%	21.02%	17.64%	35.36%	24.40%	19.51%	20.32%
Taxes	126500	126500	156672	156675	156841	156044	1710432
Insurance	33649	33649	32328	31352	30788	86377	441315
Operating Profit	-9472	384944	297641	1065342	595272	374269	4498955
Interest	900833	926251	898872	921647	913409	955443	10846812
Depreciation	696656	646656	693322	693322	693322	693322	8348980
Other Costs	152937	155141	155894	160217	157930	15803	1730562
Earnings	-1740954	-1343104	-1450447	-709844	-1169389	-1290299	-16427399
Rooms Avail.	38440	38448	37200	38440	37200	38440	453151
Rooms Sold	23000	27932	27361	32142	30838	29092	323645
Occ %	59.8%	72.7%	73.6%	83.6%	82.9%	75.7%	71.4%
Avg.Room Rate	$78.04	$78.72	$80.17	$88.03	$84.81	$82.17	$82.42
Payroll $	806931	815296	837174	885539	849266	870149	9613905
Payroll %	37.6%	31.4%	30.3%	25.0%	26.5%	27.5%	29.3%
Rooms Profit %	60.3%	66.2%	64.9%	70.8%	66.7%	63.0%	65.4%
F & B Profit %	-104.4%	-69.4%	-19.8%	0.3%	-30.4%	-2.6%	-35.5%
Food Cost %	37.6%	40.0%	29.1%	30.0%	35.1%	27.4%	32.1%
Bev. Cost %	15.7%	27.8%	22.2%	20.4%	19.1%	19.4%	18.6%

EXHIBIT 15 (b)Segmentation Report

	Jan	Feb	Mar	Apr	May	Jun
ROOMS SOLD						
Pure transient	1142	1080	1155	1428	1964	1552
Outside Res. System	440	507	435	692	765	701
Omni Classic Service		687	707	547	1101	1115
ESP	3105	2896	3826	2515	2399	1961
Special Transient	1799	2342	3339	2748	3025	2540
Mini	559	690	1364	1645	759	275
Other Packages	1534	852	1333	1294	1179	1315
F.I.T.	604	563	1340	1406	1500	1535
Association-National	154	262	406	251	164	245
Regular Corp Group	704	504	280	300	1184	1262
Bus Tours			402			
Other Groups	629	463		1090	1841	1069
Airlines	5139	7373	8018	7429	7697	8146
International Tours	160	262	922	876	958	822
Trade Shows	4122	4443	1558	1719	2475	551
Permanents	339	284	341	313	310	277
Buyers	1663	1606	1517	1196	1608	1873
Total Rooms Sold	22093	24814	26943	25449	28929	25239
Complimentary	613	755	1421	573	789	700
House Use	319	453	450	482	528	2133
Out of Order	8853	4567	3113	2967	2554	1913
Vacant	6562	4131	6513	7729	5640	7215
Total Rooms Avail.	38440	34720	38440	37200	38440	37200
AVERAGE RATE						
Pure transient	141.44	140.71	149.14	146.59	145.97	124.74
Outside Res. System	120.46	130.30	145.95	140.10	151.68	143.08
Omni Classic Service		127.48	139.22	147.46	142.11	148.98
ESP	90.48	91.27	90.41	103.66	116.30	114.34
Special Transient	69.88	75.76	80.20	84.81	88.19	79.69
Mini	67.10	67.70	70.04	70.01	72.96	78.28
Other Packages	74.96	87.39	91.37	91.83	100.64	96.46
F.I.T.	52.31	53.42	52.86	59.13	58.24	58.72
Association-National	97.78	96.21	103.18	103.73	105.26	103.44
Regular Corp Group	92.91	94.76	100.37	96.79	106.57	113.36
Bus Tours			97.65			
Other Groups	79.45	88.57		99.51	97.73	110.44
Airlines	57.88	57.49	57.35	58.09	57.42	56.74
International Tours	56.73	56.81	60.15	59.95	61.79	60.41
Trade Shows	99.79	97.78	106.97	128.63	107.95	105.10
Permanents	20.83	24.87	23.38	23.53	23.76	53.18
Buyers	87.16	91.61	91.99	95.68	96.48	97.88
TOTAL AVERAGE RATE	81.73	82.21	80.72	85.97	90.59	86.35

EXHIBIT 15 (b)Segmentation (continued)

	Jul	Aug	Sept	Oct	Nov	Dec	Total
ROOMS SOLD							
Pure Transient	766	1193	1088	2253	3298	2286	19205
Outside Res. System	435	636	514	1162	1292	1012	8591
Omni CLassic Service	189	105	162				4613
ESP	1301	1915	2125	3011	2869	1838	29761
Special Transient	3101	4309	3021	4300	3885	3124	37533
Mini	166	180	161	347	707	631	7484
Other Packages	1739	3087	1557	2353	2253	1240	19736
F.I.T.	1640	1959	1756	2621	1481	1705	18110
Association-National	154	73	2412	594	69	1988	6632
Regular Corp. Group	433	467	216	289	1084	191	6914
Bus Tours							402
Other Groups	1227	1493	2214	1981	1471	1619	15097
Airlines	8018	8192	8171	7991	7696	9034	92904
International Tours	1972	2169	2291	1672	1951	1442	15497
Trade Shows	1419	536	871	2460	1017	2179	23350
Permanents	320	311	262	417	294	280	3748
Buyers	465	1307	540	691	1471	523	14460
Total Rooms Sold	23205	27932	27361	32142	30838	29092	324037
Complimentary	722	578	352	471	782	630	8386
House Use	542	686	263	499	393	444	7192
Out of Order	4628	4272	2302	1898	841	1982	39890
Vacant	9343	4972	6922	3430	4346	6292	73095
Total Rooms Avail.	38440	38440	37200	38440	37200	38440	452600
AVERAGE RATE							
Pure Transient	179.66	143.00	176.26	139.98	129.22	113.58	139.37
Outside Res. System	134.86	133.61	139.65	144.66	138.45	132.62	138.80
Omni Classic Service	161.71	158.05	156.83				143.46
ESP	114.15	110.66	112.48	115.81	113.89	110.75	105.27
Special Transient	85.51	85.20	81.13	83.52	85.90	83.03	82.67
Mini	74.94	80.29	82.16	88.06	73.73	77.28	72.61
Other Packages	94.74	97.85	97.67	98.26	97.17	97.53	94.52
F.I.T.	58.33	58.21	58.30	57.92	59.54	58.06	57.66
Association-National	68.93	74.75	110.31	117.4	106.12	69.30	96.22
Regulal Corp. Group	126.71	110.67	105.75	110.59	121.10	120.92	109.24
Bus Tours							97.65
Other Groups	83.60	79.62	88.24	104.06	89.82	82.75	91.84
Airline	57.55	57.73	56.18	54.73	57.45	57.25	57.12
International Tours	57.65	60.49	63.50	64.24	67.57	66.80	62.38
Trade Shows	108.98	117.11	100.03	131.06	135.64	154.95	113.97
Permanents	15.10	21.33	26.76	57.84	29.05	25.10	29.28
Buyers	100.30	97.00	101.45	95.67	93.26	93.49	94.39
TOTAL AVERAGE RATE	79.85	80.84	83.27	89.29	89.28	83.44	84.71

EXHIBIT 15 (b)Segmentation (continued)

	Jan	Feb	Mar	Apr	May	Jun
REVENUES (000 OMITTED)						
Pure transient	162	152	172	209	287	194
Outside Res. System	53	66	63	97	116	100
Omni Classic Service		88	98	81	156	166
ESP	281	264	346	260	279	224
Special Transient	126	177	268	233	267	202
Mini	38	47	96	115	55	22
Other Packages	115	74	122	119	119	127
F.I.T.	32	30	71	83	87	90
Association-National	15	25	42	26	17	25
Regular Corp Group	65	48	28	29	126	143
Bus Tours			39			
Other Groups	50	41		108	180	118
Airlines	297	424	460	432	442	462
International Tours	9	15	55	53	59	50
Trade Shows	411	434	167	221	267	58
Permanents	7	7	8	7	7	15
Buyers	145	147	140	114	155	183
Total Revenues	1806	2039	2175	2187	2619	2179
% of occupancy	57.47	71.47	70.09	68.41	75.26	67.85

	Jul	Aug	Sept	Oct	Nov	Dec	Total
REVENUES (000 OMITTED)							
Pure transient	138	171	192	315	426	260	2678
Outside Res. System	59	85	72	168	179	134	1192
Omni Classic Service	31	17	25				662
ESP	149	212	239	349	327	204	3134
Special Transient	265	367	245	359	334	259	3102
Mini	12	14	13	31	52	49	544
Other Packages	165	302	152	231	219	121	1866
F.I.T.	96	114	102	152	88	99	1044
Association-National	1	5	266	70	7	138	637
Regular Coporate Group	55	52	23	32	131	23	755
Bus Tours							39
Other Groups	103	119	195	206	132	134	1386
Airlines	461	473	459	437	442	517	5306
International Tours	114	131	145	107	132	96	966
Trade Shows	155	63	87	322	138	338	2661
Permanents	5	7	7	24	9	7	110
Buyers	47	127	55	66	137	49	1365
Total Revenues	1856	2259	2277	2869	2753	2428	27447
% of occupancy	60.37	72.66	73.55	83.62	82.9	75.68	71.5

EXHIBIT 15 (c)Rooms Cost

	Jul	Aug	Sept	Oct	Nov	Dec	Total
Transient Sales	1840569	2243679	2263500	2853735	2700976	2378647	26910800
Mini Vac.Sales	12441	14454	13228	30557	52127	48765	532057
Allowance A/R	-20169	-19040	-28582	-15694	-7437	-12307	-231260
Allowance F/D	-11250	-23315	-25982	-21293	-19915	-19392	-214467
Allowance T/D	-26623	-16868	-28524	-16043	-110276	-5236	-321151
Total Rm Sales	1794968	2198910	2193640	2831262	2615475	2390477	26675979
Salaries/Wages	380976	409123	379592	420551	417961	427003	4617515
Holiday/Sick Pay	29577	12308	29550	6855	27703	42288	318212
Benefits	134213	137082	144428	140529	146923	143540	1693519
Total Payroll	544766	558513	553570	567935	592587	612831	6629246
Guest Amenities	1364	3620	3232	1500	6055	912	56892
Guest Supplies	9973	17154	18004	40514	8006	2283	194540
Courtesy Car	0	0	0	0	0	0	830
Guest Cert.	0	0	32	0	0	0	932
Dishon. Res.	0	0	6690	30165	8707	35602	87201
Laundry	57199	65006	73669	63713	88421	65128	767648
Res.Expense	13983	16815	17949	24514	25046	30003	244876
Room Commision	29809	24573	32643	35146	53811	57253	466368
Print/Stat.	840	5	2382	2048	3148	1169	34848
Supplies	3966	2285	9264	2766	12628	7603	79782
Uniforms	545	400	1424	2514	827	-454	16291
Decorations	1974	1330	2000	1495	507	2886	17440
Guest Parking	110	0	0	0	0	0	110
Security	0	14575	581	627	872	813	59129
Contract Clng.	1809	450	1776	1769	5300	-1946	22631
Night Cleaning	7974	10460	11365	10698	14200	10834	133333
Relocation	0	0	1669	0	2297	365	4331
Pers.Recruiting	0	0	0	555	0	0	870
Casual Labor	0	0	0	0	0	0	1035
Linen	20500	20500	20500	30500	40000	52719	307719
Glassware	1000	1000	1000	1000	1000	1000	12000
Euip.Rental	0	0	1914	2917	1620	5595	15818
Other Rentals	0	0	930	0	0	0	1860
Sales/Use Tax	11000	3950	4989	2712	3934	-2742	44611
Licenses	170	0	10	1195	-70	0	1310
Misc. Expense	3053	2730	4406	2655	2341	2615	37213
Total Other Exp.	165269	184853	216429	259003	278650	271638	2609618
Room Profit	1084933	1455544	1423641	2004324	1744238	1506008	17437115
	60.3%	66.2%	64.9%	70.8%	66.7%	63.0%	65.4%

EXHIBIT 15 (d)Food and Beverage Covers

	Jan	Feb	Mar	Apr	May	Jun	Jul	Aug	Sept	Oct	Nov	Dec	Total
NICOLE													
Bkfst Covers	0	1346	2310	2962	3501	0	22	0	0	0	0	0	10141
Avg Check	0	6.90	7.09	8.22	7.31	0	1.09	0	0	0	0	0	7.46
Revenue($)	0	9287	16378	24348	25592	0	24	0	0	0	0	0	75629
Lunch Covers	0	566	1254	1336	1472	0	695	895	1170	1532	1758	2342	13020
Avg Check	0	9.10	10.41	11.24	11.51	0	12.02	13.10	11.28	12.11	12.88	11.26	11.60
Revenue($)	0	5151	13054	15017	16943	0	8354	11725	13198	18553	22643	16371	151009
Dinner Covers	0	824	2382	2041	1933	0	1176	1610	2244	2472	2895	2966	20543
Avg Check	0	12.62	14.14	15.87	17.43	0	12.86	14.16	13.85	14.87	15.44	14.89	14.84
Revenue($)	0	10399	33681	32391	33692	0	15123	22798	31079	36759	44699	44164	304785
FOOD TOTAL													
Covers	0	2736	5946	6339	6906	0	1893	2505	3414	4004	4653	5308	43704
Avg Check	0	9.08	10.61	11.32	11.04	0	12.41	13.78	12.97	13.81	14.47	13.29	12.16
Revenue($)	0	24837	63113	71756	76227	0	23501	34523	44277	55312	67342	60535	531423
BEVERAGE TOT	0	10365	28855	27479	25847	0	9176	15656	24729	31848	40258	34619	248862
PARALLEL BAR													
BEVERAGE TOT	0	0	0	24682	59797	4666	22782	36914	36826	44092	46662	45416	321837
THE CAFE													
Bkfst Covers	2555	2866	1596	2239	1754	3419	3167	4769	4981	6184	5505	6029	45064
Avg Check	8.85	7.34	8.28	8.80	9.39	8.28	6.94	6.83	6.88	7.30	7.33	7.31	7.54
Revenue($)	22612	21036	13215	19703	16470	28309	21979	32572	34269	45143	40352	44072	339732
Lunch Covers	1817	1513	779	826	633	657	1230	1312	1491	989	864	515	12626
Avg Check	7.58	6.78	7.31	7.70	8.79	11.05	6.27	7.37	6.18	7.15	7.40	7.27	7.34
Revenue($)	13773	10258	5694	6360	5564	7260	7712	9669	9214	7071	6394	3744	92713
Dinner Covers	2071	1711	2332	936	788	821	869	902	889	637	213	14	12183
Avg Check	7.98	8.65	8.80	11.05	11.97	12.06	9.13	8.59	8.71	9.13	7.94	25.21	9.26
Revenue($)	16527	14800	20522	10343	9432	9901	7934	7748	7743	5816	1691	353	112810
FOOD TOTAL													
Covers	6443	6090	4707	4001	3175	4897	5266	6983	7361	7810	6582	6558	69873
Avg Check	8.21	7.57	8.38	9.10	9.91	9.29	7.14	7.16	6.96	7.43	7.36	7.35	7.80
Revenue($)	52912	46094	39431	36406	31466	45470	37625	49989	51226	58030	48437	48169	545255
BEVERAGE TOT	35037	35226	30322	17794	14839	16975	11602	9018	11225	6381	3031	4327	193777

EXHIBIT 15 (d)Food and Beverage Covers (continued)

	Jan	Feb	Mar	Apr	May	Jun	Jul	Aug	Sep	Oct	Nov	Dec	Total
ROOM SERVICE													
Bkfst Covers	1165	1098	1423	1338	1684	0	1134	1448	1977	2449	2207	1906	17829
Avg Check	6.71	7.34	8.85	8.78	8.24	0	6.06	6.39	7.27	6.55	6.63	8.44	7.37
Revenue($)	7817	8059	12594	11748	13876	0	6872	9253	14373	16041	14632	16087	131352
Lunch Covers	498	380	422	346	739	0	423	556	836	647	796	1153	6796
Avg Check	9.03	10.37	9.09	12.14	11.62	0	8.48	9.79	9.22	9.53	9.59	14.12	10.58
Revenue($)	4497	3941	3836	4200	8587	0	3587	5443	7708	6166	7634	16280	71879
Dinner Covers	752	797	1523	972	1286	0	566	1040	885	1392	1767	1452	12432
Avg Check	12.81	12.53	12.99	14.29	13.93	0	10.44	11.94	10.99	11.02	10.13	11.09	11.95
Revenue($)	9633	9986	19784	13890	17914	0	5909	12418	9726	15340	17900	16103	148603
FOOD TOTAL													
Covers	2415	2275	3368	2656	3709	0	2123	3044	3698	4488	4770	4511	42553
Avg Check	9.09	9.66	10.75	11.23	10.89	0	7.71	8.91	8.60	8.37	8.42	10.74	8.27
Revenue($)	21947	21986	36214	29838	40377	0	6368	27114	31807	37547	40166	48470	351834
BEVERAGE TOT	10973	11868	14516	9670	17466	0	5670	10893	6858	11041	10771	15406	125132
BANQUET													
Bkfst Covers	333	795	1646	1420	686	197	1627	522	2967	232	821	789	12035
Avg Check	7.90	7.05	5.03	9.17	11.36	9.80	9.84	12.00	11.63	12.44	10.78	8.22	9.49
Revenue	2631	5605	8279	13021	7793	1931	6010	6264	34506	2886	8850	6486	114262
Lunch Covers	543	1404	1100	2103	1087	899	944	906	1827	1602	1693	2121	16229
Avg Check	19.05	13.06	18.90	25.03	19.07	18.91	5.33	20.30	19.01	29.00	18.91	26.74	21.69
Revenue	10344	18336	20790	52638	20729	17000	3912	18392	34731	46458	32015	56716	352061
Dinner Covers	463	614	1855	912	2159	544	668	368	1130	941	1440	2528	13622
Avg Check	30.34	25.92	16.53	35.88	16.93	27.80	5.50	18.11	42.78	38.38	20.89	15.01	24.07
Revenue	4047	15915	30663	32723	36552	15123	3714	6664	48341	36116	30082	37945	327885
Coffee Breaks	283	207	464	2746	2341	3476	719	1461	4439	5271	4271	5754	31432
Avg Check	8.67	8.11	9.50	5.21	5.40	3.34	9.04	12.78	5.97	4.05	4.04	13.08	6.76
Revenue	2454	1679	4408	14307	12641	11610	6500	18672	26501	21348	17255	75262	212637
Reception	1623	2154	1556	1365	3497	2416	30	470	2961	3000	927	4330	24329
Avg Check	5.74	5.09	4.62	24.87	7.06	16.24	9.87	12.81	5.90	21.01	7.68	11.51	11.06
Revenue	9316	10964	7189	33948	24689	39236	296	6021	17470	63030	7119	49838	269116
Total Food													
Covers	3245	5174	6621	8546	9770	7532	3988	3727	13324	11046	9152	15522	97647
Avg Check	11.95	10.15	10.77	17.16	10.48	11.27	7.66	15.03	12.12	15.38	10.42	14.58	13.07
Revenue	38792	52499	71329	146637	102404	84900	0432	56013	161549	169838	95321	226247	1275961
Bev Rev($)	8693	10836	21998	25241	20923	19328	3761	1854	11722	31066	15666	63042	234130

EXHIBIT 15 (e)Food and Beverage Operating Figures

	Jul	Aug	Sept	Oct	Nov	Dec	Total
FOOD DEPARTMENT							
Room Service	16376	27113	31811	37553	40168	48531	351912
Banquet	77335	62135	166613	175306	96443	227564	1316624
Nicole	23507	34514	44268	55301	67338	70512	531341
Parallel Bar	0	0	0	1638	3488	5223	10349
Cafe	37613	49972	51251	58021	48439	48144	545405
Allowance F/D	-2697	-1120	-3485	-3612	-589	-426	-36206
Allowance A/R	-325	-756	-1734	-2472	-4063	-3966	-16766
Allowance T/O	-163	-1	-583	187	-256	0	-2467
TOTAL FOOD SALES	51646	171857	288141	321922	250968	395582	2700192
Cost of Sales	82474	92588	104244	121932	110470	131277	1155446
Employee Meals	-25475	-22507	-20380	-25406	-22356	-17926	-283914
Net Food Cost	56999	70081	83864	96526	88114	113351	871532
	37.6%	40.8%	29.1%	30.0%	35.1%	27.4%	32.1%
Salaries & Wages	163424	162901	198534	192486	180047	201121	2151408
Training Payroll	0	0	0	0	0	0	19776
Holiday & Sick Pay	8071	3324	12136	2193	9815	23106	116800
Benefits	60596	57878	75782	67761	64554	71960	815440
Total Payroll	32091	224103	286452	262440	254416	296187	3103424
Gross Food Profit	-37444	-122327	-82175	-37044	-91562	-13956	-1274764
BEVERAGE DEPARTMENT							
Room Service	5670	10893	6858	11041	10771	15406	125132
Banquet	3761	1854	11722	31066	15666	63042	234130
Nicole	9176	15656	24759	31848	40258	34619	248862
Parallel Bar	22782	36914	36826	44092	46662	45416	321837
Cafe	11602	9018	11225	6381	3031	2327	193777
Allowance F/D	-96	-125	-60	-19	-39	-3834	-4823
Allowance A/R	-1301	-99	-1477	-686	-170	-2266	-7231
TOTAL BEV SALES	51594	74111	89853	123723	116179	154710	1111684
Cost of Sales	8269	20791	20090	26002	22380	38257	219554
Employee Meals	-146	-201	-161	-718	-211	-245	-4428
Net Bev Cost	8123	20590	19929	25284	22169	38012	215126
	15.74%	27.78%	22.18%	20.44%	19.80%	19.40%	18.63%
Salaries & Wages	44570	41220	44415	45968	41978	39334	439897
Holiday & Sick Pay	2874	884	3385	592	3016	8109	24715
Benefits	16480	14597	16928	14567	15037	14054	160666
Total Payroll	63924	56701	64728	61127	60031	61497	625278
Gross Bev Profit	20453	-3180	5196	37312	33979	55201	271280
Function Room Rent	6900	14300	35785	46095	34130	26860	342968
Reim. Bot. Income	-4807	371	16873	18953	4480	14308	68525
TOTAL OTHER INCOME	2093	14671	52658	65048	38610	41168	411493
Gross Profit	-55804	-110836	-24321	65316	-18973	82413	-591991

EXHIBIT 15 (f) Fees and Marketing Expense

	Jul	Aug	Sept	Oct	Nov	Dec	Total
FEES:							
Management Fees	64500	77718	82244	108163	94382	94817	983776
Incentive Fees	0	0	0	0	0	0	0
Total Fees	64500	77718	82244	108163	94382	94817	983776
MARKETING							
Salaries and Wages	52148	48347	40020	46393	40196	35887	497339
Training Payroll	0	0	0	0	0	0	0
Holiday and Sick Pay	2164	292	2064	438	2059	2157	14967
Benefits	18731	16545	14637	15579	13701	12409	177751
Incentive Payments	0	0	0	0	215	0	1929
Total Payroll	73043	65184	56721	62410	56171	50453	691986
Annual Contract	0	0	0	0	0	0	25
Media	10301	958	83718	23603	2500	72007	462051
Adv. Agency Fees	220	0	0	0	0	0	220
Adv. Agency Rel	1294	79	250	0	0	78	5623
PR Agency Fees	2300	0	0	0	0	2000	39477
PR Agency Rel	1513	1072	0	0	0	5636	39535
Reciprocal Tradeout	36280	13062	7293	1793	3087	6449	160017
Printed Material	6888	2832	1890	2918	8966	4558	42522
Direct Mail	3000	0	989	34	1684	492	15725
Prep & Prod Copy	1632	451	3707	421	19109	7835	54214
Total Advertising	63428	18454	97847	28769	35346	99055	819409
National Media	25000	25000	25000	25000	25000	25000	300000
Sales Enter.	7806	7049	7493	9739	8710	11065	110959
Hotel Promos	2038	5042	5679	2439	2659	2327	45860
Gifts	0	0	130	425	0	247	987
Hotel Reps	200	200	200	200	400	200	2400
Print Mir/Dir Mail	2685	2332	2055	3982	1200	-1200	26576
Total S & P	12729	14623	15557	16785	12969	12639	186782
Relocation	0	0	0	0	0	0	1895
Per. Recruiting	0	0	60	59	0	15000	15296
Travel	637	523	2191	457	953	1169	17734
Sales/Use Tax	0	0	0	0	0	0	1567
Dues & Supcrip.	0	107	0	150	0	80	3367
Misc. Expenses	932	3865	5184	365	1029	3437	28902
Total Other	1569	4495	7435	1031	1982	19686	68761
TOTAL MARKETING EXP	175769	127756	202560	133995	131468	206833	2066948

EXHIBIT 16 Five Year Outlook and Supply/Demand Analysis

I. SUPPLY OVERVIEW

A. CURRENT

Location... The Omni Park Central actively competes with nine hotels comprising 8,442 rooms. They are the Sheraton Centre (1,845), Sheraton City Squire (720), New York Hilton (2,124), Parker Meridien (603), Warwick (500), St. Moritz (680), Essex House (700), and the Novotel (470). The Omni Park Central has 14.7% of the total supply.
Facilities... There are 15 hotels which comprise 16,119 rooms. They are the Sheraton Centre (1,845), Sheraton City Squire (720), New York Hilton, (2,124), St. Moritz (680), Essex House (700), Halloran House (652), New York Penta (1,800), Roosevelt (1,100), Milford Plaza (1,300), Summit (800), Doral Inn (650), Novotel (470), The Holiday Inn (600), and Marriott Marquis, September 1985, (1878). The Omni Park Central has 9.0% of the total supply.
Price... The Omni Park Central effectively competes with all of the above hotels depending on the time of year and market segment. However, those hotels consistently offering a price-buy are the Roosevelt, New York Penta, Milford Plaza, Holiday Inn, and Novotel.

B. ANTICIPATED FUTURE CHANGES

Hotel	# Rooms	Will Compete for	Buy Decision	Anticipated Competition
Gotham (1986?)	280	Transient	Image/location	Non-Competitve
Marriott Marquis (44th & Broadway) (April Completion)	1,878	All Segments	Facilities Location	Direct
146 W. 157th St (1987 or later) (next to Russian Tea Room)	500?	Transient	Image/Location	Direct
Barbizon Plaza	800	Closed 12-15-85		

With the completion of the New York Exposition and Convention Center, the supply within the immediate West Side could increase further during the next five years.

EXHIBIT 16 Five Year Analysis, (page 2)

II. DEMAND OVERVIEW

A. CURRENT

Demand has softened in New York City for 1985, specifically:

* City-wide occupancy decreased from 1984 (73.8%) to 1985 (70.78%) in the first six months.

  1. Location-wise demand dropped from 1984 (80.56%) to 1985 (70.21%) in Central Park South area.

  2. Price-Wise, demand dropped from 1984 (87.23%) to 1985 (73.39%) in $75-100 range.

* Vacancy rate in office/retail increase 7.1%.

  253.1 million square feet available in 1984 to 261.2 square feet available in 1985.

  145 million square feet are available in mid-town.

B. ANTICIPATED FUTURE CHANGES

Demand for the city will increase slowly with the opening of the New York Exposition and Convention Center, now scheduled for July of 1986. The construction of new office buildings in the Omni Park Central's immediate area will generate increased demand.

* Equitable Life Assurance Society's new building at 7th Avenue and 51st Street (late 1986).

* A new building on 57th Street, next to the Russian Tea Room, 72 stories to include three sections ... office space, luxury condominiums and a hotel possible with 500 rooms (1987).

* Two 70-story office buildings on 56th Street (early 1987).

* East-West Towers on 53rd Street between 6th and 7th Avenues (1987).

* A project on 55th Street, between 6th and 7th Avenues (1987).

EXHIBIT 16 Five Year Analysis (page 3)

* An office building project on 56th Street, between Broadway and 8th Avenue (1987).

* The Taft Hotel is being converted for condominiums.

* Forty-Second Street will undergo a refurbishment in the upcoming years.

Demand will be stagnant for New York City. However, the majority of the Omni Park Central's business in 1986 will be derived from an existing competition. Specifically in the individual business traveler, corporate and other group markets, the hotel will gain market share and occupancy from its direct competitors.

OMNI HOTELS
SUPPLY/DEMAND QUESTIONAIRE
(To be used to Update Mission)

Having analyzed each factor of present and future 'supply and 'demand,' please complete the following information.

I. SUPPLY/DEMAND 1985

Will the results of your findings have an effect on the balance of 1985?

A. If so, during what time frame and in what revenue producing areas?
B. If there is a change, what immediate action steps will you be taking?
C. Are the elements of rooms merchandising for the remainder of 1985 cor rect? Selective Sell Targets correct?
D. Briefly outline your room related pricing strategies for the remainder of 1985.
E. Are the positioning and elements of rooms merchandising for your hotel's banquet department and Food & Beverage outlets correct?
Are your pricing strategies correct?

EXHIBIT 16 Five Year Analysis (page 4)

II. SUPPLY/DEMAND 1986

A. Based on your Supply/Demand Analysis, please state changes you forsee in the elements of supply and demand for 1986 for each revenue producing area.

B. For 1986, what changes do you see being made in your elements of rooms merchandising and the elements of merchandising for each Food & Beverage outlet and banqueting department.

C. Please briefly outline the elements of rooms merchandising for your hotel during 1986. In addition, state your price positioning.

SUPPLY/DEMAND QUESTIONNAIRE RESPONSE

I. SUPPLY/DEMAND 1985

Will the results of your findings have an effect on the balance of 1985? Yes

A. Specifically, our transient markets are weaker than anticipated. The Buyers, Pure Transient, Outside Reservations Service, and F.I.T.'s are significantly behind our original estimates.

B. Action steps to convert the weakness are as follows:

1. Aggresively solicit competitors' Executive Plan potential buyers.

2. Spark package deals by developing special promotions.

3. Identify high rated-short term buy groups and solicit.

C. The elements of rooms merchandising are correct. The Selective Sell targets are actually being expanded.

D. We have thoroughly analyzed our pricing strategies for the remainder of 1985. After a complete competitive survey, we have decided to hold our rates through the balance of 1985. The only opportunities for rate maximization remain with the rooms merchandising process within a thirty-day period. In fact, a reduction in an ESP rate is expected to increase productivity.

EXHIBIT 16 Five Year Analysis (page 5)

E. The positioning and elements of rooms merchandising for the hotel's banquet and Food and Beverage outlets are correct.

The pricing strategies have been completely analyzed through careful cost potential and competitive survey. The result has been a lower price offering in all outlets.

II. <u>SUPPLY/DEMAND 1986</u>

A. Supply will increase through 1986. Demand will stagnate citywide. This will be the result of a slow economy and a strong dollar overseas. The transient segments will remain weak and group segments will remain price sensitive. Market share gains and occupancy/rate increases will result from solicitation of competitors' current business.

B. For 1986, selective sell targets have to be expanded to accommodate a reduced transient base. The food and beverage outlets have been positioned properly in the second half of 1985 and should remain successful. The banquet department will benefit from the increased selective sell targets for groups and a strong price/value relationship of its products.

C. The elements of rooms merchandising for 1986 will be an in-depth knowledge of the city-wide pressure points. New York City enjoys a number of city-wide sell-out periods. These time frames should be enhanced by the new convention center from mid-July onward. The key to success will be to steal competitors' business, and maximize high demand periods. In addition we will begin an active upgrade program to increase customer satisfaction and repeat business. Price positioning must stabilize until the product can be improved. Currently only two-thirds of the product is seriously competitive with existing facilities. In addition, stabilized demand presents a real obstacle to increased prices. To take business from a competitor, price flexibility is required.

EXHIBIT 17 1986 Mission and Position Statements

FOREWORD

This yearly Mission represents a broad set of directions or "marching orders" for the hotel's EOC to use its resources now to maintain the hotel at the approved level of market postion (or significantly move it towards such a postion). It represents a delicate balance among the sometimes conflicting short and long term objectives related to owners, employees, and customers. The Vice President, Operations has the responsiblity to keep the hotel's EOC Team on the proper short term objectives. This should be done within the spirit of the mission. The moment this is no longer feasible, it should be brought to the attention of the Office of the President.

I. ROOMS DIVISION

A. ELEMENTS OF ROOMS MERCHANDISING FOR 1985/1986

The primary objective of the Omni Park Central in 1986 is to progressively reposition the hotel in the market by shifting from low-rate group tours to desirable high-rate transient and corporate segments.

The hotel has three basic products, a 457 room mid-market commercial offering, 400 room standard hotel and a 400 room airline hotel.

The Omni Executive Hotel will offer a strong price/value relationship to the transient and higher rated group segments.

The Standard Hotel will offer unrenovated, clean basic accommodations for more price sensitive guests.

Finally, the airline hotel will offer the finest accommodations for the price in New York City, together with related services.

The following are the key strategies:

1. The selective sell targets will direct the merchandising and operating strategies. Flexibility will be employed at all times to insure high occupancy.
2. The advertising program will concentrate on increasing the weekend package market. Advertising will emphasize the value and uniquness of this product offering.
3. Direct Sales will concentrate on the corporate markets for both ESP and group to impact the Omni Executive Hotel. This includes an aggressive solicitation and direct mail effort. The primary success will be from the capturing of competitors' current users.

EXHIBIT 17 Statements (page 2)

4. Direct sales has the responsibility fo insure that the "Standard" and "Airline" Hotels are committed to the appropriate markets.

OPERATING MODE:

The Omni Park Central is substantially a new hotel in which the guest experience will be given the highest priority in order to support the product offering and assure the market repositioning of the hotel. Specifically, the hotel will be in the "upgrade" mode at all times. This will insure maximimum guest experience, thereby creating a base of return guests. In addition, we will take advantage of the new combined job classification provided by the union contract.

Significant emphasis will be placed on training for service. The Rooms Division will be managed in a highly cost efficient manner, resulting in a very profitable business. Most importantly, each of the three hotels will have management accountablility for the service and product rendered.

From a housekeeping and mechanical perspective, great attention must be given to maintaining the newly renovated guest rooms and public areas.

The new corporate transient program will feature benefits such as Guaranteed Availablity, Complimentary Continental Breakfast, Transportation to Wall Street and many other amenities that will guarantee a strong price/value relationship.

II. **FOOD AND BEVERAGE**

The objective of the Food and Beverage Division will be the successful continuance of the new product outlet concepts, achievment of the desired level for product and service on a consistent basis and sufficiently high volume to result in a profitable operation. All outlets will be supported by in-house collateral.

A. **BANQUET/CATERING**

The hotel will offer a much improved Banquet product and service that will appeal to the small and medium size meeting market to include breakfast, lunch, dinner, and receptions. The social market can and will be solicited for the hotel. The emphasis on the product will be a strong price/value relationship.

EXHIBIT 17 Statements (page 3)

B. ROOM SERVICE
Room Service will be provided 18 hours a day according to established Omni Standards. At this point 24 hours a day is being considered. In-room dining will be a satisfying experience, with courteous and efficent order taking, a creative menu offering, exceptionally high quality product, expeditious delivery, and meticulous preparation, as well as a daily Plat du Jour program featuring a touch of Nicole.

C. NICOLE
The thrust of Nicole, a Parisian brasserie, will be its ambience. The environment will be relaxed, unpretentious, convivial, and appealing. This will be carried through from the design scheme to the menu, to food preparation and service. The food offering will be Parisian brasserie style. Nicole will be supported by in-house promotional collateral. The emphasis here will be on a Seventh Avenue price/value relationship outlet.

D. PARALLEL BAR
The Parallel Bar will be a twofold lounge concept. After work, the working professionals of the local businesses will congregate among a full hors d'oeuvres selection, subdued contemporary music and moderate priced cocktails.

After 9 pm, the market mix of the hotel will change to reflect the "after hours" crowd of New York City, with its special flavor and ambiance. Both crowds will be serviced by attentive, upbeat employees offering a fun, new product on Seventh Avenue.

1986 MARKET POSITION STATEMENT

The Omni Park Central is a 1450 room (1257 key) first class commercial hotel which enjoys an excellent location in mid-town Manhatten at 56th Street and Seventh Avenue. The location is most advantageous in that it is in the commercial center of New York City, it is in close proximity to nearly all of the city cultural offerings and it is within the West Side area that is currently experiencing a high level of physical renovation activity. THese location advantages appeal to the multiple market segments served by the hotel and contribute to the hotel's positive image.

EXHIBIT 17 Statements (page 4)

The Omni Park Central as a renovated product, offering dramatically improved service, enters the market in 1986 with the task of establishing its new identity. The unique and strikingly attractive lobby, renovated guest rooms and corridors, two new exciting food and beverage outlets, and a bold new facade that makes an identity statement, support and complement the positioning of the hotel.

The Omni Park Central will serve multiple markets with a three tiered product line.

The Omni Executive Hotel is a 457 key, corporate commercial hotel, dedicated to the loyal corporate Executive Plan guest. These rooms are currently competitive, and all guests will be upgraded on a regular basis to begin a strong repeat clientele. This hotel is comprised of former Omni Classic Suites, Omni Classic Rooms, and newly renovated Omni Executive Rooms.

The Omni Executive Hotel competes and is priced about the same as the St. Moritz, Sheraton City Squire, Summit and Halloran House, equal to the Warwick, and below the Essex House, Parker Meridien New York Hilton, Novotel, the Marriott Marquis, and the Sheraton City Squire.

The Standard Commerical Hotel consists of 400 keys, 27 economy and 373 standard unrenovated rooms. These rooms are attractively priced for New York City, and are sold to tours, low-rated groups, buyers, and the price sensitive commercial travelers. These rooms are clean, however somewhat old and tired in that these murphy bedded rooms have furnishings and soft goods that are of a lesser qualtiy than offered in better hotels.

The Standard Commercial Hotel competes with and is priced equal to the Sheraton City Squire, below the Summit, and Novotel, Roosevelt, Penta and Holiday Inn.

The Airline Hotel is a key 400 room hotel dedicated to 100% occupancy annually. The rooms are all renovated, a mix of earlier Sheraton renovated and newly renovated Omni rooms. The rooms are on floors dedicated to the airline market for privacy and quiet. This market is critical for a strong guaranteed business base covering overhead expenses. The product, although very reasonably priced, is of very high quality. Everything is done for this market to provide the guests with a residential environment consisting of gracious hospitality and comfort. All of these amenities combined make this hotel the best Airline Hotel in the City.

The Airline Hotel competes with and is priced above the Summit, Doral, Lexington, Roosevelt, Penta, and Milford Plaza, but equal to the Sheraton Centre and the Sheraton City Squire.

EXHIBIT 17 Statements (page 5)

FOOD AND BEVERAGE

The new Food and Beverage Division of the Omni Park Central in 1986 is integral to the repositioning and success of the hotel. The improved product quality and service combine with the new outlet concepts to satisfy all desired in-house and local markets, and make a positive statement about the Omni Park Central.

Nicole

Nicole is an exciting and bustling Parisian Brasserie, appealing to the cosmopolitan customer. Nicole will be positioned as a free-standing restaurant capable of catering to the local west side residents and business people of the City. As a brasserie, its strengths will be in its product consistency and simplicity together with a Seventh Avenue price/value relationship. With the immigration to the West Side of young, upwardly mobile professionals Nicole will be a very popular restaurant. Nicole will also be a favorite for the theatre crowd, as it has a very congenial atmosphere. Both pre- and post-theatre menus will be available.

Parallel Bar

The Parallel Bar will be a twofold lounge concept. After hours, the working professionals of the local businesses will congregate among a full hors d'oeuvres selection, subdued, contemporary music and moderate priced cocktails.

After 9:00 pm, the market mix of the hotel will change to reflect the "after hours" crowd of New York City, with the special flavor and ambience.

Both crowds will be served by an attentive, upbeat employee offering a fun, new product on Seventh Avenue.

EXHIBIT 18 1986 Forecast and Marketing Budget (a)Income Statement

	Jan	Feb	Mar	Apr	May	Jun
Rooms Available	38440	34752	38440	37200	38400	37200
Rooms Sold	21224	25662	27185	29220	34519	32820
Occ %	55.2%	73.8%	70.7%	78.5%	89.5%	88.2%
Avg. Room Rate	76.60	82.17	77.31	81.15	84.43	84.54
Cash Payroll $	809187	783615	875363	872114	919769	894766
Cash Payroll %	39.0%	29.9%	32.6%	28.9%	25.1%	25.6%
Rooms Profit %	54.5%	65.9%	64.2%	67.9%	70.2%	71.1%
F & B Profit %	-48.1%	-18.3%	-18.1%	-4.0%	3.1%	3.9%
REVENUES						
Rooms	1625676	2105411	2101707	2371065	2914407	2774546
Food	196340	202542	243978	282246	339007	328169
Beverage	95389	96951	121748	133910	143323	137760
F & B Misc	26015	63656	53337	65844	75673	73207
Telephone	75366	89906	95603	101748	119823	113970
Other Income	20201	24099	25803	27344	32083	30510
Commercial Rents	39250	39250	39250	39250	39250	39250
Total Revenues	2078237	2621815	2681426	3021407	3663566	3497412
DEPARTMENTAL PROFIT/LOSS						
Rooms	885567	1386568	1349611	1510338	2046241	1973460
Food/Beverage	-139985	-54667	-66114	-16700	15001	18044
Telephone	-15924	-4760	-4172	245	7403	7636
Commercial Rents	39250	33250	39250	39250	39250	39250
Other Income	13147	15684	16855	17821	20868	19843
Operating Income	782055	1376075	1335430	1650954	2128763	2058233
DEDUCTIONS FROM INCOME						
Management Fees	62317	78654	80443	90642	109919	104922
A & G	202711	209324	225678	219777	235782	232367
Marketing	189628	173161	196618	172381	145835	146106
Energy	173627	150799	156504	134778	142157	145866
Prop. Opers.	184605	175001	182702	176847	178420	174246
Total Deduct.	812888	786939	841945	794425	812113	803507
GOP	-30833	589136	493485	856529	1316650	1254726
Taxes & Ins.	137750	137750	137750	137750	137750	137750
OPERATING PROFIT	-168583	451386	355735	718779	1178900	1116976
Interest	960000	960000	960000	950000	960000	960000
Depreciation	742500	742500	742500	742500	742500	742500
Amortization	5400	5000	5000	5000	5000	5000
Mgmt.Incent. Fee	10386	13109	13407	15107	18320	17487
Other Costs	153562	153562	153562	153562	153562	153562
Hotel Earnings	-2040431	-1422785	-1518734	-1157389	-700482	-761573

EXHIBIT 18 (a)Income Statement (continued)

	Jul	Aug	Sept	Oct	Nov	Dec	Total
Rooms Available	38440	38440	37200	38967	37710	38967	454156
Rooms Sold	28919	35219	33620	36519	29380	27269	361556
Occ %	75.2%	91.6%	90.4%	93.7%	77.3%	70.0%	79.6%
Avg. Room Rate	77.42	75.88	87.44	87.99	83.51	80.79	81.92
Cash Payroll $	845015	886711	876392	995259	928508	920803	10607502
Cash Payroll %	30.5%	27.1%	23.6%	24.4%	29.0%	30.9%	28.2%
Rooms Profit %	64.2%	88.4%	71.1%	71.9%	65.2%	63.2%	67.3%
F & B Profit %	-25.4%	-14.4%	12.9%	14.9%	0.7%	7.1%	-3.6%
REVENUES							
Rooms	2238855	2672555	2939737	3213396	2453523	3202947	29613825
Food	226855	244262	355482	381590	350276	359239	3509986
Beverage	101010	124237	150755	179683	156986	493440	1645492
F & B Misc	36445	39114	74612	97284	67938	67753	740878
Telephone	100811	122200	116636	126613	102290	95209	1260175
Other Income	27072	32770	31223	33908	27472	25663	338148
Commercial Rents	39250	39250	39250	39250	39250	39250	471000
Total Revenues	2770298	3274388	3707695	4071724	3197735	2983501	37578816
DEPARTMENTAL PROFIT/LOSS							
Rooms	1438256	1829251	2083057	2305040	1623807	1391396	19822592
Food/Beverage	-83375	-53062	66662	83527	3694	39144	-187831
Telephone	-502	10559	5607	8874	-3389	-6672	4905
Commercial Rents	39250	39250	39250	39250	39250	39250	39250
Other Income	17637	21333	20302	22053	17898	16752	220193
Operating Income	1411266	1847331	2214878	2458744	1681260	1479870	20324859
DEDUCTIONS FROM INCOME							
Management Fee	83109	98232	111540	122152	95939	89505	1127374
A & G	211146	218346	237018	246887	226882	228106	2694024
Marketing	170616	192805	179594	156828	192363	162738	2078673
Energy	152833	161120	169907	165226	160380	172286	1885483
Prop. Opers.	177045	170312	170921	183854	177123	181508	2132584
Total Deduct.	794749	840815	868980	874947	852687	834143	9918138
GOP	616517	1006516	1345898	1583797	828573	645727	10406721
Taxes & Ins.	137750	137750	137750	137750	137750	137750	1653000
OPERATING PROF	478767	868766	1208148	1446047	690823	507977	8753721
Interest	960000	960000	960000	960000	960000	960000	11510000
Depreciation	742500	742500	742500	742500	742500	742500	8910000
Amortization	5000	5000	5000	5000	5000	5420	60820
Mgmt.Incent. Fee	13851	16372	18590	20539	15998	14918	188084
Hotel Earnings	-1533896	-1146418	-809254	-573304	-1323987	-1506173	-14584427

EXHIBIT 19 1986 Departmental Sales Forecast with 1984 and 1985

	1984		1985		1986	
	Rooms	Food	Rooms	Food	Rooms	Food
Jan	1,528,965	167,923	1,773,384	109,410	1,625,676	195,340
Feb	1,729,119	167,392	1,988,393	142,407	2,105,411	202,542
Mar	1,826,616	285,626	2,105,077	207,281	2,101,707	243,978
Apr	1,763,681	207,939	2,127,316	280,701	2,371,065	282,246
May	2,214,465	287,381	2,553,605	255,115	2,914,408	339,007
Jun	2,245,664	200,309	2,103,471	125,239	2,774,546	328,169
Jul	1,691,214	112,179	1,794,966	151,645	2,238,856	226,855
Aug	1,897,599	127,862	2,198,909	171,856	2,672,556	244,262
Sept	2,176,437	197,372	2,193,640	288,141	2,939,798	355,482
Oct	2,776,100	227,677	2,831,260	321,921	3,213,396	381,590
Nov	2,340,500	189,616	2,615,472 *	250,968 *	2,453,523	350,276
Dec	1,932,125	241,689	2,390,477 *	395,582 *	2,202,947	359,239
Total	24,122,485	2,412,965	26,675,970	2,700,266	29,613,889	3,508,986

*estimated

EXHIBIT 20 Updated Competitive Analysis

MEMORANDUM

Following is the competitive analysis researched by the ESP sales office.

PENTA HOTEL - 7th Avenue and 33rd Street
Under renovation. Practically full occupancy. Corporate rate $81 single/$92 double. Rooms recently renovated, very nice. Corporate plan includes complimentary continental breakfast each morning of stay and one complimentary cocktail for entire stay. Nothing in bathrooms except soap. Rack rate is $135. No guarantee required for corporate membership.

ESSEX HOUSE - Central Park South
No drastic change since takeover by Nikko. Two types of rooms for corporate rates - single or double, Deluxe $175, Superior $185. Beautiful rooms. Superior room a bit larger and a much better view. Anyone can get a corporate rate. Other rates negotiated based on volume. No amenities. Basket of goodies in bathroom in small wicker basket. Corporate apartments and condos on premises.

EXHIBIT 20 Competitive Analysis (continued)

HOWARD JOHNSON/RAMADA INN - 51st & 8th, 48th & 8th
Location poor, not a very nice section of New York City. Rates are single or double, $75. Amenities include pool which is free to guests and safety deposit boxes in each room. Rooms in poor condition and musty.

SHERATON CITY SQUIRE - 53rd Street and 7th Avenue
Location is good. Rates are $115 to $140 for corporate rates. Amenities include upgrade, no extras. Rooms are in good condition, typical Sheraton. Consistent product.

ST. MORITZ - Central Park South
Location is good, Central Park South a definite draw for clientele. Rate is $100 single/double run of the house, $105 avenue view, $125 Park view. No amenities included in rate. Rooms musty, overcrowded, and need repair.

THE MAYFLOWER - 61st Street and Central Park West
Location is ideal, right across from Central Park. The hotel has approximately 700 rooms with a very cozy lobby. Most rooms have kitchenettes, but must be requested when making reservations. Must guarantee 50 room nights a year, no contract required. Corporate rates are $85 - $100. Rack rate is $95 - $110. Suites are spacious and nice at $135 corporate and $185 rack.

THE HARLEY HOTEL - 42nd Street between 2nd and 3rd Avenues
Hotel just changed name to New York Helmsley. It is new and very modern, touching a bit on the feminine. Practically all rooms are the same and the bathrooms are all marble with phones and full range of amenities. Must guarantee 20 nights a month for corporate program, no contract required. 790 rooms. Rack rate $115 single/double; corporate $145 single/double.

DAYS INN (formerly Holiday Inn) - 440 W. 57th Street
Turned to Days Inn last week, any changes not yet set. Corporate $79 single, $89 double; rack $86 - $109 single, $96 - $119 double. Additional $15 for king room like small suite with pull-out couch. Outdoor pool. Parking $5. Bath amenities include Crest toothpaste, Pert shampoo and soap. No other amenities.

BARBIZON PLAZA - 106 Central Park South
All rooms have small refrigerator. Only soap in bathroom. Rooms a bit tired looking but good for price. Excellent security record, special button on phone to call security in case of emergency. "Buyers' Program," $85 single, $95 single deluxe.